DISC

D0374169

- WHAT are the time-tes_____ _____ ____ ul education?

- WHICH discipline methods have been proven effective?

- HOW can minorities reach success?

- WHAT do some educators teach children in their literature and sex education classes?

- UPON WHAT foundation did the founding fathers build our nation?

- WHAT can be done to remedy some of the shocking educational practices taking place in schools across America?

These are only a few of the vitally important questions answered in SCHOOLS IN CRISIS: TRAINING FOR SUCCESS OR FAILURE?

"This excellently rendered volume is developed around the subjects of the four major crisis areas observable in public education—the areas of *Education, Discipline, Race Relations and Morals*. The book is the product of a decade of research, and is very well conceived, outlined, documented and indexed. . . .

"All who have any interest whatever in America's educational crisis *must* secure this book, read it, study it, quote and promote it.

"This book is a rare prize. Wide attention to its message can effect sweeping changes for the better in America."

Author, **Dr. H. Edward Rowe**

Schools in Crisis:
Training for Success or Failure?
Carl Sommer

Cahill Publishing Company
Houston, Texas

First printing 1984
Second printing 1984

Schools in Crisis: Training for Success or Failure?
© 1984 Cahill Publishing Co.

Printed in the United States of America

Library of Congress Catalog Card Number 83-71106

ISBN 0-9610810-0-7

Published by: Cahill Publishing Co.
              P.O. Box 91053
              Houston, Texas 77088

Contents

About the Author   xi

Acknowledgments   xiii

Part I
Introduction

1. The Crisis   3
   Educational Crisis   3
   Disciplinal Crisis   5
   Racial Crisis   6
   Moral Crisis   7
   Successful Schools   7

Part II
Educational Solutions

2. Forward with Basics   11
   Frustrated Teachers   11
   Promotional Standards   12
   Promotional Standards and Self-Esteem   14
   Teacher and Student Failures   15
   Promotional Exams   17
   Teacher Accountability   19
   New York City's Promotional Standards   21
   A New Honesty   22

3. Training for Excellence   25
   Right to Read   25
   Phonics vs. Look-Say   27
   Dyslexia   30
   New Math   31
   Math and Science   33
   Mainstreaming   34
   Gifted Children   34
   Test and Grades   36
   Truancy and Dropouts   39

4. The Educational Maze   43
   Three Basic Educational Systems   43
   Free Schools   43

Open Schools   47
Fundamental Schools   49
Progressive vs. Fundamental Education   50
Progressive and Fundamental Schools Evaluated   55
Educational Solutions   58

Part III
Disciplinal Solutions

5. Discipline Problems: The Root Causes   63
   Discipline Issues Unrelated to School   65
   Every School a Disciplined School   65
   New York City's Discipline Standards   66
   Concealing Discipline Problems   69
   Investigating Schools   69
   Schools—Habitation for Criminals?   75
   Schools—Training Centers for Proper Social Behavior   77

6. Love and Discipline   79
   Universal Need for Love   79
   Effective Teaching   80
   Authoritarian Discipline   82
   Permissive Discipline   83
   Loving Discipline   85
   Proper Balance Between Freedom and Discipline   85
   Preventive Discipline   86
   Successful Teachers   87
   A Total Disciplined Educational Environment   90

7. Discipline for Excellence   93
   Drugs for Learning and Behavior   93
   Behavior Modification   95
   Chemotherapy   97
   Corporal Punishment   98
   Effective Punishment   101
   Love and Punishment   104
   Corporal Punishment: Teachers' Reactions   106
   Supreme Court and Corporal Punishment   107
   Corporal Punishment Banned   108
   Punishment: Parents and Nature   109
   Permissive Solutions   109
   Ancient Wisdom   111
   Progressive Leaders   112
   Traditional vs. Progressive Schools   112
   Conclusion on Discipline   113

Part IV
Racial Solutions

8. Racial Progress   117
        Busing for Integration 117
        Minority School Achievement 118
        Voluntary Integration 120
        Busing Results 121
        Racial Quotas 122
        Minimum Competency Tests 126
        Bilingual Education 127
        Quota Discipline 130
        A Destroyed Generation 132
        Quality Education 135

9. Successful Schools   137
        Minority Success 137
        Achieving and Nonachieving Schools 139
        Compensatory Programs 141
        Gifted Children 141
        Fundamental Schools 142
        Progressive vs. Fundamental Schools 144
        Investigation of Schools by the Federal Government 146

Part V
Moral Solutions

10. Textbooks for Wholesome Living   155
        Textbook Fury 155
        Textbook Supporters 155
        Textbook Protesters 156
        Investigating the Textbook Controversy 157
        Textbook Reformers 160
        New History Textbooks 162
        Children's Liberation 163
        Progressive Goals 167
        Social Engineering—MACOS 167
        MACOS Evaluated 171

11. Selection Guidelines or Censorship   175
        Controversial Books 175
        New Standards 176
        Furious Parents 178
        Selection Guidelines 179
        Censorship 180

vii

Evolution vs. Scientific Creationism   182
Creationism Censored   184

12. Education for Sex or Immorality   187
SIECUS Goals   187
Three Basic Value Systems   188
A Teenage Sex Education Magazine   189
Sex Education Material   191
Nonjudgmental Sex Education   192
Sex Stimulation   193
Sex Education Results   194
Sex Educators' Claims   195
Introducing Sex Education   196
Sex Educator's True Objectives   198
Sexual Abstinence   199
Opposition to Current Sex Education Programs   201
Homosexuality—The Alternative Life-Style   204
Proper Sex Eduction   205

13. Values Clarification   207
The Alligator River Story   208
Survival Games 208
Diaries   209
Parents Questioned   210
Autonomous Children   210
Government's Moral Input   211
Promoting Positive Life Values   213

14. Moral Disintegration: Its Source   215
America's Disintegration   215
Civilizational Crisis   216
Supreme Court's Prayer and Bible Reading Decisions   216
Two Conflicting Ideologies   217
Humanist Manifesto   217

15. America's Moral Foundation   223
Separation of a National Church and
   Federal Government   223
Declaration of Faith in God   223
Enacting the Constitution   224
Presidential Declarations   226
Bill of Rights and Freedom of Religion   227
The Influence of the Bible on American Education   229
Reinterpreting the Constitution   231
State Rights   233
Separation of Church and State   234

16. A Moral America   235
    Promoting America's Moral Heritage   236
    A Narrow Ruling   237
    Prayer and Bible Reading Statute   238
    Americans and School Prayer   242
    Building a Moral Foundation   243
    The Religion of Humanism   244
    Accommodation Neutrality   245
    Three Choices   247
    Contradictory Court Decisions   247
    Supreme Court's Activism   248
    Reverse Discrimination   250

17. Schools and the Future of America   253
    Internal Disintegration   254
    Theism and Human Rights   256
    Constitutional Democracy   257
    Perpetuating America's Heritage   257
    Collapse of Civilization   260
    Three Value Systems   263
    Rebuilding America   267
    The Blackout   268
    The Silent Majority   271

Part VI
Conclusion

18. Tomorrow's Students: Actions for Success   275
    Educational Solutions   275
    Disciplinal Solutions   275
    Racial Solutions   276
    Moral Solutions   276
    Restrictive Regulations   276
    Private Schools   277
    A Time for Action   280
    Parental Rights   282
    Persistent Action   282
    Action by Educators   287
    Intelligent Action   290
    Successful Actions   290
    Men and Women of Action   297

Notes   299

Bibliography   323

Index   327

About the Author

The author has unusual qualifications for writing this book on education: He has taught high school students in New York City, counseled students and parents as a high school assistant dean of boys in a school with 3,600 pupils, worked as a foreman of a tool and die shop and managed a manufacturing plant.

Shortly after becoming a high school teacher he discovered something seriously wrong with the education his students received; for ten years he researched the problem. Though he had a college degree, in order to validate his teacher's license he attended Oswego State University, City College of New York, and New York University. While attending New York University he had the privilege of using Bobst Library, the largest research library in New York City, to help him in his investigation. His managing an entire manufacturing plant, seven years of teaching high school students, extensive researching, counseling students and parents as a dean of boys, and being a father of five children have provided him with much practical experience.

To have more time for research he sacrificed a year's salary by taking a leave of absence and was thus able to investigate the schools as a substitute teacher. In each of the five boroughs of New York City he served as an elementary, an intermediate, a junior high, and a high school teacher, teaching all grades from 1 to 12 in 27 different schools. To discover solutions to the problems plaguing American education, he sent a survey to 115 principals, 49 of whom responded. He has personally interviewed parents, students, teachers, assistant principals, and principals. Since the book covers such a multitude of problems and solutions, he has had numerous individuals, both black and white, read portions of the book: parents, lawyers, ministers, teachers, principals, a college professor, and superintendents of schools.

With his parental and managerial background the author examines the schools from without the system, and with his counseling and educational background, from within. Though exposing many current weaknesses of today's education, he constantly strives to promote practical solutions for successful schools.

Acknowledgments

I want to thank all those who have read this book and offered their useful suggestions. My wife has been exceptionally patient in bearing with me these ten years and helping to type and retype this manuscript. My children have also been helpful in clipping and filing the many articles used. I am grateful for the authors of books and articles and also the students, parents, teachers, and principals who have allowed me to probe their minds for educational solutions. Without their aid this book would have been impossible.

Part I

Introduction

Chapter 1

The Crisis

At commencement exercises across the nation untold thousands of high school graduates will receive a counterfeit diploma: a mere 12-year attendance certificate. Many of these tassel-capped students marching slowly down the aisle with lifted chins and throbbing hearts to receive their long-sought diplomas will one day come to this shocking discovery—they have been cheated of an education. It is not that they were intellectually unable to learn; rather, they were inadequately trained. A large number of these students face a bleak future because of their faulty education.

Educational Crisis

"For the 17th straight year, scholastic achievement among American high-school students has fallen to a new low," states *U.S. News & World Report* in referring to Scholastic Aptitude Tests (SAT).[1] Colleges across America have felt the impact of the verbal and math decline, insisting that inadequately trained high school graduates take remedial classes. Even bright students have been affected; some professors coined the term *straight-A illiteracy:* bright students graduating without writing competence.[2]

The *Boston Globe* after a six-month investigation reports that Boston's public school system, the oldest in the nation, may now be classified as one of the worst. One-third of the high school students taking more than two academic courses failed more than half of their basic academic subjects. Daily attendance records showed nearly one-fourth of the high school students absent. The general pattern emerged: The longer a child was educated in Boston schools, the lower he placed on a national reading test.[3]

There are reports in our nation of slight progress, but educational achievement has fallen to such an extent that these ripples of success are not enough. Here is a report from a national newsmagazine:

School test scores are rising after 9 years of decline. But don't cheer yet. Math, science achievement levels are lower than they were a decade ago.

More than a quarter of high-school graduates leave with only one year of math. And more than half have taken only one year of science.

Trained teachers are scarce. Half of those hired last year to teach math and science weren't qualified. They were certified in other fields.[4]

Educators, parents, and concerned individuals need to examine why American education has failed to train its students properly. The nation's largest school system, New York City, reports 80 percent of the eighth-, ninth-, and tenth-graders, including those college bound, failed or barely passed a writing competency test. In addition, only 48 percent of registered high school sophomores graduate; among minority students the dropout rate is even higher.[5]

Not only are students improperly taught the basics of reading, writing, and math; they are also shortchanged in history and science. Instead of a course in solid history, many students are taught a watered-down version of social science. "All the history courses my daughter has taken seem to indicate that nothing much happened before 1950," complains Thomas O'Connor, an official of the Massachusetts Board of Education.[6] "The Organization of American Historians is pessimistic about the future of its discipline," reports *Newsweek*. "Many teachers, OAH officials admit, simply find it easier to attract student interest with current events than to insist that pupils master the more rigorous skills of memorization and analysis."[7]

"America may be on its way to technological illiteracy," comments a New York Times News Service, "with most of its citizens unable to think and function effectively in an increasingly complex technical society.

"That disturbing possibility is raised by a crescendo of voices from the nation's scientific leadership . . . . The National Science Board, the government's top policy-making body for science education, has called the situation 'critical.' "[8] Another government report says that the Soviet Union, West Germany, and Japan are ahead of the United States in elementary and secondary school programs in science and mathematics.[9]

In the wake of the Sputnik challenge, the schools of America "squandered the gains in student achievement" and committed "an act of unthinking, unilateral educational disarmament." So reports the National Commission on Excellence in Education after its 18-member panel, appointed by Secretary of Education Terrel H. Bell, examined American education.

The commission spent 18 months attending public hearings, examining educational studies, and hearing a variety of experts. "Our nation is at risk," claimed the commission in its scathing report card on American education. The panel, including college presidents, high school principals, scholars, and others, gave this unanimous assessment: "If an unfriendly foreign power had attempted to impose on America the mediocre educational performance that exists today, we might well have viewed it as an act of war."[10]

Disciplinal Crisis

To discover what was happening inside New York City schools, I taught as a substitute teacher for 28 days in 27 different schools in some of the best and worst schools in the city. Some classes were orderly, but in that short time I observed students climbing on desks, tables and cabinets; throwing paper airplanes and balls in classrooms; running around the rooms and halls; yelling, fighting, and knocking over chairs and desks. While substituting, I have been threatened, been cursed, had my foot stamped on, seen a teacher assaulted, and stopped numerous fights. But this is just my personal experience.

Ann Landers printed a letter from an Iowa teacher who resigned because she was "sick of being called foul names, sick of hearing students use four-letter words, fed up on garbage and fights in the halls, and the 'you-can't-make-me' attitude."

Ann Landers responded, "Your letter sounds as if it was written in 1968. I am of the opinion that students of all ages are looking better, thinking better and behaving better. If I've been misled, I hope you teachers out there will let me know."

Did they respond?

Listen to Ann Landers as she tells it, "I'm sorry (and more than a little chagrined) to report that they have been letting me know—in strong language and large numbers. I've been told I'm clearly 'off my rocker,' 'completely out of touch,' 'crazy as a loon,' and 'living in Disneyland.'" These are some of the responses she received in one week:

From Richmond, Va: That Iowa teacher took the words right out of my mouth. I'm no quitter, but I, too, am considering resigning. These kids are more than I can take.

Armada, Mich.: I drive a school bus and "Iowa teacher" is right. Today's students are undisciplined, unmotivated and I've had it with their filthy language.

Bryan, Tex.: Most teachers are so worn out trying to maintain discipline that they have no time or energy for teaching. Kids who want to learn are being ripped off.

Royal Oak, Mich.: The public would not believe what goes on in the average classroom. Anyone who goes into teaching today should have his head examined.

Memphis, Tenn.: I've taught school for 25 years. These last five years have been the worst. Everything that isn't nailed down disappears. The language in the halls and classrooms is unprintable. (P.S. Our students are from 5 to 11.)

Chicago: I am a teacher who is also ready to quit. I have a nervous stomach from the fist-fighting in my classes. A student pulled a knife on me last week. Three teachers in our school were assaulted last month. It's a nightmare![11]

When Dr. Alfred Bloch, a psychiatrist at the University of California in Los Angeles, examined more than 200 teachers assigned to inner-city schools, he found they suffered damage far beyond mere cuts and bruises. "Bloch bases his diagnosis on a five-year study of teachers in Los Angeles," reports *Newsweek*. "His patients ranged from instructors who had been the victims of sustained verbal threats but no real violence to one woman whose hair had been set on fire by students protesting low grades." Bloch stated, "Few had received adequate support from the school system. The woman whose hair had been burned complained to the principal—and was chastised for leaving her classroom unattended. Her experiences finally led to a suicide attempt, and she has never gone back to school."

These "battered teachers," Bloch said, showed a number of stress symptoms, such as high blood pressure, anxiety, depression, headaches, lowered self-esteem, stomach trouble and disturbed sleep. The doctor discovered these teachers suffered the same kind of battle fatigue as soldiers in combat.[12] *Time* reports that in just one year more than 100,000 teachers were attacked in our nation's schools.[13]

Racial Crisis
Racial issues such as busing, racial quotas, minority discipline, and bilingual education have divided Americans. Cities have closed down schools and experienced fierce riots over racial problems. Many minorities suffer because of their inferior education. One black union official, complaining about high school graduates in his city, says some "can't even read their own names on their diplomas."[14]

Moral Crisis

Within the past 15 years there has been a dramatic change in moral behavior among the youth. Many parents are angered over their children's textbooks. In some schools children are required to read books that use the vilest language in the name of relevancy. For nine weeks, schools were boycotted in Kanawha County, West Virginia, because of textbooks. I went to Charleston to interview Alice Moore, who spearheaded the protest, and to examine these textbooks.

Parents are also disturbed over the new sexual standards being promoted by schools. To obtain information about sex education, I wrote to more than 50 sex education sources. Today America is experiencing a sexual revolution; as a result, venereal disease and unwanted pregnancies among teenagers are climbing to unprecedented heights. To combat this problem, one hears conflicting voices. Some clamor for more sex education while others blame current sex education programs for increasing this social plague. These problems will be examined.

Successful Schools

In spite of many educational failures, there are successful schools. One such school was previously a disaster; today, it is radically transformed. "Four years ago, Manierre Elementary School in Chicago's inner city had only plywood where windows used to be," reports the *American School Board Journal.* "To local educators, it was known as the 'snake pit.' Students spent their time playing baseball in the hallways, sipping wine, gambling and throwing furniture out of the windows. Only two of the 800 pupils could read. Teacher morale was understandably low; teachers had seen six principals come and go in a five-year period."[15]

Today windows have glass, litter is nonexistent, and learning is taking place. "We are 100 percent successful at the primary level in teaching reading," Principal Alice Blair told me in an interview. "Every child in this school that comes through reads." Major discipline problems no longer exist. Blair has guided these children from failure to success.

"Reading achievement in inner-city schools does not have to be as low as it ususally is," concludes a study of successful schools by the nonprofit Council for Basic Education. "A sense of purpose, relative quiet and pleasure in learning" was the atmosphere of the successful schools, noted George Weber, associate director of the council, while "disorder, noise, tension and confusion" permeated the less successful schools.[16]

In searching for the deficiencies the students already had when they entered my classes, I discovered the reasons. I probed further for answers for the national crisis. These root causes and solutions for the educational, disciplinal, racial, and moral crises facing American schools will be presented. To train successful students does not entail vast new expenditures, rather, educators need to eliminate their faulty training methods and implement those that have been proved successful.

What transpires in schools has repercussions far beyond class-rooms; it affects every aspect of our national life. America, and particularly the schools, has seriously departed from its historical past and embraced an alien philosophy. The foundational truths our forefathers stood for will be examined. America has prospered because we have followed these concepts. However, because today we have abandoned our historical past, our society and schools are facing a grave crisis. The national future will be largely determined by how the upcoming generation is taught. I urge you to take not just an outside look at education but a unique inside excursion through the largest institution in the United States. You will enter with me into various schools and classrooms to see what is happening. You will read firsthand what children are being taught in some literature and sex education classes. After revealing what is transpiring, this book will present detailed practical solutions so that together we can make our schools—institutions of success.

Part II

Educational Solutions

Chapter 2

Forward with Basics

Teaching high school students information they should have learned in elementary school left me frustrated. I wanted to teach the subject at the proper grade level, but often students could not grasp what was being offered. Unless tests were extremely simple and material was repeated over and over, many pupils would fail. Everyone makes occasional mistakes, but there was a serious educational deficiency here that was so disturbing.

Frustrated Teachers

We teachers would discuss the students' deplorable educational ability. One day I decided to probe for the exact reasons for their deficiencies. After taking a survey of one of my tenth-grade classes, I discovered the answer to the riddle.

I searched every student's permanent record and noted reading and math scores, age, and birthplace. More than half of the class had a fifth-grade reading level or lower; nearly half had a fourth-grade math level; and all students were either at the proper age or one year behind for their grade, except for one foreign student who was behind two years. After I had analyzed the survey, the mystery for the massive educational failure unfolded—automatic promotion. Students were put back a maximum of one year, then advanced regardless of their educational achievement. If students neglected to study; refused to do homework; failed tests; did not know reading, writing, or math; were absent; cut classes; or were truant—whatever they did or did not do, it made no difference—all were automatically advanced.

Often I witnessed these underachievers refusing to do the work required to pass the course. They would neither study nor do the necessary homework; in fact, some felt it was even too much effort to take out a pen and copy blackboard notes. After all, why should they? All along they had been taught that minimal effort brings success.

To this same sophomore high school class I gave a math survey test: only 8 out of 23 students could correctly add 7½ and 11⅛; five students could not write the dictated number 1,094; and for the number 785, one student wrote 70085. When comparing permanent records, I found that foreign students had higher scores in both reading and math than American-born.

Every year over one million high school juniors and seniors take the College Entrance Scholastic Aptitude Tests, which serve as a common denominator for students across America. For decades the test scores were steady, but since 1970 they have declined alarmingly. Concerned parents and educators have demanded reasons for this high rate of failure. The College Entrance Examination Board commissioned an independent panel to find out. Spending more than $750,000 in research, they produced an eight-inch-thick volume of 34 special research reports.

The committee found two periods of decline. (1) Before 1970, two new groups of students helped create the declining averages. There was a greater influx of poor people, who generally do receive lower test scores; and of women, who score lower in math. (2) After 1970, the excuse of new test-takers was no longer valid, but scores fell even more alarmingly. The panel traced the failure to a general "lowering of educational standards." Some of the reasons cited were high rates of absenteeism, grade inflation, "less thoughtful and critical reading," lack of stress on careful writing, half the former homework, lower-reading-level textbooks, and promotion that was "almost automatic."[1]

Promotional Standards

The crucial question is: What can the schools do to assure that every student receives an adequate education?

The goal to graduate properly trained students must begin, not in junior high or high school, but in the early grades. Educators should concentrate on making the first three years of schooling productive by establishing proper learning habits. In these early years children acquire their basic skills and educational foundations. Each grade in the elementary school should have a minimum level of proficiency in reading, writing, and arithmetic, and there should be a minimum standard for graduation from junior high and high school.

The first grade should prepare children for the art of learning. First grade should be considered "preparation": a time devoted to preparing children ready for second grade. After half a year in preparation, there should be an adjustment: Children who master the required material for the first half of the term will advance with the class, while those unable to do the work will be placed in another class to continue doing beginning work. Then only the children who have learned the required first year's work will be advanced to second grade; the others must remain in preparation until they are able to start second-grade work. Some children may need to spend one and a half or two years in preparation. The term *preparation* is used to minimize the negative effects of telling children they are retained.

Advancement will be based not on chronological age but on learning ability; only children who reach reading and math readiness for each grade will advance. Piaget offered sound advice when he stated that methods of education will be most productive when they are tuned to the child's natural learning abilities. However, once children are ready to learn, they should be encouraged and not left to flounder; students tend to set their standards no higher than required.

Schools should institute semiannual promotions: Children entering second grade should go into 2A, then 2B, then 3A, and so on, right through to high school. Pupils need not receive a new teacher every half year. This method permits failing students to be retained a half year instead of the customary whole year; it also allows children to enter school every half year. Children held back for two years should be put into ungraded classes or "opportunity classes." These failing children should be placed in smaller classes where they can receive special attention and continue through the school system. This procedure prevents the retention of 16-year-old students in elementary school. However, when they reach their minimum grade level, they have the "opportunity" to be placed in their proper class.

Schools should not take the hard-line position: you have failed—now suffer for your ignorance. On the contrary, utmost concern should be had for the early grades: Remedial help should be provided, and parents should be invited to a conference set up to help both children and parents. Every avenue should be explored to help students succeed in each grade. Remedial help would be used now to nip problems in the bud, instead of waiting till pupils are academically lost. Children still unable to perform in the grade should be told kindly that they are being put back a half year.

The present system of social promotion displays no great concern with pupils' success or failure; all automatically advance grade after grade. Instead of becoming alarmed over failing students, school personnel often leave underachievers alone. Consequently, many children just drift along without applying the necessary effort to learn. Automatic promotion rewards incompetence, which in turn promotes laziness and mediocrity; achievement promotion fosters diligence because it encourages and rewards students' efforts and abilities. By rejecting social promotion, schools will have to accept the responsibility for their students' learning. Classes will have to be designed to fulfill that responsibility, and teachers will have to create an effective learning environment.

Promotional Standards and Self-Esteem

Perhaps the most subtle argument for not failing students is that because children enter schools with various abilities and maturity levels, and permitting them to experience failure lowers their self-esteem and produces devastating psychological damage. Children certainly enter schools with various abilities and maturity levels— the slow learner, trying to do the work but unable; the semiliterate, coming from a foreign-language home and incapable of comprehending and expressing himself clearly; the late bloomer, acting childish and immature; the culturally deprived whose impoverished neighborhood and home have kept him from reaching his full potential; and the underachiever, having the ability but lacking inner self-discipline and motivation and thereby becomes quickly discouraged.

Students do not like to be left behind. But we must honestly ask, What procedure will prepare failing children best for their own future, being left back or being automatically promoted? A healthy self-esteem is extremely important. But is it wiser to let pupils advance beyond their ability and experience constant failure, or to let failing students be instructed by compassionate and understanding teachers and advisers that retention is not punishment but a means to help them succeed? Children retained because of lack of learning ability who then discover their ability to keep up with the class will experience a great ego boost. The greatest builder of lasting self-esteem is true success. Dr. James C. Dobson, Jr., assistant professor of pediatrics at the University of Southern California School of Medicine, says, "Make certain your child has learned to read by the end of his second year in school. I'm convinced that self-esteem has more frequently been assassinated over reading problems than any other aspect of school life. And it is all so unnecessary! . . . Every child, with *very* few exceptions, can learn to read if taught properly."[2]

"At the Gesell Institute of Human Development," reports Louise Bates Ames, the associate director of the institute, "we feel there is no need for children to be emotionally damaged when they are retained in the school grade they are already in. A slight and temporary hurt would be worth it if retention resulted in the child being placed in a grade where he could be comfortable and could do the work."[3]

Psychologist Verne Lewis of Jefferson, Iowa, questioned more than 400 parents of children who were left back. Lewis' study showed that 87 percent felt the retention was beneficial, 90 percent declared it was justified, 89 percent did not regret their decision, and 88 percent would repeat having their child retained.[4]

Automatic promotion punishes children by putting illiterates with literates, thereby causing these underachievers to remain ignorant because of their inability to function. Education, trying to be humane, has been inhumane by deceiving failing children to think they are successful. Helen Wise, president of the National Education Association, declares, "If you hold back a slow child, he will get slower."[5] But slow children are not helped when they must sit in classes and listen to incomprehensible jabberings of teachers instructing regular students, the presumption being that when teachers have some "extra time" they can help these slow pupils. These low-achieving students belong in the grade where they can function and learn.

Picture children knowing just second- or third-grade arithmetic while the teacher is instructing a class of 25 to 35 pupils in fifth-grade math. How can these children learn? They will retrogress more and more in each succeeding grade; the teacher is always instructing beyond their capabilities. Providing underachievers with 40 minutes of remedial help will assist them for their grade level; but upon returning to class they are lost again. Such students need constant remedial help. How much wiser to put children into their functional grade where education will be in harmony with their intellectual and psychological ability. This would eliminate much remedial help. Likewise, how much more profitable for students to have teachers devoting their entire time to a class at its proper grade level instead of skipping around the class and dividing their time among various levels of ability.

Social promotion is like the vain king who wanted to impress his subjects with his fishing skill. He instructed divers to hook large fishes to his line so he could boast of his achievement while the people marveled; inwardly, however, he knew better. Children who are automatically advanced, being the victims of deception, boast ignorantly of their achievement while others are amazed at their stupidity. At least the king had fish; these children's hooks are empty.

Teacher and Student Failures

Often teachers are blamed for the failures of the children, but teachers are not always at fault. Effective teaching is not an automatic mechanical response; rather, teachers must be flexible and be able to flow with the class. What profit is there if students cannot understand the teacher? Can learning take place? How can algebra be taught if students cannot add or subtract; or literature, if the majority can barely read third-grade material? Comprehension must precede learning. If students come into classes improperly trained, what can teachers do? They must start where the class is. This further lowers the level of the other students. The next grade teachers react the same way, and the dominoes continue to fall even up to the college and university level.

The *Lansing State Journal* had this letter from Ralph W. Lewis:

> Most of the arguments against minimum standards for passing to the next grade are spurious or unrealistic. The spurious arguments are often based in a superficial psychology that has been discarded by psychologists. And the unrealistic arguments are based on a time-limited concept of child as child rather than on an open concept of child as a becoming person.
>
> Only one argument can be considered now. This is embodied in the question: which is a greater hardship for a person to bear—the failure of promotion at grade three or the failure to hold a job at eighteen because of inability to read directions? Or failure in college because of a reading deficiency?
>
> Most people will agree that the third grade penalty is much less, especially since it can be cushioned and corrected so as to lead most children through it into a rapid growth phase.
>
> As a teacher of college freshmen I can tell you that the tragedies suffered by failing students are very harsh. There are not many cushions for them at this age and often there is little hope for further advanced education. When students finally discover that their troubles stem not from a lack of native ability, but from a lack of standards in their formative years, they are disillusioned and begin to wonder about the quality of knowledge and judgment in their home communities.[6]

Then there are devoted teachers who insist on course standards but are pressured by the administration to lower them. "I used to be tough and demanding, but I was told to lay off," said a high school teacher in Medford, Massachusetts. If more than 20 percent of his students fail, he is "called on the carpet."[7] Another teacher in Coos Bay, Oregon, complained about the great pressure to pass students: "If my failure rate exceeds 12%, I'll be questioned." He added, "Someone would likely ask me if I weren't expecting too much. So the failure rate goes down, but the quality and quantity of work also go down."[8] Once underachieving children have been granted success regardless of their effort or ability, it is often too late when they reach junior high and high school to help them develop successful learning behavior. Schools may salvage a few children, but it is not realistic to expect some remedial program radically to alter pupils trained for six years in permissive failure and turn them into devout students.

Often in my high school classes I tried to motivate nonachievers. With rapt attention these students listened as I enumerated incidents dealing. with the value of receiving an education and of learning how to work. They were interested, and practically all wanted to be successful, but what can be expected of students who are barely reading and doing math at a fourth- or fifth-grade level? All the good intentions they could muster would not change their ability. They were years behind in their education; to achieve at proper grade level would take an extraordinary amount of willpower and work for which they were never adequately trained. Many of these nonachievers take the easier alternative—they drop out of school.

Dr. Howard L. Hurwitz, former principal of Long Island City High School in New York City, called the remedial reading programs "sheer fakery" for high schools and colleges. "If you lose a kid in the first three years you have lost him," Hurwitz said. "The kid can never learn to read in high school. You shouldn't have social promotions. No one should be in the fourth grade who can't read."[9]

The real culprit in the educational crisis is the current system permitting nonachieving and nonworking students to advance automatically without mastering the subject material for each particular grade. The simple procedure of guaranteeing competency for each grade would revolutionize the entire educational system from elementary school through the universities. Fifth-grade teachers would no longer have students reading at the second-grade level; they could begin teaching at the proper level knowing that every child was able to comprehend fifth-grade material. High school teachers would not have students unable to do basic math or read simple instructions. Colleges would no longer have to offer remedial reading and writing; every student receiving a diploma would understand the basics. Furthermore, all students would receive tremendous benefits from having teachers who devoted their full time to the regular subject material instead of doing unnecessary remedial work.

Promotional Exams

To ensure competent students, each elementary grade should have some method of testing basic knowledge. If examinations are given and for some reason a child expected to pass receives a failing mark, another test should be offered. Some elementary school children may do poorly because they are nervous or upset; such children should be given a personal evaluation test.

To break this syndrome of success with failure, students in junior high school should have flexible scheduling as in high school, and not be automatically promoted from grade to grade whether they pass their subjects or not. There should be certain basic requirements for graduation as in high school. A Graham Down, executive director for the Council for Basic Education, gives an excellent view on what basic education should be:

> It means that all students, except the severely retarded, should receive competent instruction in all the fundamental disciplines. Basic education means that before students graduate from high school, they should at least be able to read at an eighth-grade level, write with grace and accuracy, possess computational skills, have the perspective provided by sound historical knowledge, have some acquaintance with a foreign language and its culture, some knowledge and understanding of science, and an appreciation of the role of the arts in the history of man and contemporary life.[10]

Some authorities disagree with having eligibility examinations for promotion; they would eliminate such tests altogether. Standardized tests are "like a lock on the mind, a guard at the factory gate," says NEA executive director Terry Herndon. He is against college board tests, achievement tests given to elementary and secondary school children, graduate record exams, IQ tests—in fact, any uniform test that compares large numbers of students. "The only real beneficiaries," according to Herndon, "aside from the test marketers themselves, are insecure school managers striving for comfort in their relations with school boards, legislators, and governors."

Herndon complains that "it's time to get the children out of the factory and back into the classroom where they belong." To him education is a very complex process, and hence too difficult to be assessed by standardized testing.[11]

Fears have been expressed that minimum standards will become the maximum and teachers will teach only for the tests. Certainly there are those few who will want to take advantage of any system and teach only for test results, but principals should encourage teachers to develop each student's maximum potential. Educators need to realize that there are essential skills other than just mastering the basics: analytic thinking, problem solving, logical reasoning, self-discipline, self-motivation, and developing proper moral principles.

Some are concerned over failure to evaluate the tests properly, and the ruinous effects this could have upon children. Tests must be carefully designed and evaluated so as to reflect achievement accurately. However, the danger of not having proficiency tests and standards or some method of evaluation far outweighs the few errors that are likely to appear. It is much more dangerous for schools to have low student performance and to keep pushing through thousands of illiterate children.

Teacher Accountability

Establishing standards and guidelines for the basics does not mean curtailing teachers' creativity and freedom. The guidelines should not be so stringent as to forbid teacher flexibility or to force all teachers into some particular mold. A recommended pattern should be offered for teachers who need one, but teachers should be free to use their creative abilities as long as students meet the acceptable standards. It is a system that combines discipline and freedom.

There are, of course, superior, regular, and inferior teachers. The use of standards can provide guidelines for them all. Incompetent teachers will suffer because they will be exposed as a result of standardized tests. These teachers should not be immediately eliminated; administrators should first try to assist them to succeed by supervising and counseling them on how to teach more effectively. Only when all else fails should such teachers be removed. Standards should not be a punitive device to eliminate teachers but a means to ensure the best education for all students. Nevertheless, a class is only as good as its teacher. There is no substitute for competent teachers, and there ought to be safeguards to make certain that competent teachers are in all classes.

Unfortunately in America, teachers are grossly underpaid. This causes many capable individuals to choose other occupations instead of teaching, and those who are teaching to leave the profession. Though there are many capable teachers, there are those who are incompetent. Teacher organizations need to beware of defending these incompetent teachers; otherwise the public will become antagonistic toward education and not support it as they should.

Establishing promotional standards for each grade will allow teachers to see the effectiveness of their pedagogical methods, particularly when large numbers of students have either failed or succeeded. When quality control is brought into the schools, it will become apparent which methods and materials are the most effective. While teaching reading to first-grade students as a substitute teacher in Lower East Side, Manhattan, I was surprised at how simple the work was for a class that in one month was to be promoted to the second grade. The children studied four pages from their workbook containing only three simple words: *an, pan, pin*. The workbook was overly simple and very ineffective for teaching reading. Perhaps it was no strange coincidence that the second-grade class had the second lowest reading rate in the school district.

When I asked a group of elementary school teachers what was the reason for children's low achievement, a teacher remarked, "teacher accountability." Along with others she acknowledged that they as teachers are unsupervised. Freely she admitted that being held accountable was a more taxing way to teach. Certainly not being held accountable is a much easier way to teach than having a supervisor checking one's performance. But such supervision is essential if schools want to produce competent students. One teacher complained that one's efforts are all lost when a good job is performed and next term the class receives an incompetent teacher. Ninety percent of the 49 principals who responded to my survey acknowledged the need for greater teacher supervision, and the same percentage favored teacher accountability.

The *Council for Basic Education Bulletin* reports that in Pinellas County, Florida," about one-third of the applicants for teaching jobs have failed a general knowledge test at the eighth-grade level. Confronted with such evidence, the state Board of Regents has decided to require professional competency tests before a prospective teacher can graduate from a state university."[12]

"According to the National Council of Teachers of English," notes *Newsweek*, "it is now possible for an aspirant who wants to teach high-school English to go all the way through high school, college and advanced-education degrees without taking a single course in English composition.

"Some researchers estimate that more than 50 per cent of the nation's secondary-school English teachers did not specialize in English at all during their college years."[13] When 535 first-year teachers in the Dallas school district were required to take a basic academic test for high school students, more than half the teachers failed.[14]

Professor R. R. Allen of the University of Wisconsin said that English teachers are unable to teach reading and writing skills properly because they are improperly trained: "The certification of teachers of English is largely a fraud." Allen pointed out that the "English establishment seems largely disinterested in basic skill development," and "it is arrogant and abrasive in its responses to calls for educational accountability." Then Allen analyzed the situation:

And so, my friends—Johnny can't write. And why should he be able to? Those entrusted to nurture his talents are not primarily inclined to do so, seeking instead to invite his love of literature he is largely unable to read. Teacher preparation institutions and state certifying agencies continue to sanction college English education curricula largely irrelevant to the work which teachers must do. And the English establishment stands by saying, "What we do is so immensely complex and sophisticated that no one can tell whether we do it well or not."[15]

The schools must get away from the educational philosophy that lets everyone do as he pleases. This approach of not requiring accountability from students, teachers, and administrators must be eliminated if schools want to become effective learning institutions.

New York City's Promotional Standards

Back in December 1973, New York City was hailed for establishing stiffer promotion standards. *Time* stated:

> This month, in a break with recent policy, New York City's school system announced that it will no longer promote students who lag far behind their grade level in reading ability.
>
> For the past six years, the nation's largest urban school system (enrollment, 1,490,000) has passed elementary school pupils on from grade to grade even when they have been as much as 2½ years behind the norm for their grade in reading. From now on, however, students in grades four through eight will not be promoted if they are more than a year behind. Even under the new policy, slow readers would not be forced to languish year after year in the same grade. Except in rare cases, students will not be held back more than once in elementary and once in junior high. Those who repeatedly fail to meet eighth- and ninth-grade standards will nonetheless eventually be admitted to high school.[16]

Reading this, one would be led to believe that New York City had really begun to crack down on the problem of automatic promotion—but it was still a disaster. The article stated, "Students in grades four through eight will not be promoted if they are more than a year behind." This is exactly the problem; in the early grades where educational habits are formed the children are still automatically advanced. Then somewhere between grades four and eight they can be left behind for a maximum of one year in elementary school and for one year in junior high; however, I discovered few students put back two years. Instead of learning from its past failures and instituting standards for advancement, particularly for each grade, New York City will again require promotional standards for the fourth and eighth grades.[17]

If standardized testing for the basics is utilized for promotion, there ought to be careful evaluation of the tests. This appears obvious, but I received one of my great educational shocks when assigned to mark one of these standardized tests. Students received the Nelson-Denny Reading Test for high schools and colleges, which consisted of multiple choice of five answers for vocabulary and comprehension, and a method to determine the reading rate. While marking the test I became curious as to what mark someone would receive by pure guessing. If a foreign student not knowing a word of English, or for that matter an idiot having just enough sense to pick one out of five multiple-choice answers, took the test, what reading grade would he receive? Using the law of averages, I figured out his grade. I went to the comparison chart and was dumbfounded. Something must be wrong. I could not believe the result—an 8.0 reading grade. The exact level needed to graduate from high school!

I questioned the teacher in charge of the test to make certain I had marked it properly; he assured me I was right. Then I asked the assistant principal in charge of these tests, who also affirmed that I had marked it properly. Still not satisfied, I wrote to the company that produced the test. The editor in chief of test services compared a similar test and noted that a student could get a 7.8 grade equivalent by pure guessing. "We still think there is a too-high reward on the Nelson-Denny Vocabulary Test for guessing at grade 9—and it does affect the total score upwards more than we want," he replied. "We intend to correct this with our next edition of the test."

How such a test could be devised by specialists to measure reading grades is beyond me. Fortunately, not all the reading tests are like this, for when I checked another test by using the law of averages the grade was 3.7.

A New Honesty

We need a new honesty to evaluate what is taking place in our schools. No one likes to proclaim their faults. Schools act the same as individuals—success makes front page, failures are not advertised. But no longer can America afford this deplorable situation. A full disclosure of what is transpiring is called for so schools can become the kind of institutions they were meant to be, providing a proper education for all.

All students should know the basics; otherwise the entire educational system crumbles. The massive presence of illiterate children cripples and contaminates every aspect of today's education. Its effect reaches into every level of our educational system and acts as a brake holding back learning from all students. No longer should schools be permitted to be unsupervised.

There must be a total intelligent approach to cure educational failures. This is not a costly, elaborate program. In fact, it will probably save money by eliminating many remedial teachers. There may be an initial cost in ridding the schools of ineffective books and materials. But basically, the establishing of standards is not a matter of increased expenditures; it is rather an educational concept that expects and plans for achievement from the first grade on. The time to straighten a crooked tree is not when it is old but when it is a sapling. The old adage "An ounce of prevention is worth a pound of cure" is still sound advice.

Perhaps the shock of what is happening to inadequately trained children can be best expressed by excerpts from a letter published in the *Kansas City Star*, by Herman R. Sutherland of the Sutherland Lumber Company, Kansas City, Missouri:

> In our business it is necessary that people have a good grasp of simple arithmetic, probably what would be expected of a competent sixth-grader. Constantly we are finding job applicants with a high school diploma not able to pass the simplest part of our pre-employment test. Something is fearfully wrong. How can these applicants obtain a high school certificate when they haven't even mastered grade school, simple arithmetic?
>
> Some recent inquiry has developed the astounding information that in our school system a child need not become proficient in one grade before he or she is passed on to the next one. In other words, everyone passes. I understand that this practice of just moving children through the grades year after year, without any qualifying ability being required or tested at any level, has been in force for some 15 years.
>
> As I discuss this with mature people who are not educators, they simply can't believe that this is an accepted part of the system. This flaw is so monstrous that it is hard for me to believe it is not better known and publicly appraised and debated. To me it undermines the very foundation of our nation's future. Do we want a world where children are taught that everyone passes and that whether they work and achieve or not, the rewards are forthcoming just the same?[18]

Chapter 3

Training for Excellence

In 1970 James E. Allen, U.S. commissioner of education, announced a major drive to remove illiteracy in the United States by launching the program "Right to Read." It endeavored to focus national attention on the fact that our modern technological society had close to 19 million adults and 7 million children who were functionally illiterate. Right to Read tried to coordinate federal, state, and local governments, industry, foundations, public interest groups, professional associations, schools, and adult training centers to improve reading instruction for all ages. The goal? Eliminate illiteracy by 1980.

Right to Read
In the first five years total expenditures were slightly under 40 million dollars. The administration was criticized for its slowness in attacking the problem, and Congress reacted by appropriating 413.5 million dollars for the next four fiscal years to combat illiteracy.[1]

According to *Newsweek*, the federal government "pumped $40 million into eleven New York City ghetto schools over a period of four years from 1969 to 1973. The result: all eleven schools still report much the same low achievement-test scores and high truancy rates. In Pittsburgh, Houston and San Diego, millions more have been spent on the government's attempts to tailor teaching to the needs of individual students. There has been scant success in improving schoolwide performance. . . . The failure of the affluent society of the 1960s and early '70s to improve schools—at an estimated cost of $10 billion in Federal funds—is the subject of a report in the current issue of Columbia University's Teachers College Record. Dale Mann, a political scientist at Teachers College who has been studying educational change for the Rand Corp., assembled the work of a group of social scientists who have analyzed typical Federal projects of the 1960s."[2]

In referring to this study, *Time* said, "Billions of dollars were spent in the name of those reforms, but very little concrete evidence of success could be found. Rand Corp. researchers, for example, discovered that for every study identifying a school program that worked, another equally good study concluded that the practice was

25

ineffective. To many observers, the discouraging results did not mean that the reforms had failed, just that more time—and better-run programs—were needed."[3]

The federal government has shown its great concern over the massive illiteracy problems by its .enormous appropriations. Unfortunately, it treated the symptoms instead of attacking the disease. It endeavored to eliminate illiteracy by 1980, but if the schools continue to train children in the same manner, illiteracy will not be wiped out by 1990, or by the year 2000.

When Commissioner Allen became aware of the "full dimensions of the national reading scandal," he said, "I concluded that the single most important thing I could do on behalf of the nation's schoolchildren was to establish the right of *all* children to learn to read as the educational goal for the 1970s." He talked with state education officials, teacher organizations, and other interested groups about the feasibility of the goal. To his great satisfaction, the experts assured him that the goal was achievable. Then Allen said, "*How* a school system goes about correcting reading deficiencies is not as important as that it begin *here and now* to tackle the problem."[4]

This is the exact reason why the Right to Read program will fail and all other programs have failed. The most important aspect of teaching children to read is *how* schools go about teaching them to read and learn, and this item has most often been neglected.

The way to combat illiteracy is not just to pump money into schools and hope that somehow this shotgun method will cure the nation's reading problems. A $180,000 study by the Educational Testing Service found, after reviewing 1,800 reading documents, that it was difficult to turn up a new reading-teaching method not described in a 1908 survey of methods. There has been a continuous eruption of new reading-teaching materials, but the study, financed by the U.S. Office of Education, indicated "today's teachers have been brainwashed into feeling that they must have the latest gadgets, programs and publications or they cannot teach reading."[5] Some of the reading hardware contains magic-lantern projectors, jigsaw puzzles, word dice, tutorgrams, automated flash cards with talk-back recording devices, alphabet games, "dictionary-pictionary," word games, floor games, all sorts of instructional films and cassette lessons, and the new technological wonder—the computer.

Much ruin has been caused by educational theorists sitting in their cushioned chairs far removed from reality. They push their idealistic concepts on educators to get them to try their innovative programs. The charisma of the leader causes the program to work temporarily. It is then hailed as a great success. In time it fails, and another generation of children suffers. On the other hand, education should not just live in the past and reject all innovations. There should be experimental programs for new and creative concepts, but they should be implemented only after conclusively proving their worth.

Mastery of reading is the most important educational issue. Unless a child becomes literate he is lost, for nearly every field of endeavor relies on reading mastery. With the recent unparalleled increase in human discoveries, writing and reading have become crucial to the accumulation and dissemination of knowledge. It is imperative that educational leaders provide proper methods to teach reading and supervise schools so that students truly learn how to read.

Phonics v. Look-Say

The early Egyptians developed a highly elaborate system called hieroglyphics, which consisted mainly of pictorial characters for words. The need for a simpler system was obvious, so about 1600 B.C. the alphabet was invented. Instead of being a multitude of symbols, language was reduced to basic letters and sounds. Now learning to read consisted in mastering the alphabet and acquiring the ability to learn the sounds. This method was used until the early 1800's.

Reading difficulties became acute because in the 1700's scholars, knowing little of linguistics, fixed our English. Instead of stabilizing and producing a coherent, logical system of spelling and sounds, they gave us today's language. The problem is that the scholars adapted the alphabet from Latin with its 26 letters to do the job of representing 44 sounds. Efforts to simplify and regularize our language have so far all failed.

In 1820 there was a clamor for instructional reform to incorporate a shortcut to learning to read. Thomas H. Gallaudet, director of the Hartford Asylum for the Deaf and Dumb, had been teaching children at that institution by the sight-symbol method. He endeavored to teach normal children the same way, and in 1837 a primer published by him was adopted by the Boston school system. For the next eight years the "look-say" method was used; it was a return to the hieroglyphic system of learning to read. The results were disastrous. However, look-say did not die; it went underground.

Back in the 1920's when progressive education came into vogue, educators took a new look at what was taking place in the schools. They did not like the lock-step education children received: every child learning and repeating the same things. In order to have children use adult words and sentences as soon as possible, educators reinstituted the old look-say method.

In 1955 Rudolf Flesch published *Why Johnny Can't Read*, in which he said:

> What I found is absolutely fantastic. The teaching of reading—all over the United States, in all the schools, in all the textbooks—is totally wrong and flies in the face of all logic and common sense. Johnny couldn't read until half a year ago for the simple reason that nobody ever showed him how. Johnny's only problem was that he was unfortunately exposed to an ordinary American school.
>
> You know that I was born and raised in Austria. Do you know that there are no remedial reading cases in Austrian schools? Do you know that there are no remedial reading cases in Germany, in France, in Italy, in Norway, in Spain—practically anywhere in the world except in the United States? Do you know that there was no such thing as remedial reading in this country either until about thirty years ago? Do you know that the teaching of reading never was a problem anywhere in the world until the United States switched to the present method around about 1925?[6]

Twenty years after its publication Samuel L. Blumenfeld, commenting about the book *Why Johnny Can't Read*, said:

> It is probably the single most important book on American education published in the twentieth century, because it identified and exposed to public view the cause of the most serious educational problem this country has ever faced, to wit: the inability of our educational system to teach our children to read at the level required by the complexity of our civilization. Rudolf Flesch made America aware that there was indeed an identifiable cause to what was already, in 1955, a staggering reading problem: the cause was the wholesale adoption by virtually all of our schools of the look-say or sight vocabulary method of teaching children to read.[7]

But many of the reading books utilized today still train children to read by means of the sight-reading vocabulary. How is it done? In the Lyons and Carnahan set of readers, the first-grade book has 349 new words; second-grade, 467; third, 763; fourth, 813; and fifth, 744. Words are carefully presented, and previous words are repeated over and over until fixed in children's minds by memorization. In the first three years of education, children are expected to learn 1,579 words. The Scott, Foresman set has 1,778 words for three years. This does not mean children can read any third-grade book or reader, for each book uses different words. Only words fixed by memorization can be read. Anyone dealing with memorization knows how hard it is to memorize more than 1,500 different independent words. Many children cannot master this task. Consequently, they fail to read.

Children using phonics, however, are taught to analyze an unknown word by deciphering its sounds. If children know the sound *an* and also the letters *b, c, d, f, m, p, r, t, v,* they can say each word: *ban, can, Dan, fan,* etc., even though they have never seen these words. This method eliminates memorizing each word.

Some words in our language are not phonetical and must be memorized. Critics of phonics point out these inconsistencies, as in the sound of *ough* in *rough, cough, bough, dough, through* and *thorough*. (Incidentally, this is the worst single example of sound spelling in English.) However, advocates emphasize that 85 percent of our words are phoneticlly based, and almost all the rest have partial phonic constructions.

Phonics does not say that students should not memorize; rather, along with memorization they use logic and reason to decipher words. Children who know phonics are able to read words they do not know. Take the word *procrastination:* Pupils trained in phonics will break it into parts—*pro-cras-tin-a-tion*. Since children's vocabularies far exceed their ability to read, students properly trained in phonics will discover words by themselves.

After Flesch published his book, pressure became so strong that educators added phonics to look-say. But instead of putting it first, where it would help unlock and decode the mysteries of language, they put phonics in the second grade. There, according to one leading researcher, the college-trained teacher in look-say often forgot to use it.

Dr. Jeanne Chall, professor of education at Harvard University and author of *Learning to Read: The Great Debate*, did an in-depth study of teaching beginning reading. Chall investigated the research done on reading from 1912 to 1965; examined in detail all books, teachers' manuals and workbooks offered by reading system publishers; and visited more than 300 teachers of beginning reading in the United States and England. After thorough investigation she concluded:

> My review of the research from the laboratory, the classroom, and the clinic points to the need for a correction in the beginning reading instructional methods. Most school children in the United States are taught to read by what I have termed a meaning-emphasis method (that is look-say). Yet the research from 1912 to 1965 indicates that a code-emphasis [phonics]

method—i.e., one that views beginning reading as essentially different from mature reading and emphasizes learning of the printed code for the spoken language—produces better results, at least up to the point where sufficient evidence seems to be available, the end of the third grade.[8]

Phonics should be not just a supplemental tool but a systematic approach to the entire reading program. The whole problem boils down to a simple fact—multitudes of children cannot read properly. If look-say works, let's keep it. But if it's not working, let's get a system that will work. "Forty years of this sight-vocabulary nightmare are enough," says Samuel L. Blumenfeld, author of *The New Illiterates*, "Let's get back to the alphabet and get American education back on the road to sanity."[9]

One would imagine that after such a clear disclosure from Rudolf Flesch's book educators would seriously try to remedy the reading problems. The book was copyrighted in 1955, yet nearly three decades later the same methods are being employed while reading scores continue to decline. What does this show? The tremendous sluggishness of the educational system to change in spite of evidence of failure.

Dyslexia

In recent years a new term has been coined to describe children's severe reading difficulties: *dyslexia*. To assist the dyslexic, Dr. Joyce Hood advised, "Parents can help by not demanding too much of these children or the school. Mothers and fathers can emphasize their children's strong areas so that these boys and girls can feel worthwhile in spite of their reading disability. Parents can also ask the teacher *not* to try to teach too much at once."[10]

Frank W. Freshour, assistant professor of reading education at the University of South Florida, says, "Some experts have stated the percent of 'dyslexics' varies from one-tenth of 1 percent to 40 percent. Obviously this range could not exist if there were any kind of agreement as to what constitutes this disability. Since no one knows what it is or what causes it, how can anyone's definition be wrong? As a result, any self-proclaimed expert can espouse his ideas, and this is what has happened. If the clinic gives a diagnosis of 'dyslexia' who can dispute it?" Freshour discloses some of the other terms falling under the umbrella of dyslexia: "visual dyslexia, auditory dyslexia, minimal brain damage, strephosymbolia, specific learning disability, word blindness, primary learning disability, cerebral dysfunction, neurological disorganization, and Gerstmann's syndrome."[11]

Samuel L. Blumenfeld defined dyslexia as "an exotic word invented to describe the condition of a perfectly normal, intelligent child, who can't learn to read in the way he is being taught in school."[12] Commenting about the reasons for reading failure, Rudolf Flesch mockingly said it was "due to poor eyesight, or a nervous stomach, or poor posture, or heredity, or a broken home, or under-nourishment, or a wicked stepmother, or an Oedipus complex, or sibling rivalry, or God knows what. The teacher or the school are never at fault."[13] Certainly few children have legitimate reasons for not mastering reading; according to Ruth L. Holloway, director of the Right to Read program at the U.S. Office of Education, only 1 percent of reading deficiencies are related to the child's innate ability.[14]

New Math

The "new math" was another system to enhance learning by endeavoring to teach mathematical concepts rather than mechanical rote processes. Children were to learn the meaning of math rather than simply memorize how to divide, multiply, borrow, or count decimal places.

Since the introduction of new math, scores in math have plummeted. Morris Kline, mathematics professor at N.Y.U. and author of the book *Why Johnny Can't Add*, declared, "We are producing a generation of mathematical illiterates, kids who won't know enough arithmetic to balance their checkbooks or figure out their income tax on the short form."[15]

The shocking deficiencies of high school graduates became apparent during World War II. Incoming personnel were inadequately prepared in math to be trained in radar, navigation, and other technical specialities. After the war, engineering schools recognized that incoming students needed math remedial help. In 1952 the late Max Beberman, one of the two fathers of new math and head of the Committee on School Mathematics at the University of Illinois, began devising an improved curriculum. Estimators say it takes about 25 years for a new idea to be developed and become incorporated. But in 1957 a shock wave hit the smug security of America's technology sending shudders throughout our educational system. Sputnik—the first earth satellite—was launched by the Russians. Overnight that little silver globe knocked Americans from their pinnacle of technological supremacy. Legislators and editorialists demanded that something be done, and federal agencies responded. Funds were provided for basic education, over 100 million dollars for modernization of mathematics for national security.

The money was distributed primarily to universities and other institutions to find a new approach to teaching math at all levels. The most influential was the School Mathematics Study Group (SMSG), led by Professor Edward G. Begle of Stanford University, the second

father of new math. These scholars restructured the entire curriculum from kindergarten to grade 12. New math was devised by
educators at the university and high school level; elementary teachers had little influence. However, many experts warned that implementing new math might do more damage than good.

There was no question that the approach to teaching mathematics
needed changing. With modern technology advancing at such a
rapid pace, mathematics could not remain the same. Although few
educators would dispute the value of learning the logic and development of math, many challenged the fact that social and
business applications were ignored. "Words dealing with meas-
urement, taxation, insurance, and the like," reports John H. Lawson,
superintendent of schools at Shaker Heights, Ohio, "gave way to a
new vocabulary dealing with properties of numbers, set theory, and
systems of numeration."[16] Memorization, drills, and rote learning
were replaced with the "discovery method" and "deductive logic."
The new math was designed to help students understand what they
were doing, instead of learning by the drudgery of multiplication
tables and repetitious rote methods.

The new math became a status symbol, and despite warnings
from many experts, it swept into about 85 percent of American
schools. It introduced such sophisticated concepts as sets and bases,
algebra, geometry, statistics, graphs, and laws of probability. In high
school, students were taught such college subjects as advanced
algebra, analytic geometry, topology, calculus, and a smattering of
Boolean algebra and symbolic logic.

U.S. News and World Report noted, "In the late 1950s, 'new math'
was hailed as a breakthrough in teaching a subject that generations
of children have found distasteful. By abolishing the systematic
progression from arithmetic through algebra and geometry, the 'new
math' was touted as making it easy for children to understand and
enjoy mathematics."[17] The Cambridge Conference stated that high
school graduates would have received "training comparable to three
years of top-level college training today."[18]

The new program was not a total failure. Bright students were
stimulated and challenged by the difficult curriculum. But, as
achievement scores showed, the great majority did not benefit from
the new math. One state supervisor said, "Some leave elementary
school unable to make change for a dollar."[19]

Ronald Schiller cited one reason for the failure of new math: "The
language was formidable. Addition, subtraction, multiplication and
division were taught by means of the 'commutative, associative and
distributive axioms.' A sum became a 'union of sets'; subtraction
became the 'additive inverse'; a triangle was defined as 'the union of
three noncollinear points and the line segments joining them.' "

Shiller adds, "the 'senseless abstractions' of the new math, the 'prissy pedantry which is used to give the impression of deep mathematical insight'" evokes scorn.[20] Nobel Prize-winning physicist Richard P. Feynman says, "The total number of facts that are learned is often very small, while the total number of new words may be great."[21]

James M. Shackleford, a chemist with the U.S. Environmental Protection Agency, showed his colleagues math problems from his daughter's fourth-grade math textbook. Results? His colleagues in science could not solve them! Shackleford complained that the new math spends too much time on confusing and useless mathematics theory instead of devoting time to basic arithmetic skills.[22]

In the view of Dr. Samuel L. Greitzer, professor emeritus of the mathematics department at Rutgers University, mathematics teachers should now know that new math is officially dead. "Nevertheless, there are still many educators and more teachers who appear to be unaware of this situation," he said.[23]

Math and Science

The United States is "indulging in unilateral economic disarmament," stated Glenn Seaborg, Nobel Prize winner in chemistry, former head of the Atomic Energy Commission, and member of the National Commission on Excellence in Education. The economic disarmament is caused primarily by "our failure to educate our own people in science and math to compete in a high-technology world."[24]

Paul DeHart Hurd, professor of education emeritus at Stanford University, in a paper to the National Convocation on Precollege Education in Mathematics and Science, said, "During the 1970's, the United States experienced a 77-percent decline in the number of secondary-school mathematics teachers being trained and a 65-percent decline in science teachers. Moreover, of those trained to teach science or mathematics, fewer are going into teaching; many choose to work in industry instead." Across our nation, Hurd pointed out, 50 percent of high school teachers employed "to teach math or science for 1981-82 were unqualified; they taught with emergency certificates." He gave this report of what is happening in American classrooms:

> Our children are introduced to science and arithmetic in elementary school. Of the 25 hours available for teaching in a school week, children receive, on the average, one hour of science and fewer than four of arithmetic. Students continue math in junior high, but most don't start algebra—the first rung on the ladder of higher mathematics—until the ninth grade,

and then only two-thirds do so. Science programs fare even less well: Most junior-high schools offer few opportunities to explore scientific topics in any systematic or cumulative way.

More than 3 million young people graduate from our high schools each year. Most seniors have had a biology course, a little over a third have had chemistry, but less than a fifth have had three years of science. A traditional physics course is part of this sequence for only 10 percent of high-school graduates. Only 34 percent have completed three years of math. This may help explain the 70-percent increase in remedial mathematics courses offered by public four-year colleges over the last five years.[25]

This deficiency in mathematics and science is a serious threat to American economic strength and security. *Time* reports, "Fewer than 240,000 U.S. high school students take any calculus at all, while at least 20 times as many teenagers in the Soviet Union study the subject for two years. American youngsters take eight or nine years of basic arithmetic; in most European countries, the same material is covered in two-thirds the time."[26] The future belongs to those nations that can compete in a modern, technological, sophisticated world; educators need aggressively to pursue those programs that train students for a strong America.

Mainstreaming
Another issue in public education is "mainstreaming": the introduction of handicapped children, the blind, deaf, physically crippled, and retarded, into regular classes for all or part of their schooling. Mainstreaming is profitable if children have the mental ability to function in regular classes. Otherwise they will benefit more in special education classes. The danger is that teachers may have the problem of teaching simultaneously at many levels, thereby causing everyone to suffer, particularly the handicapped.

Gifted Children
Education should make adequate provision for the underprivileged. However, there should also be adequate provision for the opposite end of the spectrum—the gifted. The popular concept that bright children will make it on their own is false. According to a U.S. Office of Education report, "Intellectual and creative talent cannot survive educational neglect and apathy."[27] Susan B. Thomas, writing in *The Gifted Child Quarterly*, says, "But what happens to children in the public school who are intellectually superior? All too often the bright child reads a library book, runs errands for the teacher, or does another twenty-five arithmetic problems of the same level of difficulty. He frequently either withdraws completely or

becomes a discipline problem. He is often ignored or treated as an average student."[28]

"A gifted child in the United States stands less than one chance in four of even being identified as gifted," commented Dr. Bruce O. Boston of the Council for Exceptional Children. "Of the country's 2.5 million gifted children, probably no more than one in 20 is being touched by some kind of program for the gifted, and that says nothing about the quality of the programs."[29]

Dr. Hilde Bruch, who has spent more than 20 years in the practice of pediatrics and then in child psychiatry and psychoanalysis, told how the "elimination of 'competition' is often accomplished by underrating the importance of intellectual achievement." She points out:

> What is often underplayed is not native intelligence but effort and striving toward achievement. There is great concern that the less gifted child may be made to feel inferior by not doing well, and the gifted child is apt to be held back to the pace of the average. Parents who want to know how they can help their children to adjust to school life so that it becomes an all-around profitable and enjoyable experience are admonished not to be too much concerned with marks in reading and arithmetic. After all, if the little fellow does not do so well in these subjects, they can take just as much pride in his prowess on the athletic field. This is a sound concept—only it has led to a reversal, that athletic ability is rated higher than academic achievement. . . .
>
> Thirst for knowledge and independent clear thinking is not encouraged—as contrasted with the vague and emotionally charged discussions and opinions exchanged on all world issues. The student who tries to learn more than is necessary to pass the next test is looked upon with suspicion as not playing the game correctly.[30]

Educators debate the concepts of aristocracy or elitism (man receives benefits because of birth), meritocracy (man receives benefits according to his ability and hard work), and egalitarianism (everyone receives the same benefits regardless of birth or effort). America has prospered largely because it has adopted the principle of meritocracy. One of the primary reasons for the erosion of educational standards is the egalitarian philosophy, which belittles individual effort. Education, instead of having as its goal the fullest development of each individual, has often produced the opposite result by dragging everyone down to a common denominator because it endeavored to eliminate the stigma of superior and inferior students. The result: Many schools have become anti-intellectual. One wonders whether today's ideal school, in failing to make children bright, is fulfilling its goal of equality by keeping everyone dumb.

To support the fullest intellectual development of every child, some industralized nations provide a longer school day for their students. In addition, they have academic high school students spend 220 days in school per year compared to America's typical 180-day school year. America's school year should be increased, for in our industralized society it is no longer essential for students to have from 2½ to 3 months off for the summer. America needs to beware, for either it provides a more rigorous educational system or it will lose its future status as a technological world leader.

To support egalitarian concepts against promoting superiority, some schools have heterogeneous grouping: Children with various abilities are put in the same class. Here they may be reading at first- or sixth-grade level. Other schools have homogeneous grouping: Children with similar abilities are placed together. The top third-grade classes can have an honor grade, with the various classes descending according to student abilities. Some object: "In ability grouping you are discriminating against slow students." Not true. This method provides a means whereby teachers can provide the best instruction to all students, bright and slow. Because of the appalling decline in Scholastic Aptitude Test scores, a report was published, "Guidelines for Improving S.A.T. Scores," by the National Association of Secondary School Principals. It concluded that one way scores could be raised would be to group students by abilities.[31]

New York City schools have many educational deficiencies. Yet, in spite of the problems, there are schools in the city that provide excellent education. Some of these superior high schools require an entrance examination; others provide homogeneous grouping by placing children in honor, regular, and modified classes. Out of the 40 finalists in the nationwide Westinghouse Science Talent Search, 11 were from New York City high schools.[32] I went to investigate which schools produced such students. Seven came from Bronx High School of Science and two from Stuyvesant High School; both are specialized schools requiring an entrance examination, which is basically a system of ability grouping.

Test and Grades

One method commonly used to reward ability and effort is the giving of tests and grades. However, some educators endeavor to eliminate tests and grades altogether, believing they are detrimental to the learning process. Education Professor Sidney B. Simon of the University of Massachusetts says, "The grading system is the most destructive, demeaning and pointless thing in American education.

It allows certain administrative conveniences—permitting assistant principals to decide who goes on probation and who can take an honors course—but it doesn't help learning." Simon's ultimate goal would be to "banish from the land the cry, 'Whadjaget?' "[33]

Some of the alternatives to grades are: (1) written evaluations: the teacher periodically describes the student's strengths and weaknesses; (2) contract grading: students decide with the teacher the course content and grading procedure; (3) performance curriculum: the teacher stipulates in the beginning of the course the work required for an A or a B, and then students work at their own speed; (4) pass-fail: a student either passes or fails the course with no intermediate grade—this has been the most popular.

Concerning common school tests, John Holt went so far as to say, "Almost all educators feel that testing is a necessary part of education. I wholly disagree—I do not think that testing is necessary, or useful, or even excusable. At best, testing does more harm than good; at worst, it hinders, distorts, and corrupts the learning process. Testers say that testing techniques are being continually improved and can eventually be perfected. Maybe so—but no imaginable improvement in testing would overcome my objections to it. Our chief concern should not be to improve testing, but to find ways to eliminate it."[34]

What is the purpose of testing? Is it solely to have students regurgitate facts so teachers can classify their pupils as A, B, C, D, and F on their report cards, or is it a valuable tool to encourage learning? One of the basic rules of education is: Learning increases in proportion to student involvement.

If a person watched a TV program about animals, he would learn a few facts. If the same individual were required to take notes for a class assignment, his knowledge would increase. If the notes were copied, and in one week a test were given, the student would learn even more. Why? In order to know the material he would have to rethink the program and memorize important facts. If, after the test, the material were presented again for a midterm and then for a final, the student would learn the most. The old rule that repetition is the art of learning is still one of the basic educational facts. Testing enables the teacher to discover how much students have learned, how active they were in the learning process, and how well the material was taught. Furthermore, tests and grades produce healthy competition, which stimulates students to study and learn.

Some people decry competition because it produces winners and losers, causes children to compare their unequal talents, creates inferiority complexes, and hurts feelings. Dr. Lee Salk, professor of psychology in pediatrics and psychiatry at the Cornell University Medical College, believes that, ideally, children as well as adults should compete against themselves. "One person's success shouldn't depend upon the failure of another," he said. "To strive to do a better job than you did before is the impetus to greatest growth."[35]

There is no justification for unjust competition that forces children to try to go beyond their abilities. Parents who lack due regard for their children's innate capacity do irreparable harm when they force their children, with an academic shoehorn, to fit their preconceived notions. On the other hand, reasonable and fair competition is an important influence in human motivation, for human nature has an element that leads people to become complacent, self-satisfied, and just plain lazy. Individuals often need encouragement to act. Imagine two teams that did not keep scores for fear of hurting one another's feelings. The thrill of sports is competition; it causes individuals to do their best in order to get the satisfaction of winning. Some educators would encourage physical or athletic rivalry but warn of the terrible effects of intellectual competition. One wonders how the battle of sports could be so beneficial while the battle of wits produces such serious consequences.

Why does achievement decline when grades are eliminated? Pupils are insufficiently rewarded when receiving only "pass" or "fail" grades. What happens when one pupil receives 100 on every test while another receives all 65's, but both get the same rating—"pass"? The student who diligently studied to achieve high marks will soon get the message that such study is useless. Let this same class receive grades, and it will achieve greater learning activity. Humans desire to succeed and be acknowledged. Grades and marks motivate students by acknowledging and rewarding their efforts. Finally, when the term is over, which students benefit the most? Indeed, if only self-competition is stressed, failing children who work at their own speed and advance to third-grade reading level in the sixth grade are really successful.

Wishing to have much free time, teachers can use the following rationale to justify their method of teaching: Good teachers need not give meaningless homework assignments to cover up faulty teaching; class time is adequate for learning. Tests are unessential and create unnecessary stress; besides, children should enjoy their youth instead of staying home doing homework and studying for tests. Such attitudes will certainly engender friendship on the part of many students. Since most children abhor work, undemanding teachers are an accommodation to their aversion. Teachers of this type, however, must guard against student reaction. They grade liberally in order to avoid criticism. Imagine classes with no homework, no tests, and high grades. How many students would object?

But it is this failure to develop proper work habits in children that is a major cause of their ruin.

Truancy and Dropouts

Joe David, describing his teaching experience in Washington, D.C., says, "Most children with whom I've worked are sensitive and easily discouraged. The slightest rejection can often shatter their fragile egos."[36] In teaching low achievers I have detected the same low frustration level; they cannot handle discouragement and they readily give up. These children have not been trained to be persistent. Eagerly they start projects, but when difficulties are encountered, discouragement enters and the projects are abandoned. They are great followers of the pleasure instinct. Many take the easy road of truancy, then the ultimate trip—dropout.

The National Association of Secondary School Principals reports that the number one problem in our schools is truancy. The average attendance in New York City schools is 76 percent. "The 76% figure is a disgrace in and of itself," states Dr. Howard L. Hurwitz, former principal of Long Island City High School in New York City. During one of the last three-month reporting periods in his school the average daily attendance was 90 percent. However, Hurwitz points out, "Even the 24% absence rate admitted by the reporting schools fails to reflect an even worse picture of actual attendance in our schools." Children report to their homerooms for attendance and then cut some or all of their classes. Hurwitz declares, "I challenge any member of the Board of Education to accompany a team of three reporters (one from each of the major dailies) to visit any one of 50 high schools I shall name (with registers of 2,000 to 4,000). Time of arrival should be about 1 P.M. on a regular school day. I predict that on that day, when the school is reporting 75% attendance, fewer than 50% of the students will be in the building."[37]

On a national average for the past decade, 26 students leave school for every 100 that graduate; but Washington, D.C., Philadelphia, Cleveland, Baltimore, New York, Detroit, St. Louis, and Chicago report that between 40 and 52 percent drop out. The problem becomes more acute because many previously available low-skilled jobs are now being rapidly phased out by new technologies. Today industries have more knowledge-oriented jobs, leaving many dropouts with the likely prospect of being jobless and dependent on public welfare—and possible involvement in criminal activities. Yet hundreds of thousands of skilled job openings go begging.[38] Edwin W. Bowers, writing in *Iron Age,* a magazine for metalworking management, says, "The National Tooling and Machining Association (NTMA) puts the current skilled worker shortage at closer to

60,000 and rising rapidly. NTMA President Harold Corner says that by 1985 the U.S. could be deficient in skilled metalcraft workers by about 285,000 persons."[39]

Strange, with all the stress on making schools so pleasant and meaningful, with educators trying hard not to damage children's— particularly slow children's—self-esteem, that these staggering numbers of turned-off youth are fleeing the comfortable institutions meant to protect them.

A South Carolina study found that the typical dropout was a tenth-grade 17-year-old white male; though reading two and a half grades below reading norm, he surprisingly never failed a grade. The reason the dropout cites for leaving school is that he dislikes it, but at the time of dropping out he is receiving in all his school majors a failing mark.[40]

What is the real solution to this immense dropout problem? "If a student knows how to read, how to compute and how to write," says San Francisco School Superintendent Robert F. Alioto, a firm believer in the traditional approach, "then he will get an ego boost that no amount of social boosting can provide in the classroom. We are conning our children if we think we can pass them up grade to grade without giving them the tools they need to get along in our society. Youngsters who don't learn the basics are doomed to failure."[41]

James E. Allen said that "for most slow learners, the trouble really started when they were not taught how to read in the critical early years. Given special I.Q. tests that depend on interpreting diagrams or pictures instead of reading, two thirds of all problem readers turn out to have average or above average intelligence."[42]

Robert E. Grinder, author of the book *Adolescence*, says it has been demonstrated that the important time to help failing children is in elementary school rather than later on. Grinder reports:

> Baymur and Patterson (1960) administered both pre- and post-experimental measures of personal adjustment, study habits, attitudes, and achievement motivation to 32 high-school juniors divided into four matched groups; one group received individual counseling, another received group counseling, a third group had a "one-session motivated experience," and the last group received nothing. No differences were noted at all. During a three-year work-study experience for potential dropouts, in which school assignments were devised to maximize success, stable pupil-teacher relations were established, counselors were always available, and afternoon jobs for pay and school credit were provided, Longstreth, Shanley, and Rice (1964) found that those who received special attention dropped out of school as often as those in regular

school programs. Honn (1965) reported similar results from a one-year Back-to-School Project in Los Angeles. In spite of individualized programs, financial assistance, vocational guidance, and close, personal relations with counselors, 70 of 105 dropped out of the project during that time.[43]

Billy Don Jackson, star linebacker for the University of California at Los Angeles, had great ambitions. Unfortunately, he is now serving a prison term for stabbing his drug dealer. Jackson, from Sherman, Texas, was one of the most valuable football players in America. Scouts from everywhere coveted him, Billy Don chose UCLA.

Billy Don had one drawback—he could not read. However, there were college classes that did not require much reading. After his freshman term he was voted by his team "most inspiring player."

By his sophomore year his honeymoon was over. His teammates discovered that he could not read; they began to tease him by challenging him to spell words. They sang "Billy Don Dumb Dumb," to the tune of "The Little Drummer Boy." He was embarrassed to go to his remedial reading class. In his junior year he would not attend all his football practice sessions and was suspended from the team. Increasingly he went to his marijuana dealer—the man he later stabbed to death.

Looking back, he regrets his crime, but he feels that his life could have been different. Now he wishes he had been made to study while attending Sherman High. "The more I got better known in town, the more each teacher didn't want to be the one to hold me back," he told the court. "They gave me better grades than I deserved." He analyzed that the core of his problem was his inability to read. Jackson claims he's not stupid; when the court gave him an IQ test, he scored 106.[44]

Children must be helped before they settle into defeatism. This is a long-range program, but if we want to train successful students, solid proven methods of learning reading, writing, and math must be implemented in the early grades. Educators should honestly evaluate their programs so that every child receives a decent education, both the slow and the gifted. To hold back bright children in the name of equality is an injustice to their freedom. True equality exists when all children, bright and slow, are given the best education to develop their native talent to its fullest. This is training for excellence.

Chapter 4

The Educational Maze

At some schools students may attend class, take a walk, or leisurely bask in the sun. At other schools pupils may be found running and playing ball in the halls, learning to read by using comic books, unlocking the secrets of math with dice and cards, or strolling about in T-shirts and patched, faded jeans. Then there are schools where discipline, patriotism, dress codes, drills, homework, tests, grades, and a heavy emphasis on the three R's prevail. These schools represent three basic educational systems.

Three Basic Educational Systems
In free schools, students have complete control.
In open schools—also known as open education, open classroom, open corridor, informal educational, integrated day, and progressive schools—students possess basic control.
In fundamental schools—also called fundamental education, traditional school, closed classroom, contemporary school, formal education, and self-contained classroom—teachers possess basic control.
Two other possibilities are worth mentioning: the situation in which teachers have absolute control while students are totally submissive; and the radical approach of Ivan Illich, author of *Deschooling*, who favors eliminating schools altogether by training youth in craft centers and using libraries as resource centers for those who wish to pursue book learning. Since these avenues are practically nonexistent, we will concentrate on examining the free, open, and fundamental schools.

Free Schools
The most famous free school is Summerhill, a small boarding school founded in 1921, in the village of Leiston, in Suffolk, England. It has about 25 boys and 20 girls ranging in ages from 5 to 15. Summerhill has been directed by A.S. Neill, and in his book, *Summerhill: A Radical Approach to Child Rearing,* he describes his principles: "The pupils do not have to stand room inspection and no one picks up after them. They are left free. No one tells them what to

wear: they put on any kind of costume they want to at any time."[1]
Newspapers have nicknamed it "Go-as-you-please School."

Neill and his wife had one main idea: "Make the school fit the
child—instead of making the child fit the school." They said they
were going to "allow children freedom to be themselves. In order to
do this, we had to renounce all discipline, all direction, all suggestion, all moral training, all religious instruction. We have been
called brave, but it did not require courage. All it required was what
we had—a complete belief in the child as a good, not an evil, being.
For almost forty years, this belief in the goodness of the child has
never wavered; it rather has become a final faith."

At Summerhill, class examinations have been eliminated and
lessons are optional. Children can stay away from classes "for years
if they want to." One boy came to the school at age 5 and left at 17,
"without having in all those years gone to a single lesson."[2] When
Herbert C. Rudman, professor of education at Michigan State
University, questioned Neill about his school, he said, "I am concerned with a *living* process" and not "whether the children learn or
not."[3]

Neill asks in his book, "How can happiness be bestowed?" He
says, "My own answer is: *Abolish authority. Let the child be himself.
Don't push him around. Don't teach him. Don't lecture him. Don't
elevate him. Don't force him to do anything.*"

Notwithstanding, even at Summerhill, Neill has found times when
he must disregard his theory. He says, "One of the school rules is
that after ten o'clock at night there shall be quietness on the upper
corridor." On another occasion, he tells how he felt compelled at a
General School Meeting "to launch a vigorous attack on the seniors
for being not antisocial but asocial, breaking the bedtime rules by
sitting up far too late and taking no interest in what the juniors were
doing in an antisocial way." However, Neill did say, "Freedom does
not mean the abrogation of common sense." In other words, though
one has rejected all discipline, authority, directions, and suggestions
for children, if this approach fails, apply common sense and use what
one has renounced.

The workshop, Neill found, was the "most troublesome department of a free school." The shop was always left open for
children, but "every tool got lost or damaged." He had built his own
private workshop, but his conscience bothered him. So he decided to
open it, and within six months not a good tool was left.

Then Neill built an extra workshop for the school that would
always remain open. He had it "fitted out with everything nec-
cessary—bench, vise, saws, chisels, planes, hammers, pliers, set
squares, and so on." Four months later, as he was showing a visitor

around the school, he went to unlock the workshop. The visitor complained, "This doesn't look like freedom, does it?"

"Well, you see," Neill said hurriedly, "the children have *another* workshop which is open all day long." When he showed his open workshop, everything was missing except the bench; even the vise was gone!

When a parent asked, "What shall I do when my boy of nine hammers nails into my furniture?" Neill counseled:

> Take the hammer from him and tell him it is your furniture, and you won't have him damaging what doesn't belong to him.
>
> And if he doesn't stop hammering then, dear woman, then sell your furniture and with the proceeds go to some psychologist who will help you realize how you made your boy a problem child. No happy, free child will want to damage furniture, unless of course the furniture is the only thing in the home that can be used for hammering nails into.[4]

Back in 1931 Ethel Mannin, in her book *Common Sense and the Child*, presented this glowing report of A. S. Neill's school:

> Let us take an actually free community of children and see what happens. I know such a community—a school of boys and girls of all ages, from three to seventeen, where there is no discipline at all, *and it is the happiest community imaginable, and nobody does any of the wild and outrageous things which theoretically take place when discipline is dispensed with.* It is a case of the theory being upset by the facts. Nobody smashes windows or jumps on the piano or wages war on the adults, for the simple reason that in such a community, the adults not being law-makers, nor set in authority, are not the enemy; when there is complete freedom there is nothing to be revolutionary about. Nobody is violent because nobody has a grievance. The desire to smash windows and knock the furniture about is the impulse of frustration; the child's way of getting back on adults. Truly it is "the law that makes the crime."[5]

Mannin certainly portrays a utopia. However, when Neill describes his own school, he frankly admits, "Furniture to a child is practically nonexistent. So at Summerhill we buy old car seats and old bus seats. And in a month or two they look like wrecks." When they decided to insulate some rooms with beaverboard, the children began to pick holes in it, and the "wall of the ping-pong room looked like Berlin after the bombardment," Neill said.[6] The school has since been taken over by an internal group of counterculturists known as the "Summerhill Collective."

Suzanne S. Fremon, author of *Children and Their Parents,* wrote about "Why Free Schools Fail": "Nine months is the average life of a free school." (The term *free* refers not to the cost but to the freedom from curriculum and discipline.) Fremon asks, "Why, then, if free schools—at least in the early and middle grades—are such fine places, do they close almost as regularly as new ones open?" She replies, "Partly because many of them, however high their ideals, are unable to put these into practice. In some free schools the atmosphere is not friendly, but edgy; many kids seem just to mope around, and there is very little indication that anyone is, in fact, learning to read."

A "major educational and psychological weakness of free schools," notes Fremon, is that "a teacher may refuse to acknowledge that as an adult he knows more than a seven-year-old student. There is in the free schools a general willingness to allow students to abandon projects when they become difficult, without helping them to overcome the difficulties. The instructors pride themselves in not imposing their values on children—a consequence of the misguided belief that a teacher shouldn't 'teach' as such but should exist solely as a 'resource person' who is available for help when a child decides he wants to learn something." She cites one instructor who "declined to teach her students how to spell, on the grounds that this would be 'imposing values' on them."[7] *Time* notes about free schools that "the number of children involved, have never been large—perhaps one-tenth of 1% of the nation's students."[8]

In 1969 there were up to 450 "free universities"—academic utopias where students and faculty could pursue any subject of interest without any pressure from grades, credits, or formal examinations. These new schools wanted to instill self-understanding, self-respect, and independent thought into the educational system. They subscribed to Educator Mark Hopkins' concept that all that is needed for education is two people and a log. "Unfortunately," *Time* points out, "some participants in the free university movement are in danger of misinterpreting that idea. Those who see no difference between teachers and students in effect reject the intellectual hierarchy that is basic to learning. Teachers, after all, are supposed to know more than students. If both are 'equal,' the result is initially stimulating and ultimately numbing. Everyone goes his way—inward."[9]

"Heliotrope, an independent free university in San Francisco," notes *Time* in describing some of the programs in these schools, "offers courses in body surfing, howling at the moon and 'bofing,' which is Heliotropese for fencing with Styrofoam foils. Santa Cruz Free University has a class entitled 'Of Course We'll Like It,' a forum that guarantees the uncritical acceptance of unpublished poems, unpurchased paintings and unaired songs. 'Let's get together and take loving care of one another's ego,' urges the course prospectus. It is hard to see how this will lead to better poems, paintings or songs. Self-indulgence could turn free universities into a travesty of education in which 'rapping' replaces research, and reason gives way to sensuality."[10] The "free university" has now fizzled out, but some of the concepts are very much alive in our present school system.

Open Schools

One of the recent trends permeating the nation's schools is "open education." The open classroom received its inspiration from the British and has been hailed as the panacea for the beleaguered American educational system. Some open school concepts and goals are as follows: Every child should become a self-directed individual and take responsibility for his own learning and behavior. In this flexible environment of freedom, children are permitted to be creative and to develop their innate abilities. Though children are free, there is guidance: at times teacher and student negotiate what will be learned; on other occasions, the child decides by himself what he will learn and then informs the teacher. Each child can learn according to his need, interests, and readiness; no set amount of knowledge is to be learned by a certain age or grade.

Some proponents of open education claim that because of increasing complexities of modern living children need to develop self-discipline at an earlier age. Open classes allow them to discover how to make proper decisions as well as how to fail; in such an atmosphere pupils are permitted to make their nonthreatening failures a learning experience toward success. Teachers must trust the child to make proper choices; the principal must trust the teacher. In this mutual area of trust, teachers as well as children are free to experiment and fail, without fear or threat of being labeled as failures. This nonfailing environment allows both teacher and child to grow, teachers being free to explore their own interests and thereby pass their learning experiences to their pupils, and children being free to learn and experiment and to become productive citizens. By this means the boredom of learning is eliminated and a joyful atmosphere is created. Work and play are no longer opposites. By transforming work into play, the educational experience has been changed from drudgery to pleasure.

Both free and open education stress that students should be free to determine how and when to learn. The difference between the two is that in free schools students are the sole determinators, whereas in the open schools the teacher still plays a significant role in learning. In free schools pupils themselves decide whether they want to read at all; open education strives to teach children to read when they are ready and at their own pace.

I visited a number of open classrooms to observe their operation. In one class the room was divided into sections, and in some sections tables and chairs were placed for children to work on their individual projects. Children were scattered everywhere; some were playing while others were working. An aide was teaching math to a group of four children in this combined first- and second-grade class. When one child decided not to do math, the aide tried to encourage him.

"Come on, don't be lazy," she admonished. But the pull of the wild was stronger than the benefits of math; the child walked away. He returned with a plastic ball and broke it over the head of another boy sitting at the table. Now a second boy left and began to play with a gun.

"You want to sit over there?" said the aide to the first boy. Then she diagnosed the boy's problem: "You're tired. Go over there and relax on the mat."

The boy with the gun returned, but she took his gun away. In the short time I observed her, she had constant interruptions with just these four children; in the end only two were doing math.

Passing another open education class in this school I observed a large group of students on the floor. When a girl left the room, I asked her what they were doing on the floor. She said the art teacher had given them the privilege of doing art or playing an organized game; those on the floor had chosen to play Probe.

In a fifth- and sixth-grade class some students were making a mural. But one boy was drawing on the blackboard, another was flying an airplane, and two youngsters were playing the game of Battleship with their chairs and desk in the hall. In this school open classroom was called "open corridor." It lived up to its title; children could be seen playing and running in the halls.

This scene I observed in a school in Manhattan that was hailed as having a good open education program. The teacher, with six years of open classroom experience, did not use the contract system. Instead she endeavored to use the "freedom with guidance" principle.

The 26 first- and second-grade pupils were noisily grouped on a carpet in the corner of the room. These are some excerpts of the conversation between the teacher and her students.

"I would like to begin. I would like to begin. Come on children. When it's quiet I will begin to talk. Children, listen. Listen, children.

Please stop it. Paul, I want that to stop. Does anyone have a good idea to write on?"

"Bullet Man," a child cried out.

"How many would like to write on Bullet Man?" the teacher asked.

Someone suggested writing about buildings. "That's an excellent suggestion. We'll use that."

"Boo," yelled some of the disappointed children.

One child wanted to write about Bugs Bunny.

"You'll write later about Bugs Bunny."

"I hate it!" the child retorted.

Another child objected, so the teacher let him write about Bullet Man. Then she instructed the class, "You can write about Bullet Man or about your favorite building in New York City."

Still there were objections. "You can write about your favorite cartoon," she finally offered the class.

As soon as they were finished they had "work period." The children scampered around the room doing anything they wanted.

Fundamental Schools

Fundamental or traditional schools offer a disciplined environment in which every child is taught the basic skills in reading, writing, mathematics, history, science, fine arts, and practical arts. The primary emphasis is on learning; on increasing knowledge; on doing research; on developing open-mindedness, logic, and deep thinking; and on encouraging self-discipline. A positive image of America and the democratic ideals upon which our nation was built are taught and held in high esteem. Teachers endeavor to develop proper conduct, good manners, neatness, courtesy, and moral development. Students are expected to be punctual, do regularly assigned homework, and turn in assignments when due. Counselors are utilized to guide students for realistic future goals.

Students in high school choose their field of interest and also have the options to take various electives. However, once a course is entered upon, they are expected to do the work and learn the material. Teachers do not wait for the "good feeling" before students become motivated to learn; tests and grades are given; students who do not measure up to course standards fail.

A disciplined atmosphere is always maintained. Students are obligated to respect the rights of others and are held responsible for their own antisocial actions. The values of individual achievement and competition are balanced with teamwork, cooperation, and citizenship.

The picture of a fundamental school as an ironclad, fully structured system with a teacher holding a rod in one hand and a book in the other, whose stern face peers unforgivingly at a group of frightened children, is false. A pleasant atmosphere can be maintained within the framework of standards and discipline. Within the concepts of fundamental education, individual projects, field trips, and outside speakers can be utilized to enrich the experiences of children. In elementary classes, there can be a science corner, an art center, and math, history, and English areas to promote the natural curiosity of children. Pupils can be instructed in groups or individually. Though children are taught to write properly by using correct spelling, grammar, and content, teachers can provide writing assignments in which pupils choose subjects of their own interest.

Progressive vs. Fundamental Education

The problem today is actually between the concepts of open education and the concepts of fundamental education; very few real free schools exist. Though we are considering open education, it is basically neoprogressivism: the old-fashioned permissiveness with a slightly new addition. Open education has eliminated the concept of "nondirective" error; a contract is made to be fulfilled within a given time, but students perform their work at their own pace and whenever they desire. In a traditional environment students are grouped according to their ability; then they are expected to learn what is taught. If they are unable to grasp the material, they are encouraged to go home and study; if they fail to understand, the teacher endeavors to assist. However, if they cannot master the material, they repeat the course.

The philosophy of open education has an excellent concept in trying to encourage children to become self-directed. But there is a deep-rooted flaw: Advocates of this system misunderstand the nature of children. They assume that *every* child, after receiving guidance, will possess the maturity to make proper choices as a disciplined adult.

The difference between free, open, and fundamental schools can be exemplified by the dietitian in charge of a school cafeteria with an ample supply of nourishing food and desserts. In a free atmosphere, children are permitted to choose anything they wish, from nourishing meats and vegetables to hot dogs, french fries, chips, soda pop, chocolate cake, candy bars, and bubble gum. In an open atmosphere, the dietitian lectures students on how to eat properly, then lets them pick whatever foods they want, all the while hoping they will choose wholesome foods. The dietitian may even stand by the meat and vegetable trays to encourage the children to take these nutritional foods, but without applying any pressure. In a fundamental atmosphere, the dietitian presents the same lecture to the children, but then each child is required to take a meat, two vegetables, and a container of milk. For dessert, the child may choose, but even here the dietitian provides tasty and nutritional servings.

What would the children choose? The majority would certainly relish the free atmosphere; it would produce the greatest immediate joy. Why would a free atmosphere be so appreciated by the children? They lack the maturity and the ability to understand what is best for their own future health. What would parents desire, or even the same children when they became mature adults? Practically all would choose the fundamental atmosphere; they know that this produces the greatest health and happiness.

Let any parents implement the self-motivating approach used in open education when they want their child to vacuum the house, and discover what will happen. Some theorists claim that in a relationship of mutual trust between parent and child the strain of confrontation will be avoided and one of the basic parent-child conflicts eliminated. Parents need to wait until the child is stimulated by that innate urge to pick up the vacuum cleaner, or they can make a contract with the child stipulating that the vacuuming must be completed within a week but leaving him to make the final decision as to exact time. It is inhumane and undemocratic for a parent to impose arbitrary decisions upon a child, thereby subverting his tender personality and creating a slavish individual. When a child does become motivated, by all means, do not criticize him for sloppy work. A nonfailing atmosphere must be provided; in this way the work experience will miraculously be turned from drudgery into pleasure.

How would a traditional mother handle the situation if she wanted her child to vacuum the house? Mother would determine that the house needs a total vacuuming every Friday, so when the child came home from school she would be expected to undertake that task. Mom would allow flexibility in scheduling if her child had some important place to go, but she would expect the vacuuming to be done that night or the next day.

Once taught how to vacuum properly, the child would be obliged to do the job right each time. If it were done incorrectly, the mother would not be afraid of damaging a tender personality by saying, "You did it sloppily." She would also say, "Now go and do the vacumming all over again—but right!"

Regardless of the child's reaction, she had to do it the way she was taught. She had a choice of which room she wanted to do first, and she had the option to use all her creative imagination on how to get the job done faster. Mom desired only that her house became clean according to her standards. Having trained her child, she expected her to work to her full potential. The impossible was not demanded, but she wanted her best.

What did this do for the child? It taught her one of life's most valuable lessons: There are times when one must work whether one feels like it or not. Many of today's youth have been destroyed because of the stress on working only when they have a good feeling, instead of learning how to discipline their life. These artificial progressive concepts do not prepare youth for the rigors of life.

James D. Koerner, speaking to the Wisconsin Education Association Council, spoke of the bandwagon of progressive education, which has never really run out of gas but still exerts a strong influence. In the early 1940's it was called "life-adjustment education." Badly battered in the 50's, it became "consumer education," followed by "education for creative leisure" and then "quality education." Now, it is "open classroom." "The history of public education in America for most of this century can be read as a history of faddishness," analyzed Koerner.[11] All these various movements can be traced back to the progressive movement of the 20's and 30's, which was the result of John Dewey's permissive educational philosophy. But though society has seen and experienced the failures of progressive education, it keeps on emerging with some new catchy title.

More than 40 years ago Dr. Leslie B. Hohman, associate in psychiatry, Johns Hopkins Medical School, and assistant visiting psychiatrist at Johns Hopkins Hospital, made this remark concerning the progressive movement in his day: "In some advanced classrooms held up to us as ideal by the propagandists, nothing that would be recognized as teaching by a reasonably conservative educator is tolerated. The wise and helpful concept that activities should spring from the initiative of the pupils is magnified into a fetish. Practically any conceivable class occupation is all right—just so long as some bubbling child proposes it out of his own 'immediate interests' without a suggestion from the teacher." He asks, "Will the 'unhampered child' always be fortunate enough to encounter in adulthood only those who will bow down at the altar of this new religion of his sacred self-activeness and creativeness?"[12]

Dr. Hilde Bruch, author of *Don't Be Afraid of Your Child*, asserts, "Many of the progressive schools make similar errors in continuing a playful, completely child-centered nondirective atmosphere." She relates how pathetic it is "to watch intelligent and eager children with a real thirst for learning and knowledge, let us say of seven or eight, become fretful and disappointed with their schools because they do not learn enough and find no real challenge for mental effort in a routine that soft-pedals the idea of 'work' out of fear of putting 'pressure' on the child or making him dislike school."[13]

The concepts of the progressive movement have been like a

cancer destroying the vitals of our educational system. Open education is the new progressive trend of today, which will produce the failures for the 80's. The utopian dreamers will then devise another progressive name and add some educational twist for the 90's. Progressiveness needs to be dealt a deathblow and proper education provided for all children. The consequence of faddish addiction to progressive ideas is that innocent students are the victims. By the droves they are leaving schools as failures because educational leaders have not implemented carefully proven methods of instruction.

The same progressive ideas are being used in many of the so-called traditional schools. There is a vast degree of interrelationship among the various methods of teaching in free schools, open schools, and traditional schools. Some open schools tend to be more free while others incorporate more fundamental-style learning; some traditional classes incorporate various degrees of free and open school principles. It is relatively easy to become deceived by titles. Educators have looked at school failures and observed that many have a traditional setting, but they neglect to realize that though the classroom is a traditional one, the learning experience taking place is a progressive one.

Instead of seeing the problem as the utilization of progressive policies, these educational leaders blame today's failures on the traditional system. So what do many of them propose as their solution? Believe it or not—more progresssive concepts! Children need more freedom and fewer restrictions. Their policies will only plunge the schools into greater disaster.

Arthur E. Salz, assistant professor of education, Queens College, New York, in an article, "The Truly Open Classroom," asks, "Why is it that most open classroom teachers I work with still feel that automatic response in arithmetic operations is vitally important" since cheap calculators are available? He then says, "Why is it that these same teachers who get most of their news information from television or radio, most of their literary stimuli from film or video-tape, and most of their real excitement in life from skiing, folk dancing, listening to poetry, or making love, still believe that reading is the most important thing kids should be learning?"

Salz assesses educational experiences: "Did I get a kick out of that experience? Was it challenging? Did it force me to do my best thinking? Was this thinking pleasurable? These are key questions. The long-range assessment is much more difficult. We have tended, in the past, to believe that what we learned in school had *practical* value in the future. In reality this was a myth. Little that we learn in school is useful in helping us control and better our environment. . . . The 'good feeling' one gets from understanding some-

thing becomes the only justification for having learned something."
And he goes on, "The overwhelming conclusion for me is that if we
evaluate experiences, both in terms of their immediate impact on the
person and on the future enrichment to his life, then all subject
matter, all domains of man's endeavors, possess equal potential for
being educative experiences. Learning science has no more inherent
value than learning sculpture; social studies is no more valuable
than basketball."[14]

Paul Goodman, who holds a Ph.D. in humanities from the University of Chicago and has written numerous books and articles,
states:

> Up to age twelve, there is no point to formal subjects or a
> prearranged curriculum. With guidance, whatever a child ex-
> periences is educational. Dewey's idea is a good one: It makes
> no difference *what* is learned at this age, so long as the child
> goes on wanting to learn something further. Teachers for this
> age are those who like children, pay attention to them, answer
> their questions, enjoy taking them around the city and helping
> them explore, imitate, try out, and who sing songs with them
> and teach them games. Any benevolent grownup—literate or
> illiterate—has plenty to teach an eight-year-old; the only prof-
> itable training for teachers is a group therapy and, perhaps, a
> course in child development. . . . It has been shown that
> whatever is useful in the present eight-year elementary cur-
> riculum can be learned in four months by a normal child of
> twelve. If let alone, in fact, he will have learned most of it by
> himself.[15]

No wonder some children are failing when educators express
opinions like these: Pleasure should be the primary goal of education. So what if students are in high school and cannot read; one
can always listen to a radio, TV, or tape recorder. Furthermore, who
needs math when computers are so commonplace? Why, learning
basketball, baseball, or ping-pong is just as valuable to some
educators as learning the three R's.

The latest educational fad is the "alternate educational program":
Parents can choose the type of school they wish for their child, either
a free, an open, or a fundamental school. This sounds like an
excellent idea, and it is a better system than the present one. But
what happens when children graduate from these different schools
with their various abilities and enter other schools? The same
problems will be encountered as before, with some children lacking
basic knowledge.

It is imperative that *every* school should ensure that each graduate be proficient in the basics. There is no excuse for a normal child entering junior high school to be deficient in the three R's. There may be different schools, responsive to various needs and abilities of students, but any school that fails to produce children with sufficient basic knowledge has no right to exist.

One reason why some students still achieve success in progressive school systems is that there are still principals, teachers, and parents fighting these concepts. Though children from disciplined homes suffer from progressive programs, many do manage to survive the system, thanks to the home—not to the school. Nevertheless, the progressive system continues. And while children are doing their own thing in the open classroom learning art and weaving, at night many weary parents are doing as one irate Connecticut mother with a child in a sixth-grade open classroom did. She took the worksheets the teacher had given her son to teach himself and she sat down and taught him.

Progressive and Fundamental Schools Evaluated

"Supporters of the open classroom," states *Newsweek*, "contend that there is still no fair system available to judge the relative effectiveness of the two methods at any given moment. Standardized testing, they say, is geared to the traditional curriculum; the open classroom produces cumulative progress academically, and, at the same time, develops immeasurably happier children.

" 'What the children are now getting cannot be measured by any conventional tests,' declares Ronald Henderson, director of the Early Childhood Education Center at the University of Arizona. . . . Yet the public may not accept this argument for very long. At the Rincon Elementary School in Livermore, Calif., children's reading scores last year were lower than for neighboring traditional schools. So, in violation of informal teaching methods, Rincon was forced this year to step up its concentration on reading.

"Open classrooms, in fact, may not be able to survive a series of such apparent testing failures. As public awareness of the new system grows, so will the number of critics who find informal teaching suspiciously similar to the 'progressive education' that overtook many U.S. schools in the '20s and '30s."[16]

Dr. Rhodes Boyson, headmaster of a 1,300-pupil comprehensive school in a deprived section of London, asserts, "There is now a tremendous body of evidence that the introduction of neo-progressive teaching methods in British primary schools (for 5-to-11 year olds) has brought a distinct fall in standards of literacy." He states that "it is only over the last 5 years that we have come to realize how really disastrous these methods have been."[17] *Today's Child* reports that "Boyson also cited a study by Bernice Martin, a

Bedford College (London) sociologist, that found that nonstructured schools had particularly adverse effects on the personality development of working class pupils, 'whom the neo-progressives pretend to hold most dear.'"[18]

Answering the question "Do open schools promote affective development?" John H. Hollifield, in *Today's Education*, says:

> Maybe they don't increase academic achievement, say proponents of open schools, but that's because their emphasis is on other development, such as creativity or self-esteem. But this study of 50 fifth graders in an open school and 50 in a traditional school gives low grades to the open school in all areas. The open-school students were deficient in academic achievement, showed significantly higher levels of school anxiety, and showed no significant increases in creativity, self-esteem, or locus of control.
>
> The open-school fifth graders had been in their school for two-and-a-half years, so the study seems to be showing long-range effects.[19]

From London the *New York Times* discloses:

> The conflict between advocates of traditional and progressive education has flared anew here with the publication of a new study praising old-fashioned methods.
>
> The debate has significance to parents trying to choose the proper schools for their children both here and in the United States, because Britain's primary school system, perhaps the most advanced in the world, has had significant influence over American education practices.
>
> The central findings of the report, which has attracted widespread attention and critical response here, are that pupils who are taught formally by traditional methods tested significantly higher in the basic subjects: reading, writing and arithmetic, were less prone to make grammatical and spelling errors, and were no worse at imaginative story writing than children in progressive classes.
>
> The report that set off the renewed conflict between the traditionalists and the progressives was written by Dr. Neville Bennett and a research team from Lancaster University.[20]

U.S. News & World Report tells about "two separate federally financed studies of nearly 40,000 students over the past three years," and one study, by Abt Associates of Cambridge, Massachusetts, "found that highly structured programs that emphasized basic skills have been much more successful than open classrooms, particularly in raising the achievement of low-income children." Interestingly, the article added, "What's more, those children in traditional classrooms apparently acquire greater self-esteem than do youngsters taught in other ways."[21]

The tragedy of these unsuccessful schools is that hordes of young men and women are walking the streets bearing the scars of the failures of the schools. Progressive education appealed to Mrs. Wolynski as she happily enrolled her four-year-old daughter, Mara, in a private school in Greenwich Village. The school attracted upper-middle-class professionals desiring to give their children a different education from the pressurized one they had received.

Children had the educational freedom not to learn, and anything that bored them they were permitted to drop. Mara Wolynski, now a free-lance writer, in writing about her experience, says, "It was school policy that we were forbidden to be bored or miserable or made to compete with one another." There were no tests or difficult times. "The way we learned history was by trying to re-create its least important elements. One year, we pounded corn, made tepees, ate buffalo meat and learned two Indian words. That was early American history. Another year we made elaborate costumes, clay pots, and papier-mache gods. That was Greek culture. Another year we were all maidens and knights in armor because it was time to learn about the Middle Ages. We drank our orange juice from tin-foil goblets but never found out what the Middle Ages were. They were just 'The Middle Ages.'"

Creativity was the way to bring happiness, so children did not learn to read until third grade. It was feared that early reading would dampen creativity. "The one thing they taught us very well," says Wolynski, "was to hate intellectuality and anything connected with it. Accordingly, we were forced to be creative for nine years." Though the school, which had 16 teachers, put a great deal of emphasis on arts, they never produced one good artist. The children were not taught techniques; it was believed that organization hampered creativity.

When these children graduated from their "Canaan," they, and also their parents, felt a deep sense of abandonment. Whichever schools the children attended afterward, they were the under-achievers and belonged to the culturally disadvantaged. One student failed in one of the worst high schools; at the age of 20 he committed suicide. Others entered mental institutions, and Wolynski adds, "they were free, once again, to create during occupational therapy."

When Mara Wolynski started high school, the school psychologist was perplexed over why she was blocking information. He wanted to give her a series of psychological tests to discover the reasons. The trouble was, she says, "I wasn't blocking because I had no information to block." She was not alone; most of her classmates were experiencing the same difficulties because of the inadequate education they had received.

Teachers were puzzled at how she entered high school. "I did manage to stumble *not* only through high school," she says, "but also through college." First she attended junior college because she was rejected by all of the other, four-year colleges. Finally, she made it into New York University, "hating it all the way as I had been taught to. I am still amazed that I have a B.A."

Puzzled parents cannot figure out why their alert, inquisitive children were returned nine years later as crippled adolescents. Some may endeavor to justify this progressive school, saying that it was just her class, but the "same bizarre behavior pattern in succeeding graduating classes" was seen, notes Wolynski.

Now she sees her 12-year-old brother attending a traditional school where he is learning college-grade math. And Wolynski adds, "I know that he knows more about many other things besides math than I do." Her 15-year-old brother was yanked out of the progressive school at the age of eight by her reformed mother so that he would not become like his sister. She also noted the superiority of the traditional educational experience he is receiving.

"And now I've come to see that the real job of school," concludes Wolynski, "is to entice the student into the web of knowledge and then, if he's not enticed, to drag him in. I wish I had been."[22]

For Mara Wolynski it is too late, but can we permit the next generation to be ruined by these disastrous concepts? The sad fact is that, though the massive failures of the schools are now common knowledge, the solution offered by many leading educators is still more progressive concepts. They have become so deceived with the cunning arguments of this philosophy that they refuse to abandon its concepts.

Educational Solutions

Discipline, standards, grades, tests, control, obedience, and work bring horror to some educators' minds. They think of freedom, self-direction, individuality, choice, self-discipline, trust, and play. But why cannot these two concepts be combined—discipline and freedom—as in a truly democratic fundamental school? This is the key to effective learning.

The ways to remedy the appalling inadequacies of students are extremely simple, and their implementation will revolutionize the entire educational system. For schools to succeed they must put an end to the last 50 years of progressive ideas, which have undermined the foundations of education. The simple solutions for the educational crisis are as follows:

1. Eliminate automatic promotion by establishing basic standards for each grade.

2. Provide graduation requirements for junior high and high school.

3. Provide competent teachers and administrators who will properly supervise and train the children.

4. Implement fundamental educational procedures of directional teaching that endeavors to develop both bright and slow children's full potential by expecting and encouraging all children to learn and study.

It is inexcusable for schools not to produce students with a basic knowledge in reading, writing, arithmetic, science, history and the functions of our government. Only as concerned parents and educators mobilize to insist on incorporating these proven educational methods will schools be able to teach our children and save our nation from further disaster.

Part III

Disciplinal Solutions

Chapter 5

Discipline Problems: The Root Causes

"A moment ago the children were calm, working," says Joe David in describing his experiences in many Washington, D.C., public schools: "Then, suddenly, without warning almost, the classroom spins into action. All the teacher sees is children, huddled in a circle, and an occasional fist which flies into the air, then lands with remarkable speed somewhere in the circle.

" 'Hit 'em good,' someone shouts.

" 'Yeah,' the crowd chants. 'Hit 'em good!'

"The teacher, who was working with a slow learner at his desk, now braces himself for combat and descends on the fighters, shouting, 'All right now. Break it up!'

"At the other end of the room, while the teacher is pulling apart the fighters, another fight rages; the teacher, still struggling to separate the first group, shouts helplessly to the others: 'All right you two. Enough!' But the noise is too loud to be heard across the room."

This was only a classroom scuffle; David writes also of fires, beatings, serious knifings, and shootings. In his five years of teaching he never felt successful. Many teachers, he says, just leave for the suburbs because of discouragement encountered in urban teaching. In one junior high school eight frustrated teachers walked out in the first semester.

Once David was instrumental in preventing a problem child from smashing a chair on the principal. Just to have a child return a borrowed pencil can present enormous difficulties; preventing disputes from enlarging takes much skill. In the process of trying to settle conflicts David has been attacked with bats, chairs, fingers, and whatever else was available.

David says that corrective measures—suspension, talks with psychologists, or conferences with parents, principals, or counselors—were ineffective. Principals simply brought the unchanged child back into the classroom; frustrated teachers often heaved the problem child back into the hall. These rejected children then roamed the school in gangs and terrorized students and teachers. Teachers protected themselves by locking their doors.[1]

For years Vincent Rubertone had a dream. He wanted to become a school teacher. He lasted three months—he returned to his former job of working with prison inmates.

At 37 years of age he entered Brooklyn College; after much sacrifice he finally graduated cum laude at the age of 51. Referring to his graduation ring he said, "This means more to me than the Hope diamond. It took 14 years to earn it."

After receiving his teacher's license, he continued to take graduate courses and three years later was appointed to Edwin Markham Junior High School, Staten Island, as a seventh-grade math teacher. Leaving his job in the Brooklyn House of Detention at an annual salary of $16,500, he became a teacher earning $9,600 a year. His school was located in a middle-income neighborhood where 85 percent of the 2,300 students were white.

The students, however, gave Rubertone a difficult time. "Every time I turned my back to the class I'd hear a piercing yell," Rubertone said. "I was new. They were taking my measure. I talked to other teachers and found they had similar problems.

"They advised me to write to the parents. I was writing 10 letters a week. A few replied, and said they'd discipline their children. If they did, it didn't make any difference in class. When I asked that one nasty kid be transferred, nothing happened."

He had 20 math students who made it a point to talk when he was talking or throw paper when he turned around to write on the blackboard. After three agonizing months in the classroom, he left without even finishing the term.

"They made it impossible for me to teach," Rubertone said. "In three months they destroyed my dream."

The principal wanted him to stay until the next term, when he would receive new classes, but Rubertone felt the atmosphere would persist. "I was getting sick," he said.

His wife became furious over his decision to leave a job that made all his education useless. But he told her, "Do you want to see me in my grave? I didn't study and struggle all these years to be a juvenile correction officer in a classroom."

Rubertone returned to his former job, working in the storeroom in the Brooklyn House of Detention. There he has ten assistants called "time men"; of working with these criminals, he said, "In the 12 years I've been there I never had a moment of trouble." Then he added, "They're always respectful and obedient."[2]

Schools can provide the best educational programs, but unless there is an orderly environment, effective learning cannot take place. Some schools have orderly classes; many achieve partial order; and at others, discipline is so lax that it can be best expressed by a former teacher's reply when someone asked how long she taught: "I haven't taught a day in my life, but I served a three-year sentence in junior high school X."

Discipline Issues Unrelated to School

In examining the root causes of the discipline crises, let us first look at those for which schools are not responsible. Students' home life is an important factor. Children who enter schools undisciplined present much greater difficulties than children from disciplined homes. Today there is a serious deterioration of the American family, not just among the poor and minorities but also among the middle class, and it affects children's school behavior. Urie Bronfenbrenner, professor of family studies at Cornell University, states, "In terms of such characteristics as the proportion of working mothers, number of adults in the home, single-parent families, or children born out of wedlock, the middle class family of today increasingly resembles the low-income family of the early nineteen-sixties."[3]

Violence on television is another important factor. An investigation by the U.S. Surgeon General's Office, after a three-year exhaustive study, reveals, "The more violence and aggression a youngster sees on TV, regardless of his age, sex, or social background, the more aggressive he is likely to be in his own attitudes and behavior. The effects are not limited to youngsters who are in some way abnormal, but rather were found in large numbers of perfectly normal children."[4]

Every School a Disciplined School

Because of such factors many people would simply dismiss the failures of schools to maintain a disciplined environment and blame the effects on parental apathy, TV, courts, standards of society, lack of sufficient funds, and the prevailing ills of society, which schools are just mirroring. Certainly these issues have an important effect on the children—there is no substitute for a good home, loving parents, and a stable society—but when children are permitted to enter first grade yelling, fighting, spitting, defying, and showing complete disrespect for teachers, schools themselves must share the blame for the discipline breakdown. They must insist on disciplined classes, even when the children are from undisciplined homes; otherwise the entire educational experience deteriorates. One of the most important duties of educational administrators is to supervise schools so that every school maintains a disciplined environment.

Teachers recognize that some classes are much more difficult to handle than others. What makes them difficult is a small core of defiant students who ruin the entire class because imposed board of education regulations prevent the teachers from exercising effective discipline. In consequence, discipline problems are increasing, in spite of school personnel efforts to maintain order. And many educators leave teaching because of frustrations involved in trying to keep order.

It has been estimated that 80 percent of teachers leave after their first year because of their inability to maintain classroom discipline.[5] William C. Morse, professor of education and psychology, School of Education, University of Michigan, says, "No one is surprised when new teachers list classroom management as their number-one problem. But today many seasoned teachers echo the same thing, and some leave the profession to avoid the daily hassle. No one can expect fewer problems in the days ahead."[6]

A high school principal cited as one of the major causes for the increase in school difficulties "lack of power on the part of the principal to remove disruptive students from the school setting." In my survey of principals, 92 percent favored "more authority should be given to school administrators to handle discipline problems." When there is a suspension at the superintendent's level in New York City, Dr. Howard L. Hurwitz points out that it takes at least 40 hours of the principal's, assistant principal's, guidance counselor's, teacher's, dean's, security guard's, and secretary's time.[7] A student who is being suspended certainly should be given a fair hearing as to the reasons why, but when the procedure is so elaborate as to take 40 hours of school personnel time, such methods only hinder effective action.

New York City's Discipline Standards
On July 8, 1974, I was gratified to read this account in the newspaper:

> The new and unanimously elected president of the City Board of Education, has announced his determination to rid city schools of goons, terrorists and hoodlums.
> The boss of the restructured, seven-man board says he's going to crack down hard on assault, theft, extortion and other crimes that have disgraced New York's public school system.
> "What we're going to try to do," he says, "is to combine peace of mind with good learning."
> There's no way a child can concentrate on study to achieve maximum performance if he, or she, is in daily fear of being mugged, robbed or beaten by vicious punks.[8]

I wrote a letter to the new president expressing my delight at his election and his desire to battle school crime. My understanding was that one could not physically apprehend misbehaving students who refused to show their identification, so as a teacher and an assistant dean of boys, I asked what authority I had to apprehend a defiant student. Our school has approximately 4,000 students, I explained, and since many of these students are unknown to us they just ignore us by walking or running away. Our only recourse is to hope to see them in class and in this way apprehend them.

I told of an incident when I was in the dean's office that concerned a girl who had been molested. After she described the attacker, some of us deans scanned the building looking for the molester. While searching in a stairwell I detected someone who met the description. When I asked for his identification, he ran away. I pursued him and saw him enter a room. A teacher was in the class, so I asked whether she knew the boy. Fortunately, the student had acted foolishly—he ran into his homeroom and the teacher gave me his name. There was no need to run away, I told him, for now I knew who he was. When I took him to the dean's office, the girl immediately identified him as the molester. My question to the president of the city board of education was: "Did I have a right to physically stop him?"

I never received a reply and so wrote to the board of education's chancellor to ask about teachers' rights in breaking up student fights. The chancellor gave the letter to the director of the law office of the board of education. In his reply he quoted one of the bylaws of the board of education: "No corporal punishment shall be inflicted in any of the public schools, nor punishment of any kind tending to cause excessive fear or physical or mental distress."[9]

The law office director added that a teacher should not violate this bylaw, but in case of being assaulted should try merely to restrain the assailant. In regard to stopping misbehaving students physically, he noted that school authorities have an obligation to maintain order; however, school disruptions can usually be handled by taking a very firm and definite stand and "proceeding through the reporting and suspension route."

His answer indicated that a teacher could use only the reporting and suspension route to apprehend students. To make sure, I wrote again, asking specifically whether I could use physical force to take an unknown student to the dean's office, or hold him if he refused to come. Receiving no reply from the law office director, I wrote again to the chancellor asking the same question. He replied that the director had sent me a letter explaining the necessary procedure and that "I do not see what more you can be told concerning the use of physical force." He believed the director's letter had been "quite explicit."

That ended the matter. Unless there is an assault or a fight, teachers cannot use physical force. How does this stricture work out in practice?

One day while I was on hall patrol an unknown student came walking nonchalantly down the steps during classtime.

"Do you have a pass?" I called out.

She maintained the same pace, walking toward the door.

"Do you have a pass?" I repeated as I went toward her.

"No!" was her indignant reply.

What did she do? She knew her rights well. As if nothing had happened she continued on her way.

I cited the authority vested in me by the board of education of the City of New York, but there I stood, helpless. I could only watch this defiant student walk away.

One day a student nearly knocked me over as he raced down the hall chasing someone. Both students stopped running and began to return, so I called them. When one became arrogant and continued walking, I asked for their identification, intending only to give them a warning about the danger of running in the halls. When one refused to stop, I stretched out my arm against the wall.

"Man, don't touch me!" he indignantly demanded.

Though my arm was out to stop him, he kept pushing, while repeatedly referring to me as "man."

His friend had his identification ready to present to me, but he told him, "Don't give it to him."

Then the assistant principal came. He also tried to get their identification. The same student still walked away. The assistant principal likewise put out his arm against the wall to block him, but the student ordered, "Man, leave me alone."

The assistant principal identified himself, but he continued to call him "man."

The boy could easily have walked away, for the assistant principal was just as powerless as I was. However, this student finally submitted and went to the office.

A dean in our school once saw two students cutting classes while he was outside the school. He grabbed them by their arms and had them turn over their notebooks for identification. By board of education standards, this dean acted illegally. What he should have done when they refused to listen was memorize their faces, then hope one day in a classroom to find them among the thousands of students.

I asked a school security guard, "What do you do if a student refuses to go with you?" He answered, "We are not allowed to put our hands on a student." Did this rule apply only in our school or were all guards so instructed? "We can only put our hands on a student when he is involved in a crime or a fight," he replied. "If a student doesn't want to show his ID card, the best we could do is to remember his face and try to follow him over to his classes."

One old-timer on hall patrol in a Bronx high school told me how he handles defiant students: "You have to humor them." Students were cutting classes and roaming about the halls, but he could not use any authority. If he did, they would react with violent anger. The secret? Use authority by gently patting them and asking them kindly to move along to where they belong. Educational leaders have put school personnel in such a position of despised weakness that many students become intensely angry even when commonsense authority is utilized.

Concealing Discipline Problems

Educational administrators must show a much greater concern over muggings, teacher assaults, rapes, and even deaths that are taking place in the schools. Amazingly, it creates difficulties for some teachers to try to convince principals and administrators that such problems exist. "Most principals are big cover-up artists," said Sonya Richman, vice-president of the Philadelphia Federation of Teachers.[10] William H. Simons, president of the Washington (D.C.) Teachers Union, called the number of unreported crimes "incredible." He disclosed that many teachers are pressured by principals not to report crimes.[11]

Teachers in Nevada have been trying to implement programs to fight the "increasing incidents of violence, vandalism, and general school disruption," noted the *NEA Reporter.* "Unfortunately, the situation here is somewhat typical of many school districts where the fact that problems exist are denied by the administration and the school board.

"In Wooster, Nevada, teachers were compelled to write an open letter to the community through the newspaper, citing repeated instances of threats, fights, vandalism, and obscenity, after their appeals had been ignored by the administration. The administration's response was that teachers were using the discipline issue as a political football and that 'the situation is really nothing out of the ordinary.' "[12]

Investigating Schools

But let someone try to investigate some of these undisciplined schools and he will meet solid opposition. My first attempts to investigate were extremely frustrating. I had to receive approval from the board of education, every school district, and every school I planned to visit. My intention was to observe the general atmosphere of the school and to interview the principal and some teachers when they were unoccupied during their lunch period. No lengthy tests or surveys were involved; the whole procedure, I estimated, would take between one and two hours. Hopefully, I could contact many schools.

The board of education readily gave me preliminary clearance, but on my first effort to visit a Brooklyn school district the deputy superintendent refused my application. She could not let me visit these schools for an estimated hour or two without first receiving a detailed analysis of my activities, which would then be submitted to the school board for approval. Assuming that this was just a diplomatic refusal, I conferred with one of the district community school officials, who advised me not to pursue the matter further. At another school district I submitted the necessary papers but never received a reply.

This resistance led me to plot an alternative course: I would interview parents and teachers outside the schools. The first school I investigated was the Brooklyn district that had required a detailed analysis of my activities. Here I met a concerned grandmother who waited daily to take her sixth-grade grandchild home for fear of her being molested. The granddaughter was the only white member in her school. During the previous term children had thrown bottles at her as she walked home, and for no reason at all some older girls from another school had tried to assault her.

The grandmother related how this term her granddaughter's teacher was having trouble with a girl in his class. When the teacher corrected the girl, she called her two brothers. The brothers came to school and plunged a knife into the teacher's back.

A paraprofessional who had for many years worked in an elementary school in this district told me that children jump, run, and scream, turn somersaults in the halls, and fight in the classes—even to the point of throwing chairs at one another.

Standing outside the school and trying to interview teachers proved very unfruitul. Though I presented my board of education identification card, teachers were extremely reluctant to discuss school conditions. Slowly I realized that schools are one of the most difficult institutions to investigate. Even as a teacher within the system, I had much difficulty entering. My request for permission from a high school superintendent to visit four of his schools for an hour or two brought this answer:

> While I am certainly sympathetic to your needs with respect to your book, I find it most difficult to provide permission for you to enter our schools at the present time.
> I am certain that you are aware that the school personnel are under a great deal of tension during these most trying times. It

would be most unwise for me to permit any additional burdens to be placed upon our personnel.

It was surely a bit humorous that a short visit from a high school teacher would produce such a strain on the staff. Hampered from investigating the schools, I fortunately discovered another method— entrance as a substitute teacher. Since I was on a leave of absence without pay to write this book, I could receive a substitute's license. No longer would I have to be "approved" by district superintendents and principals to gain entrance; the school secretaries called the needed substitutes. The suspicion I encountered in interviewing teachers outside the school changed dramatically when I inter- viewed them inside. Now that I was one of them, they freely shared their feelings.

As a substitute teacher I had the unique opportunity to roam the halls freely and observe students and teachers. A regular teacher, who is usually assigned to a room or a few rooms in a certain area, would hesitate to wander around areas of a school where he or she did not teach. But since I was a new substitute, there was not that suspicion when during my free period I would walk through the corridors of the entire school with my substitute assignment sheet in hand. When on a few occasions I was questioned, I replied, "I'm a substitute," and I just kept on walking.

After investigating schools throughout New York City, I readily understood why administrators eagerly blocked my attempts. In a modern junior high school located in lower East Side, Manhattan, with an enrollment of 1,200, I stopped a boy taking a trash can to the rear of the room to play ball. When other students wanted to play cards, I forbade them, but one student just laughed and said they always played cards. With that they sat down and began their game. Into the class walked the assistant principal, but the students continued their card game. He left without saying a word.

Students could be seen roving the halls, playing ball in class- rooms, fighting, climbing on desks and lockers, and harassing teachers trying to teach. In schools like these even the boys' and girls' lavatories are locked; in this school they had only one opened for each with an aide checking passes.

In a junior high school in Brownsville, Brooklyn, I observed only four pupils in class while the teacher was debating with other students in the hall. For some reason the teacher refused to let these students enter his class, but one just pushed his way through. The teacher closed the door; the others kept banging and kicking it. Students were scattered everywhere in this minority school. In one smoke-filled section on the top floor about 35 were congregated.

While walking through the halls during the first period in a modern South Bronx intermediate school, I noticed that already students were roaming the halls. In one large, beautiful, carpeted classroom there was a regular social studies teacher with a noisy class of students. Across the hall a math teacher had a class of chattering pupils, with two boys in the rear playing cards. Though this school was just eight months old, the art room lockers, walls, and ceiling were heavily marked with crayons.

I was substituting for the science teacher. In the modern science room two hanging wall units, apparently to hold vials for science experiments, were broken. The classroom had five sinks, but the water fixtures and various jets were missing; within two months the classes damaged all the water fixtures. Students told me what transpires with their regular teacher: They fight, climb on desks, knock over desks, and throw chairs while the teacher is teaching. They also play cards and basketball. (In classroom basketball one student sits by the sink on one end of the science table while another sits at the other sink; they shoot into each other's sink using a paper ball.) No one from the outside can observe what is going on because the door window is conveniently blocked with paper.

One science class I taught, or tried to teach, was the SP (special students): the bright seventh-grade class taking the normal three years in two. Though work had been planned for them, they did whatever they wanted; they jumped on one another, ran around the room while pushing chairs in the pathway of whoever was chasing them, and had wrestling matches, which I tried to stop. A group of boys and girls sat on the science table and loudly sang, "La la, la la," while rocking back and forth with the music. At first I was unsuccessful in getting them off the table. After a bit of persuasion they finally obeyed, then sat on a desk and sang again.

This special class of bright students returned for another period. Although I again had work prepared for them, some emptied desks and began a paper fight. Others began to run around, while some wrestled. It was bedlam. I called for the dean, but before he came I made a mental picture of the serious disturbers so I could report them. When the dean appeared, I asked whether he wanted to know the troublemakers.

"There's no reason for it in this class," he replied. He ignored the disruptions and nonchalantly walked out.

A boy who did not belong in my class came into the room. When I spoke to this six-foot-tall student, he retorted, "Shut up." When I reprimanded him for talking this way to a teacher, he said he came from Harlem and I should meet him there. He finally left the room—in his own time.

Invariably, students could be seen meandering about the halls during classtime. Although on one occasion two deans were in the hall, nothing was done about these roaming students. Once I saw a student run and fall. I thought he had tripped. I was mistaken; other students were also running and falling—they were running and sliding on the new tile hallway as though they were on ice.

In another school, someone kicked my classroom door. I opened the door and looked out, but no one was there. The act was repeated. When I related this incident to a teacher, he shared with me this nugget: Do not open the door at the first knock; if a student really wants to enter, he will keep knocking.

While teaching in the South Bronx, two fourth grade boys were arguing. Then a girl in the class pushed one into the other and a fight began. I intervened and stopped the fight. One boy then raised a chair over his head to strike the other, so I quickly went for the chair. He picked up a serving tray, and in trying to grab him I ripped his shirt sleeve. A guard and teacher appeared, but he continued his violent resistance as they removed him. When he returned to class, he threatened to bring his sister the next day because I had torn his shirt. Since I substituted only one day in each school, I had nothing to fear.

Shortly thereafter two girls began a fight. When I attempted to stop them, one girl twice stomped on my toes. While being removed by the guard, this fourth-grade girl put up a fierce struggle.

In a Queens middle-class neighborhood a principal had all elementary pupils lined up orderly and quietly outside as he addressed them. This appeared to be a well-disciplined school. The area has been changing, and the school was now approximately half Spanish and half white. The principal warned me about disciplining the children: Do not "touch them." Though the teacher was going to be absent until the end of the term, more than three weeks away, the principal had no material to offer to teach the class.

One of my third-grade girls warned me that the class was noisy, and knowing the importance of starting right I determined to obtain immediate control. After children put away their belongings, they were at once to do "class news." The assignment consisted in writing five sentences about the class. Some pupils, however, could barely write. When I asked one of the girls to write, a nearby student said, "She don't know how."

I had a spelling lesson with these third-grade children, who in a few weeks would be advanced to the fourth grade. One girl had received permission from the teacher to write only the first and last letters of each word: for the word *bat* she wrote *bt*; for *fox*, *fx*; and for *train*, *hn* (this she misspelled). Another girl wrote only the first letter for each word; even so she made many mistakes.

At the beginning of the class the students were quiet and busy.

The principal came in to observe, commenting as he left, "Fantastic!" However, this success was short-lived. Soon the class became disorderly. I told the children to be quiet, but my voice just echoed off the walls. The principal walked in and restored order. When I reported that a girl had refused to work and was causing constant problems, he said she had learning disabilities and I should do the best I could. A number of times he appeared and regained order, but as soon as he left the class would misbehave. Finally he asked whether I could handle the class; otherwise, he would have to divide it. It was an embarrassing position: Here I was as a professional teacher and being made to feel incompetent.

(When I was a high school teacher and dean, students who knew me would immediately come to order. On one occasion, on the school's Senior Day, a teacher lost control of her class, but when I walked into the class, there was silence. Although I did not yell, the students knew that if anyone caused trouble I would not hesitate to take immediate action. Mentioning to a dean I had worked with, of the disorders I experienced while substituting, called forth an astonished "This is happening in *your* class?")

The elementary school principal waited for my response to whether he should divide the class. Wishing not to be defeated, I said I would continue to try to teach. Since I was a substitute who would not be returning to this school, I complained to the principal that *he* should do something about the defiant children.

"It's your responsibility, my friend," the principal replied.

I walked around the class and pointed out five students who refused to do the assigned work. He walked out of the room and did nothing.

One girl was the class scapegoat. While she was crying at her desk, another girl came from behind and hit her in the back. I had seen what happened and told her I would report the incident to the principal. She twice stuck out her tongue at me. When the principal arrived once more and heard what had transpired, he just scolded her. As the principal left, she sneered at him.

After breaking up a fight between a boy and a girl, I told the girl, "Sit down."

"No! I don't have to," she said as she walked away. On another occasion I had two fights going on at the same time.

Someone knocked on the door and two girls opened it. A third-grade boy reached in and grabbed the private parts of one of them. One girl told me the boys do this often.

When I asked this third-grade class whether they acted so disorderly with their regular teacher, they said they did not like the teacher and they acted even worse. Going home I met another teacher, who said in referring to this school, "It's crazy, it's crazy."

She also had problems and her classes were the same. A boy in her class made a fire in a basket, and the principal did nothing about it. I asked her why the regular teacher was not coming back to her class; she believed she had had a nervous breakdown. The teacher of my class had taught for 16 years. Though she really tried to exercise class control, she was unsuccessful. The children were so difficult to handle that she would come to this teacher and ask for advice because she believed she had better control.

Schools—Habitation for Criminals?

In *New York Teacher* Jeremiah Mckenna, director of Policy Sciences Center, Inc., a research foundation organized to improve all public and private decision-making processes, says of New York City schools: "The absence of sanctions against crime outside or inside the schools has therefore transformed some of the city's schools into sanctuaries for crime. Stated another way, some of the schools are in danger of becoming *places where persons gather for the purpose of engaging in unlawful conduct.* The italicized words constitute the statutory definition of a criminal nuisance found in section 240.45(2) of the New York State Penal Law, a crime classified as a Class B Misdemeanor. There is a clear public policy against maintaining criminal nuisances, and some schools may cross that line if their student criminal element is not brought under control or removed." Some "schools, like our prisons, have become places where crime-prone juveniles are initiated into a criminal subculture and trained in criminal skills."

Not only did some schools become "sanctuaries for crime," but, Mckenna notes, it was in New York City schools that *drugs became firmly entrenched in the city.* "We know that 1968–1970 was the peak period of the city's drug abuse epidemic and that the principal contact point for the spread of the 'American Disease' was the school system," he says. "The student addict-pusher found a sanctuary in the school system, free from harassment by the police. The failure to act vigorously against the student addict-pusher exposed a generation of students to the contagion of drug addiction with disastrous results." Even though drugs were brought into the city from outside, it was primarily schools that became a haven for drug addicts and pushers.

Mckenna reports that a survey was conducted by the board's Bureau of Educational Research in 1970. It "indicated that drug use was reaching epidemic proportions among the student population. Interviews by Board of Education interviewers of known addicts who had graduated revealed that 75 percent of these addicts admitted selling drugs to their fellow students while in the school system. Nevertheless, the central board insisted on sheltering the addict population in the schools and refused to report suspected drug abusers to the proper authorities."

The city's Health Code required all public agencies, including the schools, to disclose all names of suspected drug users to a Central Narcotics Register. This register was strictly confidential, even law enforcement personnel being prevented from utilizing it. The board refused to submit names of suspected drug abusers. Board of Education Chancellor Harvey Scribner was caught "issuing an unlawful directive to school personnel ordering noncompliance with the Health Code." When board members were confronted with the issue, they withdrew the directive.

If a student took action to expose criminal elements in school, Mckenna said, it would bring "great personal risk and no results. The clear message from the school authorities is acquiescence toward criminal conduct." And he warned, "Our schools may be conditioning an entire generation in the perceived futility of positive resistance to the criminals in our midst."

In concluding his article on "Crime in the Schools," Mckenna says gloomily, "The goal of a relatively crime-free educational environment seems further off each year. The central board has thus far exhibited dreadful confusion in the goals it is pursuing in this critical area, and the upward trend in student crime makes for a pessimistic prognosis." He then predicts, "Crime in the schools, therefore, remains a bleak but certain prospect unless radically different policies and policy-making procedures are quickly implemented by the central board."[13]

The U.S. Senate Judiciary Subcommittee on Juvenile Delinquency reports, "The last decade in America has been and continues to be alarmingly and dramatically upward." There were 70,000 serious assaults on teachers in 1973.[14] The *American School Board Journal* says that within the past decade crimes against students increased by 3,000 percent and assaults on teachers by 7,000 percent.[15]

If such crime increased 100 percent, it would be serious, 200 percent would be outrageous, but figures like these?

Can we let these shocking statistics sink into our minds? Must we be told that behind each figure there is a human being suffering? Consider the victims of the 100 murders, 12,000 robberies, 9,000 rapes, and 204,000 aggravated assaults by school-age children in one year![16] Think of young children who must exercise great bladder control for fear of a toilet shakedown; the apprehensions of those who must walk in groups to protect themselves from gang attacks; the fright of teachers, parents, and children when they hear of muggings, stabbings, and rapings. But what has happened after these statistics were reported? Instead of 70,000 assaulted teachers, by 1979 students attacked 110,000 teachers.[17]

I have tried to show how powerless I was as a teacher in coping with student misbehavior because of policies forced upon me by New York City school administrators. Though courts have contributed to the breakdown of discipline, the Supreme Court has ruled that teachers can punish misbehaving children, even by the use of corporal punishment. Educators need to reverse the disastrous trend of permitting defiant children to ruin the schools. Teachers have the important function of training children to be responsible citizens. Unless educators insist on their right to maintain a disciplined environment, we will continue to see many children misbehave.

Schools—Training Centers for Proper Social Behavior

Schools have a direct relation to children's antisocial behavior. When children enter school, it is their first direct contact with society. If in school they do not learn that legitimate authorities are to be obeyed and respected, their disrespect and antisocial behavior will be demonstrated outside the school. What kind of picture is presented when teachers stand helpless before defiant children? What are children learning when they observe students cursing, pushing, fighting, and showing disregard for their classmates while a feeble teacher tries to stop them? Might prevails, not justice.

Researchers from the Institute for Juvenile Research of the Illinois Department of Mental Health in a six-year study questioned more than 3,000 teenagers about infractions, from cheating on exams to drug abuse, theft, and violence. In searching for causes of juvenile delinquency, the report noted, "Even adolescents who may say they fully share the values of their parents do not necessarily act on those values when in the company of their peers." Then the report said, "Much of the concern over juvenile delinquency can only be alleviated by changes in the institutions which process youth," and the "high schools and junior high schools loom as fatefully important institutions."[18] Besides providing children with an education, schools can do much to help society train children to engage in proper social behavior. Today, since many educators fail to incorporate proper disciplinary methods, they are in effect training children how to misbehave.

Who are the ones committing much of today's crime? The Federal Bureau of Investigation Uniform Crime Report stated that 45 percent of the serious crimes were committed by individuals under 18 years of age. These are schoolage children![19] And *Newsweek* reports this shocking statistic: "Juvenile crime has risen by 1,600 percent in twenty years."[20]

No longer can children today feel free to walk, skate, bike-ride, or travel by mass transit system as in former years. Some parks are not safe even in the daytime. In New York City policemen ride subways and stand patrol on train stations. People must carry exact change to ride buses since bus drivers demanded protection from frequent holdups. Cities have better street lighting and sophisticated crime detection equipment, but with all this juvenile crime has sky-rocketed. Has youth changed over the past 30 years, or are parents producing more violent, less intelligent children? Is it their vitamin-enriched diet, their environment, or have their genes and chromosomes been radically altered? The change has occurred in the way our society tolerates misbehavior—particularly in schools.

Something must be done to reverse the intolerable conditions existing in many schools. Criticism of schools by parents and of parents by schools does not lead to solutions. Both parents and schools have their responsibility to train children properly. There is no virtue in just wringing hands while watching multitudes of undisciplined youth being ruined. Much of the rising delinquent behavior is due to the procedures forced upon teachers by ad-ministrators. Children deserve a school environment where they can learn in freedom from fear.

American education in many schools has passed the crisis point. It is a disaster. The school conditions that I have observed and partially described are appalling; to tolerate them amounts to a crime against humanity. How many more children must be destroyed before leaders will change? To solve the discipline crises, we need a new, honest look at our schools, with an eye to changing the deplorable situation by incorporating President Truman's motto: "The buck stops here."

Chapter 6

Love and Discipline

For more than 40 years Dr. Smiley Blanton listened to people share their hopes, fears, likes, and dislikes about themselves and the world. He heard mature people trying to mend ragged ends of troubled lives; adolescents telling secret resentments and anxieties; little children indirectly describing troubles; and the elderly sharing failures, successes, and dreams of the future.

Universal Need for Love

After many years Dr. Blanton discovered one important fact: "As I look back over the long, full years, one truth emerges clearly in my mind—the universal need for love. Whether they think they do or not, all people want love."[1]

Jean Dunaway, an elementary school teacher in Memphis, works wonders with her children: "I love my profession; I enjoy children. I'm happy in my school. I haven't lost my mind; I've found a method that works for me that helps both the children and me enjoy school. I know it's not the answer for everyone, but it has cut discipline problems in my class by more than half."

Of the 30 children in her class, 80 percent are black. She claims she is not an expert; in fact, she is a low-seniority teacher who is placed in a new school and a new grade every year.

"I discovered the 'secret' when I taught first grade," says Dunaway. "I used to let the children know I liked them by a revolutionary means—I touched them."

She did a lot of hugging that year. One of her colleagues asked how she could tolerate children all around her, hugging her knees, standing on her toes, and following her the whole day. "To me, it was one more little reward of teaching children," she says.

As she moved to the fourth grade and then to the sixth, she realized how sensitive children were about feelings, bodies, and peer approval. Believing that expressing love was embarrassing for the sixth-grade children, she taught her class in the conventional way. She became cross, the children became hot and argumentative, and she began to yell.

Finally, she told the class she had to drive 35 miles to school every day in the peak of traffic and needed help. Each day she needed two things: a smile from each child to get her started in the morning, and one before dismissal to take home with her. The children were wary at first, but she went around the class collecting their smiles. If a child did not respond, she hugged a smile out, a method she does not recommend for a fiercely angry or resentful child. Though she realizes that this method is not for everyone, for her it works. It is her way of saying "I love you."[2]

Effective Teaching

Effective teaching is an art that is motivated by love for students. Some teachers show their love in an emotional way, like Jean Dunaway; others in a more unobtrusive manner. However it's shown, love must be demonstrated for a harmonious learning atmosphere.

A young girl kicked, screamed, and had tantrums to such an extent that her private tutor labeled her a "wild little creature" and a "little savage." While eating breakfast, the girl reached into her teacher's plate to grab some food, but the tutor stopped her. The girl went into a tantrum—threw herself on the floor, kicked, gave out unearthly screams, and tried to jerk the teacher's chair from under her. Undaunted, the teacher kept eating. Then the girl pinched her teacher; but every time she pinched, the teacher slapped her.

When the girl sat down again to eat breakfast, the teacher gave her a spoon. She refused to eat with a spoon and threw it on the floor. She wanted to eat with her hands. The teacher forced her off the chair to pick up the spoon, replaced her in the chair, and kept insisting that she eat with a spoon. Finally the student yielded and finished her breakfast.

The teacher persisted in order to gain her obedience and to overcome the permissive policy of her parents. The girl was so wild that she even assaulted members of her family, who had black and blue marks to prove it.

The pupil? Helen Keller. The teacher? Anne Sullivan Macy.

At 19 months of age, Helen contracted a serious disease that left her blind and deaf. For almost five years she grew, as she recalled, "wild and unruly, giggling and chuckling to express pleasure; kicking, scratching, uttering the choked screams of the deaf-mute to indicate the opposite."

To secure a teacher for Helen, her father contacted Dr. Alexander Graham Bell. Dr. Bell directed him to Perkins Institute for the Blind in Boston, where he found Anne Sullivan. Anne came to teach six-year-old Helen and until her death remained with Helen.

Anne's plan was to start slowly and win Helen's love. "I shall not attempt to conquer her by force alone," she declared. She soon discovered otherwise. Helen was not a pale delicate child. She was

large, strong, ruddy, and determined as a wild horse. Sometimes for
days she refused to have her hair combed. Force was needed even to
get her to do simple things like buttoning her shoes or washing her
face. Anne Sullivan, recognizing that her biggest problem was to
gain control over Helen without breaking her spirit, had to revise her
teaching plans. Helen was so cold and self-willed that she refused to
let Anne caress her, and everything Anne did for Helen was
accepted as a matter of course.

Anne was determined to succeed with Helen. Punishment, she
realized, would have to be applied along with her love. Helen's
parents, however, could not bear to see their child being punished,
so Anne asked to live alone with her pupil, and the parents agreed.
Off they went to live in a little homestead nearby. The experiment
began badly. The first night Anne put Helen to bed, a terrific tussle
resulted. Anne, being just as obstinate but stronger, finally won—
but only after a two-hour struggle.

The parents were permitted one visit a day, but without Helen's
knowledge. One day Captain Keller passed by and through the
window saw Helen in her nightgown, the picture of despair and
stubbornness. That day when Helen was given her clothes to wear,
she flung them on the floor. Anne let her know: If you're not
dressed—no breakfast! Here it was ten o'clock, and Helen was still
in her nightgown.

Captain Keller visited his cousin's house and tearfully said, "I've a
good mind to send that Yankee girl back to Boston." His cousin
persuaded him not to.

Within two weeks the "little savage" was transformed. She
became gentle, happy, serene, and proud of having learned to
crochet a long red chain of Scotch wool. Helen now sat on Anne's
lap for a minute or two and even let Anne kiss her, but she would not
return Anne's caresses. When Helen returned home, Anne determined to keep the ground gained by eliciting a promise from the
parents not to interfere.

Anne also taught Helen the manual alphabet by touching objects
and by finger movements in her hand. Then one day it happened. Let
Anne tell it herself:

> We went out to the pump-house, and I made Helen hold her
> mug under the spout while I pumped. As the cold water gushed
> forth, filling the mug, I spelled "w-a-t-e-r" in Helen's free hand.
> The word coming so close upon the sensation of cold water
> rushing over her hand seemed to startle her. She dropped the
> mug and stood as one transfixed. A new light came into her
> face. She spelled "water" several times. Then she dropped on
> the ground and asked for its name and pointed to the pump and

the trellis, and suddenly turning around she asked for my name. I spelled "Teacher." Just then the nurse brought Helen's little sister into the pump-house, and Helen spelled "baby" and pointed to the nurse. All the way back to the house she was highly excited, and learned the name of every object she touched, so that in a few hours she had added thirty new words to her vocabulary. Here are some of them: *Door, open, shut, give, go, come*, and a great many more.

It was a momentous day for Helen and Anne; not only because she had broken the key to language, but that night for the first time Helen of her own accord snuggled into bed with Anne and gave her a kiss.

"I thought my heart would burst, it was so full of joy," said Anne.

When Christmas came Mrs. Keller cried, "I thank God every day for sending you to us." Captain Keller took Anne's hand but was speechless.

Before Helen was ten years old, she was world renowned. Leading educators of the deaf, blind, and seeing paid compliments to Anne Sullivan Macy. Professors at Harvard wanted all teachers to know of her accomplishments.

Helen learned not only to read but to talk, and in 1904 she was graduated with honors from Radcliffe College, a difficult school even for a normal person. In braille she read French, German, Latin, Greek, and English. Years later Woodrow Wilson asked her why she chose Radcliffe when she could have entered an easier college.

"Because they didn't want me at Radcliffe," she said, "and, being stubborn, I chose to override their objections."

Her life was spent promoting better care for the blind, lecturing, and writing magazine articles and books. At 75 she told a reporter, "My birthday can never mean so much to me as the arrival of Anne Sullivan on 3rd March 1887: that was my soul's birthday."[3]

Helen's dramatic success was due to the utilization of love and discipline. Love expresses concern for children whereas discipline expresses training by guidance and encouragement. Discipline is not punishment, but it may include it. Discipline is training someone to act properly, either positively, by encouraging good behavior, or negatively, by punishing bad behavior.

There are three common methods of discipline: authoritarian, permissive, and loving.

Authoritarian Discipline

Teachers or parents domineer their children. Explanations are not given why rules must be obeyed—children's duty is to obey, not to question. When rules are broken, these grown-ups view the violation as intentional, and quick discipline is administered. Authoritarian discipline rarely uses praise or encouragement; it favors punishment to alter bad behavior.

Authoritarian teachers are firm and forceful. They are in charge. Woe to anyone who infringes on their authority. In past years these teachers walked classroom aisles with their rattan and eagerly used it against any child for the least infraction of their rules, whether intentional or unintentional. Children sat in fear as these stern teachers passed their desks. Few today would defend this dictatorial training method.

Permissive Discipline

Permissiveness is at the opposite end of the spectrum from authoritarianism. Children should be free from external control and allowed to express their own behaviors. Few demands are presented for orderly behavior. Teachers act as resource persons when children desire help, not as an active agent to change children's present or future conduct. Permissive teachers accept students' actions and impulses and allow them to govern themselves and vent their desires. Reasons are used to reach goals, but if children's actions are detrimental to others, the teacher endeavors to utilize non-punitive methods to correct misbehavior.

The strong impetus for permissiveness came shortly after World War I from the progressive movement. In 1918–19 the Progressive Education Association was formed, and one of its fundamental principles was: A child should be free to develop naturally and to develop his or her conduct by self-government.

John Dewey (1859–1952), American philosopher and educator, endeavored in an experimental school in Chicago to demonstrate a new approach to education: an educational experience based on the free and natural development according to children's interests. In the process, educators came to stress the inherent right of children to their own self-realization and self-expression. Shortly before Dewey died he reemphasized his thesis—liberty of self-realization within the bounds of the common welfare.

In *New Ways in Discipline* Dorothy W. Baruch cites some practical illustrations of the children's right to self-realization and self-expression. According to Baruch, this method allows the children's "badness" to come out and allows the "goodness" to come in.

Five-year-old Mike is returning from a school excursion. While crossing the street he stops in the middle.

Mike's teacher says, "Get out of the street, Mike; a car's coming."
Mike stands his ground stubbornly.

Quickly the teacher takes Mike by the hand and pulls him firmly onto the sidewalk.

"You dummy," Mike screams.

For two blocks he keeps repeating, "Dumb teacher! Old dummy!"

The teacher mirrors his feelings. "It looks as though you're mad at me, Mike, for having made you do something you didn't want to."

She also shows her acceptance in the good, easy tone of voice which she reinforces by saying, "It's all right for you to show me how you feel."

Baruch says a teacher or parent should see how a child feels, accept how he feels, and reflect how he feels. She presents an illustration of a father whose son, in spite of many parental implorings, goes on a hunger strike.

Today father approaches with the new look in his eye. Inside he is thinking, "Yes, I know how you feel, kid, and I'm prepared to really take it with understanding. When you tell or show me, I'm not going to scold or argue you out of it. I'm going to *accept*." To Heinie he says very simply, "You don't want to eat," reflecting what Heinie has shown.

"It's stinkin' food. I hate it. I'll throw it under the table."

"You want to throw it." Father nods.

"'Cause I won't eat it," defiantly from Heinie.

"You just don't want to," from father. His tone holds neither the sting of sarcasm nor the patience of martyrdom. He speaks with sincere kindness and his air is one of waiting, which at this moment is far better than any invitation to tell or show more.

"It's nasty. It smells. I can't stand it. I'll throw it down the drainpipe. I'll throw mom down too. I'll drown her. And you, too. You all smell, you do."

"You fell mean-mad at us."

"I'll throw all this stuff in your face."

"I know you'd like to, you feel so mean. . ."

Heinie nods and then, truculent still, eats a few spoonfuls. Gradually day by day, as he keeps on bringing out more and more of the "badness," the "goodness" increases. He eats more and eats more cheerfully, and the tirades give way to fun and laughter and a friendly recounting of recent events.

Many times this is the way it happens. When enough of the hurt and fear and anger have been released, they diminish. They stop pushing from within. They stop springing out in compulsive ways, disguising what lies underneath so that it can not be dealt with. After enough of the "badness" has come out, the "goodness" appears.[4]

It is a beautiful theory, allowing all this "badness" to come out. But strangely, children act the worst in permissive schools.

Loving Discipline

Between the extremes of authoritarianism, with its emphasis on control, and permissiveness, with its insistence on individual freedom, is loving discipline, also known as authoritative discipline or democratic discipline. It is middle-ground approach stressing control *and* freedom. Goals are set and children are expected to maintain socially accepted behavior, yet within the bounds of proper behavior they are free to express themselves.

Today's Child reports: "Authoritative parents (as opposed to authoritarian) seem to produce kids who are self-reliant, self-controlled, explorative and contented, the results of an 8-year study of middle-class pre-schoolers suggest.

"Firm and demanding yet warm and responsive, authoritative parents 'encourage verbal give and take, and share with the child the reasoning behind a family policy,' reports Univ. of California research psychologist Diana Baumrind. 'they exert firm control at points of parent-child divergence, but do not hem in the child with restrictions.' "[5]

Dr. Baumrind also found: "Whereas the parents of relatively alienated pre-school children tended to use inhibiting control, the parents of exceptionally mature children exerted even firmer control, used reason to explain their directives, and encouraged independent expression. This latter group of parents certainly did not exhibit the authoritarian personality syndrome. They were open and receptive although highly authoritative in their requirement for compliance."[6]

Grace Langdon and Irving W. Stout, in *These Well-Adjusted Children*, brought out this fact: "In one way or another all of the parents of these children echoed that statement, 'and they needed discipline.' " Of the 261 children chosen for their study these authors said, "Punishment evidently played a considerable part in the lives of all these children."[7]

Proper Balance Between Freedom and Discipline

In my research I have not found any author who supported a totally permissive or an authoritarian approach to discipline. In the example given by Dorothy Baruch, the teacher used her power to force the child onto the sidewalk away from an approaching car. Even A. S. Neill had rules in his permissive Summerhill school. Everyone recognizes some need of control. The problem is to strike a healthy balance between authoritarianism with its dictatorial control and permissiveness with its laissez-faire freedom. One can also lean lightly or heavily toward permissiveness or toward authoritarianism. The problem is the placement of the pivotal point.

The pivotal point is where freedom and discipline meet. Discipline without freedom is brutal. Freedom without discipline is license. Discipline or freedom alone is not the answer; both must be united with love. It is love that balances the delicate scale of freedom and discipline.

There are many misconceptions about love. To many people it means license, but this is a false notion; love can be firm. Anne Sullivan made tremendous sacrifices to help an unknown deaf and blind six-year-old child. Although Helen was obstinate, self-willed, and cold, Anne Sullivan's love overcame these obstacles even though she used corporal punishment. Though love may punish when necessary, it is more eager to pat a child or shake a hand. It delights to say, "Very good. Clever. Terrific! That was a good explanation. Keep up the good work."

Preventive Discipline

Loving teachers practice preventive discipline. They aim to make lessons so interesting that students are not prone to misbehave. Interest and discipline are related. As interest increases, difficulties decrease; as interest decreases, difficulties increase. Effective teachers present knowledge in an efficient and interesting manner.

Putting children into classes where they can function is an important step in preventive discipline. Automatic promotion and heterogeneous grouping greatly increase discipline problems because children with varied educational abilities will have trouble learning together. Some will find the work too easy, others too difficult. And it is often the low achievers who cause the greatest class disturbances.

Since young children need more diversion than older ones, wise teachers who see children beginning to wiggle will know it is time to change the lesson or activity. Effective teachers understand children's nature; they are always one step ahead.

Though the ideal situation is for teachers to strive for programs that prevent the need for discipline and punishment, not every lesson is so absorbing that students' tendency to misbehave will automatically be eliminated. Successful teaching trains children how to work in spite of difficult and unmotivated lessons. Once children are trained to persist in spite of difficulties, their proneness to misbehave will markedly decline.

A few hard-core rebels will refuse to behave in spite of all compassionate help. They need to be removed from a regular school because they cause untold hardships on both teachers and other students. Most often it is these hardened ones who ruin the schools and become teachers' nightmares. Control them and the schools will have harmony; let them gain the upper hand—disaster. Because a few defiant students are permitted to roam at will and to create all sorts of discipline problems, many borderline students imitate them. Placing these incorrigibles in reform school would send a strong message to all students: Schools demand discipline. Reform schools need as enforced a program of discipline and learning as regular schools. They need to have the image of being fair, extra firm, and loving. If the student still insists on engaging in antisocial behavior—then prison. Schools must demand proper behavior.

Many schools have students on drugs. Attorney General William French Smith declared that drug addiction is a major cause of crime in the United States. "I think one thing stands out for sure," said Smith concerning crime: that one of its principal "known causes is drugs."[8] The goal to reduce crime must have as its primary objective the incorporation of methods to prevent crime, and we need to start with school children.

Texas Governor Mark White favors a mandatory prison term for anyone convicted of selling drugs on a school campus.[9] What would happen if state legislators all across America passed bills making it mandatory to send every school drug pusher either to a reform school or to prison? Drug trafficking would quickly halt in schools as students witnessed drug peddlers being convicted and sent away. To protect children and to stem the rising tide of school drug use, schools must send out an uncompromising message: *We will not tolerate drugs.*

Successful Teachers

Many adults can recall teachers who always had disciplined classes while others did not. One teacher can rave and rant without results; another whispers and children respond. What is the secret of the successful teacher? Successful teachers are firm but fair. They know first impressions are important; immediately they aim at having a disciplined class. There is a firm insistence on proper behavior without bitterness. They realize that if the first trouble-maker cannot succeed, the effect on the entire class will be tremendous. These teachers are consistent and self-controlled. When they issue an ultimatum against student misconduct, it is carried out. They do not fluctuate because of unclear objectives. They know that one of the best discipline deterrents is certainty of punishment. However, some teachers tolerate certain actions one day, vacillate the next, and demand something else a week later. The moods of unsuccessful teachers determine their actions which leads to discipline breakdown.

Successful teachers despise favoritism. Reasonable, not arbitrary discipline is used. They are always ready to give an intelligent reason for their actions. Their speech does not cut and insult students. A spark of love radiates from all their conduct, including times of discipline. It is a love that chastises to help, not to retaliate.

Successful teachers always maintain eye contact with their students. They are extremely observant to prevent misbehavior, and they are always on guard to take immediate corrective action. If pupils get drowsy, windows are opened. If two children talk frequently, seats are changed. When a child does misbehave, these teachers get more response with one look than others do with their earthshaking shouts. It is the look of firmness and love; when any misbehaving child looks into those eyes, he or she had better stop— or else!

Realizing the importance of gaining immediate control, a teacher shared his secret with me. He flew into a rage over the slightest infraction. He reasoned that students would react with fear thinking that if the teacher lost his temper over a small infraction what would happen if something really tragic occurred? Another method used is never to smile at the beginning of the term. Both ways are objectionable. Good teachers do not bluff students (students are quick to spot a phoney); when they do, they take advantage of the situation. Wholesome teaching has a pleasant atmosphere, not fearful. Smile? Why not? Do teachers have to frown to prove they are serious? Successful teachers maintain a healthy balance. They know when to be serious and when to have a sense of humor. Their constant motto is:

FAIR — FIRM — LOVING

Lee Canter traveled around California teaching an unusual group of students: school teachers. They sat with alert attention as Canter explained his two-day "assertive training" program to help them maintain disciplined classes. "All the behavior problems in this country could be ended if you went into class one day and said, 'I'm not taking it anymore,'" said Canter.

For two years Canter, age 31, an instructor from the extension faculty of California State University, has trained hundreds of mostly elementary school teachers of southern California. He plans to instruct 3,000 other frustrated teachers throughout the state. "Never argue with a kid," Canter admonishes. "You'll lose—and they lose in the long run." Instead of debating, he counsels, repeat an order until it is obeyed. Also, a teacher should appear forceful by using the child's first name and should maintain eye contact when issuing commands. His firm methods have proven successful. After 18 principals and 287 Pasadena teachers were trained in using assertive authority, there was a 29 to 8 percent decline in time devoted to school discipline.[10]

It is important, in taking a no-nonsense discipline approach, that legitimate student complaints not be ignored, such as dirty lunchrooms, bad teachers, boring classes, arbitrary decisions, and overly harsh discipline. Some educators invite discipline problems because they use unrealistic standards. One mother complained to me about a principal who did not allow his elementary students to whisper in the lunchroom. She went to the principal and asked, "Why can't the children whisper?"

"If they start to whisper," the principal reasoned (most of the children whispered anyway), "then we have a whisper; then we have a yell; before you know it—we have a riot."

What is wrong with children whispering or talking in a lunchroom? One of the important aspects of loving discipline is that it is reasonable. When discipline is necessary, a student's intelligence is respected by a willingness to give an explanation. The lordship mentality of "Obey me because I said it!" is abhorrent. Some angry pupils will reject reasoned discipline and endeavor to engage in a lengthy, heated debate. Wise teachers do not yield to the temptation to force their reasoning upon a rebellious child; they know it will only increase resentment. These teachers know that reasoned discipline, even though it is rejected, does not cause lasting bitterness.

Dr. Diana Baumrind reported, "Under normal conditions, adolescents do not rebel against all authority by any means. They differentiate quite accurately between authoritarian and authoritative parental control." Baumrind told of a Swedish survey with 656 adolescents showing that "significant differences occurred in their acceptance of parental authority depending upon the reason for the directive. Authority which was based on rational concern for the child's welfare was accepted well by the child, while authority which was based on the adult's desire to dominate or exploit the child was rejected."[11]

Fear that when discipline is demanded it will cause student rebellion is ungrounded. Indeed, the opposite is the case: Discipline administered justly and firmly is appreciated. Teachers "must be the figures of authority without being authoritarian," wrote Muriel S. Karlin and Regina Berger in their book *Discipline and the Disruptive Child*. "It has been our experience, dealing with hundreds of children, that this type of teacher is what they want and need. Many, many times youngsters have come to us requesting a change of class. Perhaps three or four times this has been 'because the work is too hard.' Most of the others have words to the effect, 'I'm not learning anything. The class is too noisy.' When the discipline is lax and disorder is rife the children lose a sense of security."[12] James Dobson wrote in *Dare to Discipline*, "Teachers who maintain order are often the most respected members of the faculties, provided they aren't mean and grouchy. A teacher who can control a class without being oppressive is almost always loved by her students."[13]

A Total Disciplined Educational Environment

Schools need to implement a total disciplined system from kindergarten until graduation. As with the solutions for the educational crisis, in the early grades it is imperative to insist on a disciplined environment. The best teachers belong in these early grades to instill in children proper work and behavior habits. Theodore Roosevelt said, "If you are going to do anything permanent for the average man, you must begin before he is a man. The chance of success lies in working with the boy and not the man." If children fail to learn early how to behave, they will carry their defiant attitudes throughout their school life.

My aged barber, conversing about training children, said, "I got this tree here. If I don't put a stick there, it would grow crooked." Discipline is putting a stick beside the child to assure proper growth. Unfortunately, society and government show great concern over crooked trees and willingly spend untold billions to correct the situation. However, at the point where the sapling could have been easily straightened, they are indifferent.

Much teacher training time is spent on subject knowledge and little on classroom management, yet the latter often presents the greatest teacher difficulties. Yet the little training they receive is likely to offer the ineffective permissive approach. Teaching can be delightful, but the constant pressure to maintain order without having the needed means makes it a frustrating experience. Teachers must be provided with proper means and support to preserve a disciplined environment. Even with suitable rules and administrative support, one must recognize that there are different types of teachers. Some can handle students, some need training, and others lack the ability. Everything should be done to help failing teachers; only after all efforts are unsuccessful should they be dismissed. The wisest approach is to screen teachers carefully before employment as to their competence to teach and to maintain a disciplined class.

Effective schools require a chain of command: administrators supervising schools by periodically visiting them and insisting that *all* maintain a disciplined atmosphere; principals overseeing teachers that they *all* have orderly classes. Administrators and principals should be experts in maintaining a disciplined learning environment.

The National Institute of Education (NIE) made a study on school violence. Repeatedly these researchers found that the primary factor distinguishing safe schools from violent ones was a strong, dedicated principal who governed with "firm, fair and . . . consistent" discipline.[14]

Authoritarian discipline is universally rejected. However, often in the legitimate rejection of authoritarianism many reject proper authority. The pendulum then swings to permissiveness. History shows this pendulum swinging back and forth. Though today authority is becoming popular with the American public, many schools cling tenaciously to permissive discipline policies. Educational leaders need to implement the proven system of love and discipline, which will transform chaotic schools into institutions of learning.

Chapter 7

Discipline for Excellence

Instead of incorporating a program of discipline, some educators have altered breakfast for thousands of school children. No longer does their breakfast consist of orange juice, milk, cereal, and toast; today, drugs are a part of their regular morning diet. Not sugar-coated vitamin pills, but drugs like amphetamines, known also as the hazardous "speed." Such stimulants are to aid children to learn and obey.

Drugs for Learning and Behavior

It is well recognized that schools have educational and discipline problems. However, a host of pediatricians, neurologists, and educational psychologists have "discovered" new reasons for these massive failures: Children unable to learn are labeled "learning-disabled"; those unable to behave are diagnosed as "hyperkinetic."

"The nation's schoolchildren are suffering an 'epidemic' of learning disabilities," says Diane Divoky in the *New York Times*, "ranging from 'minimal brain dysfunction' to bad manners." Divoky notes that "in some places, such as in the Delaware Community school district in Muncie, Ind., all students have been screened and deemed learning disabled. There, the pride of the federally funded learning disabilities project is an extensive screening battery that is administered to preschoolers and high school students alike and designed to find that everyone has at least some disability.

" 'If a child got through our screens without something being picked up, we'd call him Jesus Christ,' observed project director, Fred F. Glancy Jr."[1]

Charles Mangel, co-author of *Something's Wrong with My Child: A Parents' Book About Children with Learning Disabilities*, says, "It is not uncommon in middle- or upper-class areas for some parents of children who are not doing well in school to pressure schools into designating their children as learning-disabled. Some parents of children with other handicaps, emotional disorders, for example, may do the same thing. In both instances, the intent is to lessen parental embarrassment caused by a child's performance."[2]

Diane Divoky says the learning-disability movement is an overwhelmingly middle-class one. It gives "ambitious parents a socially

93

acceptable, guilt-free rationale for their children's not making it at school or at home.

"But at the same time, the fancy diagnosis often leads to easy solutions—what one authority described as 'a prescription for drugs and a nice little program'—that only mask the very real problems of raising children who are difficult and disappointing.

"For schools, the danger is greater still. To see all children who behave badly or learn raggedly as the victims of their own neurology is to deny their right to control at least a part of their own destiny." Divoky warns about looking at every variation from the norm as a disability. Then she declares, "To treat what are in fact social problems—nonreaders and nonconformists—as medical problems is to admit the bankruptcy of the schools in finding real solutions."[3]

Barbara Bateman, an authority on learning-disabled children, notes, "Learning disability has become an incredibly successful excuse for the failure of the public schools to adequately teach those children who truly need good teaching. 'Of course we didn't teach that child; she has a disability,' is the standard line."[4] Certainly some children have learning disabilities, but the startling increase in "learning-disabled" children appears as a dignified cover-up for the failure of parents, children, and schools.

The learning disabled are children having difficulty learning. Yet authorities at the National Institute of Mental Health estimate that 3 percent, or nearly 800,000 American children, are suffering from "hyperkinetic syndrome."[5] In *The Myth of the Hyperactive Child and Other Means of Child Control,* Peter Schrag and Diane Divoky claim that there are two million such children on behavior drugs and say that the thrust for these drugs is coming from schools.[6]

These amphetamine drugs "can be highly dangerous," discloses *U.S.News & World Report.* "The argument is advanced that there have been far too few studies to prove that these stimulants are safe for young children. In fact, some doctors charge that there are such side effects as depression and stunting of growth.

"What's more, many physicians and educators fear that an entire generation of children is being turned into 'pill poppers' who are far too dependent on drug use." The article tells that the drugging of children has run into legal problems. "What is described as the first civil suit to arise out of this situation has been filed against the school system in Taft, Calif. It alleges 'coercion' by school officials, who are accused of threatening to keep children out of school unless they take daily doses of pills prescribed to them."[7]

Children receiving these drugs, usually Ritalin and Dexadrine, are classified as "hyperkinetic"; the term *minimal brain dysfunction* has also been used. Some people differentiate between a hyperkinetic child unable to control his behavior on account of organic development and a hyperactive child whose misbehavior is due to environmental difficulties. Hyperkinetic children do not suffer from a disease, are not mentally retarded, and are not so disturbed that they must attend special schools. They are basically normal children misbehaving. The issue is whether a child's behavior is due to a faulty biological or environmental function or to a defiant and stubborn nature.

Edward L. Birch, a director of special education, asks an important question: "What is to prevent the 'poor' teacher from attempting to control overactive, or healthy active behavior through referral for medical treatment?"[8] Some schools, instead of providing a disciplined learning environment, follow the new trend of labeling nonlearning and disruptive children: Those unable to read suffer from dyslexia; those with learning difficulties are diagnosed as learning disabled; and unruly children are designated hyperkinetic. Now schools have medical reasons for the educational and disciplinal crisis.

Authors Peter Schrag and Diane Divoky have a chapter, "The Invention of a Disease," in their book about the hyperactive child:

> In less than a decade, the ailment spread from virtual obscurity to something well beyond epidemic proportions. . . . Before 1965, almost no one had heard of it, but by the beginning of the '70s, it was commanding the attention of an armada of pediatricians, neurologists and educational psychologists, and by mid-decade, pedagogical theory, medical speculation, psychological need, drug-company promotion and political expediency had been fused with an evangelical fervor to produce what is undoubtedly the most powerful movement in—and beyond—contemporary education.
>
> Learning disabilities, according to some "authorities" in the field, account for nearly all school failure, most juvenile delinquency, a large proportion of broken marriages and some part of virtually every other social affliction of modern life.[9]

What can laymen say when children are diagnosed by a specialist as hyperkinetic? Now with the approval of the white cloth, schools can hide even more of their failures. Ironically, hyperkinesis is difficult even for doctors to diagnose; as one psychologist points out, the symptoms for hyperkinesis include "almost everything that adults don't like about children."[10] Now educators, instead of facing their problems head-on and correcting them, find all sorts of alibis to cover up their faulty methods.

Behavior Modification
Another recent educational method to discipline children is be-

havior modification, first introduced by psychologist B. F. Skinner and others in the 50's to describe methods used in dealing with psychotics. The term was unheard of in schools till the early 60's, and then primarily for the handicapped. Within the last decade the behavioristic approach has been used with normal school children. Dr. Bertram S. Brown, director for mental health, commenting on the widespread use of behavior modification, said, "Almost every public school near a large city or university has at least one behavior modification program."[11]

Certain concepts of behavior modification have been around for thousands of years. It is basically a procedure for reshaping undesirable behavior. Parents have used rewards (positive reinforcement) and punishments (negative reinforcement) for years to alter their children's behavior. The methods are couched in technical terms: conditioning, discriminative stimuli, aversive control, shaping, S^Ds, stimulus change, chaining, fading, extinction, and timeout.

In one method children are given tokens as rewards when they show desirable behavior. When enough tokens are amassed, they can be cashed in for candy, toys, or basketball-playing time. Once the correct behavior is achieved, rewards are decreased and verbal rewards are given. Finally, under ideal conditions, children's behavior has been so modified that they no longer require rewards or praise to maintain desired behavior.

Frances Templet was involved with a behavior modification project with her class of 10- to 11-year-old pupils, that class being chosen as the control group because she had excellent classroom discipline. Whenever children were doing their arithmetic correctly, they received checks or credit marks, which could then be exchanged for rewards.

"After a few days I noticed a change in my students' attitude toward the program," explained Templet. "The children became bored, even resentful of it. I especially noticed the more intelligent and creative kids in my class feeling this way. Finally several of the group asked for a meeting with me. In their own way they told me that the tokens and rewards were meaningless. 'These check marks don't smile or look puzzled,' said one! As each child spoke, what they were trying to say was that they didn't want to be patted on the head like a puppy when they did a task well and ignored when it was done wrong. They wanted to know why it was wrong or right. They did not want me to tell them the answers; they wanted the warm body of that adult in whom they had confidence."

Two other of her experimental classrooms likewise experienced no noticeable positive behavioral changes. Templet felt that the sponsors of the behavior modification program did not view the child as a person but as a robot. They used "a donkey-with-a-carrot-on-the-stick model to achieve 'socially acceptable behavior patterns.'" Then Templet asks, "How do we expect the child to grow up human if we treat him as subhuman?"[12]

While I was taking "Psychology of Learning," a behavior modification course required for my teaching license, the instructor emphasized that negative reinforcers should never be used. A shop teacher related a class problem he had with a boy who talked continuously. He remedied the situation by informing the boy that if he did not stop chattering the whole class would not work. (Personally, I do not favor this approach. The child who causes the problem should be dealt with individually.)

The doctor of psychology reproved him for using negative reinforcement and offered this solution: If the student talked every minute but at one time stopped talking for two minutes, he should be rewarded. When he stopped for two minutes, the teacher should aim for three or four minutes of quiet. This procedure should be continued until the behavior was altered. For rewards it was suggested that the student receive candy when he was progressing. To this suggestion the down-to-earth shop teacher replied, "Then I would have the whole class talking." The class roared with laughter.

Chemotherapy

Certainly school children need to have their behavior modified so that educators can teach properly. The problem is, how far will educators go to modify humans? The use of stimulant drugs for hyperkinetic children is just the tip of the iceberg; drugs to increase memory capacity and change motivation are also under consideration. Observers warn that chemotherapy is just entering the schools and such drugs will play an ever increasing role. Mind control or brainwashing is also accomplished by use of psychosurgery and electroconvulsive therapy. As one physician commented, "Pneumonia can sell only so much penicillin, but once human behavior is seen as a disease, there are no limits to the problems that can be treated with drugs."[13]

Not all doctors agree on using drugs for treating unruly children. Dr. Sidney Walker, a neuropsychiatrist, remarked, "It may well be that stimulant drugs produce greater harm in the long run than the hyperactive symptoms they are meant to control."[14]

Amphetamine problems were discussed in *A Federal Source Book: Answers to the Most Frequently Asked Questions About Drug Abuse*, which asks, "Are there any special difficulties in the treatment of stimulant abusers?"

"The 'speed freak' is a difficult patient to rehabilitate. Although he may want to stop using the drug, his 'high' is so intense that he is attracted to the enormous euphoria that he obtains from the chemical. Persons who seem to have broken the speed habit often relapse." The *Federal Source Book* also reveals, "Sweden has a major problem with the amphetamine-like substance, phenmetrazine. It was introduced as a 'safe'· weight reducing pill, but for the past 10 years its illicit use has been increasing." Now Sweden has virtually abolished medical use of this drug; nevertheless, illegal laboratories and sources from other countries provide amphetamines for the addicted.[15]

There was a time when the school was supposed to fit the child and all sorts of new programs were incorporated to accommodate children. Today, a new trend emerges: Make the children fit the school—drug them into submission.

Imagine the diagnosis Helen Keller would have received from some of today's psychiatrists and pediatricians! That poor girl would have been labeled a severe hyperkinetic and given the maximum drug prescription. Anne Sullivan broke nearly every rule that modern educational theorists advocate. She saw that Helen was being ruined by her parents' permissive policies and initiated a program to conquer her stubbornness. When Helen refused to listen, she insisted on obedience. When Helen pinched her, she used corporal punishment. Yet deep within Anne Sullivan was that sincere love for Helen—a love that utlimately conquered. Anne Sullivan incorporated the proven system of love and discipline, or rewards and punishment, then continued a program of discipline for excellence.

Corporal Punishment

Just mention something favorable about corporal punishment to some modern educators and see what happens. This is the reaction I received in my required behavior modification course:

"You're not going to force me to change my psychology. If you want to beat your children you could, but I'm not going to have you act like this."

I wanted to answer my infuriated psychology teacher, but she indignantly silenced me, "Now listen to me!"

She continued to give me a severe tongue-lashing, and knowing the folly of reasoning with one in anger, I quietly listened. Then curtly dismissing me, she snapped, "Next!" to another waiting student.

In amazement I walked away at the reaction of this doctor of psychology.

The incident was initiated on a previous occasion when I expressed belief in the use of corporal punishment in training children. She expressed her strong disapproval. Ironically, in class she proved the effectiveness of punishment when she told us about an experiment. A group of rats were placed in a T maze, which resembled a race track, and trained to obtain their food in the easiest manner. The rats were divided into three groups; they were to be trained by different methods to take a longer path to obtain their food. Every time the first group took the short way they were withdrawn when they came close to the food; the second group found a barrier placed in their way; the final group received an electric shock every time they went the short way.

The teacher asked which method was the most effective: no reward, barrier, or punishment? After hearing and reading all the negative remarks about punishment, I eliminated punishment as the most effective. When the teacher asked for answers, I responded, I guessed wrong; punishment was the answer. The teacher listed the results on the blackboard: withdrawn rats—took 230 times to be trained; barrier—82 times; punishment—6 attempts.

When the teacher presented her views about the ineffectiveness of negative reinforcement, I expressed the opinion that punishment was effective when administered in love. Since I was the father of five children, I had on numerous occasions practiced love and discipline and observed positive results. She challenged my statement about corporal punishment and categorically stated that no modern psychologist believed in it. On learning that I had recently acquired a book on child rearing advocating spanking, she asked to see it.

The following class I gave her *How to Parent*, by Dr. Fitzhugh Dodson. First she checked author credentials. As the book stated, he "earned his A.B. *cum laude* from Johns Hopkins University, his B.D. *magna cum laude* from Yale University, and his Ph.D. from University of Southern California. He is founder of the nationally famous La Primera in Torrance, California." Next she wanted to know if he was a psychologist. Indeed he was—a child psychologist, and psychological consultant of his own nursery school. I then showed her Dr. Dodson's statement:

> Many parents also have the impression that modern psychology teaches that you should not spank children. Some psychologists and psychiatrists have actually stated this idea in print. However, as a psychologist, I believe it is impossible to raise children effectively—particularly aggressive, forceful boys—without spanking them.[16]

My teacher declared that this was just an opinion of a psychologist and had no scientific backing. I countered by recalling the rat experiment, which proved that punished rats learned much faster.
"That's rats, not people!" she bristled.
Previously she had given illustrations about rats, pigeons, cats,

and other animals to support her theories. Now when an experiment contradicted her concepts, she stated that rats were not people. Certainly, caution needs to be exercised in applying animal experiments to humans; nevertheless, I saw no value, I told her, in studying rats if we could not apply the lessons to humans. This doctor of psychology became so infuriated that she resorted to that tongue-lashing and twisted my whole concept of love and discipline.

Following this event I began an extensive research on discipline. After going through hundreds of volumes, I readily understand why so many psychologists and educational leaders have taken such a strong anti-corporal punishment stance. In *Changing Children's Behavior*, John D. Krumboltz and Helen B. Krumboltz said, "Punishment may produce intense fears and anxieties which may last a lifetime."[17] John E. Valusek noted, in *People Are Not For Hitting*, "It is my contention that childhood spanking is the major seed-bed of much of the world's violence."[18] An article in the *Education Digest* stated, "Leading the revolt is a National Education task force which recommends that corporal punishment be phased out by the beginning of the 1973–74 school year. Following months of study, the task force—representing teachers, students, and administrators—found that physical punishment as a disciplinary measure causes more harm than anyone ever imagined."[19]

The NEA *Report of the Task Force on Corporal Punishment* presented these statements: "The effect of repeatedly and righteously inflicting physical pain is likely to be more detrimental to a teacher's mental health than learning other ways of dealing with frustrating circumstances would be."[20] B. F. Skinner is quoted as saying, "In the long run, punishment, unlike reinforcement, works to the disadvantage of both the punished organism and the punishing agent."[21] According to the report, the obvious evidence was so weighty "that corporal punishment is used, not because it has proven to be effective, but because its ineffectiveness has not been thoroughly understood and accepted."[22]

Others say that corporal punishment does not eliminate undesirable behavior but only temporarily suppresses it. Freudian psychologists have presented the view that corporal punishment, particularly on the buttocks, may produce sexual deviations, causing the child to become a flagellomaniac. It is claimed that the buttocks are an erogenous zone, and when a child is punished, sexual stimulation is effected. One physician went so far as to claim that beating the buttocks can lead to brain damage: Spanking can dislodge tiny fat particles, which may in the future cause blood clots in the brain. She also said that headaches, dizziness, forgetfulness, and difficulty in concentrating can occur.[23]

Effective Punishment

These are a few of the many statements made by the anti-punishment advocates. However, there have been studies showing the effectiveness of punishment. Richard L. Solomon, in *American Psychologist*, exposed the error of Skinner's comment in 1948 in *Walden Two*: "We are now discovering at an untold cost in human suffering—that in the long run punishment doesn't reduce the probability that an act will occur." And the error of the Bugelskis, who in 1956 stated, "The purport of the experiments . . . appears to be to demonstrate that punishment is ineffective in eliminating behavior." Solomon admired "the humanitarian and kindly dispositions contained in such writings. But the scientific basis for the conclusions therein was shabby, because, even in 1938, there were conflicting data which demonstrated the great effectiveness of punishment in controlling instrumental behavior. For example, the widely cited experiments of Warden and Aylesworth (1927) showed that discrimination learning in the rat was more rapid and more stable when incorrect responses were punished with shock than when reward alone for the correct response was used."

Solomon tells how in "spite of this empirical development, many writers of books in the field of learning now devote but a few lines to the problem of punishment, perhaps a reflection of the undesirability of trying to bring satisfying order out of seeming chaos. . . .

"Perhaps one reason for the usual textbook relegation of the topic of punishment to the fringe of experimental psychology is the widespread belief that punishment is unimportant because it *does not really weaken habits*; that it pragmatically is a *poor controller* of behavior; that it is extremely *cruel* and unnecessary; and that it is a technique leading to neurosis and worse. This legend, and it is a legend without sufficient empirical basis," caused a "lack of concerted research on punishment from 1930–1955."

Solomon cites a strange situation, in that "punishments are asserted to be ineffective controllers of instrumental behavior;" yet they are "often asserted to be devastating controllers of emotional reactions, leading to neurotic and psychotic symptoms, and to general pessimism, depressiveness, constriction of thinking, horrible psychosomatic diseases, and even death!"[24] Is it any wonder that psychologists and educators reading these early unscientific conclusions had such strong reactions against punishment?

Dr. Justin Aronfreed of the University of Pennsylvania psychology department was the recipient of many honors. One such one was the National Science Foundation Senior Postdoctoral Fellowship at the Center for Advanced Study in the Behavioral Sciences. "I've always been interested in how human beings develop a conscience," he said. "Obviously, you can't find out much about that from animals. So I decided to study children—to try finding out just how punishment teaches them to control their behavior. And I began my studies because research on the effects of punishment has been so neglected."

In summarizing these studies Aronfreed stated, "*Any* kind of explanation that makes a child consciously connect an undesirable act with an unpleasant punishment will help suppress the act. But you get the most suppression if you connect the punishment with the child's *intensions.* If you catch him with a piece of forbidden cake in his hand, for instance—you don't tell him you're punishing him for taking the cake but, let's say, for wanting to eat somebody else's share." Many years ago, Aronfreed related, research on animals showed the punishment was undesirable. Certain educators, psychiatrists, and social philosophers claimed that punishment brutalized a child, and that permissiveness was the answer. Psychoanalytic theory put the blame for neuroses on punitive, traumatic childhood experiences. Many parents, often the better educated, were influenced by these theories to reject punishment.

"Now speaking as a parent myself," said Dr. Aronfreed, "it's quite clear that punishment can be tremendously effective in changing conduct and values. That's how we become socialized. So why did the early animal studies produce such discouraging results? For one thing, the investigators used punishment to try suppressing behavior that was in the service of a strong biologial drive. Starve a rat for 24 hours, put him in a box where he can get food only by pressing a lever, then shock him when he presses it, and of course the shock won't be very effective in suppressing the lever-pressing. And many of the early studies forced animals to make very difficult discriminations. There's reason to think that if you punish human beings for behavior that is prompted by the need for survival, you'll get effects like those in the early animal studies. But human beings are very rarely placed under this kind of stress. When they *are*—in concentration camps, for instance—behavior taught and sanctioned by society tends to break down."

Beginning in the 50's much work was done on animals proving the effectiveness of punishment. Aronfreed's experiments confirmed that punishment is likewise effective in children. As he cheerfully observed, most people have more sense about raising children than the psychiatrists and psychologists advising them.

The general conclusion Aronfreed draws from his studies on punishment is this:

> The effects of punishment are not capricious, but predictable
> from theoretical models. Under certain conditions, punishment

can be a very effective way of controlling a child's behavior. We should try to learn why punishment is useful on some occasions and not others. And we shouldn't reject its use on the basis of emotional prejudice and incorrect assumptions.[25]

In *Psychology Today*, Donald M. Baer, professor of human development and psychology at the University of Kansas and research associate of the Bureau of Child Research, cited examples of the effectiveness of punishment: "In general, behaviorists have found punishment to be one of the fastest, most effective techniques available for helping people rid themselves of troublesome behaviors."

The reasons for much of the revulsion, he says, were due to the truly inhumane punishment of "headmasters with canes, slave masters, prison turnkeys with whips, bullies, orphanage overseers, snake-pit mental hospitals." Baer notes how "in recent years, researchers have reported successful results using punishment to cure such diverse problems as smoking, tics, suicidal ruminations, jealousy, thumb-sucking, nail-biting, homosexuality, exhibitionism, alcoholism, dangerous wall-climbing and habitual coughing."

Dr. Baer criticizes society's reaction to this scientific discovery of the value of punishment: "By the usual standards of science these findings ought to evoke admiration: scientists successfully applied research findings to problems that had not responded to therapy and they relieved patients of misery. Had the findings been a vaccine against some disease, there would have been headlines and congratulations. But the treatment is not called 'vaccination,' it is called 'punishment.' The word brings with it images of anger, whips, screams. So instead of celebrating a new scientific advance, we feel apprehensive; we look for a hint of sadism."[26]

Unfortunately, many educators and psychologists have been trained to consider punishment in the light of the false conclusions of Skinner and Freud. Then one psychologist quotes another until the *legend* of the ineffectiveness of punishment is claimed to be a scientific fact beyond disputation. The NEA *Report of the Task Force on Corporal Punishment* quoted this authoritative statement by Henry A. Waxman: "Psychologists are unanimously agreed that corporal punishment is a totally ineffective disciplinary device."[27] However, psychologist Donald M. Baer concludes:

Punishment is not a barbaric atavism that civilized men must always avoid. It is a legitimate therapeutic technique that is justified and commendable when it relieves persons of the even greater punishments that result from their own habitual behaviors.[28]

Today's Child reports: "Let's not sneer at spanking as an aid to discipline, says the director of Univ. of Chicago Child Psychiatry Clinic, but let's not overdo it either.

" 'An occasional good whack on the seat' can do a lot to convince a young skeptic that his parents mean what they say, observes Dr. John F. Kenward. Used sparingly, a spank serves as a kind of shock treatment which shows a child that he's gone too far."[29]

Love and Punishment

Researchers have shown that humane punishment is effective. Other researchers, to prove corporal punishment ineffective and detrimental, produce studies showing that though many criminals were severely beaten by parents they still committed crimes. Anti-punishment advocates, however, fail to differentiate between highly punitive parents and their authoritarian discipline and parents who mete out punishment with love.

How can one punish in love? If a two-year-old has been warned to stay away from a hot stove, a loving parent will slap the hand if the child reaches out to touch it. It is an expression of parental love to give the child a temporary sting and a lesson in obedience rather than see the child burned. A child who runs into the street after being warned may receive a sound spanking from a loving parent. Parents would rather inflict corporal punishment than see their child crippled for life. But why punishment? Because corporal punishment is of short duration and extremely effective.

Take a class of 30 third-graders in which an unruly failing child repeatedly refuses to sit down and delights in disturbing and hitting other children. If the teacher believes corporal punishment is dehumanizing, he may take this approach:

"I know how you feel. You hate the class. You wish the teacher were dead."

Then to relieve the child's inner frustration he redirects the child's energy by using a nonpunitive approach. "Instead of hitting others, kick the play box, or the chair, or anything else. Say, 'I hate you,' or whatever you want, but don't kick anyone."

What will the other children learn with this teacher when an unruly child is not effectively chastised? They will learn that misbehavior is not punished; some will instead be tempted to imitate the disturbing conduct.

Suppose the same boy has a teacher who practices loving discipline. The teacher tells him, "I know how you feel, but you cannot leave your seat and hit others because you are mad." Firmly and lovingly he insists that the child return to his seat and sit down.

Later, as the class is doing art work, the teacher takes the child aside and tries to help him learn the material he is failing. In spite of the teacher's efforts, the boy again leaves his seat and hits another student. The teacher gives him a warning: "The next time you hit someone, I will take this paddle and give you a spanking."

The child disregards the warning. The teacher then has the child bend over and applies a few strokes with the paddle. The child cries and returns to his seat. Both the boy and the class know the teacher is in authority. Now with an orderly class a learning atmosphere prevails.

Objections arise because in resorting to corporal punishment the teacher is modeling undesirable behavior by the use of force. However, the teacher realizes that *all* 30 children have rights, and it is undemocratic to let *one* child violate the rights of the other 29. All societies have laws preventing individuals from engaging in anti-social actions. They have police, judges, courts, and jails to apprehend and punish offenders of basic human rights. When a child insists on fighting and disrupting the class, it is a matter of justice to punish him. Far from modeling undesirable behavior, the teacher is modeling justice against misbehavior.

Concerned teachers do not use corporal punishment as the only way to punish a child. There is also reprimand, detention, withdrawal of privileges, isolation, assignment of special tasks, or expulsion. Simply taking a child aside often does wonders. Sometimes there are hidden reasons why children cause problems. Often students are transformed just by having their parents notified of their misbehavior.

When corporal punishment is used, it should be done with intelligent love. It is not a device for teachers who have tried everything and whose nerves have reached the flash point—then they "haul off and give the kid a good whack to put him in his place." In this case the teacher feels guilty, and the child cries, despises his punishment, and looks for revenge. Punishment administered unjustly is scorned.

A few teachers will abuse corporal punishment. The solution, however, is not to eliminate corporal punishment but to make sure abusers are dealt with effectively. Policemen are known to abuse their weapons; should elimination of nightsticks and guns be the goal? Cars cause many highway deaths; shall we go back to walking as the only mode of travel? In one year, 55,000 individuals required hospital emergency room treatment resulting from playground injuries; should we close all playgrounds? The solution is not elimination but the incorporation of proper safeguards.

Corporal punishment should be neither always the first nor the last resort. Each situation should be evaluated on its own merit. Teachers need to know how to maintain a disciplined learning atmosphere. Once they are properly trained and have the authority to maintain order, there will be little need for corporal punishment. It can be readily observed in disciplined classrooms how seldom punishment is required, but if a child does misbehave, immediate intelligent action is taken. For a serious infraction children know they are likely to experience the paddle.

Opponents of corporal punishment speak of a child in a Boston school who was beaten on a hand that had an infected finger and consequently spent three days in a hospital. No one in his right mind would condone hitting a child's hand when he had an infected finger. But strangely these antipunishment advocates show grave concern over an infected finger or bruised buttocks yet maintain silence over the multitudes of children who are harassed, mugged, beaten, knifed, and even raped and killed in undisciplined schools.

Many individuals have been spanked in their childhood. Looking back on these experiences they do not despise their parents or the punishment. In fact, sometimes they say, with a twinkle in their eye, "I deserved a lot more." I visited a large Christian camp in the Adirondacks to interview 25 youth ranging from 13 to 21 years of age about the effects of parents' using the biblical principle of "applying the rod." All expressed extremely favorable attitudes toward the spankings they had received. The general feeling was summed up by a 17-year-old girl who was planning to enter college—the discipline was natural. Resentment over corporal punishment could not be detected, even among the youth still under parental control.

Corporal Punishment: Teachers' Reactions

As has been shown, the proper use of corporal punishment is an effective device to correct misbehavior. Nevertheless, permissive educational leaders have tried for years to bar its use from schools. Though there are some 60 anti-corporal punishment groups, a survey conducted by NEA showed that 72 percent of teachers favored corporal punishment.[30] It is amazing that teachers constantly bombarded with anti-corporal punishment materials can still, in the majority, favor its use. One teacher cleverly analyzed the situation: "The farther away you are from the classroom, the less you think corporal punishment is needed."

The *American Teacher* reports that in Pittsburgh, in spite of a downpour, more than 1,000 teachers and paraprofessionals demonstrated for strengthened discipline and security measures in city schools. Teachers were angry after a pupil who assaulted a teacher was allowed to return to class a few days later. They wanted "firm action to deal with assaults on teachers, on other staff, and on students," reported President Al Fondy of AFT Local 400. "If there is an assault on a teacher, the student should be transferred or suspended for the balance of the school year."

One of the demands the union presented was that corporal punishment be restored. "Absence of paddling," Fondy said, "particularly at our elementary schools and middle and junior-high schools, has been a major factor in the deterioration of discipline conditions in our schools. Restoration of this alternative for dealing with certain disciplinary infractions could go further than any other single step toward improving school-discipline conditions and toward reducing suspensions."[31]

School crime became so rampant in Los Angeles that California Attorney General George Duekmejian in an unprecedented lawsuit charged school officials with inflicting cruel and unusual punishment on children by forcing them to attend city schools. In bringing this civil suit against county agencies, mayor, city council, and police in the nation's second largest school district, the state is trying to compel schools to protect their children. Duekmejian says, "My primary goal is the restoration of our public schools as islands of safety in which students can pursue their learning without fear."

To combat the rising crime, Los Angeles has reinstated corporal punishment after prohibiting it four years ago. In a statewide survey of more than 800 parent-teacher associations, 85 percent of the parents and teachers supported corporal punishment. When Los Angeles school principals were surveyed, 89 percent favored reinstatement of corporal punishment.

Board member Bobbi Fiedler, asked about the effectiveness of corporal punishment, replied, "On an issue like this, experience is perhaps the best teacher. In Los Angeles schools, corporal punishment was ended in 1975. Since then there has been more fighting, more obscenity and a general disregard for good behavior. There has been not only increased lack of respect for adults, but children have exhibited greater hostility toward each other as well. We are facing a tremendous increase in the violence on our school campuses."[32]

Supreme Court and Corporal Punishment

In October 1975, corporal punishment was brought before the United States Supreme Court; it was ruled that teachers may spank misbehaving pupils—even over parental objections. In January 1976, the House of Commons likewise rejected a bill to abolish corporal punishment in British schools.

Then in April 1977, the United States Supreme Court decided that spanking of school children by teachers did not violate the Constitution's Eighth Amendment on cruel and unusual punishment. Writing for the majority, Justice Lewis Powell said the prohibition against cruel and unusual punishment was applicable only to prisoners and "the schoolchild has little need for the protection of the Eighth Amendment." Justice Powell then added, "The openness of the public school and its supervision by the community affords significant safeguards."

The Court stated that the "prevalent" rule is derived from common law, whereby teachers may use "reasonable but not excessive" force to discipline children. School officials using unreasonable or excessive force, the Court said, are almost everywhere subject to possible criminal or civil liability. The Court further ruled that when teachers use corporal punishment, students do not need to have a hearing before receiving their punishment.[33] (In Dade County, Florida, it is prescribed that wooden paddles should not exceed two feet in length by four inches in width by one-half inch in thickness. The number of strokes for elementary and for high school students is also stipulated.)[34]

Corporal Punishment Banned

Most states have never acted on the use of corporal punishment, but New Jersey, Maryland, and Massachusetts have statutes forbidding it. New York State permits corporal punishment; however, when Irving Anker, chancellor of the New York public school system, heard of the Supreme Court ruling, he said it would not affect the city Board of Education's prohibition against corporal punishment. "It is our view that corporal punishment is both dehumanizing and counterproductive,"[35] commented the chancellor.

Fritz Redl and William W. Wattenberg wrote, in *Mental Hygiene in Teaching*, "A number of states and cities very wisely have made physical punishment illegal. In such school systems both teachers and children survive very nicely. The fact is that whippings, slappings, beltings, and paddlings can accomplish nothing that cannot be achieved better by some other method. The very conditions which physical punishment involves violate the known requisites for producing a psychologically justifiable result."[36]

New York City educational leaders can boast that corporal punishment has been banned for decades, but they cannot deny the horrible conditions existing in many of their schools. Since teachers have been stripped of their powers to restrain physically and punish pupils, many find it extremely difficult to maintain disciplined classrooms. According to *Time*, a number of other cities have "banned spanking in public schools," and they are: "Pittsburgh, Los Angeles, Chicago, San Francisco and Washington, D.C."[37] (Los Angeles has recently restored it). In retrospect, one can recall that it is in many of these same cities that experience the greatest amount of violence.

To imagine what it is like to teach in New York City schools, envision teachers' hands tied behind their backs as they stand helplessly before unruly children. Often students mock teachers' impotence. Were teachers given in loco parentis (teachers acting in lieu of parents) to administer reasonable control and punishment to disruptive children, it would transform the schools and have a much greater impact than many costly programs to help delinquent youth. But to some educational leaders it would be utterly intolerable to allow teachers to use their discretion to apply corporal punishment. One wonders why these same leaders take so little positive action against the tragic undisciplined conditions existing in some of their schools?

The action they occasionally use is to suspend children who cause serious discipline problems. Then they play musical chairs, sending children from one school to another. The most seriously unmanageable are eventually sent to a school for emotionally handicapped children. In one such school, I substituted as a buddy teacher. For just 130 first- to third-grade pupils there were 12 classes, 12 teachers, 12 paraprofessionals, and 4 buddy teachers who visited the various classes. Clearly, a few had problems, but the majority were simply undisciplined. In a second-grade class a regular paraprofessional and I had 10 pupils. When the children began running and hitting each other, the paraprofessional tried desperately to control the situation, but the children were totally disrespectful. Although I wanted to take the first one who misbehaved and paddle him to obtain order, under no conditions was I allowed to do so. We were finally saved by the dismissal bell.

Punishment: Parents and Nature

The American public has been so deceived regarding corporal punishment that one is made to feel ashamed to admit one believes in it; or worse, practices it. Nevertheless, Ross D. Parke, of the University of Wisconsin, says, "According to a large scale study of child-rearing, 98 percent of the parents interviewed occasionally used physical punishment to control their children."[38]

Even animals use punishment in the training of their young. Hens and mother birds peck at their chicks and nestlings to correct them; mother bears cuff their cubs vigorously when they misbehave; when calves become too boisterous in getting milk, the mothers butt them. Nature also operates on the principle of obedience—happiness; disobedience—punishment. Nature takes no backtalk. Expose body gently to the sun: suntan; overexpose body: sunstroke. Nature strikes quickly and effectively, and mankind learns quickly to abide by its rules.

Permissive Solutions

There is an instinctive revulsion to pain. This is the reason punishment is so effective in training children. Physical or psychological pain causes unpleasant feelings to change behavior. Strangely, permissive leaders protest the serious consequences of physical pain yet in the same breath advocate psychological pain. The NEA Task Force recommends, "Quiet places (corners, small rooms, retreats)" could be used as a short-range solution to avoid corporal punishment; also "privileges to bestow or withdraw." It advocates "social workers, psychologists, and psychiatrists to work on a one-to-one basis with disruptive students or distraught teachers"; also parent education programs, student human relations councils, student involvement in decision-making processes in the schools, increased human relations training—and "full implementation of the *Code of Student Rights*."[39]

Imagine the psychological results from some of these programs as opposed to the results from a teacher who, acting *in loco parentis*, tells a child, "If you hit another child once more you'll get a spanking." The child misbehaves, receives a temporary sting, and all is forgotten, whereas the child disciplined with progressive concepts must parade from teacher to principal to parent to psychologist to psychiatrist to social worker, etc. While the child is parading about to these specialists trying to diagnose and alter his conduct, he continues to misbehave, influences others to do the same, causes bedlam in the classroom, frustrates the teacher, and hinders effective learning. Which method is truly humane and creates the least psychological damage?

In *Today's Education* a teacher describes a situation in which David Evans, a sixth-grade student, was consistent about three things—he came to school, fought, and swore. His father was an alcoholic, his mother was busy with her lovers, and he was virtually reared by older street gangs. Being a victim of an inner-city deprived life, at age 13 he was already on probation for stealing.

A sincere but vain effort was made by the teacher to help David adjust to school. The teacher became exhausted and bruised from breaking up fights. The school counselor, Mr. Wright, also tried to help David, but the boy would sulk in his office and reenter the class unchanged. The situation became so difficult that school authorities finally contacted the courts to have him sent to a correctional home.

Then a dramatic change occurred. David was involved in a fight, and the teacher finally became fed up with the situation. He threatened David with his size, his fighting ability, and his own inner-city experience. David was terrified. His swearing stopped. He even said, "Yes, sir; no, sir," to the astonishment of the teacher, who never dreamed that he knew these expressions. The following week his class, as the teacher described it, was "total bliss."

In the midst of this change, the plans for David to enter the correctional institution were approved. David strongly protested, and his teacher too now wanted him to stay. In discussing the situation with Mr. Wright, the teacher wanted to appeal to the courts to give David another chance because of the dramatic change in David's behavior. Nevertheless, Mr. Wright decided that David would benefit more from being placed in an institution with trained personnel; "quieting a child by using threats," he believed, was wrong.

Off to the institution David went, never again to be seen by his teacher. But David, he heard, had reverted to his old behavior.

Today's Education presented the reactions from educators to this incident. One response was from a speech and language specialist and the president-elect of a Texas Classroom Teachers Association: "The teacher's threat of physical punishment may stop David's deviant behavior temporarily," he said, "but it will not necessarily help him develop the values and attitudes he needs to remain in and benefit from a public school classroom." Then he concluded, "Perhaps what David needed was an alternative school environment sponsored by the school district whose purpose was achievement through valuing and self-control rather than correction through incarceration."[40]

That the teacher altered David's behavior was not important. The crime is that the teacher used the threat of punishment; therefore he was wrong regardless of the outcome. The facts are no longer the issue; what matters is whether teachers' actions harmonize with educational leaders' permissive philosophy.

Ancient Wisdom

A statement made by a king 3,000 years ago contains more wisdom than can be found in scores of books and articles published by many modern educators and psychologists. The story is told that in the beginning of the king's reign God appeared to him and said, "Ask what you wish me to give you." The king requested not riches, or long life, but wisdom to judge his people. God, highly pleased with his unselfish request, promised him there would be no one before or after him who would attain to his greatness. The man was King Solomon, and under his rulership Israel achieved its golden era. In Proverbs 29:15 King Solomon wrote,

> The rod and reproof give wisdom: but a child left to himself bringeth his mother to shame.

What contrast of this ancient wisdom to today's. Solomon advocated the use of corporal punishment, and for thousands of years millions have proven its effectiveness. In some schools it has been totally eliminated; in others its abolition is being sought. Permissive educators want to dismiss corporal punishment as one of the archaic brutalities of the past. But look at today's schools and observe the fruits of modern wisdom.

In addition to using the rod, King Solomon advised reproving children. When children misbehave they are not to be just punished but reproved. Reasons are given why their actions were wrong. Schools should follow this ancient wisdom. They should have reasonable standards of behavior; children should be instructed in these standards; then corporal punishment should be permitted for noncompliance. It is "the rod and reproof" that gives wisdom.

Finally, Solomon strikes at the very core of progressiveness: "A child left to himself bringeth his mother to shame." Children need to be trained in the way they should go and not left to flounder according to the whims of their immature feelings.

Progressive Leaders

The American public has pinpointed the main problem in the schools as discipline. However, I fear that progressive leaders have bulldozed the majority of people into thinking traditional methods of love and discipline embarrassingly old-fashioned. The silent majority needs to be awakened to the fact that their beliefs about discipline are up-to-date and highly effective. It is because educational leaders have rejected these proven methods and substituted methods of permissiveness and license that the schools are in ruins.

James Harris, president of the largest teachers' union, the National Education Association (NEA), said schools themselves are to be blamed for the present problems of vandalism and violence. He told a Senate subcommittee that the reasons include depersonalization, alienation, outmoded discipline practices, racial hostility, and society's use of violence as a means of reaching solutions. Harris then gave the typical progressive reasons for failures, which are really the solutions: "the increasing dependency on short-range measures, such as corporal punishment, suspension or expulsion, police in the schools, and detention/isolation, is particularly depressing," he said. "Schools which rely on traditional methods of school discipline in isolation are traveling on a different path than young people today, and the gap between the institution and the students is widening because communication in such situations has become virtually impossible."[41]

The problem is not that traditional schools and young people today are on different paths but that the progressive schools have destroyed the effective well-worn path.

Traditional vs. Progressive Schools

Often it is the traditionalist demanding discipline that is labeled a vicious, brutal, undemocratic beast, robbing children of their liberty and freedom by insisting on obedience. Yet in traditional schools are found harmony, peace, and freedom for *all*. In such schools children can be seen laughing, playing, and enjoying living. On paper it may look harsh not to handle hard-core delinquents with kid gloves. But visit schools where love and firmness are combined, and you will find a delightful atmosphere. Then visit progressive schools with their overemphasis on students' rights, and you will witness in many an atmosphere of hate and fear. Why? Because in classes with insufficient authority to punish misbehavers each child must defend himself. As a result a natural pecking order occurs, each child fighting for his class position and the strongest finally achieving overall authority. Even though the pecking order becomes established, violence continues, with fighting among those who want to advance their standing.

Independence and freedom are excellent virtues when exercised within bounds of mutual respect. In disciplined classes there is legitimate authority to enforce this right; disruption results in immediate correction. Traditionally, teachers had authority to act under a legal and moral sanction of *in loco parentis*. Today's preoccupation with children's rights, particularly those of disruptive children at the expense of teachers, parents, and legitimate authority, is destroying schools.

Conclusion on Discipline

In conclusion, the traditional methods of being fair, firm, and loving are as effective today as they have been for thousands of years. Children will never be harmed with that proven treatment. What is needed is a school reform movement that will reject the progressive model that has caused the great havoc not only in our schools but in all of society.

With permissive discipline children fear their classmates. With authoritarian discipline children fear their teachers. Both are to be rejected. The solution? Love and discipline.

Simple? Yes! Very, very simple. This is not a costly program; it is a simple no-nonsense approach that expects orderly schools. We need to demand that administrators and principals provide a disciplined learning atmostphere, encourage preventive discipline techniques, give teachers *in loco parentis* authority, permit corporal punishment, and remove the few hard-core troublemakers. Once a proper system of discipline is established, every teacher should be expected to maintain a disciplined class. In this disciplined atmosphere schools can once again provide quality education for all.

Part IV

Racial Solutions

Chapter 8

Racial Progress

Seven-year-old Linda Brown lived within four blocks of an all-white school in Topeka, Kansas. Instead of attending her neighborhood school, she was forced to walk six blocks, cross the busy Rock Island railyards, and travel 15 more blocks to an all-black school. Her father, Minister Oliver Brown, enraged that his daughter had to be bused so far, unsuccessfully tried to enroll her in the nearby all-white school. Having failed, he filed a lawsuit in 1951. The lower courts declared that segregated schools were legal, but the case was brought before the Supreme Court. In 1954 Chief Justice Earl Warren solemnly read the unanimous decree: "Separate educational facilities are inherently unequal."[1]

Busing for Integration

Since that decision a second revolution has occurred in American education. Because of busing, both North and South have experienced numerous court decisions resulting in school closings and fierce riots. Some people have argued that since 44 percent of American children take buses, with only 3 percent for integration purposes, the issue is really, as Professor Thomas F. Pettigrew of Harvard remarked, a "polite, culturally sanctioned way to oppose the racial desegregation of the public schools."[2]

Two well-known congresswomen had a heated debate over busing.

"I never bought a home without looking first to find out about the schools my boys would attend," said Republican Edith Green of Oregon. "If the Federal Government is going to reach its long arm into my house and say, 'We are sorry but your children are going to have to be bused 30 miles,' I say the Government has gone too far."

"Let me bring it right down front to you," answered Brooklyn's black Democrat Shirley Chisholm with fiery emotion and scorn. "Your only concern is that whites are affected. Where were you when black children were bused right past the white schools?"[3]

Despite the rhetoric about racial harmony and cooperation, our nation is still divided. The volatile busing issue has been a vital issue causing this separation. The problem is not simply busing children but forced busing determined solely by skin color. When, in 1951,

Linda Brown could not attend her neighborhood school because she was black, the Supreme Court ruled she could. Today, reverse discrimination occurs, and white children are often forced to bypass their neighborhood schools solely because of their color.

Most Americans believe separate racial schools are detrimental. On the other hand, many strongly object to their loss of freedom to send their children to neighborhood schools. Schools need strong community and parental ties; the greater the parental access to schools, the greater the school's effectiveness. In many schools parental involvement is lacking, and busing children miles away only further prevents more parents from participating.

The opposite side of the issue concerns minority students condemned to inferior neighborhood schools. In 1949, when the "separate but equal" school system policy was in effect, Clarendon County, South Carolina, spent $179 a year for each white child compared to $43 for each black child.[4] However, when, in 1966, Johns Hopkins sociologist James S. Coleman completed his massive report analyzing more than 600,000 children and 60,000 teachers in 4,000 schools, he found that schools attended by whites and minorities differed less in physical facilities, curriculums, and teachers than anyone had suspected. His conclusion: "Family-background differences account for much more variation in achievement than do school differences."[5]

Minority School Achievement

Though schools may differ little in their physical plant, there is a vast difference in educational achievement among schools. When City University of New York implemented the admission standard that all high school graduates must have an eighth-grade reading and mathematics ability, they found that 40 percent of entering students had been failing the test since 1971. Of these students, the *New York Times* reports, "72 percent of the black students sampled scored below eighth-grade level in either reading or math ability, that 65 percent of Hispanic students similarly scored below that level and that 20 percent of the whites did."[6]

A black minister of a successful Harlem church told me how delighted he and his wife were when across their street a new school was built for their son to attend. At this school his son was at the top of his class. Through an open enrollment plan, other neighborhood children attended another school. These children, the father observed, were not outdoors as often as his son was because of their homework; his child, however, received little homework. Questioned about homework, the son said he had none.

Even though the child was the brightest in his class, the father felt his son was being shortchanged. Through the same open enrollment plan he transferred the boy to an old school in a predominantly Jewish neighborhood. He was the only black child in the school, and he did terribly. The work was extremely difficult; he just cried in class. The father asked why he was acting this way.

"I don't understand the work," the son complained. "They seem to be so far ahead."

He was in the fourth grade, yet in this school he was barely toeing third-grade level. In his father's view the neighborhood school had victimized him: Whereas in the former school he had been top of the class, now he was at the bottom. The father believed that an obstacle can be made either a stumbling-block or a stepping-stone, and being a determined man, he chose stepping-stones. Instead of giving up, he worked tirelessly with his son to repair his deficient education. The son met the challenge and graduated on a par with the other students.

Educational achievement and standards in many minority schools are disastrous. Most parents do not object to having minority children in their local schools, but they violently object when their children are forced out of their neighborhood schools to attend nonlearning and undisciplined schools, which are often in unsafe neighborhoods. The busing issue is a racial problem only because the government has made race a criterion; objections would arise to mandatory busing even if all races were the same. Regardless of reasons given, no concerned parents, whether black or white, want their child bused from a good neighborhood school to an inferior one.

Think of concerned parents who are required to send their children to undisciplined schools. The objection can be raised: "What about the parents living in these neighborhoods?" Certainly they deserve good schools. But the solution is not for these parents to insist that their children be bused out of their inferior schools while outside children are compelled to attend their undisciplined schools. Rather, these parents should band together and insist that their neighborhood schools have quality education in a disciplined environment. Parents deserve the freedom to choose the neighborhood and school they desire and not be forced by reverse discrimination to commit their children to detrimental environments.

One family, Al and Mildred McCauley, became so upset over forced busing that they kept their three children—David, 15, Danny, 14, and Debbie, 10—at home. Their boys would have had to get up at 6:35 A.M. to ride a bus for 50 minutes to reach a ghetto school 22 miles away in Louisville, Kentucky.

"They won't go there—ever," Mrs. McCauley vowed.

Their major complaint was the inferior education their children would receive and the school discipline problems they would encounter. They have also heard of crimes, stabbings, and rapes in the

Parkland neighborhood. The McCauleys realize the desire for blacks to want better schools, but they reasoned, "Why don't they just upgrade their schools? I just can't see sending my children in there to get a lower education so that *they* can get a better one."[7]

Carl Merchant refused to have his 13-year-old daughter attend a school located in a black neighborhood in Pontiac, Michigan. He does not consider himself a racist. "I work with black guys in the shop, and they're as much against busing as I am," he said.

Because of his refusal to send his daughter to the appointed school, Merchant was brought to trial. His primary defense was his concern for the safety of his daughter. Pontiac's police chief likewise bore witness that the school was situated in a high-crime area—even the police traveled in pairs.

"I couldn't bring myself to let my daughter go down into that environment," declared the father.

Nevertheless, Merchant was convicted of "educational neglect," and his in-laws were given custody of his daughter.[8]

Voluntary Integration

Allowances can be made for parents whose children are zoned for inferior schools and who hope to have them attend better schools by incorporating a voluntary transfer system. Newspaper columnist William Raspberry recommends adoption of a policy whereby students can attend any school that will improve racial balance. If schools implemented such a program, he notes, they would "not generate the fear-spawned opposition that busing has generated."[9]

Portland, Oregon, has a voluntary transfer system. So far, 2,700 pupils, mostly black, have taken advantage of the opportunity to go to white neighborhood schools. A white exodus has not resulted since white children were not forced to attend predominantly black schools.[10]

To foster better racial relations, magnet schools can be utilized, and children from various neighborhoods can enter these specialized schools to participate in their unique programs. Trotter High School, in Boston's Roxbury ghetto, was staffed by some of the best teachers in Boston; it had an innovative and exciting curriculum, including a fine arts course. Before the busing disruption, it had two-thirds blacks and a long waiting list for whites. In the Dallas suburb of Richardson, the previously all black Hamilton Park Elementary School is balanced, with 289 white and 265 black students. It is a magnet school with outstanding courses in gymnastics, drama, and music with a 16:1 pupil-teacher ratio.[11] Many of the colleges are naturally integrated because of the specialized programs they offer.

Busing Results

Many minority parents are rightly concerned that their children receive a proper education; nevertheless, many receive a permissive educational experience. Instead of promoting a program of quality education in a disciplined environment, much money is spent on forced busing. Minority parents are often deceived into thinking their children are now in "good" schools after being bused; in reality, their children often receive the same permissive education as in their former schools.

Two critics of busing came from two black women, Biloine Whiting Young and Grace Billings Bress, who have studied the history of school desegration since its inception in 1954. In the educational journal *Phi Delta Kappan*, they showed from several studies that integration had a "lack of significant effect on black achievement" in schools. "For 20 years the national remedy for low minority achievement has been busing for integration—the faith that if the correct racial mix can be provided in a classroom, problems of low achievement and racial tension will disappear.

"Such a 'solution' now appears to have been dangerously simplistic, creating expectations it has, so far, been unable to satisfy. Further, mandatory busing has contributed to the racial and economic segregation of our cities on a scale undreamed of in 1954, to the extent that in many there are no longer enough white pupils to integrate."[12]

As a result of forced busing, "resegregation" is taking place North and South as whites flee to the suburbs leaving the city schools to the minorities. Some prejudiced parents have put their children into private schools, but the majority of parents choose private schools to avoid having their children receive an inferior education in undisciplined schools. The majority of private schools have an open-admissions policy. What appeals to many parents is that private schools stress morality, have a disciplined learning environment, and offer back-to-basics approach to education.

When busing began in Detroit in 1971, the schools were 60 percent black; today they are 82 percent black. In Richmond the schools have switched from 55 percent white to 82 percent black, while Boston has changed from 60 percent white to 60 percent black since the implementation of busing. After integration, Atlanta black enrollment spiraled from 59 percent to 90 percent and Washington, D.C., from 57 percent to 92 percent.[13]

In 1966 University of Chicago sociologist James S. Coleman issued a pioneering report indicating that children from slums benefit when attending middle-class schools. His report was the basis for much of the federal school desegregation effort. Today, he no longer favors compulsory busing because it has forced an exodus of white children from cities or to private schools leaving the public schools more segregated than ever. "The only honest way to proceed in something like this," Coleman remarks, "is to ask, 'Is this the kind of regulation that I would want applied to me? Would I be willing to have my child sent to a school in the metropolitan area which is determined, not by my judgment, but by the school district, and I can't do anything about it unless I move away?' I think that very few of us, because we care very strongly about our kids' education, would be willing to answer 'yes' to those questions."[14]

"What's wrong with compulsory busing is that it's a restriction of rights," Coleman further objects. "We should be expanding people's rights, not restricting them."[15] He finds it understandable that both black and white parents resist sending their children to schools "where 90 percent of the time is spent not on instruction but on discipline."[16]

Derek A. Bell, former black civil rights lawyer who supervised 300 cases of desegregation while with the NAACP Legal Defense and Educational Fund, Inc., and now dean of the University of Oregon Law School, said, "My contacts with blacks convince me that they want quality and effective schooling, they don't want the inconvenience of busing."[17] UCLA Professor Thomas Sowell, also black, stated that busing black children is a terrible mistake because it did not help black achievement. He contends that the quickest way for blacks to improve their schools is to implement strict discipline and get rid of the few troublemakers who prevent the majority from learning.[18]

Racial Quotas

Instead of strict discipline and a program of quality education to guarantee minority progress, permissive leaders have another solution: Keep the program of automatic promotion and provide more freedom and rights. When minorities cannot make college grades, blame the colleges for racial bias. Minorities are failing, they say, not because of their inferior education but because of the way tests are worded and on account of different cultural background. Educational standards must now be lowered to allow a fixed percentage of minorities into higher education. Some legislators in Maryland proposed that state bar examinations be eliminated as a requirement for law graduates to obtain a license to practice. Their reason was that black applicants were failing the tests disproportionally to whites; they claimed these tests were not "job related."[19]

The Boston Latin schools, which opened the doors of higher learning to generations of Irish, Jewish, and Italian children, have been forced to lower their standards. These two schools were not part of the busing dilemma facing Boston; they were city-wide schools that required a rigorous entrance examination. These schools were integrated having between 7 and 9 percent black enrollment. When Federal Judge W. Arthur Garrity, Jr., discovered that they did not reflect the racial composition of the city, he ordered the schools to disregard test scores and admit 35 percent minority students.[20]

Allan Bakke, a Marine Vietnam War veteran and an honor college student, decided to become a doctor. Though having a promising career as a space-agency engineer, after hours he took premed courses and worked as a hospital volunteer. At age 32, Bakke applied to the University of California Medical School at Davis, but was twice rejected. He discovered that though he ranked far above other accepted students he was rejected because he was white, instead of being black, Hispanic, or Asian American. Out of the 100 applicants, 16 places were reserved for "disadvantaged students," which could include whites but never did. In their average aptitude percentile rankings the 16 students enrolled in 1973 scored 35 in science, 46 in verbal skills; Bakke scored 97 in science, 96 in verbal skills.

Bakke filed a lawsuit, *Regents of the University of California v. Allan Bakke*, charging racial discrimination on the grounds of the equal-protection clause of the Fourteenth Amendment: "No State shall . . . deny to any person within its jurisdiction the equal protection of the laws." The issue had become so complex and explosive that nearly 60 separate legal briefs had been filed by "friends of the court," the largest number of briefs in Supreme Court history.[21] After a long-awaited decision, the Supreme Court rejected rigid racial quotas but allowed race to be considered as a factor for special consideration.

"One of the most serious dangers of the QUOTA doctrine," warns Bayard Rustin, the black president of A. Philip Randolph Institute, "is that it will perpetuate the stereotypical and profoundly mistaken view that Blacks lack the ability and the will to make it on their own." Rustin analyzed that the quota system would automatically cause the "dominant White society to question the abilities of all Blacks, including the overwhelming majority who have succeeded because of their intelligence, skills, and self-discipline."[22]

Permitting minority students to enter colleges with lower standards because there is a lack of a representative sampling, and permitting such students to graduate, will have grave repercussions. Who will respond to these minority professionals on a free and open market where they will have to withstand competition? If an individual, whether black or white, is deathly sick and has the freedom to choose between a minority doctor who perhaps advanced because of lowered standards and another doctor required to pass the original standard, whom will he choose? The minority doctor may have been the brightest in his class, but patients do not check school records. All they know is that members of a certain race were permitted to enter these institutions with lowered standards. To be on the safe side, many will avoid these doctors—not because of racial prejudice but because of racial qualifications.

The end result will be that all minority doctors will bear the permanent stamp of racial inferiority, thereby causing generations of minorities to suffer. The same outcome will result for lawyers, engineers, architects, or persons in any other field where standards were lowered; finally, all minorities will bear the scar of racial inferiority.

When Rosa Cuevas heard about Allan Bakke, she declared: "Hurray for Allan Bakke! I am a Spanish-American female who will apply to medical school next fall. I have a 3.9 average (out of a possible 4.0). I do not want sixteen slots reserved for people like me. I want to be selected on the sole basis of my achievements."[23]

John Hope Franklin, a black professor at the University of Chicago, said:

> I, for one, would want to know how my physician stood in his class and on his board examinations. Who would want to place his fortune or his sacred honor or even his life in the hands of an attorney, whose only record shows that he was exposed to the study of the law for the prescribed three years and that a state board certified him with no evaluation of his performance to practice law? The spirit of egalitarianism that would make us all lawyers or physicians or economists on the basis of our membership in the human family not only reflects irresponsibility but is counter-productive of the true objectives of a democratic society.[24]

As more and more minorities graduate with lowered standards, there will be an increasing cry from top minority students who suffer from the stigma of intellectual inferiority. Here is a complaint by David L. Evans, a senior admissions officer of Harvard and Radcliffe colleges:

> So much has been written about the illegitimacy of special recruiting efforts for minority students, black students' disillusionment and "reverse discrimination" that the mere *presence* of blacks at selective institutions has more and more begun to imply substandard credentials or relaxed admissions policies. Why is this? One reason is the almost total absence of news-media coverage of the successes of black students. This one-sided coverage has, in many cases, become an excuse for

inaction and a belief that nothing can be done without "lowering
the standards."

Harvard and Radcliffe Colleges have no special programs for
minority students, but the more than 400 black undergraduates
here have not escaped this unfair criticism. . . .

Although averaging above the 94th percentile on the Scholastic Aptitude Test, and thus belonging to the cream of the crop of
all college-bound teenagers, black students who come to
Harvard far too often receive the coolest, most ambivalent
reception given to any upwardly-mobile ethnic group that has
ever entered these ivied walls. The polite black student still finds
some of his white peers suspicious and probing.

"They are often trying to silently confirm that 'awful something,'" explains one black student, "so even a casual conversation takes on a nasty competitiveness. I feel I have to be wary of
making the little mistake that will confirm what they are
seeking—proof that 'reverse discrimination' is what brought me
here."[25]

It is unfortunate when top-quality minority students have to
defend their status. This is, however, a natural consequence when
government forces schools to lower standards to achieve a certain
percentage of minorities. Russell Kirk, editor of the *University
Bookman,* points out, "Washington is using the force of law to
compel colleges to hire underqualified and unqualified persons as
professors merely because they are members of one 'minority' or
another."[26]

In 1965 President Lyndon B. Johnson launched the federal
affirmative action program. At Howard University, President Johnson said, "You do not take a person who, for years, has been hobbled
by chains and liberate him, bring him up to the starting line of a race
and then say, 'You are free to compete with all the others,' and still
justly believe that you have been completely fair."[27] This is true. On
the other hand, one does not take the person and start him in the
middle of the race and declare him a winner. Really to help this
unfortunate individual one should make special effort to train him
until he can begin the race at the starting line. Then, when everyone
competes equally, he can emerge as a true winner.

Few would object to seeking out talented minorities and providing
extra help so that they can compete on an equal footing for college
and employment. Objections arise when double standards are
applied, solely on the basis of race. A Gallup poll showed that 83
percent of all respondents, and 64 percent of the nonwhite ones,
opposed racially based preferential treatment for colleges and employment.[28]

When a great shortage of minorities occurs in a certain field, special classes can be provided so students can reach the necessary standards to enter specialized schools. Qualifications are not lowered; rather students are upgraded to meet standards. Upon graduation these students can then effectively compete with their peers. Instead, minority students are often pushed through the educational system whether they learned or not. St. Louis University instructor Ernest Calloway remarked about black students, "The expectation of the teacher is very low. One of the problems is raising the expectations so the child will be told, 'You *can* learn. You *will* learn.' "[29]

Eugene V. Rostow, professor of law and former dean of Yale University Law School, said he pioneered recruitment programs in black colleges and summer-school programs for promising black students so that they could "come into law school better prepared to compete in a basis of equality." His program was to "help those who've been disadvantaged without threatening the standards by which all should be judged."

To the comment "Advocates argue that reverse discrimination is the fastest way to help minorities recover from years of mistreatment," Rostow replied, "No, it isn't. What happens very often with a quota system is that you get a large attrition rate. If you take in a lot of people who really can't do the work, you find that many of them drop out. They are bitter, bruised and badly hurt by their experience."[30]

Programs are needed to help minorities achieve, not stopgap measures that destroy them. For too long these issues have been improperly handled. It is time educators faced the problem squarely and promoted realistic racial prosperity.

Minimum Competency Tests

One of the most popular trends in education today is the minimum competency movement. A panel appointed by the government to explore the movement reported that it deplored the idea of statewide testing before students could be awarded a diploma. One reason cited for rejecting the tests was: "If success on tests—for purposes of graduation or promotion—is achieved by four-fifths of a suburban school system but only one-third of a central city's system, the consequences could be serious for domestic tranquillity as well as social equity in a world where a high school diploma, regardless of intrinsic meaning, is frequently a ticket to particular jobs."[31]

The argument that many inner-city children will fail to obtain a diploma in comparison to suburban children should be the exact reason for demanding competency standards. After seeing these high rates of failure, inner-city parents and educators should be saying, "Let's have the facts. We welcome any device helping us realize our shortcomings; for by understanding our weaknesses we can upgrade our schools." Unfortunately, there are those who believe that minority success can better be achieved by rejecting exposure of educational failure.

The report released on the Educational Testing Service, *The Reign of ETS: The Corporation That Makes Up Minds,* written by Allan Nairn, stated that ETS's tests are biased against minorities and lower-income students. ETS president William Turnbull replied, "Nader and Nairn wrongly blame the tests for showing that minority students are less well prepared in school than majority students . . . . The tests do not create the difference; they reveal it."[32]

When black columnist William Raspberry heard that half of Washington, D.C., first-, second-, and third-grade students had failed the promotional tests, he was quite sure of the reaction. "I thought we'd have a sprinkle of blame-placing, a dash of explanation, several dollops of criticism of inadequate parents, and then: a half-baked campaign to get rid of the tests that brought us the bad news in the first place."

Instead, superintendent James Guines inaugurated a drive to recruit 1,000 volunteers to tutor most of the nearly all black children. Then Raspberry wryly commented, "It is such a sensible step that I'm astonished anyone thought of it. Its obvious premise is that the children can learn—even if they haven't learned all they should have learned so far. It also accepts the principle that children who haven't mastered one grade ought not to be promoted to the next one."[33]

The tenth annual Gallup poll on the public's view of education indicated that "those who are most likely to have children who fail in their school-work—poorly educated parents—are the ones most in favor of requiring students to pass tests for promotion."[34]

Bilingual Education

Another program instituted to help particularly minority foreign-born students is bilingual education. Instruction is mostly in Spanish to accommodate the large population of Puerto Rican, Cuban, and Mexican children. In addition, there are to be 61 other languages, including the many tribal languages of the American Indians and Eskimos. Children are taught in their native tongue while English is learned as a second language. It is claimed that by gradually having children master both their native tongue and English they will be encouraged to remain in school. Previously, schools had an effective program called ESL (English as a Second Language), which encouraged students to learn English quickly, rather than depend on their native tongues. Bilingual programs do not emphasize English, as the ESL program does.

A Spanish paraprofessional told me that in her school bilingual classes for American-born Spanish children are conducted in Spanish except for the study of English. She said that people favoring bilingualism are those who anticipate returning to their own country, not those planning to stay in America.

In the South Bronx a bilingual teacher voiced his opposition to the bilingual program (he stressed English, not Spanish). He showed me papers written by two Spanish children in this country only one and a half years, and I was amazed at their excellent English. Nevertheless, when school authorities observed him teaching, he was instructed to teach children more Spanish.

In another South Bronx school I interviewed a group of Spanish bilingual teachers. One teacher of many years' experience believed the bilingual program was detrimental. However, the younger teacher supported the program; she had come to this country at the age of 15 and knew how difficult it was to learn. The experienced teacher remonstrated, "If they would have had a bilingual program you never would have went to college."

The purpose of bilingual programs is to teach subject matter to foreign-speaking children handicapped in English. Yet both these teachers disclosed that in their junior high school only 1 out of 50 students in the bilingual program could not speak English; all had been born here or had come to this country when very young. The *New York Teacher* states, "The U.S. Office of Education claims that only one-third of the students enrolled in bilingual classes were of limited English-speaking ability. In the preliminary report, the study claimed that 85 percent of the Title VII project directors who were surveyed said that children were kept in the program after they are able to function in English."[35]

Frank E. Armbruster, a director of interdisciplinary studies and author of *Our Children's Crippled Future*, says in his detailed study:

> We began by examining the urban school systems at the beginning of this century, the last period when large numbers of predominantly rural people swarmed into our northern cities. During this time, northern-city schools saw vast numbers of pupils who spoke no English. In New York 53 percent of the children came from families where no English was spoken, and 72 percent of the city's entire population was first- or second-generation immigrants. Similar situations existed in Philadelphia, Chicago, Cleveland, Boston, Milwaukee, and Buffalo, as well as many smaller coal, iron, and mill cities throughout the East. . . .
>
> Classrooms housed up to eighty or ninety pupils. Teachers were from earlier immigrant groups but spoke only English in class and often as not are said to have despised the unwashed

newcomers. Yet the schools upheld the standards and taught the essential subjects of middle-class America. The pupils learned to read and write, and learned basic grammar, arithmetic, history, and geography by the sixth grade—which was as far as most children went in those days. . . .

The Great Depression era again saw high student/teacher ratios (about 30 to 1); many schools with second-generation immigrants whose parents couldn't speak English (and those who could had generally gone only to the sixth grade); and little money for education "specialists" or for schools in general. Yet pupils who couldn't read by the seventh grade in those days were virtually unknown. They could also do long division, knew history, geography, could write compositions, and scored some of the highest grades on ninth-grade academic achievement tests we have ever seen. Most states had strictly enforced laws that kept pupils in school until they were sixteen, but these big, tough kids were orderly, for slum, or mining patch, behavior, grammar, and dress were left at the schoolyard gate. Middle-class standards were maintained, and even "Manual Arts" program students had to take and pass one year of algebra, one year of geometry, two years of a foreign language, three years of real history, and four years of English, including composition and American and English literature. During World War II, these were the boys who had those high aptitude test scores.[36]

Millions of former immigrants have learned through our schools and become assimilated into our nation. Now, with bilingualism, these children will have greater difficulty functioning in society. For many, bilingualism compounds learning problems; foreign children, who often have enough difficulty learning one language, must now learn two languages!

Knowledge of English is still essential for opportunity in America. Certainly non-English-speaking children should be helped over the rough transition period and encouraged to learn their parents' culture and language—in ESL and foreign-language courses. But the current bilingual program helps to polarize nationalities and is ineffective in helping children learn and master English. It is another permissive method making it easier for children to adapt but creating future hardships.

A *New York Times* editorial casts additional light on the difficulties of bilingualism:

Viewing the growing language conflict in Canada, Americans can be grateful that this country has no great region of non-English-speaking citizens such as the Province of Quebec. . . .

Many other difficulties have grown out of Canadian bilingualism. Hostilities are fanned by requirements for French-speaking quotas in Government offices and even for whole units in which French must be spoken. . . . It has proved a political curse in Belgium, an endless source of friction in ethnic patchwork countries like Yugoslavia and a cause of bloody massacres in India. Only in little Switzerland does it not seem to have been a millstone.

Immigrants to America have naturally formed language enclaves, but the sooner their children have learned to think, speak and write in English, the greater has been their mobility, the better their chances of success and the freer their country from the friction of clashing cultures. This is not to deny the need to tide Spanish-speaking children over a rough transition period in New York's school system. It is rather to urge that it not be allowed to encourage a language separatism that can only grow more harmful with the years.[37]

Quota Discipline

Another racial issue is the disproportionate amount of minority punishment. More than a million chidren are suspended from public schools for disciplinary reasons each year, and black students are punished twice as much as any other group. Sex discrimination also exists: Boys far outstrip girls in receiving disciplinary action.

Superintendents of New York City schools were told by the school chancellor to monitor ethnic data in student suspensions because of the demands of the Office of Civil Rights. Some of the high school principals were cited because of the high percentage of a certain ethnic group. Ted Elsberg, president of the Council of Supervisors and Administrators, said, "Essentially, what does monitoring of suspension by ethnicity mean? It means that the offenses—be they mugging of students, beating of teachers and supervisors, drug pushing or whatever—are deemed less important than the ethnic label of the offenders.

"Maintenance of discipline in the schools for the sake of pupils of all origins becomes irrelevant. Quotas *never* made any sense."[38]

Scott D. Thomson, associate secretary of the National Association of Secondary School Principals, claims the problem is not racial prejudice, for "blacks are suspended more often than whites even in schools that have black administrators." In his opinion, "The life style of black kids simply gets them in trouble more. Traditionally, the white kid succeeds by following the rules, while the ghetto kid gets ahead by acting tough."[39] Eugenia Kemble, special assistant to the AFT president, says, "The proportionality argument—in suspensions, testing, credentialing—is emerging as evidence of discrimination. But we need to know how many of the suspended children—black or white—are from broken homes, live in single-parent families, have suffered from child abuse, and neglect, or are from families with incomes below the poverty level. I would be willing to wager a guess that if these factors were looked at across racial lines, many of them would prove to be much more crucial determinants of suspension than race."[40]

However, the government is often not interested in facts; it simply wants everything to look proper on paper. Imagine a school having 30 percent black, 20 percent Hispanic, 5 percent Oriental, and 45 percent white, with a 50 percent male and 50 percent female population, at the end of the school year it could report to the government that suspensions and disciplinary actions perfectly matched these figures. Utopia!

Perhaps a 5 or 10 percent deviation could be allowed to show flexibility. What will such a program of "quota discipline" produce? If a school with 50 percent minority and 50 percent white students has 75 minority troublemakers and 100 white troublemakers, what should it do? Search for 25 minority students to punish or let 25 white students go free? If another school has had too many minority students sent to the dean's office, should it send a notice around: "Please note: Minority quotas have succeeded the allotted number; we will take only white students until further notice."

Yet there are minority individuals who rightfully complain of the soft treatment their people receive. One such person is Omar Blair, a black member of the Denver Board of Education who protested about double standards: "Teachers don't discipline black students because they say they are afraid of the consequences. Black students roam the halls and are ignored. Teachers allow black kids to talk back to them and won't do anything about it. In contrast, white kids would be sent to the principal."[41] A white teacher in Charlotte, North Carolina, said, "I wasn't even aware that I was going easier on blacks than whites until a black student mentioned it to me. He said I was not yelling at them as much and asked if I were afraid of them. I guess I was afraid black students would take it as a threat."[42]

In New York City many of the minority schools have much greater discipline problems; consequently, when the students enter other schools they transfer their learned undisciplined behavior. Contrariwise, a high school where I was a dean had a good number of Chinese students, who caused very little difficulty. Will this school fall under the government ax for being discriminatory if it does not reach the quota for Chinese?

Government quotas for discipline can only be a disastrous policy. It prevents teachers from implementing proper disciplinary procedures where students of another race are involved for fear of being labeled prejudiced. The end result? Minority students suffer.

Teachers and school officials face a dilemma: On the one hand, minorities complain that their children are not disciplined the way whites are; at the same time, the government charges that too many minority children are being punished. The solution is not to count colors but to reject racial figures as a criterion for taking disciplinary actions. It is far wiser to attack racial discrimination whenever it rears its ugly head.

A Destroyed Generation

The effect of lack of discipline and low educational standards has been calamitous—a generation of minorities has been destroyed by the inferior education they received. Today, because of the busing issue, exodus of the middle class, high crime, and other economic factors, many cities have an increasing population of minorities and high unemployment. The *New York Times* reports, "Despite chronic unemployment among young blacks that now officially exceeds 40 percent—some estimates range upward of 70 percent—there has been no agreement among experts about how to avert what could become a human disaster in which millions of blacks become adults with no hope of ever finding jobs with a future."[43]

"A new generation of ghetto youths is casting a long shadow across many of America's big cities," states *U.S. News & World Report*. "Poorly educated for the most part and lacking in job skills, such black youngsters are drifting by the hundreds of thousands toward aimless lives of poverty, drugs, crime and violence—in effect, closing their minds and turning their backs on the outside world.

"These young people are a minority within a minority."[44]

Andrew Billingsley, president of Morgan State College in Baltimore and an expert on black family life, says, "We have young people in our black communities 30 years old or so who have never held a job. We are thereby developing a permanent jobless subsociety, the implications of which are far too dangerous to imagine."[45] The high level of unemployment has had its impact on the criminal behavior of the youth. A study made by the Law Enforcement Assistance Administration comments that the present level of violence of black teenagers is "without precedence."[46]

In looking behind the disturbances in Detroit, where the majority of the city's 1.4 million people are black, including the mayor and many high officials, one finds that there are few family men in their prime managing to hold on to a steady job. According to the Census Bureau, black families have been splitting up at a growing rate in the ghettos; nearly half the children in Detroit are living with one parent—usually the mother—or with relatives, and the chances are both mother and children are on welfare. Unemployment of black youth in Detroit is estimated to be from 50 to 75 percent. *U.S. News & World Report* describes the terrible conditions:

Many nonworking Detroit youngsters have been out of school, either as dropouts or graduates, for years and still haven't landed their first job. Others who did try no longer bother to look, preferring instead to scratch out a living on the streets as "con" artists, petty criminals, drug pushers, pimps and prostitutes.

Even if there were jobs for everybody, sizable numbers of black youths probably still would not be working.

Some just don't want to work. Far too many, say Detroit businessmen and black leaders, are trying to enter the job market with no skills, little appreciation for the "work ethic," and without even the fundamentals of an education. They're simply unprepared to hold a job.

Those in close touch with ghetto youth point out this: In all their growing-up years, no one has explained to such young-sters what it means to come to work on time, or how to co-operate with fellow workers, take supervision or separate personal problems from their job.

Largely because of inadequate preparation in job skills and attitude, only a handful of young disadvantaged blacks who land jobs are successful in keeping them.

In one hiring program aimed at helping members of Detroit gangs, a mere 20 per cent of those hired were still on their jobs a month later. Almost all of those who stuck with it had been gang leaders before. One is now making over $300 a week as a plant supervisor.

Black leaders here blame the schools for failing to do a better job of educating these youngsters—and many criticize them-selves for not insisting on quality education.

Some high-school graduates "can't even read their own names on their diplomas," complains a black union official. . . .

There is growing criticism, too, over what is being stressed in the predominantly black public schools. Too much emphasis, critics argue, is being put on instilling "black pride" in these young people and not enough on teaching them to read, write and do simple arithmetic.

"The educational system has deteriorated terribly in this city," comments Tom Turner, a black who is president of the Detroit AFL-CIO Council. "And I suppose the black community is partly responsible."

He says the problem started decades ago when blacks, lured

from the South by the prospect of high-paying employment in factories, migrated here by the tens of thousands.

They eventually pushed out of the traditionally black East Side into the northwest and far-west sections of the city. White families in those areas moved to the suburbs, leaving the neighborhoods and the schools with a black majority. This fall the schools have a 76 per cent black enrollment.

Mr. Turner continues: "What the black community did—tragically in retrospect—was to insist that the school board lower the standards of the system to the level of the black students instead of raising the black levels to the existing standards."

Those wanting to go on to college have been especially cheated, critics contend. On their college-entrance tests this year, Detroit students scored among the nation's lowest.*[47]

In Detroit, as the article reveals, one can observe the results of permissiveness: children not trained to work, no insistence on quality education, automatic promotion where some high school graduates "can't even read their own names on their diplomas," neglecting to teach children the three R's, and lowering the standards for the minorities. Results? College-bound youth is one of the worst in the nation, and poorly educated youth are drifting "toward aimless lives of poverty, drugs, crime and violence."

Patrick J. Buchanan writes about the schools in Washington, D.C.:

By dollars spent, D.C.'s schools should be among the nation's best. Twenty-five years ago, when the city spent about $250 per pupil, we did indeed boast of some of the finest public schools in America. Now, the taxpayers shell out $1,800 per student (fourth among the top 20 cities in America) and ours is arguably the lousiest public school system in the United States. Nineteen of every 20 kids in attendance are black. They are being robbed as systematically as the taxpayers footing the bill.

Take discipline. As a Fortune Magazine writer who studied the city described it, "The public school system is a shambles. Violence is commonplace. Absenteeism in the upper grades averages 21%. The cost of replacing broken windows comes to $620,000. . . ."[48]

A most pathetic incident in relation to inferior education has to do with a Washington, D.C., black student graduating as valedictorian

---

*Excerpt from *U.S. News & World Report.* Used by permission.

from Western High School, which Buchanan says was "one of our best public highs." While at high school he had a straight A average; but when he tried to enter George Washington University, he scored so low on the Scholastic Aptitude Test (SAT) that he failed the entrance exam. His verbal score placed him in the lowest 13 percent of college-bound seniors; his math score put him in the lowest 5 percent. The administration was puzzled by the wide discrepancy between his high grades in school and his low SAT score. The university administered a different test, and the result was the same!

Superintendent of schools Vincent Reed speculated that in a school plagued with discipline problems he might have had his grades inflated because he behaved. When Joseph Ruth, George Washington's dean of admissions, was asked what went wrong, he replied, "My feeling about a kid like this is that he's been conned. He thinks he's a real scholar. His parents think he's a real scholar. He's been deluded into thinking he's gotten an education."[49] The seriousness of the situation lies in the question: If the valedictorian did so poorly, what level of achievement could the other students possess?

Minority youth need a proper education to find meaningful employment. But the government must be careful to promote incentives to train minorities and not force industries to hire unqualified help. Pressure in the latter direction will compel industries to flee to areas rich in capable help. Some persons may object and insist on having success now, claiming they have suffered long enough. But what has instant success produced? Minorities are suffering and alienated more than before.

Quality Education

Implementing a program of quality education that will assure all minority students a proper education is not an instant success program, as the racial quota system tries to be. But what if such a program were incorporated in minority schools so that *all* children were expected to know the basics for each grade level? A school located in a ghetto area with grave social problems would certainly have more difficulties attaining such goals. The remedy is not to water down the curriculum to ensure that children experience success; rather, it is to spend extra time and effort to help them succeed. If achievement promotion and reasonable educational standards are established and minority children are trained to work and learn to compete on their own, then when entering employment or higher education they can unashamedly declare they have achieved on their own merits. With such achievements the future for minorities will be bright.

With racial quotas utilizing lowered standards, results are instantaneous. However, the future will be bleak for minorities, even for those who have achieved on their merits. Every minority person will suffer the permanent label of inferiority, and his children's children will bear the scar of this stigma. They may fight the label, but the fact that they were permitted to enter schools and graduate with lower standards cannot be altered.

Minorities have not had their full share of the American dream. To partake of the benefits of this land, they must avoid the easy solutions that guarantee quick success. Minority leaders must demand a proper education, a disciplined environment for their neighborhood schools, and challenge students to take difficult courses.

Our nation needs a healing of the races. I long to see the day when all races will freely share, work, and live together as fellow human beings in love and harmony. It was a great encouragement to me to find, in some of the all-black schools of Ocean Hill-Brownsville, Bedford-Stuyvesant, and Harlem, children not possessing a bitter racial spirit. Herein lies hope to provide these and other minorities a bright future. Yet we live in a world that practices racial hate and discrimination. The way to end discrimination is not by pampering minorities with progressive policies that cause racial deterioration but by fighting discrimination itself.

We may look at ghetto neighborhoods with their shattered buildings, fenced stores, and grinding poverty, but we must never forget that living here are people—people with dreams, visions, and aspirations just like ours. The education they have been subjected to has made it impossible for them to succeed. They have been trained for failure. America needs to train a new generation, and to provide *every* race with a program of quality education.

Chapter 9

Successful Schools

A few years ago, a Chicago elementary school was a teacher's nightmare. Less than 1 percent of the pupils could read; undisciplined students roamed about and played ball in the halls, drank liquor, gambled, and damaged the school. Within a period of five years the school had six principals. Teacher morale was understandably at low ebb.

Minority Success

Even though still a ghetto school, where 90 percent of the students' families are on relief or other assistance, now all windows have glass, litter cannot be found, children do not roam the halls, pupils read, and teachers look forward to teaching. The change: Alice Blair. A former black teacher with 17 years' experience with inner-city children, plus another three years as an assistant principal, she took charge of Manierre Elementary School and dramatically altered it. Blair told the secret of her success: "The teachers have very high expectations," she said. "I have demanded, and I don't want teachers on the staff who don't have those kind of expectations for the success of these children either in the behavior of the youngters or in the academic achievement of the children. If I don't glean from the interview that they feel that black children can succeed, and that they have a contribution to make to that success, then I don't want them" The assistant principal is white, and the staff is 60 percent white and 40 percent black. Alice Blair made a special effort to secure black male teachers so that children from welfare families would get to know successful black male adults.

At her first staff meeting she told teachers she believed in some very simple ideas. "One of them is that all children can learn; and all black children can learn. I knew from experience, what worked with black ghetto kids, and I showed my staff members how to make success possible for children who rarely experience success." Blair noted, "Black inner-city children from welfare families have a special need for security. They can't expect stability and security from home, so it must come from school. It is important for children to be able to anticipate what happens next in school and we follow routines religiously." This plan proved very successful.

"My children in school now compare to white and middle class black schools in terms of achievement," Blair said. Subjected to a heavy phonics approach to reading, all children at primary level read successfully. The reading problem now is with low achievers who enter from other Chicago schools. Blair has these lagging children held back until they meet the reading grade; she insists that they attend summer school. Children with severe reading problems create most school problems, she found, but now that children experience reading success, there is little need for discipline. Once order is achieved, new children learn good behavior from others. When children enter this disciplined environment and misbehave, correction is immediately administered.

Parental cooperation is important in a successful school. At Manierre when children fail to do their homework, parents are immediately notified. Parents of preschool children meet daily to study child development. One parent-teacher conference achieved a 100 percent turnout.

Alice Blair recognizes that blacks suffer much from permissiveness. Schools do not insist that children learn how to work. Blair related this incident: "When I was an assistant principal in an integrated setting in Michigan City, Indiana, where the school population was only about 11 percent black, I discovered that there was much more leeway given to black youngsters when black youngsters broke the rules. When I became the assistant principal, for at least a year, there was quite a disturbance in the community because I demanded from black youngsters that they had to meet the same standards that the white youngsters in that school had to meet." Then Blair analyzed the situation: "By saying that they could not meet them, you were saying they were inferior." And added, "I have demanded of them." She does not want sympathetic teachers to feel sorry for these children because they are poor and black and cannot do any better.

The *American School Board Journal* noted about Blair:

> Don't mistake her modesty for timidity. Blair's favorite motto is posted in the school's main office: "If God had believed in permissiveness, He would have given us the Ten Suggestions." Students know that their principal suspends rule breakers without hesitation, and teachers are familiar with the story of Blair's first day on the job—when she asked the school's secretary where 25 of the school's teachers were. "Don't worry," the secretary assured her," the teachers generally come in a little late around here."
>
> "Not any more they don't," Blair said as she picked up the

telephone to request 25 substitute teachers from the city's central personnel office.

Questioned about her basic complaint regarding the permissive philosophy, she told me, "Not to control. It just leaves control to some agency of our society. We don't control them in the schools, then the police will have them. We cannot excuse ourselves because parents don't control them. We have a responsibility for five hours of the day, and we must not only control them but educate them." But to "control them, we have to have order first. There is no way you can teach in disorder and permissiveness." She cleverly analyzed that permissiveness is an "abandonment of our responsibility." Because of her success, Blair has been advanced to the district superintendency.[1]

Achieving and Nonachieving Schools

Daniel Klepak, director of the New York State Office of Education Performance Review, conducted a study on the reasons for the wide discrepancy in reading achievement in two predominantly black elementary schools. Both schools had situations and problems mirroring the poverty of their environment. However, the successful school had an efficient, achievement-oriented principal with an experienced teaching staff; the underachieving school was deficient in such leadership. The *New York Times* editorialized, "Conditions in the successful school were actually inferior to those of the failing one: it was more crowded, had more pupils per teacher, and its children came from families with even lower incomes. . . . Mr. Klepak's conclusions—that good leadership, experienced, well-planned teaching and faith in the children's capacity are crucial—are hardly revolutionary. What renders them significant is the chronic reluctance of school systems to take a hard and self-critical look at the success and failure of their own strategies."[2]

Americans have traditionally believed that schools make a difference in students' achievement. However, some studies have found reasons elsewhere: James Coleman ascribed achievement to family background; Arthur Jensen, primarily to heredity and race; and Christopher Jencks, mainly to luck. Certainly these studies contain elements of truth. Nevertheless, George Weber, former associate director of the Council for Basic Education, developed the hypothesis that in several American inner-city public schools children were successful in learning to read. He received a grant from the Victoria Foundation and discovered four such schools: P.S. 129 and P.S. 11 in New York City, Woodland School in Kansas City, and Ann Street School in Los Angeles. He wanted to find some common factors for their success. Weber came to these conclusions: "Their success shows that the failure in beginning reading typical of inner-city schools is the fault not of the children or their background—but of the schools. None of the successes were achieved overnight; they required from three to nine years. The factors that seem to account for the success of the four schools are strong leadership, high expectations, good atmosphere, strong emphasis on reading, additional reading personnel, use of phonics, individualization, and careful evaluation of pupil progress."

Concerning the level of discipline in these schools, Weber notes, "The good atmosphere of these schools is hard to describe. And yet it is difficult to escape the conviction that the order, sense of purpose, relative quiet, and pleasure in learning of these schools play a role in their achievements. Disorder, noise, tension, and confusion are found in many inner-city schools at the elementary level. I have been in schools where such conditions prevail, but, over-all, the four successful schools were quite different."[3]

Ronald Edmonds, researcher for the Harvard Graduate School of Education, has identified five factors similar to George Weber's for successful schools: emphasis on basic skills, standardized testing, orderly environment, authoritative leadership, and high expectations of students by teachers.

When students in grades 2 through 11 were tested in Baltimore public schools in 1978, their average score in reading was 20.2 months behind the national norms and in math, 17.4 months. Four years later, the reading lag was 5.7 months and math 0.3 month. What happened? Columnist William Raspberry reports, "The heart of the program is simple enough: tough standards and tender concern."

Baltimore superintendent John L. Crew tells the story: "We had our people write learning expectancies in reading, writing and math for each grade, so that each teacher would know exactly what was expected. . . . We made it a matter of policy that every child would have homework. Then we began placing our children according to their test results. Students who scored less than 40 percent on the reading proficiency test, for example, were assigned a reading clinician in addition to their regular language arts program."

An example of his tender love and tough standards, which caused the remarkable change, is Crew's introduction of a reading-through-drama program so that poor readers could act out plays. However, in midyear Crew dismissed three principals.

"A lot of the things I'm doing now," he says in explaining how these changes could be made, particularly among blacks, "I couldn't have done in the 1960s, even though I'm black myself. In the '60s, everything was develop-at-your-own-rate, whole-child, progressive education and 'relevancy.' We were wrapped up in educational innovation and decentralization and a lot of political issues, with really no defined goals and objectives. As educators, we are learning that you must have structure and objectives, or your program simply won't work."[5]

Compensatory Programs

Educators and governmental leaders have tried to help minorities to achieve. *U.S. News & World Report* tells how "large expenditures by all levels of government have gone into 'compensatory' programs at schools in low-income areas to help upgrade scholastic achievement and to narrow the disparities between blacks and whites, and between poor and middle-class youngsters.

"So far, however, test scores have not shown that a significant improvement results from programs of this sort."[6]

Why do programs like Head Start, Follow Through, and Title I of the Elementary and Secondary Education Act show such small gains? It is like carefully growing flowers in a hothouse, then placing them in an unattended garden. Children cannot have an initial successful training program and then be placed in an unsupervised and undisciplined environment.

Certain compensatory programs *have* managed to be successful, and *Educational Leadership* presents the results of the Metropolitan Applied Research Corporation in a report to the Select Committee on Equal Educational Opportunity of the U.S. Senate:

> An analysis of successful "compensatory" or "educational enrichment" programs reveals that these programs are "successful" only when they succeed in imposing upon a particular school and classroom the pattern of essential ingredients of an effective educational program—systematic and specifically defined sequentially developed curricula; high expectations for the students, and acceptance of them as individuals who can perform in terms of high standards; effective teaching and diligent supervision; and regular evaluation and reinforcement of strengths.[7]

According to this report, the few successful programs were conducted in exactly opposite manner to the progressive approach that is so prevalent in today's education. Such programs of supervised education are beneficial to *all* races, not just minorities.

Gifted Children

An article titled "Advanced School Goes Back to Traditional Teaching Methods," appeared in *Today's Child* back in 1961: where "an elementary school whose pupils' intelligence quotients average out to 150-plus has announced a radical change in its approach to the education of intellectually gifted children. Next September students attending Hunter College Elementary School, where chief entrance requirement is a minimum I.Q. of 130, will find less 'democracy' in the classroom and more protein in the academic diet, less emphasis on 'enrichment' and more stress on mastering academic subject matter.

"Among other drastic changes-to-come will be a return to letter grades—A, B, C, D and F—after years of progress reports . . . 'There has been too much misinterpretaion of 'democratic' procedures in the classroom,' says Dr. L. T. Camp, school principal. 'Educators haven't used good judgment in working with children's expressed interests and needs. Intellectually gifted children are still kids and need a firm hand to instruct and guide them.' "[8]

Seventeen years later I interviewed Dr. Stanley Seidman, principal of Hunter College Elementary School. When shown the report of the Metropolitan Applied Research Corporation on successful compensatory programs, he agreed with that approach. In teaching these highly gifted children, he said, the staff philosophy is "individualization with direction and guidance."

Fundamental Schools

James K. Wellington, manager of organizational development for the Arizona Public Service Company, spoke at Arizona State University "A Look at the Fundamental School Concept." Fundamental schools, he says, are increasingly being adopted in cities across America:

I wrote to several individuals who were deeply involved with the fundamental concept within their community. The response was excellent and I would like to share this response with you.

I can say at the outset that in each one of the schools that I wrote to, and from those who responded, the fundamental school has been a success and improvement has been definite and measurable. . . .

Fred Hechinger, a longtime education editor of the New York Times, writes of his experiences in investigating the fundamental school in Palo Alto. When Hechinger first learned that a basically liberal community such as Palo Alto had concluded that it was desirable to establish a structured traditional alternative, he was skeptical. He fretted that Palo Alto citizens had accepted the idea that education "can be good only if it tastes like bitter medicine."

But after visiting Palo Alto's more structured alternative school, Hechinger concluded that "disenchantment with the latest neoprogressive wave can lead to a rational, rather than reactionary, search for conservative answers." At Palo Alto's basic education alternative school, Hechinger noticed an "air of courtesy" and a "low noise level." Children, he said, seemed less frantic and appeared relaxed rather than regimented or submissive. And parents seemed pleased, partially because reports on student work in progress, but not grades, were sent home every Friday, augmented by quarterly report cards which were graded.

Wellington describes the high success of pupils in various fundamental schools and the overwhelming parental support for these schools. He then states, "So, you can see that I am a believer in the fundamental concept because of the excellent record that has been achieved by those schools and by those states who have gone to the basics, or the fundamental concept."[9]

John Marshall Fundamental School, K–8, opened in Pasadena in September 1973, and grades 9–12 were added the following year. The school emphasizes discipline, respect, and patriotism; mastery of basics with reading instruction based on phonics; homework for all levels; and the development of creative abilities. Their guidelines states: "Under no circumstances will vandalism, violence, destructive acts, intimidation, extortion, harassment, malicious disturbances, or any flagrant disregard for law and order be tolerated, condoned, or excused." To enforce these goals they use: "loss of privileges, detention, special tasks, corporal punishment in and out of school, suspension, adjustment transfer, withdrawal from school and expulsion." Teachers are expected to maintain complete control at all times.

The high school division has a Planned Program of Study that is divided into 12 majors: Art, Business Education, Communications, Consumer Education and Homemaking, Engineering and Technology Education, English, Foreign Language, General Education, Mathematics, Music, Science, and Social Science. Students can choose a vocational or professional goal that will prepare them to enter an occupation, advanced studies at a junior college or technical school, or a four-year college or university. Each major has subdivisions in which students can choose their field of specialty. For example, under the major of Business Education the electives are Accounting, Data Processing, General Business, Clerical and Secretarial. After deciding their majors, students take the required subjects and choose electives.[10]

In 1970 the Pasadena Unified School District had forced busing;

as a consequence, school achievement rapidly declined to an all-time low. Many students left the schools, thereby creating a situation in which integration would never be achieved. When a new board was elected in 1973, forced busing was terminated for voluntary integration. In the same year, John Marshall Fundamental School was organized. Leaders of teachers' organizations, various progressive educators, and others favoring forced busing put up a desperate struggle to destroy the fundamental school and foil attempts to implement an academic accounting system. The new school board hoped its efforts would reverse the trend of academic failure; opponents eagerly looked for signs of failure.

After five years, the downward trend in school achievement was reversed, and the elimination of forced busing stemmed white flight. To the chagrin of fundamental school opponents, the school is now voluntarily integrated and reflects the racial and socioeconomic makeup of the entire district. Parents were not opposed to integration when assured that their children would receive a quality education in a peaceful environment.

Richard Vetterli, Ph.D., author of *Storming the Citadel: The Fundamental Revolution Against Progressive Education,* in writing about John Marshall Fundamental School says, "John Hardy, black educator and trustee of the Pasadena School Board, campaigned for election to this post in 1975 on a platform of opposition to forced busing and progressive education. It is his contention that what black children—and all school children for that matter—need is not compensatory education gimmicks or artificial forced integration schemes but fundamental education."

Progressive vs. Fundamental Schools

For Pasadena's minority children progressive education, Vetterli says, has been "tragic." When children end "kindergarten there is a distinct difference between black and white students when compared to the national norm." The gap progressively widens between black and white children until "by the eighth grade Pasadena's black students are, in effect, 3.5 years behind their fellow white students in reading, over 4 years behind in language, and over 3 years behind in mathematics." When these students reach twelfth grade, the gap becomes even wider. "Court mandated forced busing has placed students in the same classroom who may differ in academic competence as much as 4 to 6 years. This problem is not peculiar to the Pasadena Unified School District, for across the nation similar and worse conditions can be documented."

However, at Marshall Fundamental School black students showed amazing ability on the Cooperative Primary Test scores. "The reading and language norms for the first, second and third grade classes at Marshall," says Vetterli, "where the students are over 40% black, topped the national norm in every class in each of the three grades." He tells how "in first grade mathematics at Marshall, 75% of the students scored above the national norm. In first grade reading, approximately 78% of all students scored above the national norm." Similar results were achieved at Sierra Mesa Fundamental School, where 42 percent of students are black; in grade 1 they scored in reading and math 83 percent and 76 percent respectively above the national norm. Vetterli then adds an important fact: These high scores are achieved because black students, representing more than 40 percent of the students, make a "significant contribution to the high test scores—unlike the district as a whole, where the large number of black students assure district test scores averaging below the national norm in most instances."

Vetterli states how "fundamental educators in Pasadena maintain that forced integration schemes, such as forced busing, are also counterproductive. Not only has forced busing failed to improve education, integration or racial understanding, its effects have been universally negative." Also, "fundamental education is demonstrating what progressive education has universally failed to do, that black children can achieve academically, often spectacularly so. The Pasadena experience demonstrates that fundamental education is beneficial to all children across all levels of academic ability and socio-economic background."

The fundamental schools in Pasadena are also "characterized by high test scores, creative achievement, respectful students, neatly dressed faculty and administration, orderly classrooms and clean campuses." Likewise, "other district schools, such as the highly acclaimed Burbank School, which basically follows the fundamental approach, consistently achieve respectable test scores, and are characterized by high student and faculty morale.

"On the other hand, Audubon School, one of the most 'open' and 'Progressive' schools in the district, registers achievement test scores that are tragically low. Given the school's inordinately high socio-economic status, the inordinately low test scores place Audubon at or near the 'bottom' of the district academically." Dr. Vetterli then states:

Fundamental education has always been effective. Before the saturation of American education by the Dewey revolution of permissive, progressive education, fundamental education had helped to make the United States the most literate and advanced nation in history.

Did the success of the fundamental school bring a revolution to the educational system at Pasadena? Listen to what Vetterli says: "Ironically, while many school district officials from far and near come to Pasadena to visit the fundamental schools and learn their methods, causing fundamental education to spread to other areas and school districts, forced-busing and progressive-education militants in our city have 'moved heaven and earth' in an attempt to destroy the fundamental schools. This effort to destroy the fundamental school program has been through court action, telephone threats to parents who enroll their children in fundamental education, to published falsehoods concerning the methodology of fundamental education."[11]

Investigation of Schools by the Federal Government

One of the strongest indictments concerning the serious erosion of educational excellence has come from the federal government. Secretary of Education Terrel H. Bell commissoned an 18-member panel to "examine the American educational system and to recommend reforms." The commission "based its findings on papers commissioned from a variety of experts; existing studies of education; letters from those volunteering their opinions about needed reforms; descriptions of notable educational programs; and testimony at eight meetings, six public hearings, two panel discussions, a symposium, and a series of meetings around the country." Following are excerpts of their findings:

An Open Letter to the American People
A Nation at Risk:
The Imperative for Educational Reform

Our nation is at risk. Our once unchallenged preeminence in commerce, industry, science, and technological innovation is being overtaken by competitors throughout the world. This report is concerned with only one of the many causes and dimensions of the problem, but it is the one that undergirds American prosperity, security, and civility. We report to the American people that while we can take justifiable pride in what our schools and colleges have historically accomplished and contributed to the United States and the well-being of its people, the educational foundations of our society are presently being eroded by a rising tide of mediocrity that threatens our very future as a nation and a people. What was unimaginable a generation ago has begun to occur—others are matching and surpassing our educational attainments.

History is not kind to idlers. The time is long past when America's destiny was assured simply by an abundance of natural resources and inexhaustible human enthusiasm, and by our relative isolation from the malignant problems of older civilizations. The world is indeed one global village. We live among determined, well-educated, and strongly motivated competitors. We compete with them for international standing and markets, not only with products but also with the ideas of our laboratories and neighborhood workshops. America's position in the world may once have been reasonably secure with only few exceptionally well-trained men and women. It is no longer.

Our concern, however, goes well beyond matters such as industry and commerce. It also includes the intellectual, moral, and spiritual strengths of our people which knit together the very fabric of our society.

International comparisons of student achievement, completed a decade ago, reveal that on 19 academic tests American students were never first or second and, in comparison with other industrialized nations, were last seven times.

Some 23 million American adults are functionally illiterate by the simplest tests of everyday reading, writing, and comprehension.

About 13 percent of all 17-year-olds in the United States can be considered functionally illiterate. Functional illiteracy among minority youth may run as high as 40 percent.

Many 17-year-olds do not possess the "higher order" intellectual skills we should expect of them. Nearly 40 percent cannot draw inferences from written material; only one-fifth can write a persuasive essay; and only one-third can solve a mathematics problem requiring several steps.

There was a steady decline in science-achievement scores of U.S. 17-year-olds as measured by national assessments of science in 1969, 1973, and 1977.

Between 1975 and 1980, remedial mathematics courses in public four-year colleges increased by 72 percent and now constitute one-quarter of all mathematics courses taught in those institutions.

The Department of the Navy, for example, reported to the Commission that one-quarter of its recent recruits cannot read at the ninth-grade level, the minimum needed simply to understand written safety instructions. Without remedial work they cannot even begin, much less complete, the sophisticated training essential in much of the modern military.

Paul Copperman has drawn a sobering conclusion. Until now, he has noted:

Each generation of Americans has outstripped its parents in education, in literacy, and in economic attainment. For

*the first time in the history of our country, the educational
skills of one generation will not surpass, will not equal,
will not even approach, those of their parents.*

In contrast to the ideal of the learning society, however, we
find that for too many people education means doing the
minimum work necessary for the moment, then coasting
through life on what they have learned in its first quarter. But
this should not surprise us because we tend to express our
educational standards and expectations largely in terms of
"minimum requirements." And where there should be a coherent continuum of learning, we have none, but instead an
often incoherent, outdated, patchwork quilt.

We conclude that declines in educational performance are in
large part the result of disturbing inadequacies in the way the
educational process itself is often conducted.

Secondary-school curricula have been homogenized, diluted,
and diffused to the point that they no longer have a central
purpose. In effect, we have a cafeteria-style curriculum in
which the appetizers and desserts can easily be mistaken for
the main courses. Students have migrated from vocational and
college-preparatory programs to "general-track" courses in
large numbers. The proportion of students taking a general
program of study has increased from 12 percent in 1964 to
42 percent in 1979.

The amount of homework for high-school seniors has decreased (two-thirds report less than one hour a night) and
grades have risen as average student achievement has been
declining.

In many other industrialized nations, courses in mathematics
(other than arithmetic or general mathematics), biology, chemistry, physics, and geography start in grade 6 and are required
of *all* students. The time spent on these subjects, based on
class hours, is about three times that spent by even the most
science-oriented U.S. students, i.e., those who select four
years of science and mathematics in secondary school.

In England and other industrialized countries, it is not unusual for academic high-school students to spend eight hours a
day at school, 220 days per year. In the United States, by
contrast, the typical school day lasts six hours and the school
year is 180 days.

In most schools, the teaching of study skills is haphazard and
unplanned. Consequently, many students complete high school
and enter college without disciplined and systematic study
habits.

Our recommendations are based on the beliefs that everyone

can learn, that everyone is born with an *urge* to learn which can be nurtured, that a solid high-school education is within the reach of virtually all, and that life-long learning will equip people with the skills required for new careers and for citizenship.

We recommend that state and local high-school graduation requirements be strengthened and that, at *a minimum, all* students seeking a diploma be required to lay the foundations in the Five New Basics by taking the following curriculum during their four years of high school: (a) four years of English; (b) three years of mathematics; (c) three years of science; (d) three years of social studies; and (e) one-half year of computer science. For the college-bound, two years of foreign language in high school are strongly recommended in addition to those taken earlier.

We recommend that schools, colleges, and universities adopt more rigorous and measurable standards, and higher expectations, for academic performance and student conduct, and that four-year colleges and universities raise their requirements for admission. This will help students do their best educationally with challenging materials in an environment that supports learning and authentic accomplishment.

Standardized tests of achievement (not to be confused with aptitude tests) should be administered at major transition points from one level of schooling to another and particularly from high school to college or work. The purposes of these tests would be to: (a) certify the student's credentials; (b) identify the need for remedial intervention; and (c) identify the opportunity for advanced or accelerated work. The tests should be administered as part of a nationwide (but not federal) system of state and local standardized tests. This system should include other diagnostic procedures that assist teachers and students to evaluate student progress.

Students in high schools should be assigned far more homework than is now the case.

The burden on teachers for maintaining discipline should be reduced through the development of firm and fair codes of student conduct that are enforced consistently, and by considering alternative classrooms, programs, and schools to meet the needs of continually disruptive students.

Placement and grouping of students, as well as promotion and graduation policies, should be guided by the academic progress of students and their instructional needs, rather than by rigid adherence to age.

Persons preparing to teach should be required to meet high

educational standards, to demonstrate an aptitude for teaching, and to demonstrate competence in an academic discipline. Colleges and universities offering teacher-preparation programs should be judged by how well their graduates meet these criteria.

Salaries for the teaching profession should be increased and should be professionally competitive, market-sensitive, and performance-based. Salary, promotion, tenure, and retention decisions should be tied to an effective evaluation system that includes peer review so that superior teachers can be rewarded, average ones encouraged, and poor ones either improved or terminated.

It is their America, and the America of all of us, that is at risk; it is to each of us that this imperative is addressed. It is by our willingness to take up the challenge, and our resolve to see it through, that America's place in the world will be either secured or forfeited. Americans have succeeded before and so we shall again.

A close examination of this report will reveal that the problem plaguing American education is that schools have been inundated with progressive concepts. Instead of establishing high educational standards, the commission discovered, for "too many people education means doing the minimum work necessary for the moment," and in "most schools, the teaching of study skills is haphazard and unplanned."

The commission recommends these fundamental concepts: (1) There should be achievement promotion and ability grouping; thus "placement and grouping of students, as well as promotion and graduation policies, should be guided by the academic progress of students and their instructional needs, rather than by rigid adherence to age." (2) Students need to be challenged with higher requirements to achieve an adequate education by having stricter high school graduation standards. (3) "Students in high schools should be assigned far more homework." (4) Achievement tests "should be administered at major transition points from one level of schooling to another." (5) Teachers should "meet high educational standards" and be held accountable. Their "salary, promotion, tenure and retention decisions should be tied to an effective evaluation system." (6) Schools should have "firm and fair codes of student conduct that are enforced consistently."

It was this same report that said, "If an unfriendly foreign power had attempted to impose on America the mediocre educational performance that exists today, we might well have viewed it as an act of war."[12] Schools in crisis: training for success or failure? The answer is obvious—many students are being trained for failure. We need to reverse this trend.

There is, however, a great danger. The commission made a plea for increased funding for education. Some people will see this as the major issue and insist that the cure for educational ills is an increase in federal, state, and local taxes. *Education Week* says, "But some of those who responded to the report—including spokesmen for the nation's two largest teachers' organizations—said its recommendations could not be met without increased federal assistance."[13] There is a definite need for increased funds to be appropriated for teachers to receive an adequate salary, for far too many are grossly underpaid. But if the government is not careful it will repeat the mistakes of the past; it will shoot money at the problems and expect this shotgun method to be the remedy. Then after a number of years it will set up a commission to investigate the results and conclude that for every program that succeeded there were others that failed. Meanwhile schools will continue to decline. Or if increased funding is not available, many persons will feel it is hopeless to try to change the failing educational system.

But money is not the cure. The cause of the disease is the permissive progressive educational policies. The remedy is simple: There must be an educational reform movement that will eliminate the progressive policies and implement the disciplined fundamental educational concepts that have been proven successful.

Within one month after the National Commission on Excellence in Education issued its report, another task force of 41 elected officials, corporate and labor leaders, and educators, came to this conclusion, "We have expected too little of our schools over the past two decades—and we have gotten too little. The result is that our schools are not doing an adequate job of educating for today's requirements in the workplace, much less tomorrow's."

The officials of the National Task Force on Education for Economic Growth, chaired by Governor James B. Hunt of North Carolina, reported: There is a "real emergency" upon us that is caused by world competition, and a "deep and lasting change" is needed in the schools. They recommend an "action plan" for kindergarten through grade 12 should be developed by governors and state educational leaders; and that school officials should eliminate social promotion, and set "firm, explicit and demanding" requirements for homework, attendance, grades, and discipline.[14]

Again it can be seen that the major issue facing education today is whether educators will continue using progressive educational policies or change and implement fundamental principles.

It is important that this fact be understood; otherwise the fight throughout the next decade will be over increased funding to improve the educational deficiencies instead of rooting out the progressive leaders and their policies, which have brought on this massive decline.

Successful schools are possible. Although there are those who vehemently oppose fundamental schools and their concepts, many Americans are choosing this type of school for the pragmatic reason that it is producing positive results instead of failures, as has been demonstrated in many districts around the country. Concerned individuals must be willing to face the opposition to fundamental education and incorporate these tried and proven methods in schools across America. The future of our nation depends upon the training we provide for all our children.

Part V

Moral Solutions

Chapter 10

Textbooks for Wholesome Living

Textbooks created such a volcanic eruption in Kanawha County, West Virginia, that schools were boycotted for nine weeks with more than 15,000 out of 45,000 children absent at one time. Some 10,000 coal miners and other workers staged sympathy strikes; Charleston's transit system was closed down; 30 protesters, including ministers, were arrested; violence flared as rocks were thrown, windows broken, and tires slashed; two dynamite blasts went off; two men were shot, one critically; and schools were firebombed.

Textbook Fury
The cause of such fury? Alice Moore, a school board member and mother of four school-age children, and her husband, a Church of Christ pastor, began to examine 300 basic and supplementary readers. The books, worth half a million dollars and already purchased according to a five-year textbook adoption plan, were to be used from kindergarten to twelfth grade. Parents read the approved books with such alarm that, in an area with a student population of 45,000, some 12,000 individuals signed petitions opposing them. Customarily, when the school board met they usually had less than 25 onlookers. But when the board was scheduled to make its final decision, nearly 2,000 parents attended to protest these books. The meeting room was too small; most of the 2,000 stood out in the rain to express their disapproval. The board split 2 to 2, and Albert Anson, the lame-duck member of the board, cast the deciding vote to approve the books. As a result, a school boycott was initiated lasting nine weeks.[1]

Textbook Supporters
Supporters of the textbooks claimed they were relevant, pictured the real world, and prepared students for a place in that world. Kanawha County school superintendent Ken Underwood vowed angrily he would not remove any books; he likened the protest to book-burning days of Nazi Germany. He resisted parental efforts, claiming that their actions would clothe teachers with academic straitjackets. He asked whether the Charleston school system

155

should give rose-colored glasses to students by presenting only the pleasant facts of life, which would abolish "our responsibility as educators by letting students leave school with a distorted—perhaps unhealthy—view of the world as it exists."[2]

Others expressed their opposition. The *American School Board Journal* reported, "The most populous and prosperous county in West Virginia was experiencing a school book-banning war more complex and fanatical than any in recent U.S. history."[3] James Lewis, a minister in one of Charleston's churches, said, "The books in question are creative books, written with the intention of helping our children discover the truths." He explained that "these books open up a world of opinion and insight," and were "not un-American or ungodly." The problem, said Lewis, is that "this country is experiencing a religious crusade as fierce as any out of the Middle Ages. Our children are being sacrificed because of the fanatical zeal of our fundamentalist brothers who claim to be hearing the deep, resonant voice of God."[4] A *New York Times* editorial appraised the situation: "Even here in the heart of the Appalachian coal fields, where the airwaves are full of emotive radio preachers' fire and brimstone and roadside signs carry the bullet pocks of beery Saturday night automobile snipers, the Fundamentalist bill of particulars seemed too thin to many this week to explain the near chaos that is still disrupting Kanawha County and West Virginia's capital city."[5]

Textbook Protesters

In response to those opposing the textbook removal, Elmer Fike, president of the Business and Professional People's Alliance for Better Textbooks and president of Fike Chemicals, said, "Naturally, the liberals try, as they always do, to cloak themselves with intellectualism and paint their opponents as ignorant but this charge just won't hold up." Fike objected that the textbooks contained little that was inspiring or uplifting; attacked civilization's social values; pitted blacks against whites, stirred racial animosity; dwelled on sex in such a manner as to encourage promiscuity; taught throughout the theme of pacifism, without ever suggesting that some wars were worth fighting because of intolerable conditions; and concentrated on the sordid while failing to motivate upward.[6]

Christianity Today, one of the leading conservative religious magazines, commented, "Because the West Virginia protests were inspired by 'fundamentalists' identified as such, one of the few remaining minority groups that are targets for ridicule, and because the protestors object not only to material that has to be recognized as blasphemous and insulting to their religious views but also to many other things that elsewhere are considered normal and representative literature, it has been even easier for observers to label the

Kanawha County protests as blatant attempts at censorship by a group of religious fanatics. In doing so, such observers fail to grapple with issues deserving closer scrutiny."[7]

In the *Borger News-Herald* Mel Gabler said the textbook protesters were portrayed as "indulging in fire-bombing, shooting and other violence;" but he pointed out that nearly all the violence had been against the protesters, not by them, and that the two shootings and two bombings of automobiles were against parents protesting textbooks.[8]

In evaluating the Kanawha situation, *Wall Street Journal* observed, "A reading of some of the textbooks indicates that we may owe the demonstrators a vote of thanks. The appalling third-grade volume of the D. C. Heath series on reading and grammar entitled *Communicating* consistently deals with frightening themes."[9]

Investigating the Textbook Controversy

After reading about this conflict, I decided to investigate the matter firsthand and flew to Charleston. While there I examined the controversial textbooks and for approximately three hours interviewed Alice Moore, who spearheaded the protest. The major criticisms, she said, were of the teacher's edition, so that parents viewing their children's books were unable to know what teachers were discussing in class. The objections were not against the one or two unpleasant stories the books contained, Moore said, but rather to the constant diet of negativism; the undermining of parent-child relationship, morals, and religious faith; and the teaching of situation ethics.

Some people portrayed the protesters as ignorant hillbillies and religious fanatics; others presented them as parents concerned with the social and moral values their children were taught. To gain a true perspective, the following sampling will show some of the controversial material offered to these children. Under the caption "Talking About Your Own Ideas," a Communicating series published by D. C. Heath and Company, three objectives are listed for the teacher: "(1) to discuss personal experiences or ideas; (2) to tell or write about an experience or idea; (3) to read what one has written." The eight-year-old children are asked in their textbook the following questions:

1. Most people think that cheating is wrong, even if it is only to get a penny, which is what Shan did. Do you think there is ever a time when it might be right? Tell when it is. Tell why you think it is right.

2. Have you ever cheated or stolen something? What happened? How did you feel when you did it? How did you feel after you did it? Did you get caught? If so, tell about this too.[10]

Parents object when their eight-year-old children are asked to justify cheating and resent having teachers probe their private lives. In the same book the children are instructed to make their own myth:

> There are a lot of puzzling things in our world:
> 1. Why do we have pain?. . .
> One way to make up a myth is to think of a question like one of these. Suppose your question is *Why do men have pain?* Now, imagine a time when man did not have pain. Pretend that the first men on earth went around without ever feeling pain. Next imagine that some kind of god walked among men and something happened. Maybe a man did something bad or made a bad mistake. Because of this the god punished men, giving them pain for the rest of their days.[11]

Anyone acquainted with the biblical story of Adam and Eve can see a near perfect correlation. Across the nation millions of homes and thousands of churches hold to the literal account of Adam and Eve. These parents do not want their children to be encouraged "to make up a myth" about a god that tends to undermine their faith. Then the sixth-grade Communicating series mockingly describes a group of religious people as "shuffling Holy Rollers at an all night inspiration."[12]

In the same book children are taught how to use "standard" and "nonstandard" English. "Rewrite the paragraph below so that it looks like 'standard' English to you." The example presented is the antisocial reaction of a young bully who justifies his stealing:

> When I was five years old, I was just about the biggest kid in kindergarten. I didn't take no lip from nobody, not even in first grade. My mom, she said I just growed and growed like a sunflower. So I guess that's what give me this view of life I seem to have took. I weren't mean by nature. It just seem to me that, you know, I can get anything I want just by taking it. Nobody ever stop me.[13]

One of the junior high school books adopted by the school board was a three-act play, *Scripts 3*, published by Houghton Mifflin Company. It was to be read aloud by 12- and 13-year-old children. The play shows Arthur and Ernie conversing about Clifford Truckston, who was getting drafted next month and had got his girl "knocked up." Clifford was going to "get four other guys to swear she'd put out to *them*, too, but then he decided he'd better do the honorable thing and get her an abortion."

ARTHUR. (*A great effort to be nonchalant and keep up his part of the "man of the world" act.*) I'm gonna be *really* careful from now on!

ERNIE. A guy's gotta be. (*A very short pause.*) Did your old man ever take you into the bedroom and give you the old pep-talk? About women and diseases and all?

ARTHUR. No, he never.

ERNIE. Mine did. He really did. Only he waited till I was twelve, for Godsake! All I could do to keep a straight face.[14]

The following scene is found in Act Two:

ERNIE. Okay! That's all you had to say! They would've stopped talking about their goddam problems, but you didn't want them to stop and listen. You were scared they'd hear you!

ARTHUR. (*Turning on him, viciously.*) Get out of here, you sonofabitch! Get out! (*He rushes* ERNIE, *who turns and exits up the steps to the yard with* ARTHUR *pushing him.*) Get out, God damnit! Get OUT![15]

Here are some additional phrases children will learn in junior high from this approved play: *hell, fat old bitch, by God, work your ass off, stupid son of a bitch,* and *Christ, no.*[16] Some of this wording is repeated over and over. All the previous textbook materials were shown to me when I visited Charleston.

These and other selections aroused citizens of Kanawha County. From this protest the dispute has spread to dozens of communities throughout the nation. The board of Island Trees School District in Long Island, New York, banned certain books from junior high and high school libraries because they contain "obscenities, blasphemies, brutality and perversion beyond description" and "materials offensive to Christians, Jews, blacks and Americans in general." Representative Norman F. Lent of New York supported the board's decision, and its responsibility for determining what schools taught. Lent wanted to discover what would happen if he submitted excerpts from these banned books for insertion into the *Congressional Record.* He received this reply: "The Joint Committee of Printing, after reviewing the excerpts submitted, has refused to print the same. The general rules governing the *Record* prohibit the inclusion therein of profanity, obscene wording or extreme vulgarisms."

Lent viewed the *Congressional Record's* refusal to print these excerpts as support for his position that the board's action was proper and that no infringement of the First Amendment was involved. If individuals wanted to get these books, they could obtain them from public libraries and bookstores, said Lent.[17] In a 5-to-4 decision in *Board of Education, Island Trees Union Free School District No. 26 v. Pico,* The U.S. Supreme Court did not define the precise constitutional limits but did decide that school officials may be required to defend their motives in federal court.[18] The school board dropped its ban on the books in order to avoid "judicial control" of its school libraries. Now when anyone checks these books out, they are required to notify parents.

U.S. News & World Report cites the following excerpts found in school libraries and on approved lists in Montgomery County, Maryland, to which parents objected unsuccessfully:

From *Manchild in the Promised Land*, by Claude Brown:

> But the chick was really something—she couldn't see anybody knocking her off just one time. . . . She just kept forcing me. . . . When she got high, all she wanted to do was screw and screw. . . .

From *Real Magic*, by P. E. I. Bonewits, on "How to Cast a Lust Spell":

> There is a particular person you really want to go to bed with but he or she isn't interested. . . .
> You surround yourself with the sounds, smells, lights, textures and colors that remind you of pure, unadulterated lust! . . . You imagine the target as passionately assuming a sexual position, ready and willing. . . . Wait as long as you can to build up your lust to its peak, and then fire. . . .
> Some readers might think that this is merely a description of sexual fantasy. It's more. . . . In a lust spell, any orgasm is a mere side effect on the way to the real goal, which is the discharge of psychic energy to affect someone else's mind.[19]

Textbook Reformers

Among the leaders in stressing educational and moral excellence in textbooks are Mel and Norma Gabler. Their concern over textbooks was aroused when their son Jim came home from school and asked his father a question concerning states' rights and the Constitution. As the father told his son, the Tenth Amendment to the Constitution provides that powers not delegated to the United States by the Constitution nor prohibited by it belong to the states and their people.

"That's not what my textbook says," replied Jim.

Jim brought his history textbook home the next night and proved his point. The parents examined the book, along with others, and were shocked. This episode started the Gablers on their tedious and meticulous work of examining textbooks 20 years ago. Today, they head a nonprofit organization, Educational Research Analysts, in Longview, Texas, with a staff of seven workers.

Jimmy Brown says, in the *Gladewater Mirror*, "The Gablers are not by any stretch of the imagination self-righteous busybodies, intent on entering the twilight zone of censorship. They are intelligent, cheerful people who simply take the time to become deeply involved." The Gablers "have built a solidly respected reputation as perhaps the most authoritative and expert public school textbook reviewers in Texas. Their work, now a fulltime task, has earned them a great deal of publicity, many honors—and quite a number of verbal brickbats. But now, when the Gablers speak out on a textbook a great many important people listen intently. More often than not these days their recommendations are accepted." They have more than 300 different printed forms covering textbook content as well as the largest assortment of textbook reviews in the nation. They have jointly received the Texas Outstanding Citizenship Medal for 1973, and at the National Congress for Educational Excellence, which is composed of approximately 350 affiliated parent groups, they were awarded the Outstanding Parent Leadership Award in 1976.[20]

"We've been concentrating on parents," Mel Gabler told me in an interview, "because we've found wherever parents do get concerned, educators give in, but other than that they ignore parents."

Their influence is also enhanced because Texas is the nation's largest textbook purchaser, spending up to 30 million dollars a year. Because the state exerts a strong influence on publishers that desire their market, many textbooks have been altered to meet Texas specifications.

Though deeply concerned that patriotism and morality have been severely downgraded in recent years, the Gablers also examine textbooks for facts, skills and knowledge. Norma Gabler says teachers have been handicapped by many poorly written textbooks. "I feel review of textbooks is one of the most important things I've ever done," she says. "I don't think there's anything more valuable than the mind of a child. A child is only as informed as what he reads and studies. In the final analysis this determines the kind of men and women they will become.[21]

Norma Gabler objects to the new role given to mothers in current textbooks. "They give the impression that a woman becomes a slave in marriage." She notes "They also act as if motherhood is second-class, a burden, when that's the highest privilege a woman can have. My point is that they're trying to force women into a role reversal that's against our culture and tradition and in some instances against the Bible."[22]

In their perusal of textbooks, the Gablers found this selection from a rhyme book entitled *The Inner City Mother Goose* for nursery children:

> Jack be nimble, Jack be quick. Snap the blade and give it a flick. Grab the purse—it's easily done. Then just for kicks, just for fun, plunge the knife and cut and run.[23]

In reviewing a group of five high school textbooks on sociology and psychology, Mrs. Gabler said that they heavily favored legalizing homosexuality. Many of these books also downgrade free enterprise, traditional American standards, religion and prayer, the home and family life. A high school psychology textbook, *Behind the Mask: Our Psychological World*, suggested this:

> To truly induce completely creative thinking, we should teach children to question the Ten Commandments, patriotism, the two-party system, monogamy and the laws against incest.[24]

New History Textbooks

In a fifth-grade history book, *Search for Freedom: America and Its People*, published by Macmillan (Benziger), Norma Gabler found that on several pages a few sentences were devoted to George Washington, whereas the late film star Marilyn Monroe received six and a half pages. She said, "We're not quite ready for Marilyn Monroe to be the mother of our country." The more than six-page spread included photos and personal background on Marilyn. "Most of the questions at the end of the chapter were related to her and specifically about her marriages, for example, what she liked about being married." Gabler was unable to see how this could be "pertinent reading material" for fifth-grade history students.[25]

Norma Gabler tells an incident showing how textbooks have changed: "Mel and I read in the new histories that George Washington had a violent temper—period. We didn't know. We couldn't argue with the book until we found the same statement in an old history book by the same publisher, with an added qualification: 'George Washington had a violent temper, *but* he kept it under masterly control.' You see how the new history casts doubt on his leadership?

"We find examples like that all through the new histories. Our heroes are constantly put down and obscure characters put in to prove the author's point."[26]

Mrs. Gabler found that history texts demoted national heroes, minimized important historical events, dwelt on the frivolous, and made students feel ashamed of their national heritage. When comparing modern histories with old ones, she wondered, "Has history changed or have the new books changed history?"[27] Historian Frances FitzGerald supports Gabler's perception of altered textbooks. "Textbooks published since the 1960s," says FitzGerald, "contain the most dramatic rewriting of history ever to take place in American schoolbooks."[28]

A fifth-grade book, *Many People, One Nation* (Random House, 1973), had this to say about our American heritage:

> No nation on earth is guilty of practices more shocking and bloody than is the United States at this very hour.
>
> Go where you may and search where you will. Roam through all the kingdoms of the Old World. Travel through South America. Search out every wrong. When you have found the last, compare your facts with the everyday practices of this nation. Then you will agree with me that, for revolting barbarity and shameless hypocrisy, America has no rival.[29]

"Textbooks today major in the defects and faults of our government," says Norma Gabler, "in our free enterprise system, and in our society. Too often they decline, or refuse to point out, the successes and achievements of our system. The mild patriotism, if any, with their indoctrination in the weakness and problems of our American system has made our youth think, 'The American system has failed. It must be replaced.'

"And we parents wonder why some young people are dedicated to the destruction of our American way of life.

"Each generation has the responsibility to pass their heritage to the succeeding generation. As parents, we have fallen down. Today's youth have received a distorted version of our heritage. It is late, very late—but not too late.

"We, the parents, should demand that a true and unbiased picture of the American system be presented to our young people. If this 'equal time' plan could be used in textbooks and in the schools, we guarantee that young Americans will develop a keen appreciation for the heritage which is theirs.

"If not, we will soon see a real revolution and the death of a great nation.

"The training we give our children is important—very important—for youth holds the key to the future of this nation."[30]

Children's Liberation
Instead of a positive program of training there are those who advocate greater freedom:

In the outside world, kids should be able to:

Smoke and drink. Some state laws say a person must be 16 to buy cigarettes and 18 to drink liquor. Once they have been made fully aware of the possible health hazards, all kids should be allowed to drink and smoke. . . .

Vote. Thousands of senile, alcoholic, and mentally ill adults can vote. So why can't kids?

Statements from an underground press? Communist newspaper? Speech from a far-out radical? No. These statements are from an educational magazine my son received in seventh grade.

The article, "No Kidding? Kids' Lib Is Coming?" by Steven A. Otfinoski, was in the magazine *Read*, published by Xerox Education Publications. The author quoted Dr. Richard Farson, a California psychologist, and other liberationists in their support of giving children the right to drink, smoke, and vote.

Otfinoski wrote how American minorities have gone liberation mad, but the "biggest minority group of them all—80 million—has been the slowest to pick up a protest sign." Who were these poor depressed minorities? The kids reading the article—this time it included my son.

Dr. Farson said today's children are "patronized, ignored, dominated, and abused" by adults. But the article does not stop at student rights; it gives the doctor's and other liberationists' concepts of how parents should treat their children at home:

Stop babying. Kids should not be talked down to, treated like infants, or made to do things their parents don't do. For instance, they shouldn't be forced to "clean their plates" at dinner when their parents can eat what they want.

Give them a choice. Children from troubled homes now must either stay with parents they often hate or enter a detention home—although they haven't committed a crime. These kids should be able to make their own choice of where to live, whether it be with relatives, friends, or by themselves.

To counteract these comments, and apparently to show impartiality, the magazine quotes Ann Landers on Kids' Lib:

DEAR ANN LANDERS: I am writing to tell you about a new group that I am trying to start. It is called *Kids' Lib.*

We want the right to express ourselves without being told we are too young to know anything. We also want the right to smoke and drink if we want to at age 13.

I saw a man on TV the other night who gave me this idea, and a lot of my friends think it's neat. He said kids at age 13 should be able to handle their own money, choose their own clothes, and pick which parent they want to live with if there's a divorce. Will you back me up?

DEAR KIDS: No way. You are adding apples and oranges and getting bullfeathers. I agree a 13-year-old should be able to express his opinions, pick his own friends, and handle his own money (an allowance, in most cases), and the judge often will allow a 13-year-old to decide which parent he wants to live with. All those things are reasonable, but that crock about 13-year-olds being allowed to smoke and drink is strictly for the birds—the loons, that is. Forget it, buster.[31]

I complained to the substitute teacher at my son's school and to Xerox Corporation; Xerox corporation replied and sent me the teacher's edition of *Read*. To generate class discussions, teachers were encouraged to take a children's poll. It was suggested that the following be put on the blackboard: "The right to vote, smoke, choose your own bedtime, quit school and work, and take only the school courses you want to. Then take a hand vote as to who wants what. After the votes are tallied, you might ask students to defend their position for or against a particular right."[32]

Imagine school situations in which 12-year-olds are discussing the parental prerogatives of whether children should have the right to smoke, choose their own bedtime, and quit school. So long as schools give both sides to any question, it appears, anything becomes legitimate material for discussion, even whether parents should be obeyed or not. In good faith millions of parents send their children to schools, yet in some classrooms their parental authority is being questioned.

"ON THE RISE across the U.S. is a 'children's liberation' movement that is forcing the nation's elders to sit up and take notice—often in disbelief," notes *U.S. News & World Report.*

"At least four national organizations of attorneys and countless public-welfare groups have joined the fray in behalf of the 68 million Americans under 18 years old—whom some libertarians call the country's 'most oppressed minority.'

"At times, the movement resembles a pint-sized version of the youth revolt that shook campuses in the past decade.

"One underground pamphlet, which the National Association of Secondary School Principals says has been distributed at many high schools, mixes current concerns about students' rights with warmed-over rhetoric against defoliation in the Vietnam War. This 'school-stoppers textbook' tells disgruntled students 61 ways to shut down their schools—including burglary and arson."[33]

The Children's Rights Organization in Playa del Rey, California, the majority of whose members are under 18, was founded by Morley Cowan, a psychotherapist and family counselor. One of its positions states, "Alternate home or living environments must be given Youth, who will have freedom of CHOICE where and with whom they reside." The question was raised concerning the inadequate knowledge of young people on how to live alone. The solution: "That will be the first change in the School curriculum. Grade 7. Course #1: How to live alone. How to cook. How to shop. Where to catch a bus. How to avoid being cheated. Same argument used against freeing slaves is used against freeing Youth."[34] (Notice Youth is capitalized.)

Progressive Goals

In the progressive 30's, Ethel Mannin said in *Common-Sense and the Child*, "Parents, nurses, and teachers are the natural enemies of the child because they are the destroyers of its freedom. They represent authority from the beginning."[35] But in the 70's, John Holt, who has taught in Colorado, Massachusetts, and California, and has written many popular educational books and articles, set forth these progressive goals for children in his book *Escape from Childhood:*

I propose instead that the rights, privileges, duties, responsibilities of adult citizens be made *available* to any young person, of whatever age, who wants to make use of them. These would include, among others:

1. The right to equal treatment at the hands of the law—*i.e.,* the right, in any situation, to be treated no worse than an adult would be.
2. The right to vote, and take full part in political affairs.
3. The right to be legally responsible for one's life and acts.
4. The right to work, for money.
5. The right to privacy.
6. The right to financial independence and responsibility— *i.e.,* the right to own, buy, and sell property, to borrow money, establish credit, sign contracts, etc.
7. The right to direct and manage one's own education.
8. The right to travel, to live away from home, to choose or make one's own home.
9. The right to receive from the state whatever minimum income it may guarantee to adult citizens.
10. The right to make and enter into, on a basis of mutual consent, quasi-familial relationships outside one's immediate

family—*i.e.*, the right to seek and choose guardians other than one's own parents and to be legally dependent on them.
    11. The right to do, in general, what any adult may legally do.

Referring to the age of voting, Holt says, "When I say that I want all young people to be able to vote, older people ask with amazement, disbelief and even anger whether I mean children of any age. That is exactly what I mean. I am talking not just about the sixteen-year-old vote but about the six-year-old vote. I think a six-year-old who wants to vote ought to be able to vote."

Holt elaborates on his guaranteed income plan: "What I propose is that such an income should be guaranteed, not just to all adults, male or female, single or married, but to all children as well, down to an early age—as early as the child wants to receive it. For obviously the right to leave home, to travel, to seek other guardians, to live where they choose, and alone if they choose, cannot be an active or meaningful right for most young people unless they can get the money they need to live. Some will object that this much financial independence might weaken family ties. But the state ought not to use the threat of poverty as a glue to hold the family or other personal relationships together."

Holt also proposes "to allow all people to use what drugs they want," and says that "ALL PEOPLE, INCLUDING young people, should have the right to control their own private sex lives and acts."[36]

Social Engineering—MACOS

One of the most daring attempts at reshaping American children has been directed through the implementation of the federally subsidized course called MACOS (Man: A Course Of Study), for fifth-grade children. The development of MACOS began in 1963 when the National Science Foundation (NSF) was given a federal grant of 4.8 million dollars. More than 50 commercial textbook publishers refused to market the course because of its high expense, objectionable content, and philosophy. Finally, the Educational Development Center marketed the program, but only after the NSF provided the center with an additional 2.16 million dollars; by 1974 MACOS was taught in 1,700 schools in 47 states.[37]

Initially, MACOS sold well, but as parents became aware of the program, protests and resistance arose. Because the federal government subsidized the program, Congressman John B. Conlan of Arizona brought the issue of MACOS before the House of Representatives. Conlan proposed an amendment to "reassert congressional authority over NSF curriculum activities to stop what is shaping up as an insidious attempt to impose particular school courses and approaches to learning on local school districts—using the power and financial resources of the Federal Government to set up a network of educator lobbyists to control education throughout America." He noted that the NSF provided a special 80 percent reduction in the normal royalty to Curriculum Development Associates so that "MACOS would sell and undercut competition from other curriculum materials available in the private sector."[38]

Congressman Conlan spoke before the House of Representatives:

> Mr. Chairman, MACOS materials are full of references to adultery, cannibalism, killing female babies and old people, trial marriage and wife-swapping, violent murder, and other abhorrent behavior of the virtually extinct Netsilik Eskimo subculture the children study.
>
> Communal living, elimination of the weak and elderly in society, sexual permissiveness and promiscuity, violence, and other revolting behavior are recurring MACOS themes.
>
> This is simply not the kind of material Congress or any Federal agency should be promoting and marketing with taxpayers' money.
>
> The course was designed by a team of experimental psychologists under Jerome S. Bruner and B.F. Skinner to mold children's social attitudes and beliefs along lines that set them apart and alienate them from the beliefs and moral values of their parents and local communities.[39]

The following material is from various MACOS books about the Netsilik Eskimos to which elementary school children are exposed:

Adultery and Wife Swapping

> Husbands have a very free hand in their married life and it is considered to be quite in order for them to have intercourse with any woman whenever there is an opportunity. ("The Netsilik Eskimos," MACOS Volume I, p. 117)

> If a man is about to set off on a journey and his wife is sick or unable to go with him, he may borrow the wife of his song partner to take along, giving his own wife in exchange. This kind of wife-exchange is necessary in the kind of life the Eskimos lead. ("A Journey to the Arctic," MACOS Booklet 18, p. 23)

> Two men who become song partners . . . are so closely bound together that they can exchange wives if they choose. ("A Journey to the Arctic," MACOS Booklet 18, p. 38)

Cannibalism

The wife knew that the spirits had said her husband should eat her, but she was so exhausted that it made no impression on her. She did not care. It was only when he began to feel her, when it occurred to him to stick his fingers in her side to feel if there was flesh on her, that she suddenly felt a terrible fear; so she, who had never been afraid of dying, now tried to escape. With her feeble strength she ran for her life, and then it was as if Tuneq saw her only as a quarry that was about to escape him; he ran after her and stabbed her to death. After that, he lived on her, and he collected her bones in a heap over by the side of the platform for the purpose of fulfilling the taboo rule required of all who die. ("The Netsilik Eskimos," MACOS Volume I, pp. 97–98)

Divorce and Trial Marriage

Divorce is common as long as there are no children, and there are women who go through seven or eight trial marriages before they finally settle down. ("The Netsilik Eskimos," MACOS Volume I, p. 115)

Female Infanticide

[The Netsilik Eskimos] would like to have many sons and few daughters. If a baby girl has not already been promised as a future wife, her family may feel that they cannot provide for her. If there is no family to adopt her, it is their custom to allow the child to die. ("A Journey to the Arctic," MACOS Booklet 18, p. 24)

I talked to several Netsilik women in one camp about the children they had. One had borne eleven children—four boys and seven girls, of which four girls had been allowed to die at birth. ("A Journey to the Arctic," MACOS Booklet 18, pp. 24–25)

Senilicide

When we spoke of Eskimo murder, Father Henry told me about a man now at Committee Bay who had come to him one day, and, after the usual tea and silence, had said to him suddenly: "I took the old woman out on the ice today." It was his own mother that he had driven out and set down at sea to freeze to death. He was fond of her, he explained. He had always been kind to her. But she was too old, she was no longer good for anything; so blind, she couldn't even find the porch to crawl into the igloo. So, on a day of blizzard, the whole family agreeing, he had taken her out, and they had struck camp and gone off, leaving her to die. ("Old Kigtak," MACOS Volume 7, p. 18)

We have a custom that old people who cannot work anymore should help death to take them. ("Songs and Stories of the Netsilik Eskimos," MACOS Booklet 16, p. 44)[40]

During the congressional debate over MACOS, Congressman Annunzio said, "As a former teacher in the Chicago public school system, and as a parent and grandparent, it is my firm conviction that our schools should be seen as an extension of the family function which instills moral standards in children. The exposure of children during their formative years to these vagaries of other civilizations and cultures without appropriate perspective constitutes a condemnation of the moral standards of the Judeo-Christian culture which have made this Nation so great."[41]

In contrast, Congressman Ottinger said that under the test to which MACOS was subjected "the Holy Bible would not pass. It is just as easy to show out-of-context examples of murder, adultery, et cetera in the Bible as in MACOS."[42] But there is an important difference between the Bible and MACOS: The Bible condemns murder and adultery; MACOS justifies immoral behavior.

MACOS is a subtle attack on our social moral values foisted upon impressionable 10-year-old children. For example: When Arfek left his old mother-in-law Kigtak, who was half-blind and crippled, to "crawl over the ice and catch up if she could;" he "had no choice but to leave Old Kigtak behind." The people "have a custom that old people who cannot work anymore should help death to take them." So Old Kigtak thought of this and decided, "Why hang on as a burden to her children."[43] And in support of their behavior: "You see, it is not that we have hard hearts but that the conditions of life here are merciless and to survive in a land of ice and snow sometimes we must be without pity."[44] In the teacher's edition a suggestion is made for interested classes to role-play the act of senilicide of Kigtak and to present "reasons for their opinions."[45]

Infanticide is justified. Boys are valued much more than girls because of their ability to obtain necessary food. Wife swapping is defended because "they are so closely bound together that they can exchange wives if they choose. . . This sharing of responsibilities is necessary in the nomadic life the Eskimos live."[46]

There would be few objections to having a history course spend time on various cultures even if some had cruel and inhumane practices. However, when the worst acts of the human race—senilicide, infanticide, suicide, and promiscuity—are justified, as Congressman Conlan pointed out, in "a subculture group with only 30 or 40 people in it," and "a culture that is so low that even the other Eskimos do not want to associate with this clan," one realizes the serious implications of such material.[47]

Perhaps schools should also rationalize the ancient practice of placing jars containing infants in the walls of new houses to bring blessings from the gods, or the use of temple prostitutes by worshippers, or the act of widows of India throwing themselves upon their husband's funeral pyre. With such reasoning one could even exonerate Hitler in his extermination of the Jews and other "misfits" to develop a superior race. Stalin and Mao Tse-tung could be hailed as benefactors; though they murdered millions, their brutal acts benefited communism.

Imagine children taught to empathize with a culture that practiced wife swapping, adultery, and the killing of infants and the elderly. These impressionable children may one day have to make similar difficult decisions. What should they do when their parents become old and feeble? Should they deprive their family of comfort to take care of them? They will long have forgotten this social studies course, but the subconscious approval of senilicide will remain. Parents should not be shocked if their children ignore their agonies because of the sacrifices entailed. Indeed, children may even condemn their parents for trying to make themselves a burden upon them. After all, the good Netsilik parents who were a hindrance were to "help death to take them." So parents should be good—hang themselves or go out into the cold and let themselves be frozen to death. If some leaders have their way they may allow parents to die with dignity; they will provide painless gas chambers. Quite a contrast to our historic Judeo-Christian ethic: "Honor thy father and thy mother."

MACOS Evaluated

When the National Council for Social Studies issued a report on MACOS, it had the audacity to state that this course fostered "decision-making and other analytical skills, multi-cultural understandings, sensitivity to human relations, strengthening of human compassion and love for and appreciation of the family and its role as a personal and social institution."[48]

Rhoda Lorand, a psychologist with a Columbia University doctorate in educational psychology, does not agree that MACOS strengthens human compassion and love for family. "It is incredible that this exercise in sadism should be foisted upon a captive audience of children who are undergoing the crucial process of adaptation to our culture and civilization," says Lorand. "Equally incredible is the fact that a program so lacking in awareness of children's emotional development and needs, as well as in the purposes of education and the processes of character development, should have been given government support."[49]

Sheilah Cambell Burgers, who taught MACOS in Sheffield, Massachusetts for one year, flatly declared, "I refused to teach it again." She told how "after having read nine teachers' manuals and 31 books, after having seen the 21 course films several times, and after having worked with 75 fifth-graders, I felt that MACOS not only restricted academic freedom but also inhibited the development of my students by presenting a negative, one-sided and dishonest picture of man. In short, MACOS is a brainwash—clever, well-executed, and lethal.

"The method of teaching is inquiry. The teacher asks questions; the student finds answers.

"All answers are found in course books and films. Outside sources cannot be used because material concerning the course content (the social structure of the herring gull, salmon, baboon, and the Netsilik Eskimo) is understandably non-existent at the fifth-grade level. Input and output are thereby totally controlled.

"Books cannot leave the classroom. Except for projects, homework is discouraged. Manuals are kept at school for professional use only. Adult intervention, therefore, is minimal."

The children also play a simulation game: Hunt the Seal. As Burgers tells it, the game "takes a week to play. The victor must procure enough seals to insure his own survival. He can do this only by starving his co-players. The price of survival is killing; the lesson is re-enforced by the story of the old woman who was left on the ice to die because she could not contribute to her society.

"The book word for this is 'senilicide,' a tough word for fifth-graders, but they got it. They approved and defended abandonment of the old woman. At this point I deviated from the manual and asked one of the children what he would call this act in terms of his own culture. He gulped and answered, 'murder.'" When Sheilah Burgers was confronted with having departed from the manual, she says, "I was reprimanded for infusing irrelevant questions into the program."[50]

Courses like MACOS, says Dr. Onalee McGraw, coordinator and spokeswoman for the National Coalition for Children, in speaking before the Senate subcommittee that controls the NSF's budget, have caused functional illiteracy and social and moral uncertainty in today's high school students. These "hip" literature and behavioral social studies courses have been substituted for geography, history, economics, English, and hard sciences. McGraw blames the educational philosophy of these contemporary courses that question and discard parents' views, moral standards, and religious beliefs as being largely responsible for America's severe social youth problems.[51]

MACOS is not just an anthropology course. It is a subtle social engineering and psychotherapy program whereby 10-year-old children are molded to accept humanistic concepts. The course suggests that man's values and behavior are determined by specific environmental pressures as opposed to theistic principles. MACOS implies an evolutionary and mechanistic philosophy of relativism that denies traditional American values based on the Judeo-Christian heritage. Consequently, it dehumanizes man and humanizes animals by implying that man has evolved from lower animals and has received his social behavior from them. Then, through open discussions, man's antisocial actions are rationalized.

Due to the religious zeal of progressive educators to resocialize school children to accept morals contrary to those of the majority of Americans, loud voices within our nation are demanding action to stop this undemocratic incursion into school children's minds. Today a battle rages between liberal educators who insist on having academic freedom while charging parents with censorship, and parents who demand selection guidelines while charging progressive leaders with social engineering.

Chapter 11

Selection Guidelines or Censorship

One of the hottest issues in the textbook controversy is: Who controls the education of children, parents or schools? When 11 books were removed by the Island Trees School District because they contained material "offensive to Christians, Jews, blacks and Americans in general," the *New York Teacher* remarked that this act "is regarded by the teachers as an outrageous incursion on academic freedom and a clear contract violation."[1] According to the *New York Times*, "Ira Glasser, executive director of the New York Civil Liberties Union, said that the Island Trees ban was part of a recent 'epidemic of book censorship' in New York and 11 other states directed by 'self-appointed vigilantes' who do not have the 'insight to understand their educational mission.'"[2]

When newspapers report on controversial textbooks, their standards do not permit them to print the language children are forced to read in schools. Many parents, therefore, receive a distorted view of the issues. They hear charges of censorship and attacks on academic freedom, but often they are not fully aware of what is really said in these controversial books. With great hesitation I included the profanity found in various books. But if children are required to read such school material, I finally reasoned, then parents should know what is in today's books so they can make intelligent decisions as to whether they want their children reading it.

Controversial Books
Following are excerpts from two books that Island Trees school board members believed should not be school material:

When the plane was safely aloft, the machine that was Billy's father-in-law asked the quartet to sing his favorite song. They knew what song he meant, and they sang it, and it went like this:

In my prison cell I sit,
With my britches full of shit,
And my balls are bouncing gently on the floor.
And I see the bloody snag
When she bit me in the bag.
Oh, I'll never fuck a Polack any more.

In the same book Billy visits a Times Square bookstore:

> Billy was mildly curious as to what could possibly have been kept hidden in such a place. The clerk leered and showed him. It was a photograph of a woman and a Shetland pony. They were attempting to have sexual intercourse between two Doric columns, in front of velvet draperies which were fringed with deedlee-balls. (Kurt Vonnegut, Jr., *Slaughterhouse Five*)[3]
> "Now there is one thing I want to tell you that is directly related to this. To be sure, I have never understood it and I don't believe that I ever will. But I have seen it work and it may be that you brothers can understand it, and it may prove useful to you, it may help you to make it. There is a sickness in the white that lies at the core of their madness and this sickness makes them act in many different ways. But there is one way it makes some of them act that seems to contradict everything we know about whitey and shakes many blacks up when they first encounter it. . . . There are white men who will pay you to fuck their wives. They approach you and say, 'How would you like to fuck a white woman?' 'What is this?' you ask. 'On the up-and-up,' he assures you. 'It's all right. She's my wife. She needs black rod, is all. She has to have it. It's like a medicine or drug to her. She has to have it. I'll pay you. It's all on the level, no trick involved. Interested?" (Eldridge Cleaver, *Soul on Ice*)[4]

New Standards

No wonder those school officials were upset: racial slur ("Polack"), human and animal sex, and the disgusting lie that there is a sickness in the white race that black sex can cure. The standards for today's authors of children's books have been drastically changed. Jane Yolen, author of thirty-five books, teacher, and lecturer on writing children's books, has received numerous awards and honors for her work. In the professional magazine the *Writer*, Yolen presents these instructions for people who plan to write children's books:

> Don't get mired in that deepest kind of quicksand, belief in the *taboo*. There are no longer any taboos in children's books, except that of bad taste. (And depending upon your taste, you might say that even that has fallen by the wayside.) What was once not even whispered in the parlor, and only snickered at in the barroom, is now legitimate fare for young readers.
> The old-fashioned view that certain things should be taboo for children simply because they are young is no longer in style.

Librarians, who are often caricatured as conservative, accept this, too. . . .

So all the deadly sins, plus sex, death, drugs, drunkenness, divorce, poverty, hunger all have become the subjects of children's books.[5]

Take the book *Go Ask Alice*, which the Island Trees school board also wanted removed from their high school library, as an example of why so many parents are upset. This book is an actual diary about a middle-class 15-year-old drug user who ran away twice from home. The book ends with her desire to go straight; however, three weeks after she decided to stop writing her diary, her parents found her dead at home from unexplained causes. Here are some excerpts children will read from this book:

What a fantastic, unbelievable, expanding, thrilling week I've had. It's been like, wow—the greatest thing that has ever happened. Remember I told you I had a date with Bill? Well he introduced me to torpedoes on Friday and Speed on Sunday. They are both like riding shooting stars through the Milky Way, only a million, trillion times better.

Tranquilizers are the greatest.

Then Richie showed me how to smoke, Richie told me to suck in open-mouthed gulps to mix as much air in as possible. And I was so relaxed! I don't think I've been that relaxed in my whole entire life! It was really beaufitul.

Richie is so good, good, good to me and sex with him is like lightning and rainbows and springtime.

I don't mind pushing at high school because the stuff is sometimes kind of hard to get and the kids usually come up and ask me for it. Chris and I just supply it from Richie. He can get whatever is their bag, barbs or pot or amphetamines or LSD or DMT or meth or anything.

The goddamned rain is even worse than yesterday. It's like the whole sky is pissing on us. I tried to go out once, but my cold is so bad I was chilled to my ass before I'd even gotten to the goddamned corner.

I feel awfully bitched and pissed off at everybody. I'm really confused. I've been the digger here, but now when I face a girl it's like facing a boy. I get all excited and turned-on. I want to screw with the girl, you know, and then I get all tensed-up and scared, I feel goddamned good in a way and goddamned bad in a way.

Another day, another blow job. The fuzz has clamped down till the town is mother dry. If I don't give Big Ass a blow he'll cut off my supply. Hell, I'm shaking on the inside more than I'm shaking on the outside. What a bastard world without drugs![6]

Furious Parents

Reading "literature" like this makes many parents furious. We must understand that it is not parents creating the disturbance but overzealous educators and publishers endeavoring to destroy the traditional moral system and force a new set of social values upon children. The determination of educational leaders to have children read vile books has created this backlash of public opinion.

One of the excuses used by those who support vile books is: "You don't understand the book because you have never read it through." With that they try to silence the critics; but it does not take much insight, after reading some excerpts, to tell whether school children should have a diet of such material. "But it's true and relevant—it pictures the world like it is," is another excuse. The fact that something is true or relevant does not mean schools have the license to make it available. Should schools include books on *How Successful Pimps Operate; Crime and Drugs—The Way to Wealth; How to Destroy Schools; Sexual Experiments: Detailed Illustration on Ultimate Sexual Satisfaction?*

Parents are becoming increasingly angry because of what is transpiring in schools. They want their parental rights respected in what is made available for their children. They want books that will build strong minds and inspire their children to wholesome living. However, many administrators take the position that they, as professionals, should determine curriculum content. William P. Haubner of the Teacher-Rights Division, National Education Association, has expressed it this way: "Selection and presentation of materials falls within the purview of the profession. You don't tell a carpenter which saw or grade of wood to use. If you let inexperienced, unsophisticated, unknowing people make the decisions, teaching quality will be impaired."[7]

Much of what Haubner says is true. Nevertheless, though the buyer does not tell the carpenter how to build his house, he does tell him what he expects as a finished product. Parents should not enter classrooms and tell teachers how they should teach, but they do have a *right* to demand that their children leave school properly educated, disciplined, and without having their moral standards ridiculed and destroyed.

Normally, if a carpenter does poor work, one seeks another. When parents send their children to public school, however, most have no alternative except to spend thousands of dollars for private education. Since not everyone can afford private schools, parents are forced to send their children to public schools. Furthermore, these schools belong to the taxpaying public, and it is the public's right to insist that educational procedures properly train children.

Selection Guidelines

Since there are forces determined to undermine the traditional American way of life and to impose their degenerate concepts upon children, there should be definite guidelines to protect community standards. Such guidelines should:

(1) Forbid material encouraging racial hatred, profanity, criminal behavior, drugs, sexual promiscuity, and religious animosity.

(2) Promote the generally accepted standards of proper English, good citizenship, patriotism, the common values of our historical heritage, and the laws of the land.

The Texas Board of Education issued a set of guidelines that put publishers on notice that world history textbooks "shall depict the role of the United States in world history in a positive manner." The publishers were also ordered to explain in the developments of the 20th century "the positive aspects and effects of American capitalism upon the world" and the "hardships of life under both fascist and communist dictatorships."[8]

With properly enacted guidelines, educators will have ample academic freedom to choose textbooks. Some educators, however, object that guidelines will halt effective education and limit academic freedom. They should realize that only because educational leaders have violated the normal parental trust in schools are such guidelines needed. It is rather strange that educators' choice of books is called a legitimate selection process defending academic freedom, whereas when parents object they are said to be imposing censorship. Where is the parents' academic freedom to help determine the type of books for their children? In all fairness, who has more rights, parents, or educators who teach children a few hours a day?

George Weber, a former editor for the *Council for Basic Education Bulletin,* says, "Traditionally, professionals were content to stay out of controversial areas in the classroom and to permit the schools to reflect community values. If they were not content with this position, they were at least reconciled to it, since school authorities usually insisted upon it. Today, some professionals feel that it is their duty or right to change the values and attitudes of children and young people 'for the better'—in whatever way the professionals define 'better.' "[9]

One objector to parental decisions said, "Censorship imposes a value system on students." True! So does our Constitution. America does have a value system, and many parents are violently opposed to its destruction.

Jeffrey St. John, writing in the *Tacoma News Tribune*, reports:

The National Educational Association (NEA) is the major proponent of a humanistic educational philosophy. It is viewing this revolt in Charleston and other states over content of textbooks as the first serious challenge to its power and control to determine content without consent of parents. NEA has managed to convince the business community and the government of this state that the issue is one of book burners vs. enlightened education.

In reality, however, it is a conflict between the authoritarian educational establishment and angry, confused parents who are fast realizing that they have increasingly little control over their children once they are forced by law to send their children to public school.

The educational establishment as represented by NEA is confronted with a demand from parents in the urban, sub-urban, and now rural areas like Appalachia that education must cease being a privileged elitist sanctuary and open its door to the demands of parents for democratization. This parental demand is particularly ironic since NEA has consistently asserted that its educational credo is to serve democracy.[10]

When George Gallup asked, "When parents object to books or material in textbooks on grounds of religion, politics, or race or sex discrimination, how much consideration should be given to the parents' views in deciding whether to keep these books in the school?" 5 percent did not reply, and only 7 percent replied, "None."[11] If 88 percent of the parents want their views to be considered in controversial subjects, where is democratic justice when leaders take such a strong arbitrary stand that teachers should be the sole determiners of the textbooks used?

Censorship
William Murchison, associate editor for the *Dallas Morning News*, reported a controversial Texas textbook adoption meeting:

A great commotion arose in Austin last week as the state textbook committee met to choose public school textbooks. You might have supposed a horde of Klansmen, with tattoos and sloping foreheads, to have been marching on Texas, spreading desolation and illiberality as they went.

The commotion was all about book-burning. The Texas literary establishment sees the bonfires flickering again. "We are living," writes Kaye Northcott of the Texas Literary Institute, "in the worst era of censorship since the McCarthy days." You always know, when the horrific name of McCarthy is brought up, that the subject is a grave one. . . .

If the Gablers went around incinerating textbooks, they would make broad and convincing targets. But they do nothing of the kind. They merely insist that textbooks reflect the community's basic norms—such norms anyway as the Gablers *hope* the community affirms.

At the Austin read-in much merry sport was made of the Gablers' objections to "open-ended (classroom) discussion," wherein students are left to pursue their own intuitions about complex social issues. If I read the Gablers rightly, their objection is not to intellectual inquiry—it is to putting young minds ashore on strange islands devoid of recognizable landmarks and guideposts.

Miss Northcott submits that "a free society depends on a vigorous and uninhibited exchange of ideas." I, as a First Amendment man, hereby declare that she is bang on.

But whatever way all men were created, all ideas manifestly weren't created equal. Some ideas (e.g., democracy) are infinitely better than others (e.g., Marxism). A public school is a public institution, supported by public tax money. It has the right, indeed the duty, to take stands—to come down firmly on the side of such ideas as the community finds truthful and nourishing.[12]

Mel Gabler brings this interesting insight to the censorship problem:

CENSORSHIP is an issue. Textbooks have been heavily censored BEFORE reaching classrooms.

(1) CENSORED of cheerful, kind, encouraging, or uplifting content.

(2) CENSORED of content favorable to our free economic system.

(3) CENSORED of most of the benefits of our Nation.

(4) CENSORED of the greatness of our Nation's founders.

(5) CENSORED of absolute values, such as morality.

Then Gabler adds, "This censorship has NOT been by concerned parents. REPEAT, not by protesting parents."[13]

Censorship has become such a loaded word that anyone declaring belief in censorship conjures up visions of demented intellectual misfits. But what is censorship? It is simply the act of forbidding the use of certain objectionable materials. Every responsible individual believes in censorship. Anyone claiming that naked children pictured in pornographic magazines should not be published or used in schools believes in censorship. The basic issue, therefore, is not censorship versus noncensorship; it is, rather, by what standard should books be censored or selected?

Evolution vs. Scientific Creationism

Amazingly, though educational leaders demand academic freedom for themselves and are extremely liberal in regard to discipline, rights of children, morals, sex, and knowledge in general, for years they have strongly censored the concept of scientific creationism as a viable alternative to the theory of evolution. Dr. Henry M. Morris, director of the Institute for Creation Research, San Diego, California, who has taught in five major universities, is a popular lecturer and debater for special creation, and has written 22 books, says:

> When creationist parents object to the exclusive teaching of evolution in the public schools, they are usually informed that all scientists are evolutionists and that their belief in creation is based solely on religious faith in the book of Genesis.
>
> Both statements are wrong. There are today thousands of qualified scientists who do not believe in evolution (over 500 in the Creation Research Society alone) and the number is increasing rapidly.
>
> As far as religious faith is concerned, evolution requires a higher degree of faith in events which are unobservable, unprovable, and unreasonable than does creation. . . .
>
> There is definitely no scientific proof of evolution, and all the available scientific data fit at least as well (and usually better) in the creation model. Consequently, by all standards of academic freedom, civil rights, and scientific objectivity, the creation model ought to be accepted on at least an equal basis with the evolutionary philosophy in all our public schools and other tax-supported institutions.
>
> If the evolutionist objects that the concept of a Creator is itself "religious," he should be reminded that the concept of no creator is equally religious. Atheism requires a much higher degree of faith than creationism, since it negates the fundamental scientific law of cause-and-effect.
>
> Naturalistic evolutionism requires its followers to believe that randomly moving particles of primeval matter had the ability and knowledge to develop a complex universe of living organisms, and even to evolve intelligent creatures who could exercise faith in evolution! Creationism at least postulates a first cause which is competent to explain such effects.[14]

Dorothy Nelkin writes in the *Scientific American* about the "The Science-Textbook Controversies": "Most textbook controversies issue not from rural folk in Appalachia but from middle-class citizens, many of whom are technically trained." She says further, "It is not accurate to dismiss the critics of science textbooks as being merely an antiscience fringe group."[15] The fact is that creationists' basic argument is scientific—they claim that an unbiased scientific examination of fossils and living evidences supports special creation, not evolution.

In 1925 Clarence Darrow faced William Jennings Bryan in the famous Scopes trial in order to defend the right to teach evolution. Ironically, more than half a century later, groups in many states are now defending their right to teach scientific creationism.

Attorney Wendell R. Bird prepared a resolution for a "Balanced Presentation of Evolution and Scientific Creationism," stating "The theory of special creation is an alternative model of origins at least as satisfactory as the theory of evolution, and that theory of special creation can be presented from a strictly scientific standpoint without reference to religious doctrine." He points out that "school districts in at least five states are currently teaching both theories of origins or are implementing instruction in both theories."[16]

Objectors to scientific creationism try to claim separation of church and state to support their insistence on a strict evolutionary teaching of origins. Supporters of creationism, however, reject the view that special creation is uniting church and state. They claim: (1) They are not proposing to teach a Genesis account of creation. (2) Creationism is as scientific as evolution. (3) Thousands of qualified scientists and professionals are adherents of the theory. (4) They do not forbid the study of evolution; their desire is equal time to expose students to a two-model approach to origins to enable students to make an intelligent choice between evolution and creationism.

ACLU has been in the forefront of the battle to eradicate any trace of scientific creationism in public schools. However, one of its lawyers, Robert F. Smith, after closely following creationist literature, lectures, and debates for five years, made this frank confession:

> Based solely on the scientific arguments pro and con, I have been forced to conclude that scientific creationism is not only a viable theory, but that it has achieved parity with (if not superiority over) the normative theory of biological evolution. . . . Creationists have been scrupulous to adhere to strict discussion of science alone. Not religion! Statements to the contrary are false. . . .
>
> Contrary to the allegations . . . no creationist professors are seeking to "require public schools to offer courses and text-

books that support the literal Genesis account of creation." Nor can it be legitimately suggested that scientific creationists are "disguising fundamentalist religion in scientific jargon," or that they are working for some covert "advancement of sectarian religion."[17]

Dr. John N. Moore, professor of natural science at Michigan State University, taught evolution but upon reexamination of facts rejected evolution for creationism. As a result of his studies, he began to collect material on theistic creation. "Now hundreds of references have been acquired," he says, "indicating that reputable scientists in each decade since Darwin's book was published have been critical of evolution." Moore then asks this puzzling question: "Why didn't my professors inform me of that when I was an undergraduate in college?"[18]

When the American people were asked in an Associated Press–NBC News poll whether public schools should teach both the scientific theory of evolution and the biblical view of creation, 76 percent voted for both theories; only 8 percent favored the strictly scientific theory.[19]

Creationism Censored

"Three high school biology textbooks," reports the *New York Times*, "have been rejected for use in the New York City public schools because of what Board of Education officials say is an inadequate treatment of the Darwinian theory of evolution.

"The publishers of two of the three books have been told that their books are additionally unacceptable because of what school officials termed an uncritical endorsement of the creationism theory, which is based on the Bible." Following are excerpts which caused the New York Board to "reject" these books:

Another hypothesis about the creation of the universe with all its life forms is special creation, which gives God the critical role in creation. In some school systems, it is mandated that the evolution and special-creation theories be taught side by side. That seems a healthy attitude in view of the tenuous nature of hypothesis. (*Natural Science: Bridging the Gap*, Burgess Publishing Company, Minneapolis.)

Some people believe that evolution explains the diversity of organisms on earth. Some people do not believe in evolution. These people believe that the various types of organisms were created as they appear. No one knows for sure how the many different kinds of living things came to be. But many people have developed theories to explain how this diversity may have come about. (*Life Science,* Prentice-Hall, Englewood, N.J.)[20]

Educational leaders have for decades eliminated facts that contradict the theory of evolution and censored scientific creationism. Now when parents object that textbooks promote anti-Americanism, religious mockery, racial slurs, profanity, drugs, and immoral sex, they cry suppression of academic freedom.

Protesters of today's textbooks are not on some witch-hunt trying to impose sectarian beliefs. These parents are not listening to the cries of suppression of academic freedom; they are demanding *responsible* academic freedom. They are greatly disturbed that educational leaders have used public schools as forums to censor our historical, social, and cultural values in order to reshape student behavior. Many parents believe that society, particularly the schools, should uphold high ethical, moral, and civic standards and not descend in the name of relevancy to the baser elements of our culture; these parents want proper selection guidelines. Since the Supreme Court has recognized the right of communities to establish their own standards for materials, parents are demanding their rights by insisting that teachers be provided with textbooks that will build, not destroy, our heritage.

Chapter 12

Education for Sex or Immorality

Within the past 15 years our nation has experienced a sexual revolution that has altered life-styles of millions of Americans. Today there are a proliferation of flourishing free-love groups; experimentation with group marriages; extensive pornography; free and open homosexuality, college coed dormitories; sex commercialization by newspapers, magazines, books, billboards, radio, television, movies, and plays.

In 1964 the National Education Association and the American Medical Association jointly endorsed a proposal that students from kindergarten to high school should receive health education including full information on sex and family life. By 1969 at least 60 percent of American schools had incorporated some formalized sex education program. Then in 1969 a bitter controversy arose among various groups concerning school sex education. The controversy focused primarily on SIECUS (Sex Information and Education Council of the U.S.), which has been in the forefront of the promotion of sex education and has served as a clearinghouse for sex information.

SIECUS Goals
SIECUS has proclaimed this as its purpose:

To establish man's sexuality as a health entity; to identify the special characteristics that distinguish it from, yet relate it to, human reproduction; to dignify it by openness of approach, study and scientific research designed to lead toward its understanding and its freedom from exploitation; to give leadership to professionals and to society, to the end that human beings may be aided toward responsible use of the sexual faculty and toward assimilation of sex into their individual life patterns as a creative and re-creative force.[1]

Newsweek stated in 1969, "SIECUS has no more subversive objective than promoting healthier attitudes toward sex among youngsters and adults alike."[2] In contrast to what SIECUS proposes as a healthy attitude toward sex, a SIECUS study guide, *The Sex Educator and Moral Values,* by Isadore Rubin, reveals this organization's true attitude and purpose:

Whether we like it or not, it has become increasingly clear that most of our sex values have left the core of our culture and entered the arena of competing alternatives. For the first time the monopoly once held by an absolutistic, religiously based sex ethic has now been destroyed. Today, a number of contending value systems exist side by side in the open market place of ideas, competing for the minds of young and old alike. . . .

Merely to mention the various aspects of sexual behavior is to indicate how broad are the disagreements about their morality and about the extent to which they should be proscribed by law and social regulation: masturbation, contraception, abortion, sterilization, artificial insemination, petting, premarital inter-course, homosexuality, the double standard, pornography, and so on. . . .

Since no one at present can see with any certainty what is best sexually in all respects for both the individual and society, it seems best at the present time to follow the counsel of David R. Mace and encourage the open and honest expression of opinion by people of widely differing viewpoints; to create a genuine open forum. No possibility of consensus exists in a country as large and diverse as we are, and it does not seem fruitful to try to attain it.[3]

Since a wide range of opinion currently exists concerning various sexual acts, even those that were once regarded as strongly immoral, SIECUS attempts to promote a nonjudgmental attitude. Dr. Mary Steichen Calderone, executive director of SIECUS, describes her philosophy: "Sex is not something you do but something you are. To me, there is no controversial subject in sex. Anything that exists is here, and therefore we must explore it, understand it, and learn as much as we can about it."[4]

While speaking to a group of boys at Blair Academy in New Jersey, Calderone said, "What is sex for? It's for fun." When newspaper reporter Gloria Lentz questioned Dr. Harold I. Lief, a SIECUS presi-dent, about Calderone's statement, Lief said that "her speech was taken out of context" and neither he nor SIECUS advocated free love. Upon further questioning, Lief responded about premarital inter-course, "We believe in responsible relations. Now, those can occur premaritally. We're not saying that they can't. Very often kids think they're being responsible, but they're not. There are situations in which premarital intercourse may be growth producing—there are many in which the relations may be destructive."

Three Basic Value Systems
Lief believes that students should be instructed in the three basic

value systems: "The traditional morality, situational ethics of Joe Fletcher, and the anything goes, fun morality. They all should be taught—they all should be examined. Every child should know there are these three basic value positions and should be allowed to figure out for himself what ought to guide his behavior."[5] As I examined sex education literature from more than 50 organizations, they reflected the same nonjudgmental concepts as SIECUS. The prevailing moral philosophy is situational ethics: There are no moral absolutes; each situation determines the rightness or wrongness of an act. Therefore, any sex act mutually consented to is permissible and good; however since such an act can lead to VD and unwanted pregnancy, an extensive sex education program is needed. This "new morality" is promoted in schools across America.

A Teenage Sex Education Magazine

SIECUS materials are written primarily for educators, but materials are available for adolescents. *What's Happening* is a teenage sex information magazine published by Emory University School of Medicine, Department of Gynecology and Obstetrics Family Planning Program, Atlanta, Georgia. It puts sex education principles as promoted by SIECUS and other organizations into practical terms for todays' youth.

In the article "Dr. Caplan Talks to Teens," the doctor answers the questions "Should I have sex? How do I decide?" with this counsel: "The best way to decide whether or not to have sex, is to learn what sex means to you. Learn what you think is right or wrong. This means accepting that we are all equally capable sexually, and ought to decide the issue for our own reasons and not someone else's.

"REMEMBER: SEX NEVER PROVES ANYTHING. And that's what can make it so nice."

Sex education literature usually presents both positive and negative views. Dr. Caplan warns teens: "It pays to understand ourselves and know why we are having sex with others. If we do it for someone else's reasons (pressure from a partner, going along with the crowd, the only way to get loving, etc.) we are not being fair to ourselves and will often end up getting hurt. It is RIGHT to say 'no' if it's not in your own best interests to have sex."

Then Dr. Caplan presents the positive view for unmarried teenagers: "If we have sex for our own reasons, and have carefully considered birth control, VD risks, and other consequences, and if we feel good about it, then there is nothing wrong with sexual activities."

The magazine discusses various subjects related to sex education.

Masturbation

If you have guilt feelings, don't masturbate. If your choice to masturbate is based upon facts, "then you are perfectly free to do whatever feels right at any time."

Methods of Birth Control

Various birth control methods are pictured and information is presented concerning their use and effectiveness. They are: condoms, foam, IUD (intrauterine device), birth control pills, diaphragm with jelly or cream, rhythm method, and withdrawal. In describing the rhythm method the article says, "A teenager, who has regular 28-30 day cycles . . . can use a fairly simplified version of the rhythm method. She can limit intercourse to the first two-three days after her period and to the three-four days just before her period when she can tell the period is coming soon."

It's Your Right to Decide

The subtitle is "What to do About an Unwanted Pregnancy." Three choices are presented: Keep the baby, put the baby up for adoption, or have an abortion. The writer stresses, "EARLY ABORTIONS ARE SAFER ABORTIONS."

Homosexuality

To the question "Is homosexuality unnatural?" the author writes, "Some experts say no, others say yes. Some say it is a natural variation of human sexuality, while others note that it goes against the instinct to reproduce."

In answer to the question "Are homosexuals sick?" the article states, "No. Calling homosexuality a sickness comes from a value judgment, not medical evidence. Some gays do have psychological problems (just like straights do), often caused by the pressure of being 'different' in an intolerant society. Homosexuals use the word 'gay' to mean being free from shame, guilt, misgivings, or regret over being homosexual—liking who you are and what you do."

VD—True Stories from Three Teens

Facts and fables concerning syphilis and gonorrhea are presented. In describing an incident the author says, "When a girl like Missy starts having intercourse regularly, sometimes she can get an infection with some of the symptoms of VD without her having VD at all. Her body has to adjust to this new part of her life. Missy's boyfriend was too quick to think that she was being unfaithful."

Advice is offered to prevent VD; the author adds, "AND MOST IMPORTANT: It is old fashioned to be ashamed of having VD, and to be too embarrassed to go to the doctor. Most doctors are understanding and treatment is confidential.

"The only thing dirty about having VD is spreading it."

Sex Words

There is an alphabetical listing of various sex words. The definition of *virgin* states, "VIRGIN usually refers to a woman who has not had sexual intercourse. Approximately 50% of U.S. teenage women have not ever had intercourse. It is not 'right' or 'wrong' to be a virgin. Each person must decide what is best for them."

In the article "Sex Is More Than Getting Down," a story is told about a group of students sitting together on school steps talking about sex. Anthony gives his reasons why a boy has sex: to show a girl he digs her, to discover whether she really likes him, and sometimes to get a feeling. The boys and girls talk freely about loneliness, using protections, becoming pregnant, getting a baby to get back at mama, and receiving instruction from father about using a rubber.

Darlene tells why she has sex: "Yeah, well I like it when a boy tries 'cause it makes me feel like I'm pretty and sexy, but I won't do it unless we're pretty tight and we have some protection."

Then David looks at Diane and says, "When two people care about each other, and take responsibility for what might happen, sex can be beautiful."

The message children receive is this: Have all the responsible sex you desire, but avoid pregnancies or contracting VD. The dream for these "sex for fun" advocates is to see developed a vaccination against VD and a pill capable of painlessly aborting any unwanted pregnancies. Society can then live in sexual utopia!

Perhaps the best description of a sex educator's concern is a centerfold picture of a pregnant man with this question: "Would you be more careful if it was you that got pregnant?" Beneath the picture are the words "Protect Your Lover—Wear A Rubber!"[6]

Sex Education Material

These excerpts were taken from "For Kids Only," by William Block; the material was developed for New Jersey's K-12 sex education curriculum.

Sex Life Skill Sheets

Draw the world's largest penis. Do a guided imagery on your own, using the following idea:. . . If I had the world's largest penis. . . .

Copy the picture of mother and father making love. . . .

For those who want to dig deeper into their minds and want help with an explicit lovemaking film. . . . A guided sexual

imagination trip. . . . You are ready for genital sex. . . . Feel
your nakedness against the sheets of your bed. . . . Feel
another body alongside yours.[7]

In Howell, Michigan, the following was presented to seventh-grade
through ninth-grade children in their sex education course.

The man has something that we call a penis. It is something
like a finger and it hangs in front of his body between his legs.
Most of the time it hangs there quite loosely. But, when he is
attracted to his wife in love, then the penis becomes hard and
firm and it stands erect, kind of right angles with the rest of his
body. And this happens so that it will be able to fit easily into a
special place in a woman's body that was made for it. This
special place in a woman's body we call the vagina. It's an
opening between her legs. And when she wants him to show her
that he loves her the vagina becomes kind of wet and slippery so
that it will be easy for the penis to enter it . . . . the penis moves
back and forth inside the vagina until from the end of the penis
there comes a kind of milky fluid and we call this, when this
happens, we say that the man is having an ejaculation. And this
makes the man feel real good. And the woman, too . . . she feels
good all over, too.
    As for the creams, foams, and sprays, they are notoriously
unsafe. It is surprising that they are being sold as safe contraceptives. Finally, there is the oldest safe commercial contraceptive on the market, the condom or rubber, as it is commonly
called, which is used by the man. These are quite safe. But
accidents result from careless use or a defect in the very thin
latex rubber that they are made from.
    Only you can decide for yourself whether you want to take the
chances that are involved in finding the ultimate sexual satisfaction.[8]

Nonjudgmental Sex Education
Many sex educators fail to realize the grave dangers in trying to
teach sex from a nonmoral point of view. They believe that by
presenting all the facts and letting children decide their own moral
values in an atmosphere of freedom they are imparting valuable
knowledge. But when teachers are nonjudgmental concerning pornography, prostitution, premarital sex, abortion, and homosexuality,
in reality they are condoning them as acceptable adjuncts to traditional sexual behavior. *No* individual can claim moral neutrality. One
is either *for* or *against* responsible sex; *nonjudgmental sex education
is immoral sex education.*

Dr. Melvin Anchell tells how, under the guise of freedom, "students are encouraged to go overboard in a tolerance for perverts." A normal person has a natural reaction of shame and disgust to perverted sexual acts, but "when disgust turns to sympathy," notes Anchell, "the normal individual becomes defenseless."[9] *Time* reports that in 1969, 42 percent of college students believed homosexuality morally wrong, as opposed to only 25 percent five years later. In 1969, 57 percent of the noncollege youngsters held that premarital sex was wrong; five years later, only 34 percent.[10]

Sex Stimulation

When students receive sex information without proper moral guidance, many will put into practice John Dewey's philosophy of "learning by doing." After receiving detailed instructions on the mechanics of sex, they will take the next step and try out their newly acquired knowledge. One does not put a 12-year-old behind the wheel of a Corvette to train him to drive a car when the legal age for driving is 17. Once he feels the surging of the engine and the exhilarating effect of controlling a car on a superhighway, he will never be satisfied until he drives the car himself. Training should coincide with the legal age for driving; at 12 years of age a child should be taught the dangers of attempting to drive without a license, not how to drive. Just because some young teenagers may have stolen a car and gone joyriding, it provides no reason for schools to give driver education to children entering their teens. Schools should teach the dangers of premarital sex, not the techniques of sex. Besides, this free discussion of intimate sexual experiences between boys and girls breaks down their ingrained modesty and wall of inhibition that civilized people have upheld for thousands of years to prevent premarital sexual experimentation.

Some sex educators discredit the claim that sex education stimulates experimentation. Mary Susan Miller, trustee of the American Association of Sex Educators and Counselors (AASEC), says, "Parents are afraid that sex education will lead their children to promiscuity." But, Miller declares, "The opposite is true. The person who is truly sex-educated is able to make a lasting and satisfying relationship because he is confident of his ability to love and to be loved; he has come to terms with his sexuality."[11]

When Antioch college instituted coed dorms, associate dean Jean Janis rationalized, "The more responsibility you give students, the more they are able to assume." As *Time* noted, "Most school officials maintain that coeducational living does not lead to increased sexual activity. According to Stanford Psychologist Joseph Katz, an incest taboo develops in coed dorms as a result of a brother-sister relationship between the residents."[12] However, five years later *Time* disclosed that coed dormitories had become so popular "that more than half the nation's resident college students now live in them," and that at one eastern college "47% of the women had sex in the dorms" and "42% of the men."[13]

Sex was so abundant at another college that a law student dismissed sexual relations as a legitimate reason for living together. "After all, sex is pretty freely available," he said, and added, "You don't have to start living together to have sex."[14] George Thorman, assistant professor at the Graduate School of Social Work, University of Texas, cited sex education as one reason why so many college students were living together: "Delaying sexual relations and gratification doesn't make much sense to a generation sophisticated in the knowledge of contraception. Given the ready availability of birth control techniques, couples are more inclined to become sexually involved and to experiment with a wider range of sexual behavior, including living together."[15]

In the *New York Daily News* Ken McKenna tells about a worker who spent more than 20 years caring for girls with unwanted babies. The worker found that the girls' overconfidence with sexual knowledge had convinced them "that they know all about sex, so they experiment. Then, they go too far with their experiments."[16]

A 24-year-old London school teacher taught her grammar school pupils about sex. One day 20 of the boys in her sex education class put into practice what they had learned in the classroom—they raped her.

"I didn't know what to do," she said, in describing the incident. "There they were, coming at me, naked, excited. . . ."

"We didn't think we were doing anything wrong," said one boy when questioned about raping the teacher. "Didn't she spend the whole year telling us how to do it, when to do it, and how much fun it would be?" Two hours later the principal found her on the floor.

When the young teacher applied for the position in London, she was not overly concerned when told that part of her job would be sex education. "Now that I look back on it all," she said, "I guess it is a bit stupid. There I am describing all their sexual functions in a great amount of detail—so it's only natural that they should get ideas."[17]

Sex Education Results

As a result of another sex education course in Phoenix, Arizona, *U.S. News & World Report* says, a mother "was 'turned off' when she saw her son, aged 12, trying to demonstrate on his 4-year-old sister what he had learned in classroom about intercourse."[18]

Sex education lobbies have existed in Sweden since 1954. Ten years later the *Los Angeles Times* stated, "The King's physician, Dr. Ulf Nordwall, and 140 eminent Swedish doctors and teachers signed a concern over sexual hysteria in the young. The petition asserted that this problem appeared to be a product of sex education, and it was now the business of the schools to correct it."[19] Professor Jacqueline Kasun of Humboldt State University says, "In Sweden, for example, where sex education has been mandatory since 1956, the illegitimacy rate (the number of illegitimate births per thousand families of childbearing age), which had been declining, subsequently rose for every age group, except for the older group which did not receive the special sex education. Swedish births out of wedlock are now about 31 per cent of all births, the highest proportion in Europe, and two and a half times as high as in the United States."[20]

Professor Kasun reports, "In Humboldt County [California], where we have several 'model' programs and government family planning, expenditures per person have been much higher than in the nation, and adolescent pregnancy has increased ten times as much as in the nation. The reason this increase in pregnancy has not resulted in an increase in births is that Humboldt County has had a greater than one-thousand percent increase in teenage abortions during the past decade, more than fifteen times the rest of the nation."[21]

In Denmark pornography was legalized in 1967, three years later sex education was compulsory, and in 1973 abortion on demand up to 12 weeks was permitted. Laws against homosexuality, indecent exposure, and statutory rape were eliminated. These are the results within the past ten years: Assault rape increased 300 percent; abortions increased 500 percent; illegitimacy doubled; VD among those over 20 years of age increased 200 percent; in those 16 to 20 years of age VD increased 250 percent; and in children under 15 years of age VD increased 400 percent.[22]

Sex Educators' Claims

Many persons are deceived by claims of sex educators. Leaders say sex education should be sound, thoughtful, responsible, and productive of a positive self-identity. A beautiful concept, but public school sex education has adopted moral relativism, which produces the exact opposite results: By releasing sexual inhibitions it has helped to create the rampant adolescent sexual activity. Educational leaders, instead of stopping this immoral sex education, cite the extensive sexual activity they helped to create as a rationale to provide *more* sex education!

Sol Gordon, professor of child and family studies at Syracuse University, Syracuse, New York, and director of the Institute for Family Research and Education, says, "Now for a statistic that may shock: Current research suggests that more than 50 percent of adolescents in this country will have engaged in sexual intercourse by the time they are graduated from high school."[23] *U.S. News & World Report* states, "The National Alliance Concerned With School-Age Parents reported that the highest increase in pregnancies was occurring among white girls under 15, while Planned Parenthood's Alan Guttmacher Institute found that one fourth of American 15-year-olds and one tenth of 13-year-olds have had sexual relations. In Washington, D.C., and other major cities, adolescents—some as young as 12 or 13—are joining the ranks of streetwalkers."[24]

Sol Gordon feels that Americans should face the facts and attempt to fathom the reasons behind adolescents' premarital relations, instead of severely chastising children for such affairs. "Thus, our society seems to succeed only in barring children from the information they seek about human sexuality, from the contraceptives that perhaps they should have, from the laws that would protect their interests."[25]

Rosalie Cohen, a media-center coordinator of New Rochelle, New York, public schools, and Claire Rudin, a health services coordinator of Nassau County, New York, admonish with regard to the venereal disease pandemic, "If the schools fail to heed the warning, about two million youngsters will have been allowed to run the risk of blindness, arthritis, sterility, and pain caused by gonorrhea, and some 250,000 will have risked insanity, paralysis, heart disease, disfiguration, and death from syphilis."[26]

When sex education was heatedly debated in 1969, *Newsweek* reported, as "perhaps the most persuasive case" for sex education, a warning by Dr. Charles W. Socarides, a Freudian analyst specializing in treating serious sexual orders: "No aspect of life is untouched by the rich benefits and rewards of fulfilled sexuality, or conversely by the impoverishment and disability which emerges from disturbed sexuality. In doing away with sex education we may be throwing away untold benefits that will probably come from the programs, including a decrease in crime, violence and lives blighted by sexual maladjustments."[27] Sex education remained in schools; the appalling, unprecedented increases in criminal and immoral behavior speak for themselves.

The *Washington Evening Star* cautions that if there were no sex education programs we would have "the back alley and the washroom, with its guarantee of misinformation, anxiety, and needless, lasting guilt."[28] But what has sex education done? It has taken back-alley sex and coated it with respectability. Previously, students knew immorality was from the gutter; now, by the attempted nonjudgmental teachings of sex educators, it has gained social approval.

Introducing Sex Education

Sex educators have deceived many parents with their subtle

promotional tactics. Initially, a soft approach is utilized to incorporate the program. Then, when the beginning opposition fades and sex education is secure, the program becomes enriched and introduced into other schools. Once established, it is extremely difficult to remove. As a high school teacher and parent I was ignorant of the extent of high school sex education.

It is no wonder that objectors to public school sex education have been labeled extremists, called closed-minded, accused of possessing sexual hangups and of being misled by rumor-spreading fear groups. The literature produced by sex educators could easily delude its readers. Some of the program titles are: Science and Health; Family Life and Sex Education; Family Life Program; Health Instruction; Family, Personal, and Social Health Education; Sociology, Marriage, and the Family; Human Growth and Development; Toward Maturity; Preparation of the Individual for Life; Personal Growth; Social Hygiene; Family Living; Preparation for Parenthood; For Life and For Love; Human Relations. Or sex education may be hidden in a biology or hygiene course.

In 1969 sex education ignited tempers in numerous school districts across the nation. At that time educators were planning to introduce sex education into New York City elementary schools. As a parent, I attended a meeting at our local elementary school to hear a speaker describe the program; the prospect of having my children take sex education courses caused me no great alarm. I was given the *Public Schools of New York City Staff Bulletin* on "Family Living Including Sex Education." (Note the careful approach used to introduce sex education.) "The immediate spark for the formal initiation of work in this new curriculum area was touched off on April 19, 1967. On that date, the Board of Education unanimously adopted a resolution," which authorized "the preparation of 'a suitable program of instruction for all pupils in appropriate grades in the area of family living.' The resolution further stated, 'this course of study shall include a sensitive presentation of the importance of understandings of sex as it relates to wholesome living; to ethical, emotional and social maturity; and to the reproductive process.'"

The *Bulletin* also contained a message by Bernard E. Donovan, superintendent of schools:

> In order that our students may develop the background and understanding needed to arrive at sound answers, we again ask the full cooperation of each district superintendent and unit administrator in using the District Advisory Committee to build firm ties with the home, religious institutions, area groups and other responsible agencies in order to involve more students and their parents in the program. We also ask that, at the local level, emphasis be placed on adequate teacher-supervisor

training and on closer cooperation with colleges, health centers and hospitals.

The possibilities for helping young people through the program of "Family Living, Including Sex Education" are unlimited. By adapting the curriculum so carefully designed with the help of recognized outside authorities, a sensitive teacher can build the sound values, the basic knowledge, and the social and emotional stability which students will need—without infringing on those areas that are not primarily within the prerogative of the school but reserved for the home or religious institution.[29]

Can fault be found with such a program? Parents generally favor sex education, and it should come as no great surprise that a 1969 Gallup poll showed 71 percent favored public school sex education.[30] But upon investigating the program, I discovered that the overriding issue was not sex education per se but the moral framework educators used to teach sex.

Sex Educators' True Objectives

Six years later when I investigated the current sex education program one of my children was to have in hygiene, I was shown the New York City curriculum guide, *Family Living Including Sex Education.* Above the topics "Unhappy marriages, divorce, venereal disease, prostitution, out-of-wedlock pregnancies, abortion, homosexuality, pornography and mass media influences sexual behavior" an asterisk referred to a small-typed statement at the bottom of the page: "Important: Develop from a factual point of view."[31]

Previously the curriculum guide had stated, "It is difficult to be non-judgmental and somewhat objective about sex. Yet, the teacher's non-judgmental objectivity is a requirement for helping youngsters to sort out confusions and to develop slowly a set of internally integrated values which may be relied upon as bases for important decision making immediately and in the future."[32] If teachers must be "non-judgmental" and "develop from a factual point of view" the subjects of venereal disease, prostitution, pornography, out-of-wedlock pregnancies, abortion, and homosexuality, then they are in reality forbidden by the board of education to say that these matters are improper.

When Robert Johnstone, chief of the New York State Education Department's Bureau of Elementary Curriculum Development, was asked how a school handles a discussion about premarital relations, he said, "We can tell the children that premarital intercourse is illegal but we can't tell them it's right or wrong."[33]

At Evander Childs High School in the Bronx I took a science class to the library, where approximately 250 students were asembled to view a VD film produced by the New York State Education Department.

"I like my sex," remarked a boy in the film.

The boy discussed what he would do if he got into trouble when having sex: If he liked mountain climbing and became injured, he would not stop mountain climbing—he would just be more careful.

The film presents a family scene in which a mother discovers that her son has VD. She rages and marches furiously about the house cleaning everything her son has touched. In her fury she wants to throw her son out. The understanding father enters the room and calms the mother. He then has a heart-to-heart talk with his son.

After discussing the problem the father asks, "What are you going to do the next time?"

"Next time you got to check the chick out," the son answers.

With this the film ended. A nearby girl loudly remarked, "What an ending!"

At this school I questioned some girls about their sex education courses. One said that on controversial subjects the teacher did not give his opinion. In her class she had to role-play a prostitute; when the subject of prostitution was discussed, she said most students favored it.

Is it any wonder informed parents vehemently oppose sex education as currently taught? Public school sex education is a perfect course for parents who are unconcerned whether their child engages in premarital sex, prostitution, or homosexual relations. Undoubtedly, many teachers discourage such acts, but if they do, they violate board of education guidelines.

Though this repugnant "sex for fun" philosophy has proliferated in our nation's schools, millions of Americans repudiate these immoral concepts and hold to our historic ethic that sexual relations belong only in marriage. Children once heard from parents, ministers, and teachers that sex belongs only in marriage, and it was the neighborhood degenerate who advocated premarital sex. Today, schools have joined the degenerate in promoting sexual license.

Sexual Abstinence

If sexual abstinence before marriage were taught, there would be no need for an extensive kindergarten to grade 12 sex education program. Children should be taught to abstain from sex, instead of being shown how to have "safe sex" by the use of the pill, condom, IUD, diaphragm, jellies and foams—and then if they do get caught how to diagnose and obtain help for VD or to abort the fetus. Furthermore, if teachers would discourage premarital sex instead of encouraging it by their nonjudgmental instructions, thousands of youth would be spared the crippling effects of VD and the torturous decision whether to kill or retain their unwanted child.

Donn Byrne, professor of psychological sciences and chairman of the social-personality program at Purdue University, says: "There are 11 million teen-agers in America today who have sexual intercourse from time to time. No more than 20 percent of them use contraceptives regularly. The result is almost 700,000 unwanted adolescent pregnancies a year, followed soon after by 300,000 abortions, 200,000 out-of-wedlock births, 100,000 hasty and often short-lived marriages, and nearly 100,000 miscarriages.

"One might think that increased availability of contraceptives, together with competent sex education programs, would reduce these figures substantially." However, since research proves otherwise and our nation is experiencing an epidemic of sexual experimentation, Professor Byrne suggests: "A simple call to celibacy is not likely to help much; effective contraception seems more promising. And since information, emotion, and imagination all influence the use of contraceptives, we should use all three in our educational efforts.

"Accurate, complete information about contraceptives should be a part of everyone's education before and during adolescence. The information should be specific and include considerations of the problems of unwanted pregnancy and explicit details about obtaining and using each type of contraceptive.

"Any child-rearing, educational, or therapeutic practices that lessen guilt and anxiety about natural sexual functions should be encouraged. This can be done without advocating any particular lifestyle. The assumption should be simply that human beings would be healthier and happier if they could react to sex without fear and self-blame."[34]

As Professor Byrne points out, the present sex education program is a failure. What should educators do now? Teach traditional values of chastity, the sure cure? Never! We must now provide "complete information about contraceptives" to every pupil "before and during adolescence." But in order to free students from religious hangups, sex educators must rid them of their feelings of "guilt and anxiety about natural sexual functions."

No longer should educators provide just sex information. They should teach children the immoral value that they should react to premarital sex "without fear or self-blame." Initially, sex education was to be nonjudgmental, but since this has failed, the program should now be taught positively: Get rid of your guilt and anxiety when engaging in natural sex; you will be "healthier and happier."

Opposition to Current Sex Education Programs
As one author aptly said, "It is one of life's little ironies that the very people who share the most responsibility for the problems are now being called upon to furnish the remedy. It's a little like trying to cure a sick man by giving him more of the medicine that made him sick!"[35] But *Newsweek* points out, "The opposition to sex education has won the support of some prestigious professionals. Dr. Rhoda Lorand, a New York child analyst and author of a psychology book on sexuality for older adolescents, 'Love, Sex and the Teenager,' believes that many of the teaching materials used in the courses are overstimulating—if not downright pornographic—and can do untold harm to the child's sexual development."[36]

Lorand states in an article, "The Betrayal of Youth," that the increase in illegitimate births is a cause for concern. However: "Scare headlines have created the erroneous impression that there is an 'epidemic' of teenage pregnancy. The Alan Guttmacher Institute, an affiliate of Planned Parenthood, has issued a report entitled: 11 MILLION TEENAGERS, *What Can be Done About the Epidemic of Adolescent Pregnancies in the United States?* Those who did not examine the report naturally assumed from the title that 11 million teenage girls were pregnant.

"Investigation discloses, however, that the statistic of 11 million refers to the total number of boys and girls between 15 and 19 years of age who are estimated to have had sexual intercourse, of whom 4 million are girls.

"The heading appearing in the report, 'one million teenagers become pregnant each year'. . . . The Guttmacher Institute obtained the shockingly high figures by including the *entire* population of females between 15 and 19. Thus, of the one million pregnant teenagers widely assumed to be unwed, close to half were married (of the 430,000 married teenagers included in the figure, 100,000 gave birth within 8 months of marriage)."

Lorand tells how in 1976 "almost 70 percent of white teenage girls were virgin," and in 1971 "approximately 80 percent had been virgin." She adds: "The resistance by the majority of girls in the United States to the ubiquitous and insistent pressure to have intercourse, reveals the depth of the feminine need for love, devotion and commitment as prerequisites for sex. Revealed too, are the strength and prevalence of the Judeo-Christian ethic, despite the unceasing efforts of the sex lobby to convince parents, teenagers and educators that it is obsolete.

"It would be a tragic mistake for our schools and government agencies to continue to go along with the thinking of the sex lobby (for whom, it must be conceded, an epidemic of chastity would be an unmitigated financial disaster) and attempt to convince young boys and girls that premarital coitus is inevitable."[37]

Lorand also unmasks what sex educators fail to teach: "Most revealing and instructive are the *omissions* from this very detailed discussion of sexual activity and its possible consequences. They are: the great risks of sterility, especially to girls, from gonorrhea and from IUD-caused pelvic inflammation. No mention is made of the fact that the latest VD scourge, genital herpes is not only painful and dangerous, but incurable at the present state of medical knowledge. Not only does it make a girl eight times more likely to develop cervical cancer, but it may result in her giving birth to a baby that is blind, brain-damaged, suffering from other central nervous system impairment, or dead, even ten years in the future when she may be happily married. One finds no reference to those facts nor to the proven connection between early teenage coitus and cancer of the cervix, coitus *under age 18 having been found to be crucial*. One looks in vain for a word of warning about other proven facts: the risk of cervical cancer is greatly increased by multiple partners, by frequent coitus and by coitus with promiscuous males."[38]

Time   gave this report on "herpes, an incurable virus":

After chastity slouched off into exile in the '60s, the sexual revolution encountered little resistance. Indeed, in the age of the Pill, Penthouse Pets and porn-movie cassettes, the revolution looked so sturdily permanent that sex seemed to subside into a simple consumer item. Now, suddenly, the old fears and doubts are edging back. So is the fire and brimstone rhetoric of the Age of Guilt. The reason for all this dolor: herpes, an ancient viral infection that can be transmitted during sex, recurs fitfully and cannot be cured. Also known as the scourge, the new Scarlet Letter, the VD of the Ivy League and Jerry Falwell's revenge, herpes has emerged from relative obscurity and exploded into a full-fledged epidemic.

Spurred on by two decades of sexual permissiveness, the disease has cut swiftly through the ranks of the sexually active. "The truth about life in the United States in the 1980s," says Dr. Kevin Murphy of Dallas, one of the nation's leading herpes researchers, "is that if you are going to have sex, you are going to have to take the risk of getting herpes." An estimated 20 million Americans now have genital herpes, with as many as half a million new cases expected this year, according to the Centers for Disease Control in Atlanta.

Those remarkable numbers are altering sexual rites in America, changing courtship patterns, sending thousands of sufferers spinning into months of depression and self-exile and delivering a numbing blow to the one-night stand. The herpes counterrevolution may be ushering a reluctant, grudging chastity back into fashion.[39]

Creeping over the horizon is another epidemic. Back in 1979 doctors in New York and California began to see young homosexual men with a rare cancer found only in men over 50 and a rare form of pneumonia. By April of 1981 doctors began to realize that a new epidemic was emerging; they reported their findings to the Centers for Disease Control (CDC) in Atlanta. Four months later 70 homosexual men were found to have contacted the disease—of these, half died. By the end of 1981 the disease spread to 180 people in 15 states, included were 15 heterosexual men and women.

By June of 1982 other unusual cancers were discovered among homosexual men. CDC warns that among homosexual and heterosexuals it is reaching epidemic proportions. Doctors believe that drug use and sex with strangers contribute to the spread of the disease. In July, 1982, the disease was officially given a name: Acquired Immune Deficiency Syndrome (AIDS). They also discovered that Haitian immigrants and hemophiliacs have come down with the immune disorder.

AIDS now has claimed 450 victims, three new ones are being reported every day. Among those who have contacted the disease— 19 percent have died within one year of diagnosis, 70 to 80 percent after 2 years. Less than one year later, CDC claims 1,450 victims— 558 deaths. The epidemic has now been doubling every six months.[40]

Besides the dangers of contacting diseases because of promiscuous sex, Dr. Max Levin, psychiatrist at the New York Medical College, further emphasizes the dangers of the current sex education programs: "But, sadly, many of our sex educators, even among those who are highly respected, seem (in my opinion) to be confused and they are leading our youngsters astray. I disagree with the SIECUS position that sex education 'must not be moral indoctrination.' . . . I speak not as a clergyman but as a psychiatrist. There cannot be emotional health in the absence of high moral standards and a sense of human and social responsibility. I know that today morality is a 'dirty word' but we must help our youth to see that moral codes have meaning beyond theology; they have psychological and sociological meaning."[41]

Dr. Melvin Anchell, author of *A Second Look at Sex Education*, wrote: "Today's sex education . . . the type that the American Association of Sex Educators and Counselors has in mind . . . causes irreparable harm to the sexual and mental development of young people.

"Comparing civilized sexuality with the sexuality proposed by sex educators shows that each diametrically opposes the other.

"The most fundamental psychological principles regarding human sexuality are completely disregarded in the sex training foisted on students by the new hierarchy of sex educators."[42]

Homosexuality—The Alternative Life-Style?

Viable societies have condemned premarital sex, adultery, homo-sexuality, prostitution, pornography, and other acts of sexual abuse. Today, militant gays want not only to pursue their own life-style but also to be able to propagate their behavior as an acceptable alternative. The "Gay Rights Platform," drawn up by A National Coalition of Gay Organizations in Chicago, demands "Federal encouragement and support for sex education courses, prepared and taught by Gay women and men, presenting homosexuality as a valid, healthy preference and lifestyle as a viable alternative to heterosexuality."[43]

The San Francisco School Board banned discrimination due to sexual orientation. Then two years later they voted that the family-life curriculum was to recognize homosexual life-styles.[44] The New York City Board of education and the United Federation of Teachers (UFT) declare they will protect the rights of homosexuals to teach in the schools. Initially, New York City's "Family Living Including Sex Education" course was to promote "a sensitive presentation of the importance of understanding of sex as it relates to wholesome living";[45] less than ten years later, the New York City Gay Teachers Association claims to have 300 members in city public schools.[46] And Dr. Howard L. Hurwitz reports: "There is the teacher at the Louis D. Brandeis High School, in Manhattan, who flaunts her moral pyromania and is indulged by the school's principal, Murray A. Cohn. The teacher states in the Gay Teachers Association 'Newsletter' (Feb. '83) that she has been successful in the 'subversion' of her school and hopes to encourage others.' Her 'subversion' consisted of pressuring the school librarian into placing 18 pro-homosexual books on the library shelves."[47]

A minister explains that parents' concern about homosexuality "is not centered on psychiatry, pedagogy or predjudice but on morality. Main-line Christians and Jews see homosexual practice as sharply offensive to God's order, leading to personal alienation and misery." He then points out, "Teachers *are* role models to children. As homosexual teachers 'come out of the closet,' pride in their practice will be explicit—especially if new civil rights laws guarantee their positions. . . . Parents have every right—without prejudice—to re-sist classroom influences that flatly contradict their decisions in the moral education of their children."[48]

In support of preventing homosexuals from teaching children the United States Supreme Court let stand a Washington State court ruling that allowed a Tacoma high school social studies teacher to be dismissed on the grounds of "immorality" when school officials discovered he was a homosexual.[49]

Dr. Melvin Anchell warns, "Sex educators and pornographers are taking over the sexual indoctrination of children." Then he states, "Misinformed sex-educators must be stopped from filling the minds of our forthcoming generations with perverted sexual ideas."[50]

Proper Sex Education

Parents should not be deceived by the warm, loving approach of sex educators in their promotion of "freedom of choice." Their soft manner betrays the heinous message that is destroying the values of American youth. Sex education programs that advocate moral relativity should be replaced with the historic American ethic of chastity. To support the need for intimate instruction, sex educators tell of unwed pregnant girls ignorant of human reproduction. The fact that some parents are negligent in training their children in sexual matters does not license public schools to promote an extensive non judgmental sex education program. In the traditional biology or science courses children can be taught the facts of birth and the dangers of pregnancy and VD, without delving into the controversial subject of birth control. Should such efforts fail, parents should withdraw their children from public school sex education programs. The action may cause their children initial embarrassment, but it is better that they learn to stand for moral convictions than hear instructors teach the acceptance of immorality.

Perverted sex acts should be condemned as defined by state legal statutes. *U.S. News & World Report* discloses that "32 states still have laws on their books defining sodomy as a crime, and the Supreme Court last year upheld the constitutionality of such laws."[51] There are also state statutes that make sexual relations outside of marriage criminal offenses. When schools teach that adultery, fornication, homosexuality, and prostitution are acceptable life-styles, they are in effect teaching children to engage in criminal behavior and impairing the morals of minors.

Youth as well as adults need information about sex. Our entire being pulsates with its message, and a proper understanding of sex is essential to human happiness and fulfillment. Some people endeavor to portray sex as evil, but sex is amoral. It is what one does with sex that determines whether it becomes evil or good. The rampant commercialization of sex, the epidemic of VD, and the extensive increase in unwed mothers show the vital need for proper sex education.

"For more than 25 years I have worked with teen-age girls in trouble," states Eunice Kennedy Shriver, executive vice president of the Joseph P. Kennedy, Jr., Foundation. "And I have discovered that they would rather be given standards than contraceptives. Indeed, only recently I went to a center for teen-age girls where the teacher asked what they would like to discuss most. Human biology? Infant care? Physiology of childbirth? Family planning? The girls showed no interest. Then the teacher asked: 'Would you like to discuss how to say 'no' to your boy friend without losing his love?' All hands shot up.

"These girls want to believe in values. They are thirsting for someone to teach them." Shriver then adds, "Teen-agers want their parents, their teachers, their political leaders to stand up strong for values. And this includes the values of love and sex."[52]

Schools should teach boys and girls to love and respect one another by upholding the high ideals of sexual restraint. The advantages of controlling the fiery sexual urges till marriage disciplines the individual with regard to future sexual temptations. One of the reasons our nation is suffering an epidemic of family breakdowns is that many husbands and wives have never been trained in their youth to discipline their passions. What will happen to tomorrow's families if children are being trained to accept pornography, premarital sex, prostitution, adultery, and homosexuality as normal? How can healthy families exist?

But this is teaching morals. Of course! Since when is upholding morals evil? Telling a child not to cheat, lie, steal, or kill is also teaching morals. Likewise, when educators teach from a nonjudgmental view, they *are* also teaching morals—moral relativism: There is no universal right or wrong; each individual chooses his own standards. When sex is taught in the concept of moral relativism, it is no longer just an innocent sex education course; it is rather an education for immorality.

The choice is not whether to teach morals or not; it is which morals to teach. Educators should teach proper values as contained in their state laws and from our historical theistic heritage. When they do so, schools will once again be bulwarks for morality.

Chapter 13

Values Clarification

Undoubtedly, many parents reading this material about sex and values will be alarmed and will demand that schools teach morals. Well, do not be shocked—educators are already one step ahead of you. They recognize the great concern of parents and leaders over the increasingly immoral behavior of youth. When Gallup polled the American public on whether they wanted "instruction in the schools that would deal with morals and moral behavior," 79 percent favored such studies.[1]

But rather than discard their program of sex education, educators have launched a new program of moral education: "values clarification," which Amitai Etzioni, director of the Center for Policy Research, called "the hottest new item in post-Watergate curriculums."[2] *Newsweek* reports that "more than 300,000 classroom teachers have attended workshops and summer institutes to learn how to teach the courses, and at least 6,000 school systems have offered values programs."[3] Now if troubled parents are concerned about having their children trained in proper behavior, educators can proudly show that they are aware of the problem and are teaching children to develop right values. Relieved parents will now think their children are at least being taught appropriately.

By now, after exposure of the progressive educational leadership, one should become suspicious when the educational wolf wears the sheep's clothing of morality. True to the nature of permissive educators, values clarification is another subtle program that further alienates children from their parents and destroys children's already fragile value system.

Values clarification stresses that teachers should not moralize. "We must not try to indoctrinate youngsters with our values," says a *Guide Book for the Teaching of Controversial Issues*, prepared by a Bronx school district, "but rather provide them with practice in critical thinking. Our students should be provided with opportunities to analyze, clarify and work out their own set of values. Thus, we shall achieve one of the major objectives of our educational system, the development of an effective citizen in a democratic society."[4]

As with sex education, children are asked their opinions on premarital sex, lovemaking, contraception, homosexuality, trial mar-

207

riages, and other sexual issues. *Values Clarification*, by Sidney B. Simon, Leland W. Howe, and Howard Kirschenbaum, acclaimed as the most widely known and used book in the new field of values education, cites a strategy that "illustrates how difficult it is for any one teacher to say, 'I have the right values for other people's children.'"

The Alligator River Story

Once upon a time there was a woman named Abigail who was in love with a man named Gregory. Gregory lived on the shore of a river. Abigail lived on the opposite shore of the river. The river which separated the two lovers was teeming with man-eating alligators. Abigail wanted to cross the river to be with Gregory. Unfortunately, the bridge had been washed out. So she went to ask Sinbad, a river boat captain, to take her across. He said he would be glad to if she would consent to go to bed with him preceding the voyage. She promptly refused and went to a friend named Ivan to explain her plight. Ivan did not want to be involved at all in the situation. Abigail felt her only alternative was to accept Sinbad's terms. Sinbad fulfilled his promise to Abigail and delivered her into the arms of Gregory.

When she told Gregory about her amorous escapade in order to cross the river, Gregory cast her aside with disdain. Heartsick and dejected, Abigail turned to Slug with her tale of woe. Slug, feeling compassion for Abigail, sought out Gregory and beat him brutally. Abigail was overjoyed at the sight of Gregory getting his due. As the sun sets on the horizon, we hear Abigail laughing at Gregory.[5]

After hearing this story, the children are to "privately rank the five characters from the most offensive character to the least objectionable."[6] They are divided into groups of four to discuss the pros and cons of each character. Imagine immature boys and girls debating the pros and cons of sex to gain favor in a nonjudgmental atmosphere.

In Maryland, school children in a tenth-grade home economics class were to role-play this situation: "A boy with several years of schooling ahead of him is confronted by a girl he has been dating. She tells him that he is the father of her expected child, and she demands that he marry her. If neither professes to love the other, what should they do?"[7]

Survival Games

Morals education examines and probes many other controversial issues. One such activity is "survival games." Children are divided into groups. Suddenly World War III begins, with bombs dropping everywhere. People are running for shelters, and the class group is in charge of these shelters. A desperate call is received from a fallout shelter where ten people want to enter, but to survive the necessary three months there is enough space, air, food, and water for only six. The group has exactly one-half hour to decide which ones will enter before they themselves must seek protection. Here are the individuals:

1. Bookkeeper; 31 years old
2. His wife; six months pregnant
3. Black militant; second-year medical student
4. Famous historian-author; 42 years old
5. Hollywood starlette; singer; dancer
6. Bio-chemist
7. Rabbi; 54 years old
8. Olympic athlete; all sports
9. College co-ed
10. Policeman with gun (they cannot be separated)

The teacher distributes copies of this list to the class and then counts down: 15-, 10-, 5-, and then 1-minute warnings.[8] Instead of seeking ways to find out how to save all ten, children are asked to decide who will die. This is an ideal strategy to teach early the doctrine of the individual's right to die with dignity—euthanasia. Dr. Thomas Goldeke, superintendent of schools in Howard County, Maryland, has banned survival games in his district. He says they "are not educationally sound for students in our kindergarten through grade 12 programs."[9]

Diaries
Another strategy values clarification uses is to extract information by probing student private lives by means of personal diaries. Children can choose among various diaries, including one on their religious habits. Then the diaries are shared with the class while the teacher asks a series of values-clarifying questions. Simon, Howe, and Kirschenbaum say, "Perhaps *the* best place to find the data for values-clarification activities is in the students' own lives. Diaries is a strategy that enables the students to bring an enormous amount of information about themselves into class to be examined and discussed."[10]

In this program children are expected to expose even their most sacred religious beliefs and to defend them before their classmates. Barbara M. Morris in *Why Are You Losing Your Children?* asks a series of questions: "Upon what foundation can immature, impressionable children make wise decisions about the religious beliefs parents have passed on to them? Who, in the secular classroom will help immature children to defend religious beliefs they hold, but may not as yet fully understand? Does not such meddling constitute a serious and indefensible violation of the principle of church and state, and an invasion of individual and family privacy?"[11]

Parents Questioned

The *Council for Basic Education Bulletin* tells how ninth-graders were asked to fill out this questionnaire:

> Do your parents seem to respect your opinion?
> Do your parents tend to lecture and preach too much to you?
> Do your parents have confidence in your abilities?
> Do they [your parents] really try to see your side of things?
> What is the most difficult subject for you to discuss?

The *Bulletin* then says: "In all fairness, most schools do not do this kind of thing. We believe that the proper answer to those who do is: 'None of your business!'"[12]

Autonomous Children

Everything the child has been taught is taken apart and clarified: religion, sex, family, parents, feelings, attitudes, problems, etc. Nothing is personal or sacred. Values clarification often places children into dilemma situations in which they must make decisions between two wrong choices. Instead of teaching positive morality it stresses situation ethics. Values clarification also indoctrinates children until they lose their sense of shame over evil and accept degenerate behavior as normal. The pros and cons of drugs, sexual perversions, lying, stealing, euthanasia, and suicide are likely to be discussed while nonjudgmental teachers carefully avoid imposing their values. The immature child is to be autonomous and must determine his own value system. Barbara Morris declares:

> The values you have passed on to your child—the values he comes to school with, must be clarified. They are not acceptable "as is" because you did the unforgivable—you decided for your child, because it is your God-given responsibility and right—what values you want him to hold. Those imposed values which he did not choose freely must be clarified. He must decide, immature and unwise though he may be, whether or not he wishes to keep, modify or discard what you have taught him.

Values clarification involves exposing personal, private values of the child to the scrutiny of his peers in the classroom. Your child's values are forced through the "meat grinder" of public exposure and group discussion. . . .

It's up to him to decide, with the help of the pooled ignorance of his peers and the influence, intentional or not, of the teacher, whose own value system may or may not coincide with yours. As the emerging Humanist child, he has a right to achieve maximum individual autonomy. He has a right to voice in the formation of his own values, even before he is capable of making sound judgements.

The effect of values clarification is to drive a wedge between parent and child, child and authority and between child and religious beliefs. It is a powerful vehicle for chaos and alienation. Without exaggeration, it sets up a battle between you and the school for the very soul of your child. Considering that the school claims him as a captive audience for five or more hours a day, five days a week, who do you think is winning the battle?[13]

Government's Moral Input

Dr. Harold M. Voth, Menninger Foundation psychiatrist, chief of staff of the Veterans Administration Medical Center in Topeka, Kansas, and clinical professor of psychiatry at the University of Kansas Medical School, was asked to evaluate the government's Title X sex education curriculum materials. His conclusion: Eliminate the materials as soon as possible. Originally the program was to provide birth control and venereal disease information, he noted; however, values clarification, psychodrama, role playing, homosexuality, and other deviate lifestyles, and issues such as "social atom" and "adult astrology chart" were included.

Many of the methods proposed in these manuals, Voth notes, "are used in other settings as psychotherapeutic techniques," and it is extremely dangerous to put them "in the hands of teachers and others, many of whom are neither personally nor professionally qualified to provide guidance for developing young people." He says these techniques provide "militant, aggressive individuals" opportunity to promote behavior that the American majority abhors. "The so-called sexual revolution," he declares, "is just that—it is a revolution which is being led by a small number of militant, rebellious, personally and sexually disturbed individuals who are sufficiently clever to impose their views on the unsuspecting. I believe much of the content of the manuals I reviewed derives from this revolution."

Values clarification was cited by Voth as an example. Though it stresses neutrality, a "careful reading of the resource materials reveals subtle and at times outspoken advice to the student to challenge all the existing values of the established system. One of the exercises reviewed for this hearing advocates the adolescent establishing complete autonomy—i.e., independence—from his family." This taxpayer-funded program, he says, is to veer students "away from those solid values which have evolved over the centuries and have stood the test of time and experience."

Voth states that "values clarification exercises introduce a great number of possible experiences to students who otherwise might never have thought of carrying out such behavior." Then Voth says frankly that such programs "do not make sense in terms of Title X nor do they have any place in our schools. The latter remark is based on my understanding of personality growth and functioning as a result of 30 years of psychiatric and psychoanalytical experience."[14]

Richard A. Bauer, Jr., associate professor at Cornell University, says, "A substantial body of scholarly criticism of values clarification has arisen that in many ways corroborates and reinforces at least some of the objections that have been raised by parents." Bauer goes on, "It is for this reason that I shall summarize here the major criticisms that have appeared in this scholarly literature and on the basis of them argue that values clarification should not be used in the public schools or by such quasi-public agencies as Scouts, Planned Parenthood, and 4-H."

Following are excerpts of his reasons why values clarification should not be used:

> But what the proponents of the method have quite overlooked is that at the deeper methodological level of what philosophers call "meta-ethics" (that is, critical analysis and theory about the nature of ethics or values as such), their claim to neutrality is entirely misleading, for at this more basic level, the authors simply *assume* that their own theory of values is correct. That is, they assume that all values are personal, subjective, and relative and cannot be known to be true or false, good or bad, right or wrong, except by and for the individual directly involved.
>
> Putting all of this together, it is fair to conclude that the proponents of values clarification are *indoctrinating* students in their position of ethical subjectivism and relativism.
>
> Many philosophers, theologians, and ethicists, for instance, hold, contrary to values clarification, that values can be *known* to be true or false, right or wrong, not just for the individual making the value claim but in a more general sense.
>
> All of this points up a disturbing implication: underneath the

apparent freedom and tolerance of values clarification lies a dimension, almost certainly unintended by the authors, of potential intolerance and tyranny. When all is said and done, freedom, tolerance, justice, and human dignity are not values that we can know to be right and true or for which we can present valid arguments or good reasons. They are simply choices some people make, and values clarification theory in principle indicates no way for us to be clear about whether they are better choices than such opposite values as tyranny and intolerance.

Biblical religion regards the love of God and the service of one's fellow human beings as the highest goals of man. But values clarification's emphasis on self-fulfillment and action on the basis of one's own desires and preferences stands in direct conflict with this religious value. In reference to human behavior, it presents its own "religious" view of life, a view that centers in the individual and his or her own self-fulfillment. Philosophically, the author's view is a form of hedonism.[15]

In his conclusion, Bauer says that values clarification "threatens the right to privacy of students and their families"; uses state power to coerce students to participate in psychotherapy; is biased "against authority, traditional morality, and a sense of duty and self-sacrifice"; and is a "religious" position.

Promoting Positive Life Values

We cannot stand idly by and watch the systematic destruction of American youth to become totally demoralized to the point of accepting perverted sex and degenerate behavior that current nonjudgmental sex education and values clarification programs are propagating. What promised to be a gentle breeze in the subtle promotion of family living just a decade ago has now become a destructive tornado with outspoken homosexuals teaching children. We need to examine the source of the school's moral deterioration and study America's moral foundation to restructure our educational system in order to promote positive life values.

Chapter 14

Moral Disintegration: Its Source

America is experiencing its greatest dilemma since its birth 200 years ago—a crisis of values. In the past 20 years our nation has been shaken by a bitter Vietnam War controversy, Watergate, rampant street crime, arrogant organized crime, lopsided criminal justice, strife-torn cities, blazing ghettos, bitter racial riots, assassinations, bribery of high-ranking officials, polluted environments, wild melees on college campuses, and unprecedented brazenness of undisciplined youth.

America's Disintegration
In this period of unrest, black militants, Spanish-speaking minorities, and American Indians have demanded their rights. Joining in the fray for rights are men, women, children, welfare recipients, mentally ill, handicapped, radicals, and gays. With the new liberation movement came the great sexual revolution, in which total freedom became the vogue. Sex standards, chastity, modesty, marriage fidelity, and virginity became passé; while premarital sex, adultery, pornography, open prostitution, topless and bottomless bars, and even complete nudity were accepted. Venereal disease mushroomed and illegitimate births skyrocketed, and abortion became the accepted solution for unwanted children.

Pressure and confusion were generated over traditional family structures, frustrating and dividing families. The courts, instead of promoting family togetherness during these periods of tension, granted greater freedom to separate and divorce; the unprecedented surge in family breakdowns resulted in nearly one divorce for every two marriages. Some fathers have been demanding—and receiving—the custody of their children, yet in a rising number of cases neither parent wants the child. Abuse of dangerous drugs and alcoholism soared among teenagers. Yearly a minimum of one million youth, largely from middle-class homes, run away from home; other frustrated young people commit suicide, now the second leading cause of death in people between the ages of 15 and 24.

In contrast to the serious deterioration of values within the past 20 years, there were remarkable discoveries and technological advances: A quarter of a million miles away, a man walked on the

215

moon and set up the American flag while the awestruck world watched on TV. A space ship landed safely on Mars about 35 million miles from earth, diagnosed soil samples, and sent the information back for scientific analysis. Open heart surgery, organ transplants, transistorized circuits, miniaturized computers, satellite communications, space shuttles, and laser beam technology were developed.

Civilizational Crisis

In the midst of this remarkable technology, America experienced a civilizational crisis that fragmented our nation. The schools, plagued for decades with progressive concepts, quickly joined the liberation movement promoting greater student freedom. Leading educators yearning for a more egalitarian society permitted standards to vanish, the end result being an appalling decline in student achievement. Nevertheless, guaranteed success was provided, causing the soaring rate of illiterate graduates.

Standards of behavior changed and disappeared. Traditional parental values were razed, and the new standard became "If it feels good, do it." Acceptance of all moral systems became the mode, leaving students powerless to create a coherent system of constructive values. With this new rootless pluralism, our nation and schools began to disintegrate. Cheating, dishonesty, disobedience, stealing, crime, and immorality became widespread. Concerned individuals ask, "What can America do to stop this terrifying decline in national morality?"

To the founding fathers, religion and government were twin necessities to maintain a moral society. At the same time, they were firm in their insistence on separation of a national church and the federal government. They had a vision of a firm reliance upon God, who gave mankind unalienable human rights, and of a government that was responsible for securing these rights. The early American leaders laid our national foundation upon a theistic value system, which produced a high standard of morality and brought about a coherent bond between home, place of worship, community, and school.

Supreme Court's Prayer and Bible Reading Decisions

In 1962 the United States Supreme Court, in *Engel v. Vitale*,[1] outlawed state-mandated prayers. In 1963, in *Abington School District v. Schempp*,[2] the Court ruled against state-mandated Bible reading in public schools. These Warren Court decisions had a far greater impact than just the surface issue of saying a prayer or reading the Bible in school. Though for many years there had been a steady erosion of our theistic heritage, the Court's rulings dealt a deathblow to the traditional value system. Though the Supreme Court did not say that the historic theistic ethic was outlawed, many educational leaders considered the decisions an official governmental rejection of our moral legacy as the criterion for the school's ethical system. This rejection acted as a wedge between society's common moral standards and schools and created a moral vacuum in the educational system. For decades the progressive movement's teaching of secular humanism had tried to dominate educational philosophy; following the Supreme Court's school prayer and Bible reading decisions, atheistic humanism quickly filled the moral vacuum and became the substitute for our traditional value system. Since 1962 it can be clearly observed that schools have been overtaken with humanistic permissive policies. At the same time America began to experience an escalating flood of immoral behavior.

Two Conflicting Ideologies

What the American public needs to understand is the root cause of the school crisis. Throughout this book the conflict between two ideologies has been revealed: one advocates permissiveness, freedom without responsibility, instant gratification, no tests, no homework, free and open classrooms, automatic promotion, profane textbooks, parental disrespect, laxity toward misbehavior, lowering of standards, situational ethics, maximum individual autonomy, sexual license, euthanasia, right to suicide, anti-Americanism, and atheism. The other favors discipline, *in loco parentis* concept, law and order, freedom with responsibility, work ethic, academic excellence, knowledge of the basics, tests, homework, achievement promotion, parental respect, decent textbooks, sexual purity, patriotism, and theism.

Humanist Manifesto

The conflict is between humanism and the traditional American value system based upon a theistic ethic. Once this humanistic philosophy is understood, it becomes clear that its progressive teaching has permeated not only our schools but our society, and it continues to be the archenemy of educational success and national morality. The humanists have produced two manifestos describing their beliefs. The first was published in 1933, one of its chief architects being the philosopher and educator John Dewey, father of the modern progressive educational system. Because of new events a second manifesto was published in 1973. A careful reading of these documents will reveal their destructive philosophy. Following are some excerpts:

Humanist Manifesto II

Preface

The next century can be and should be the humanistic century. . . .

Traditional moral codes and newer irrational cults both fail to meet the pressing needs of today and tomorrow. False "theologies of hope" and messianic ideologies, substituting new dogmas for old, cannot cope with existing world realities. They separate rather than unite peoples.

Religion

We believe, however, that traditional dogmatic or authoritarian religions that place revelation, God, ritual, or creed above human needs and experience do a disservice to the human species. Any account of nature should pass the tests of scientific evidence; in our judgment, the dogmas and myths of traditional religions do not do so. Even at this late date in human history, certain elementary facts based upon the critical use of scientific reason have to be restated. We find insufficient evidence for belief in the existence of a supernatural; it is either meaningless or irrelevant to the question of the survival and fulfillment of the human race. As non-theists, we begin with humans not God, nature not deity.

Too often traditional faiths encourage dependence rather than independence, obedience rather than affirmation, fear rather than courage. More recently they have generated concerned social action, with many signs of relevance appearing in the wake of the "God Is Dead" theologies. But we can discover no divine purpose or providence for the human species. While there is much that we do not know, humans are responsible for what we are or will become. No deity will save us; we must save ourselves.

Promises of immortal salvation or fear of eternal damnation are both illusory and harmful. They distract humans from present concerns, from self-actualization, and from rectifying social injustices.

Ethics

We affirm that moral values derive their source from human experience. Ethics is *autonomous* and *situational*, needing no theological or ideological sanction.

The Individual

The preciousness and dignity of the individual person is a central humanist value. Individuals should be encouraged to realize their own creative talents and desires. We reject all religious, ideological, or moral codes that denigrate the individual, suppress freedom, dull intellect, dehumanize personality. We believe in maximum individual autonomy consonant with social responsibility.

In the area of sexuality, we believe that intolerant attitudes, often cultivated by orthodox religions and puritanical cultures, unduly repress sexual conduct. The right to birth control, abortion, and divorce should be recognized. While we do not approve of exploitive, denigrating forms of sexual expression, neither do we wish to prohibit, by law or social sanction, sexual behavior between consenting adults. The many varieties of sexual exploration should not in themselves be considered "evil."

Moral education for children and adults is an important way of developing awareness and sexual maturity.

Democratic Society

To enhance freedom and dignity the individual must experience a full range of civil liberties in all societies. It also includes a recognition of an individual's right to die with dignity, euthanasia, and the right to suicide.

World Community

We deplore the division of humankind on nationalistic grounds. We have reached a turning point in human history where the best option is to *transcend the limits of national sovereignty* and to move toward the building of a world community in which all sectors of the human family can participate. Thus we look to the development of a system of world law and a world order based upon transnational federal government.

Humanity as a Whole

In closing: The world cannot wait for a reconciliation of competing political or economic systems to solve its problems. These are the times for men and women of good will to further the building of a peaceful and prosperous world. We urge that parochial loyalties and inflexible moral and religious ideologies be transcended.[3]

The implementation of this humanistic philosophy shows why schools face their worst crisis. One can wonder why patriotism and American history are downplayed in classes while the negative aspects of national leaders are magnified; but when one realizes humanists "deplore the division of humankind on nationalistic grounds" and "look to the development of a system of world law and a world order based upon transnational federal government" it becomes clear that patriotism hinders a one-world government.

Humanism claims, "Ethics is autonomous and situational, needing no theological or ideological sanction" and "In the area of sexuality, we believe that intolerant attitudes, often cultivated by orthodox religions and puritanical cultures, unduly repress sexual conduct." No longer should anyone be perplexed why textbooks encourage lying, contain profanity, and mock religious faiths while sex educational courses promote premarital sex, abortion, homosexuality, adultery, and prostitution—these are humanistic values.

For humanists, "The world cannot wait for a reconciliation of competing political or economic systems to solve its problems," so they "urge that parochial loyalties and inflexible moral and religious ideologies be transcended." An excellent method to speed the process of the humanization of the world is to alienate children from parents' value systems. The children's liberation movement, which stresses children's rights to smoke, drink, quit school, work, disobey parents, and choose where to live, is an excellent vehicle to promote humanistic aims.

Values clarification, which puts all values into a nonjudgmental blender, is an ideal method to make the next century a "humanistic century." In *Values Clarification*, the most popular book on this subject, coauthors Sidney B. Simon, Leland W. Howe, and Howard Kirschenbaum inform readers, "For a list of materials currently available and workshops offered in the values-clarification area, write to the Adirondack Mountain Humanistic Education Center."[4] It is humanists who promote values clarification.

A perfect humanistic tool to train 10-year-old children is the social studies course MACOS (Man: A Course of Study). This one-year course justifies adultery, wife swapping, cannibalism, suicide, the slaying of female babies, and the killing of the elderly. Since books are conveniently left in school, the parents' damaging value system cannot counteract course contents.

The humanists' strongest attack is against "traditional dogmatic or authoritarian religions that place revelation, God, ritual, or creed above human needs and experience." They declare, "As non-theists, we begin with humans not God, nature not deity," and "Promises of immortal salvation or fear of eternal damnation are both illusory and harmful." Consequently, humanists try everything to rid children of these "harmful" religious teachings. One such attack concerns the book *Biology: A Search for Order in Complexity*, put out by Zondervan Publishing House, which endeavors to present both the theory of evolution and scientific evidence for creation. Adoption of this book by a number of states, *Eternity* magazine reports, "has stirred the anger of many uptight evolutionists, who apparently want to 'burn' the Zondervan creation-oriented text."[5] The book was developed by the Institute for Creation Research, and its magazine, *Acts & Facts*, states, "The American Humanist Association, under the inspiration and leadership of its president, Bette Chambers, has launched a drive against efforts of creationists to convince educational authorities to teach the scientific evidence for creation in public schools."[6]

It is strange that when parents object to textbooks containing obscenities, ridiculing religious faiths, promoting antipatriotic sentiments, and supporting degrading sexual practices they are labeled fanatical censors, yet humanists who attack textbooks that provide children an option to believe in scientific creationism or evolution claim they are supporting the constitutional concepts of separation of church and state. When one understands the humanist manifesto, it is no longer strange; now the entire educational puzzle begins to make sense—humanists freely censor books that teach traditional morality based on our theistic heritage. They are staunch atheists and tolerate nothing that contradicts their theory and provides students with the "detrimental" teaching that God exists and provides moral standards.

Once humanism is understood, it becomes evident that this philosophy is the source of America's moral disintegration and has caused the grave social crisis. To produce moral citizens, we need to reject humanism as our educational philosophy and restore the moral values that made our nation successful.

Chapter 15

America's Moral Foundation

Many Americans are concerned over society's moral disintegration and desire a restoration of positive values. America's past reveals a nation founded upon faith in God, which provided the necessary moral principles and positive values. However, the Supreme Court's rulings against public school prayer and Bible reading had the effect of erecting a monumental wall between God and state. Many individuals agree with the Supreme Court's decision; others at first agreed but now oppose; some just dismiss the issues as insignificant. Nevertheless, an examination of the ramifications of this rejection of our historical theistic culture clearly reveals that it is the basic cause for the ruin of our schools and nation.

Separation of a National Church and Federal Government

I readily sympathize with Americans who believe that the separation of church and state means that theistic concepts for secular education needs are unconstitutional. When I started this book I held to the same view, but after delving into school social problems, pondering a national value system, and examining America's heritage, I realized I was greatly mistaken. Our constitution supports the concept of separation of a national church and federal government; it does *not* support the concept of separation of God and state.

As Americans we are now so confused over the concept of separation of church and state that we have come to believe it is undemocratric and unconstitutional to express our faith in God in a public institution. This is *not* what the founding fathers had in mind when they wrote the Constitution. It is of utmost importance for solving the educational crisis to understand the basic structure of our Constitution and American heritage. The colonial leaders possessed great wisdom when laying the foundation for our nation, and unless we understand their principles, we stand little chance of solving the crises facing us.

Declaration of Faith in God

On July 4, 1776, fifty-six men, willing to sacrifice their wealth and lives for the freedom of America, signed the Declaration of Independence. An examination of the opening and closing paragraphs of

223

the Declaration of Independence clearly reveals that they also made
it a declaration of faith in God. They did not believe in separation of
God and state.

> When in the Course of human events, it becomes necessary
> for one people to dissolve the political bands which have
> connected them with another, and to assume among the
> powers of the earth, the separate and equal station to which
> the Laws of Nature and of Nature's God entitle them a decent
> respect to the opinions of mankind requires that they should
> declare the causes which impel them to the separation. We
> hold these truths to be self-evident, that all men are created
> equal, that they are endowed by their Creator with certain
> unalienable Rights, that among these are Life, Liberty and the
> pursuit of Happiness. . . .
> We, Therefore, the Representatives of the United States of
> America, in General Congress, Assembled, appealing to the
> Supreme Judge of the world for the rectitude of our intentions,
> do, in the Name, and by Authority of the good People of these
> Colonies, solemnly publish and declare, That these United
> Colonies are, and of Right ought to be, Free and Independent
> States . . . And for the support of this Declaration, with a firm
> reliance on the protection of divine Providence, we mutually
> pledge to each other our Lives, our Fortunes and our sacred
> Honour.

The first paragraph declares the concept of God as "Creator" and
the self-evident truths "that all men are created equal" and are
"endowed by their Creator with certain unalienable Rights." The last
paragraph contains an appeal to the "Supreme Judge of the world"
and, "for the support of this Declaration," attests to "firm reliance on
the Protection of divine Providence."

Enacting the Constitution
The American Revolution was won, and on May 25, 1787, the
Constitutional Convention met in Philadelphia's Independence Hall
with George Washington in the president's chair. Thirteen colonies
came to be united. Even though most had English as their common
language, each representative came with his separate independent
traditions. A number of colonies had large foreign-speaking popula-
tions with their own newspapers and school systems; the majority
had state-established churches. Previous attempts at consolidation
had failed. The sessions dragged on for three and one-half months
through the hot, muggy summer. Disagreements were so severe
that the convention verged on total collapse; it appeared that 13

separate nations might emerge instead of a unified country. In the midst of this hopeless situation, 81-year-old representative Benjamin Franklin, from Pennsylvania, arose and said:

> In this situation of this Assembly, groping as it were in the dark to find political truth, and scarce able to distinguish it when presented to us, how has it happened, Sir, that we have not hitherto once thought of humbly applying to the Father of lights to illuminate our understandings? In the beginning of the Contest with G. Britain, when we were sensible of danger we had daily prayer in this room for the divine protection.—Our prayers, Sir, were heard, and they were graciously answered. All of us who were engaged in the struggle must have observed frequent instances of a Superintending providence in our favor. To that kind providence we owe this happy opportunity of consulting in peace on the means of establishing our future national felicity. And have we now forgotten that powerful friend? or do we imagine that we no longer need his assistance? I have lived, Sir, a long time, and the longer I live, the more convincing proofs I see of this truth—*that God* governs in the affairs of men.* And if a sparrow cannot fall to the ground without his notice, is it probable that an empire can rise without his aid? We have been assured, Sir, in the sacred writings, that "except the Lord build the House they labour in vain that build it." I firmly believe this; and I also believe that without his concurring aid we shall succeed in this political building no better than the Builders of Babel: We shall be divided by our little partial local interests; our projects will be confounded, and we ourselves shall become a reproach and bye word down to future ages. And what is worse, mankind may hereafter from this unfortunate instance, despair of establishing Governments by Human Wisdom and leave it to chance, war and conquest.
>
> I therefore beg leave to move—that henceforth prayers imploring the assistance of Heaven, and its blessings on our deliberations, be held in this Assembly every morning before we proceed to business.[1]

His motion carried. Every day, morning prayer was offered for divine assistance. The change was dramatic. New wisdom emerged, the deadlock was broken, and shortly after a compromise was reached. By summer's end the Constitution was adopted; it became

---

*"God" is twice underscored in Benjamin Franklin's manuscript.

a notorious document for individual freedom and justice. To this day both houses of Congress begin their morning sessions with prayer.

Presidential Declarations

On April 30, 1789, George Washington declared in his first inaugural address:

> Such being the impressions under which I have, in obedience to the public summons, repaired to the present station, it would be peculiarly improper to omit in this first official act my fervent supplications to that Almighty Being who rules over the universe, who presides in the councils of nations, and whose providential aids can supply every human defect, that his benediction may consecrate to the liberties and happiness of the people of the United States a Government instituted by themselves for these essential purposes, and may enable every instrument employed in its administration to execute with success the functions allotted to his charge. In tendering this homage to the Great Author of every public and private good, I assure myself that it expresses your sentiments not less than my own, nor those of my fellow-citizens at large less than either. No people can be bound to acknowledge and adore the Invisible Hand which conducts the affairs of men more than those of the United States. Every step by which they have advanced to the character of an independent nation seems to have been distinguished by some token of providential agency.[2]

In the same year, George Washington issued this Thanksgiving Day proclamation:

> Whereas it is the duty of all nations to aknowledge the providence of Almighty God, to obey His will, to be grateful for His benefits, and humbly to implore His protection and favor; and
>
> Whereas both Houses of Congress have, by their joint committees requested me "to recommend to the people of the United States a day of public thanksgiving and prayer, to be observed by acknowledging with grateful hearts the many and signal favors of Almighty God, especially by affording them an opportunity peaceably to establish a form of government for their safety and happiness":
>
> Now, therefore, I do recommend and assign Thursday, the 26th day of November next, to be devoted by the people of these States to the service of that great and glorious Being who is the beneficent author of all the good that was, that is, or that will

be; that we may then all unite in rendering unto Him our sincere and humble thanks for His kind care and protection of the people of this country previous to their becoming a nation;. . .

And also that we may then unite in most humbly offering our prayers and supplications to the great Lord and Ruler of Nations. . . .[3]

In his dissent in *Engel v. Vitale*, Justice Stewart notes that "each of our Presidents, from George Washington to John F. Kennedy, has upon assuming his Office asked the protection and help of God."[4] On March 4, 1797, John Adams, our second president, said:

And may that Being who is supreme over all, the Patron of Order, the Fountain of Justice, and the Protector in all ages of the world of virtuous liberty, continue His blessing upon this nation and its Government and give it all possible success and duration consistent with the ends of His providence.[5]

On March 4, 1805, Thomas Jefferson, our third president, said:

I shall need, too, the favor of that Being in whose hands we are, who led our fathers, as Israel of old, from their native land and planted them in a country flowing with all the necessaries and comforts of life; who has covered our infancy with His providence and our riper years with His wisdom and power, and to whose goodness I ask you to join in supplications with me that He will so enlighten the minds of your servants, guide their councils, and prosper their measures that whatsoever they do shall result in your good, and shall secure to you the peace, friendship, and approbation of all nations.[6]

On March 4, 1809, James Madison, our fourth president, said:

In these my confidence will under every difficulty be best placed, next to that which we have all been encouraged to feel in the guardianship and guidance of that Almighty Being whose power regulates the destiny of nations, whose blessings have been so conspicuously dispensed to this rising Republic, and to whom we are bound to address our devout gratitude for the past, as well as our fervent supplications and best hopes for the future.[7]

Bill of Rights and Freedom of Religion
Such were the sentiments of the founding fathers concerning the

separation of God and state. They freely believed in a public expression of faith in God and prayer. In the Constitution, Amendment I of the Bill of Rights states:

> Congress shall make no law respecting an establishment of religion, or prohibiting the free exercise thereof; or abridging the freedom of speech, or of the press, or the right of the people peaceably to assemble, and to petition the government for a redress of grievances.

When statements made by the fathers of our nation are compared with the Bill of Rights concerning separation of church and state, it is obvious that the Constitution they formulated never meant separation of God and state.

Various phrases have evolved with regard to the function of government and religion: "separation of church and state," "strict and lofty neutrality to religion," "wall of separation between church and state," "religion and government to remain each within its respective sphere," "neither support for religion nor hostility to religion," and many more. All have been coined outside the language of the Constitution. What the First Amendment does say is "Congress shall make no law respecting an establishment of religion, or prohibiting the free exercise thereof." The phrase "separation of church and state" is not a legal, constitutional statement. What is proper is that a national church and the federal government are not to be established; or the organization of a national church is to be separated from the national government. However, today it has been construed to mean that no teaching, views, insights, or values of the church can permeate or be accepted in public or governmental institutions; this position violates the very Bill of Rights it aims to protect by suppressing the rights of individuals freely to exercise their faith.

Early American history reveals the mind of colonial leaders who wrote about government and the establishment of religion. They had no intention of separating the influence of their religious faith and government. Justice Black, writing the opinion of the Supreme Court in *Engel v. Vitale*, said, "Indeed, as late as the time of the Revolutionary War, there were established churches in at least eight of the thirteen former colonies and established religions in at least four of the other five."[8] Not until 1817 did disestablishment take place in New Hampshire, 1818 in Connecticut, and as late as 1833 in Massachusetts.[9]

In 1892, after analyzing the place of Christianity throughout our history, the Supreme Court said in *Church of the Holy Trinity v. United States*:

There is a universal language pervading them all, having one meaning; they affirm and reaffirm that this is a religious nation. These are not individual sayings, declarations of private persons: they are organic utterances; they speak the voice of the entire people. . . . These, and many other matters which might be noticed, add a volume of unofficial declarations to the mass of organic utterances that this is a Christian nation.[10]

In *Vidal v. Girad's Executors*, 1844, the Supreme Court in the opinion of Justice Joseph Story affirmed Christianity as a "part of the common law of the state."[11] From the Congressional Research Service of the Library of Congress, *The Supreme Court Opinion in the School Prayer Case (Engel v. Vitale): The Decision, the Reaction, the Pros and Cons*, comes this statement:

Joseph Story thought that while the "no establishment" clause inhibited Congress from giving preference to any Christian sect or denomination, it was not intended to withdraw the Christian religion as such from the protection of Congress. Thus, in his *Commentaries on the Constitution* he wrote:

Probably at the time of the adoption of the Constitution, and of the amendment to it, . . . the general, if not the universal sentiment in America was, that Christianity ought to receive encouragement from the state, so far as was not incompatible with the private rights of conscience, and the freedom of religious worship. An attempt to level all religions, and to make it a matter of state policy to hold all in utter indifference, would have created universal disapprobation if not universal indignation.[12]

The Influence of the Bible on American Education
Agreement or disagreement with these sentiments is not the issue; history proves that our nation was based on Christian concepts. Our first colleges, Harvard, William and Mary, Yale, and Princeton, were founded upon religious principles. During the colonial period children's education was largely church sponsored; along with the three R's, the fourth R, religion, was held indispensable to a proper education. For years the Bible was the only textbook, and when it was replaced, the first textbooks contained much biblical material. For 150 years the celebrated *New England Primer* was the outstanding public school textbook; 87 percent of it was composed of selections from the Bible.[13]
Many early educators and government leaders regarded schools as the chief transmitters of the American ethic of moral and spiritual

values to undergird society. They had daily Bible reading because they considered the Bible one of the most important textbooks for teaching the oldest principles of virtue, morality, discipline, patriotism, and neighborly love. Though stressing nonsectarian schools, they claimed that the Bible did not promote sectarian beliefs since it was not aimed at winning adherents to any particular creed or faith; it was an instrument to produce secular state benefits. For this reason many states have for years allowed and encouraged prayer and a nondenominational Bible reading. For example:

Massachusetts: The school committee shall require the daily reading of some portion of the Bible in the common English version; but shall never direct any school books calculated to favor the tenets of any particular sect of Christians to be purchased or used in any of the town schools. (*General Statutes* 1859, Ch. 38, Sec. 27, Acts 1855. Ch. 410.)

Kansas: No sectarian or religious doctrine shall be taught or inculcated in any of the public schools of the city; but nothing in this section shall be construed to prohibit the reading of the Holy Scriptures. (*General Statutes* 1905, Sec. 6816.)

Michigan: Religion, morality, and knowledge being necessary to good government and the happiness of mankind, schools and the means of education shall forever be encouraged. (*Constitution* 1909, Art. XI, Sec. 1.)

North Dakota: The Bible shall not be deemed a sectarian book. It shall not be excluded from any public school. It may at the option of the teacher be read in school without sectarian comment, not to exceed ten minutes daily. No pupil shall be required to read it nor be present in the schoolroom during the reading thereof contrary to the wishes of his parents or guardian or other person having him in charge. (Political Code 1899, Sec. 754, Laws of 1890, Ch. 62, Sec. 134.)

Benjamin Weiss in his book, *God in American History*, says, "All fifty states of the United States of America have expressed dependence on Almighty God for their preservation and strength. A statement of the faith of the framers of the constitution is included in the preamble, or a reference is made to their faith in God in the body of the constitution of the individual states." Weiss also points out, "Their dependence on Almighty God was more than an act in extreme emergency or on occasions when the leaders felt they had exhausted their own strength and ability. This great Christian ideal was woven into these constitutions when the leaders of the different commonwealths were in deliberation planning the structure of a state."[14] For instance, the preamble of the New York State Constitution says, "We, the People of the State of New York, grateful to Almighty God for our Freedom, in order to secure its blessings, DO ESTABLISH THIS CONSTITUTION."[15]

Woven into our national life are the indelible imprints of our faith in God as found in the Bible. Bernard Eugene Meland, professor at the University of Chicago, says, in *The Realities of Faith: The Revolution in Cultural Forms,* "A full account of the evolving cultural experience of the west would reveal the Bible to be the primary document of western culture. . . . The Bible, and its tradition, has a priority in our cultural experience which no other document shares; it cannot be dissolved or denied without serious loss and possible radical dissolution of the controlling sensibilities of our common life."[16]

As late as 1952 the Supreme Court held, "We are a religious people whose institutions presuppose a Supreme Being."[17] Our nation was founded by individuals using the Bible for their value source to undergird our government. The presidential, judicial, and legislative branches of government are a system of checks and balances provided from the biblical belief in the fallibility of man; many statutes and criminal laws can likewise trace their origin to biblical principles. Because of our religious heritage the government provides many religious aids: Both houses of Congress and the armed services have chaplains, the president is inaugurated with prayer, religious properties are tax exempt, and "In God We Trust" is stamped on our currency. When in 1954 the words "under God" were inserted into the Pledge of Allegiance, the House report stated that these words in no way violate the First Amendment but recognize "the guidance of God in our national affairs."[18]

Reinterpreting the Constitution

The reason the Supreme Court outlawed school prayer and Bible reading was not the First Amendment. Justice Brennan, in his concurring opinion in *Abington School District v. Schempp,* said, "No one questions that the Framers of the First Amendment intended to restrict exclusively the powers of the Federal Government." He then added, "Whatever limitations that Amendment now imposes upon the States derive from the Fourteenth Amendment."[19] The Fourteenth Amendment, enacted shortly after the Civil War to protect all American citizens, reads,

. . .No State shall make or enforce any law which shall abridge the privileges or immunities of citizens of the United

States; nor shall any State deprive any person of life, liberty, or property, without due process of law; nor deny to any person within its jurisdiction the equal protection of the laws.

In 1940 the Supreme Court interpreted the Fourteenth Amendment this way in *Cantwell v. Connecticut*: "The fundamental concept of liberty embodied in that Amendment embraces the liberties guaranteed by the First Amendment. The First Amendment declares that Congress shall make no law respecting an establishment of religion or prohibiting the free exercise thereof. The Fourteenth Amendment has rendered the legislature of the states as incompetent as Congress to enact such laws."[20]

To restrict the federal government the colonial leaders enacted this last amendment to the Bill of Rights: "The powers not delegated to the United States by the Constitution, nor prohibited by it to the States, are reserved to the States respectively, or to the people." But the Supreme Court's interpretation of the Fourteenth Amendment ruled that states were now incompetent to decide whether religion and morality are necessary for good government and mankind's happiness, and whether schools should encourage them in accordance with individual rights of conscience. In reading the Fourteenth Amendment one finds it difficult to understand how the Supreme Court made its ruling. But even if the amendment did apply to the states, then, since the intent of the First Amendment was to forbid the establishment of a national church, the Fourteenth Amendment should only forbid the establishment of a state church. It should not stipulate that public schools cannot permit Bible reading in order to derive principles and convictions for freedom and justice. By restricting the expression in public schools of the beliefs of God-fearing Americans the Supreme Court has in effect violated the First Amendment's free exercise clause.

Walter Berns, professor of political science and author of numerous books and articles on constitutional theory, says in *The First Amendment and the Future of American Democracy*:

> Prior to the adoption of the Fourteenth Amendment (or, more precisely, prior to the time when it was held to embrace the religious provisions of the First Amendment), the Supreme Court lacked all supervisory authority over the states in religious matters. Whether the states imposed religious tests for voting or holding office, or required or permitted their schools to teach the tenets of any faith or to conduct prayer services or to read from the Bible at designated devotional ceremonies, or with their financial support discriminated against other than Christian churches or even among the various denominations

of Christians—all these were questions "to be acted upon according to [each state's]* own sense of justice. . . ." The First Amendment by itself left "the whole power over the subject of religion . . . exclusively to the State governments."[21]

Edward S. Corwin, considered one of the most respected of our constitutional scholars, comments, "The historical record shows beyond peradventure that the core idea of 'an establishment of religion' comprises the idea of *preference*; and that any act of public authority favorable to religion in general cannot, without manifest falsification of history, be brought under the ban of that phrase."[22] Professor Berns adds, "The First Amendment forbids a national church and any preference in the aid or recognition extended to religion; applied to the states by way of the word 'liberty' in the Fourteenth Amendment, it forbids state churches and state preferences and, therefore, sectarian state schools."[23]

State Rights

Harold O. J. Brown, in *The Reconstruction of the Republic*, remarks, "The United States Constitution is not a source of fundamental values. It is an instrument whereby fundamental values can be protected, defining the procedures, principles, and methods whereby government can function to allow the people to give content to their lives. But the Constitution itself cannot give that content."[24]

Since states were given the power to define fundamental values, these values are definitely absent in the Constitution. Looking at the Constitution alone leads to false conclusions; the framers carefully stated in the Bill of Rights that whatever was not delegated by the Constitution was reserved to the states. Since Christianity—and values derived from this belief—was not mentioned in the Constitution, the federal government had no jurisdiction over it. The concept of separation of church and state has been repeated so often that many Americans believe it comes directly from our Constitution or the Bill of Rights. Americans need to be awakened that this sentiment is unconstitutional. Our government was established on religious principles, and it favored the uniting of the influence of the church and state.

The early leaders adopted the First Amendment: "Congress shall make no law respecting an establishment of religion, or prohibiting the free exercise thereof." They carefully sought to avoid the error of Europe of having a centralized national church, while still maintain-

*Author's brackets.

ing the right of individual states to choose their own value system, even to the point of having state-supported churches and state-mandated prayers. Today most Americans would favor religious liberty and voluntary prayers instead of state-dictated prayers; however, framers of the Constitution left these decisions to citizens of individual states, not to the Supreme Court.

Separation of Church and State

There is a country in which the constitution does dictate in very forceful words the concept of separation of church and state. It is found in Article 52 of the Constitution of the Union of Soviet Socialist Republics:

> Citizens of the USSR are guaranteed freedom of conscience, that is the right to profess or not to profess any religion, and to conduct religious worship or atheistic propaganda. Incitement of hostility or hatred on religious grounds is prohibited.
> In the USSR, the church is separated from the state, and the school from the church.[25]

It is obvious from a study of American history that the Supreme Court's interpretation concerning saying a prayer or reading the Bible in public schools is a flagrant violation of the intent of the Bill of Rights. Today the Constitution has been falsely construed to imitate communist Russia's constitution as regards separation of church and state. A new honesty is needed in examining our Constitution and its meaning. From a nation founded on the conviction that "In God We Trust," we have degenerated to the point where practically every vestige of a definite proclamation of faith in God has been removed from public education.

Chapter 16

A Moral America

Peter Berger, professor of sociology at Rutgers University, writing in the *New York Teacher*, analyzes the historic relationship between God and state:

> Unlike the French republic and other democracies modeled upon it, the American state was not conceived in a secularist mode. From the beginning there was a complex but intimate dialogue between the social contract of the republic and the sacred covenant of the churches. Thus the purpose of the First Amendment to the Constitution was to protect pluralism and religious liberty, not to insulate the state from religious influences. It is only since World War II that an overtly secularist tendency has developed in America. This new secularism has succeeded in influencing both the courts and agencies of government on various levels.
>
> The decision of the Supreme Court declaring prayer in public schools to be unconstitutional was a symbolic climax of this development. . . .
>
> What is more, recent trends have come perilously close to a new "establishment of religion"—to wit, the legal establishment of the quasi-religion of secularism. This would be a violation of the religious liberty of large numbers of Americans. Even more seriously, though, it would be an act of social suicide on the part of the American System.
>
> Has the American System lost the capacity to survive? A negative answer is overwhelmingly plausible if one looks at the immense capacities of the American economy, the inventiveness of American science and technology, the resilience of the country's political institutions, and the human qualities of its population. All of these resources—material, human, and institutional—will not prevail, however, without a resurgence of the American spirit. This will require political and intellectual leadership of a sort that has been painfully lacking in recent years. It will also require a revitalization of those institutions that have always been the matrix of beliefs and values in the society. Among those institutions the churches occupy a central place.[1]

235

Where should the line be drawn between God and state? The complete divorcement of God from public affairs has been catastrophic—it has destroyed America's moral foundation. The founders of our nation had the right concept. They recognized the ethic that was the predominant belief of the people as a basis for national morality.

Promoting America's Moral Heritage
How can the essential moral framework the Constitution so carefully provided for the United States be restored? First, every God-fearing parent, teacher, administrator, and leader in any capacity should immediately do everything legally possible to promote our moral heritage. There is a definite danger of overreacting to the Supreme Court's decisions and considering everything lost. Instead of being on the defensive, we should be on the offensive, mounting an aggressive campaign to restore our moral foundation and refusing to yield the smallest fraction to atheistic humanism and other forces that are destroying the nation.
In the *Engel* decision, Justice Black said:

> There is of course nothing in the decision reached here that is inconsistent with the fact that school children and others are officially encouraged to express love for our country by reciting historical documents such as the Declaration of Independence which contain references to the Deity or by singing officially espoused anthems which include the composer's professions of faith in a Supreme Being, or with the fact that there are many manifestations in our public life of belief in God.[2]

Teachers should use historical material and patriotic anthems showing how our forefathers' faith in God molded our government and contributed to America's success. Historical documents, songs, and materials can generate questions about our theistic heritage, and teachers are free to answer them. Teachers should refuse to allow their classes to read vile books; they should insist on decent literature. Proper work habits and moral standards should be instilled into children from the "many manifestations in our public life of belief in God."
Teachers can communicate ideas concerning religion, but they cannot indoctrinate. Creative teachers know how to differentiate between teaching about religion and sectarian indoctrination. Teachers should boldly declare their faith in God and the American system of government, whose foundation is the self-evident truth that men are "endowed by their Creator with certain unalienable rights."

A Narrow Ruling

When the Supreme Court made its decisions in *Abington School District v. Schempp* and *Engel v. Vitale*, most educators interpreted the rulings to mean that it was illegal for a teacher to read the Bible for moral training or to pray. A strict reading of each decision will reveal that it was a very narrow ruling; only state-mandated Bible reading and state-mandated prayers were outlawed.

In *Abington School District v. Schempp*, two cases were combined. The Commonwealth of Pennsylvania by law required, "At least ten verses from the Holy Bible shall be read, without comment, at the opening of each public school on each school day. Any child shall be excused from such Bible reading, or attending such Bible reading, upon the written request of his parent or guardian." From a Maryland code the school board provided the "reading, without comment, of a chapter in the Holy Bible and/or the use of the Lord's Prayer." The Court said that "these companion cases present the issues in the context of state action requiring that schools begin each day with readings from the Bible."[3] It was these state actions that were declared illegal.

What was made illegal in *Engel* was the action taken by New York State in directing the Union Free School District principal to cause the following prayer to be recited by the class: "Almighty God, we acknowledge our dependence upon Thee, and we beg Thy blessings upon us, our parents, our teachers and our country."[4]

Justice Black in his decision said that the government "should stay out of the business of writing or sanctioning official prayers and leave that purely religious function to the people themselves and to those the people choose to look to for religious guidance."[5] Today some schools are obeying this injunction by not "writing or sanctioning official prayers"; instead, they permit teachers the freedom to say prayers while allowing dissenting students to leave.

However, in two federal district courts judges ruled that a teacher-initiated prayer (*De Spain v. De Kalb County Community School District*)[6] and a student-initiated prayer (*Stein v. Oshinsky*)[7] were both illegal. These decisions are not binding on the entire nation; in only 2 out of the 11 federal circuits that the decisions were made. When the *De Spain* case was brought before the Supreme Court on appeal, at least five Supreme Court justices decided not to review the case. Their refusal to hear the case does not make the federal court's decision law for the nation, but it does reveal a dangerous trend: that they are leaning toward eliminating all school prayers. If the Supreme Court ruled against all school prayers on constitutional grounds, it would display an ironic twist of reasoning: When the Constitution, which is the Supreme Court's guideline, was formulated, the leaders encountered such insurmountable obstacles to achieving unanimity that they relied on prayer for its completion. Furthermore, each day in the same Supreme Court the justices stand as one of the officials prays, "God save the United States and this Honorable Court."[8]

High school students in Lubbock, Texas, were allowed with supervision to gather voluntarily either before or after regular school hours for any educational, moral, or religious purposes. The American Civil Liberties Union in Lubbock challenged the policy as unconstitutional. The issue was whether students could meet for Bible discussions just as they could gather for a history club or a debating team. The Fifth Circuit Federal Court upheld ACLU's contention.

The case was brought before the U.S. Supreme Court in *Lubbock School Board v. Lubbock Civil Liberties Union*. Supporters of the school board, including 24 United States senators, stressed that voluntary activities in public schools must also include freedom for religious functions. The senators filed a petition to the Court saying that "if students can meet voluntarily to discuss Jean Paul Sartre's reasons for disbelief in God then surely they should be able to meet to discuss Saul of Tarsus' reasons for belief in God." The Supreme Court refused to review the case.[9]

Prayer and Bible Reading Statute

Because of recent trends in removing voluntary religious activities, school prayers, and the alarming moral deterioration in schools, the American people need to press their members of Congress to vote for a prayer and Bible reading statute that would return to states their right to return to these practices if they want them. In promoting such a statute it should be stressed that this is not an addition to the Constitution; rather, it is a restoration of what was originally in the Constitution. Supreme Court Justice William O. Douglas declared in *Zorach v. Clauson*, "We are a religious people whose institutions presuppose a Supreme Being."[10] The foundation of America was built upon the Bible, and our early leaders relied on prayer for the nation's prosperity.

Attempts by Congress to restore the theistic heritage to schools by amending the Constitution have never achieved the required two-thirds majority vote of both houses. If a prayer and Bible reading amendment should pass both houses, it still would need ratification by three-fourths (38) of the states. One such amendment that Congress failed to approve, was section One of the Becker amendment:

Nothing in this Constitution shall be deemed to prohibit the offering, reading from, or listening to prayers or biblical scripture, if participation therein is on a voluntary basis, in any governmental or public school, institution, or place.[11]

This amendment would have forced all states to allow prayer and Bible reading. Although this is not an unwholesome concept, it is not in keeping with the Constitution our forefathers formulated. In this amendment the federal government is dictating to the states what they should do in the area of religion. We need an amendment that would restore to each state its constitutional right to have prayer or Bible reading if it so desires. Such an amendment could read,

> Nothing in this Constitution shall be deemed to prohibit the states from permitting the offering, reading from, or listening to prayers or biblical scripture, if participation therein is on a voluntary basis, in any governmental or public school, institution, or place.

This amendment is exactly the same as the Becker amendment, except for four words: "the states from permitting." With such an amendment, each state would have the liberty to decide on this important issue, in accordance with the government the founding fathers formulated. Such an amendment would not put one prayer in any school; it would simply allow state government and its citizens to decide. Once such an amendment passes, concerned individuals of each state can press for the historical principle of permitting teachers to lead children in nondenominational prayer and to instill into children the high moral standards from our biblical heritage.

President Ronald Reagan spoke to the American people about supporting a constitutional amendment permitting voluntary prayer for all states:

> We thank the chaplain of the Senate for that blessing. It's an inspiration for me to see all of you, Protestants, Catholics, members of the Jewish faith and others, who are gathered here at our national home to pay homage to the God in whom we trust. . . .
> I said before that the most sublime picture in American history is of George Washington on his knees in the snow at Valley Forge. That image personifies a people who know that it's not enough to depend on our own courage and goodness. We must also seek help from God our father and preserver.
> Abraham Lincoln said once that he would be the most foolish man on this footstool we call earth if he thought for one minute he could fulfill the duties that faced him if he did not have the help of one who is wiser than all others.

The French philosopher Alexis de Tocqueville, visiting America 150 years ago, marveled at Americans because they understood that a free people must also be a religious people. Despotism, he wrote, may be able to do without faith, but freedom cannot.

Today prayer is still a powerful force in America, and our faith in God is a mighty source of strength. Our pledge of allegiance states that we are one nation under God, and our currency bears the motto "In God we trust."

The morality and values such faith implies are deeply embedded in our national character. Our country embraces those principles by design, and we abandon them at our peril. Yet in recent years well-meaning Americans, in the name of freedom, have taken freedom away. For the sake of religious tolerance they've forbidden religious practice in our public classrooms.

The law of this land has effectively removed prayer from our classrooms. How can we hope to retain our freedom through the generations if we fail to teach our young that our liberty springs from an abiding faith in our Creator?

Thomas Jefferson once said Almighty God created the mind free. But current interpretation of our Constitution holds that the minds of our children cannot be free to pray to God in public schools. No one will ever convince me that a moment of voluntary prayer will harm a child or threaten a school or state.

But I think it can strengthen our faith in a Creator who alone has the power to bless America.

One of my favorite passages in the Bible is the promise God gives us in Second Chronicles: If my people which are called by my name shall humble themselves and pray and seek my face and turn from their wicked ways, then will I hear from heaven and will forgive their sin and will heal their land.

That promise is the hope of America and all our people. . . . Changing the Constitution is a mammoth task. It should never be easy. But in this case I believe we can restore a freedom that our Constitution was always meant to protect. I have never believed that the oft-quoted amendment was supposed to protect us from religion—it was to protect religion from Government tyranny. Together let us take up the challenge to reawaken America's religious and moral heart, recognizing that a deep and abiding faith in God is the rock upon which this great nation was founded.

Thank you all again, as I say, for being here, and God bless you all.[12]

In spite of the many benefits of voluntary prayer, there are individuals who object. John Herbert Laubach, in his book *School Prayers*, reports that "Rabbi Joachim Prinz, President of the American Jewish Congress, concluded that a theory of moral encouragement by national promotion of religion was 'false both in theory and practice.' He condemned governmental manipulation of religion designed to 'maintain and propagate specific, and often transitory, societal codes.' While he believed that religious truths grew out of profound faith and that religion strengthened moral responsibility, he doubted that the needs of a particular society, as embodied in 'public school religion,' could produce beneficial effects."[13] Professor Paul Freund of the Harvard Law School claims, "A school prayer at best would face the dilemma of being so bland as to be meaningless, what some have called a 'to whom it may concern' sort of prayer, or so sectarian as to be divisive and to some repelling."[14] Professor Kauper of the University of Michigan Law School states, "Ritualistic practices, whether prayers of Bible reading without comment, supported by the compulsive power of the State, contribute little to the development of any genuine religious piety for ethical conduct and may, indeed, have the effect of cheapening and degrading religion."[15]

Others object that permitting prayer and Bible reading will begin to establish a state religion, violate minority rights, force the minority to support religious exercises, and lead to formalism. Then there is the problem, which version of the Bible should be read? To avoid such issues, a simple solution has emerged—eliminate all prayer and Bible reading.

Certainly some touchy issues can arise if schools permit prayer and Bible reading, but one must remember that before the Supreme Court ruled on prayer and Bible reading, public schools did work and generations of upright citizens were trained. Each generation has its misfits; however, an impartial look at public schools today reveals a massive moral deterioration. Generally public schools did not force sectarian beliefs upon children. The Christian ethic was chosen for national morality because it was the predominant belief. Since Judaism was also derived from biblical beliefs, some schools allowed children to read from Protestant, Catholic, or Jewish versions of the Bible. Prayer and Bible reading in schools will not establish a church or a secularized civil religion. It merely acknowledges that we are a nation under God and we seek his aid through prayer and recognize the Bible as a source book for a sound ethical system. Furthermore, a prayer and Bible reading statute would prevent the constant nibbling by humanist forces to rid schools of our godly heritage and replace it with humanistic goals.

The reason Bible reading was held illegal in *Abington v. Schempp* was that the Court considered such an exercise a religious ceremony. Simply reading a few verses from the Bible is not for the purpose of a religious ceremony or of establishing a sectarian religion; it is strictly for promoting moral guidelines. Since America was grounded on biblical principles, we want to perpetuate this wholesome moral foundation by permitting voluntary Bible reading. Think how the great principles of the Ten Commandments would benefit our nation: God is to be honored; God's name is not to be taken in vain; one day is to be kept sacred; parents are to be honored; and murder, adultery, stealing, bearing false witness, and coveting are forbidden.

Instead of audible prayer, some schools feature a period of silence, during which children are permitted to do whatever they desire. Surely this is better than no prayer, but it is not the solution. Why is reinstating audible voluntary prayer and Bible reading in a public institution such an important concept? It gives official recognition that America was founded on theistic principles, we need God's help to exist as a free people, the source of our values is not humanism but theism, states have the option to permit teachers to instruct children in proper values from our theistic culture, and schools can promote the values that the safety and survival of our society require.

It can be argued that, since public schools are not compulsory, parents have the liberty to send their children to private or parochial schools to be indoctrinated in the value system of their choice. For many, however, public schools are compulsory; parents simply cannot afford the expense of private schools. The question goes even deeper than just the issue of freedom of choice: "What right does government have to spend public tax money supporting atheistic humanism, while telling theists to spend their own money for private education?" The question can be reversed by atheists: "What right does government have to take public tax money to support theistic values while telling atheists to spend their money for private education?" The answer is simple—our nation was founded on theism, not atheism. Public schools only endeavor to perpetuate our historical godly heritage.

Americans and School Prayer

In spite of the opposition, *Time* reports that the "latest Gallup poll indicates that 76% of Americans are willing to go even further and approve a constitutional amendment allowing school prayers."[16] Only 15 percent opposed such an amendment, while 9 percent were undecided.[17] Even William J. Murray, son of Madalyn Murray O'Hair, whom his mother took to the Supreme Court to ban state-mandated prayers, issued a public apology for his actions in removing such prayers. He said in a letter that he had wasted 33 years of his life because he did not have faith in God. Murray then stated:

> I pray that I may be able to correct just some of the wrong I have created. The part I played as a teen-ager in removing prayer from public schools was criminal. I removed from our future generations that short time each day which should rightly be reserved for God. Inasmuch as the suit to destroy the tradition of prayer in school was brought in my name, I feel gravely responsible for the resulting destruction of the moral fiber of our youth that it has caused.[18]

Many individuals have been changing their attitude concerning school prayer. The leaders of the 13 million Southern Baptists have reversed a position they held for many years. By a margin of 3 to 1 they endorsed President Reagan's constitutional school prayer amendment. Charles Stanley, initiator of the resolution, said, "Prohibiting prayer and Bible reading in public schools is only one step in the demoralizing of America."[19]

When Senator Jesse Helms was attacked on the Senate floor because of his judicial prayer bill, he declared, "I want a senator to stand up and identify one child in this country who has ever been harmed by voluntary prayer in the public schools." No one responded.[20]

Building a Moral Foundation

Throughout history there has been belief in a greater power available for man to live an ethical life, and public schools have encouraged children to seek this power. Public schools did not teach children how to obtain this power; they taught only that it was available and left it to the home and religious institutions to teach and formalize particular tenets. For this reason, a nonsectarian school prayer and Bible reading was considered a legitimate expression of our nation's civil faith.

One of the pressing issues is who should determine the prayers and Bible readings. This should be left to each state to decide. Some states may want to prescribe certain prayers that have already been written and portions of the Bible to be read; others may want to leave the issue to individuals in charge, with the stipulation that whatever they choose should be nonsectarian.

Individuals who believe that prayer and Bible reading for moral inspiration should not be in public schools need to answer this question: "From what source should our nation and our educators derive their morality standards?" To stipulate that educators should not teach morals would make it impossible to teach many subjects adequately. Without moral standards teachers could not declare any act right or wrong.

Others advocate that, since we are a pluralistic society, government and schools should be neutral; all moral views should be equally presented to permit students to choose their own value system. On the surface this appears fair, but should educators teach that lying, stealing, euthanasia, premarital sex, abortion, pornography, and prostitution are acceptable if a child so chooses? When schools take the neutral position, they are promoting humanism. It is impossible to be morally neutral. Paul Hirst expresses this point forcibly:

> Whether we like it or not, the whole enterprise of education is, from top to bottom, value-ridden. It is surely just nonsense to think otherwise. The very selection of what is to be taught involves major judgments of value. To teach the chosen content involves attention to standards of value of many kinds. Schools are institutions which involve complex human relationships where not only moral ideas but also patterns of moral conduct are being shaped. There must be rules and principles governing the functioning of the institution if it is to be a civilized community at all, let alone an educational one.[21]

The Religion of Humanism

Morals originate either from God or from man. The issue is not whether schools are morally neutral but *what* moral system shall be taught. It used to be a theistic one; now humanism reigns. But humanism is an atheistic system of belief and falls into the category of being a religion and therefore unconstitutional. Congressman John B. Conlan was able to add an amendment to the foreign studies and language development portions of a Title II bill that forbade grants to any project "involving any aspect of the religion of secular humanism." The *Congressional Record* presents Conlan's speech:

> Mr. Chairman, this amendment prohibiting taxpayer support for any educational program or activity involving any aspect of the religion of secular humanism is a legislative and constitutional necessity.
>
> The amendment touches the heart of the concept of academic freedom—a concept which in some circles has been virtually destroyed by the false assumption that the "secular humanist" stance taken by many administrators and teachers in public educational theory and practice is fundamentally religiously "neutral."
>
> Nothing could be further from the truth.

The U.S. Supreme Court stated clearly in the 1961 decision in the case of Torcaso against Watkins that secular humanism is a religion—a world and life view.

The highest court perceptively declared in this case that:

> Among religions in this country which do not teach what would generally be considered a belief in the existence of God are Buddhism, Taoism, Ethical Culture, Secular Humanism, and others.

Secular humanism declares that there is no God, that man is his own god. Educators advocating a secular humanist view consistently excluded from the classroom any teaching of moral and ethical principles based on the Judaic-Christian belief in God.

Historically, the increasingly vehement attack upon and exclusion of certain Judaic-Christian Biblical views of origins and ethics has falsely been thought to be the upraising of the banner of "Scientific or humanistic neutralism."

But we must remember that in Abington against Schempp, in 1963, the U.S. Supreme Court again ruled that—

> The Government may not establish a "religion of secularism" in the sense of affirmatively opposing or showing hostility to religion, thus "preferring those who believe in no religion over those who do believe."[22]

Though the common concept of religion is to render service and worship to God, the Supreme Court has defined religion as a system of values from which individuals derive their world views, whether theistic or atheistic. Even the preface of *Humanist Manifestos I and II* states, "Humanism is a philosophical, religious, and moral point of view."[23] We must not forget that it is illegal to teach secular humanism in schools and show hostility toward religion. What the Supreme Court has declared unlawful is that public schools cannot have (1) state-required prayers (*Engel*), (2) state-mandated Bible reading (*Schempp*), and (3) on-premise religious training (*McCollum*).[24]

Accommodation-Neutrality

Many teachers, school administrators, and lower courts are laboring under the delusion that public schools must be strictly neutral toward religion. The government's position is one of accommodation-neutrality toward religion. In other words, government should favor religion when it does not violate the First Amendment. Supreme

Court Justice William O. Douglas, in the 1952 *Zorach* decision, stated the principle of accommodation-neutrality:

> When the state encourages religious instruction or cooperates with religious authorities by adjusting the schedule of public events to sectarian needs, it follows the best of our traditions. For it then respects the religious nature of our people and accommodates the public service to their spiritual needs.[25]

Officials who forbade any religious influence in schools would also violate Justice Douglas' decision. He commented on the probable result if the state were not to accommodate religion:

> To hold that it may not would be to find in the Constitution a requirement that the government show a callous indifference to religious groups. That would be preferring those who believe in no religion over those who do believe. . . . But we find no constitutional requirement which makes it necessary for government to be hostile to religion and to throw its weight against efforts to widen the effective scope of religious influence.[26]

As recently as 1976, accommodation-neutrality was further enhanced when Justice Blackmun declared in *Roemer v. Maryland Public Works Bd.,* "The Court has enforced a scrupulous neutrality by the State, as among religions, and also between religious and other activities, but a hermetic separation of the two is an impossibility it has never required."[27]

Though accommodation-neutrality is a part of our nation's law, yet the interpretation of the Court's ruling regarding prayer and Bible reading had a devastating effect upon our theistic values. What emerges is educational leaders tried to make public schools walk the impossible razor edge of moral neutrality. However, the presumption that state and schools can be neutral, neither favoring nor opposing religious faith, is an illusion. There are only two moral positions and both are religious—theism or humanism: one moral system must be chosen.

Godly educators and parents need to resist and expose the religion of humanism in schools and promote the Supreme Court's rulings to accommodate religion. But what happens is opponents cite Supreme Court rulings that suppress methods of supporting theism. For this reason it is important for educators and parents to convince Americans and Congress of the necessity of restoring state rights to permit school prayer and Bible reading and hence officially establish our historical theistic value system.

Many persons will automatically reject this proposal, not because they have thoroughly examined the issues, but because of the false belief that our government supports the total separation of God and state. To promote such a statute effectively there must be a movement to educate Americans so they understand their historic roots that the United States has a government whose foundation is built upon faith in God.

Three Choices

Three fairly defined choices concerning religion and education are evident:

1. Prayer and Bible reading are necessary in public schools for the development of proper character.

2. Parents desiring religious moral direction should send their children to private sectarian schools.

3. Religion should be taught in the church, Sunday school, and home; schools should be strictly secular.

For many years the first principle, using prayer and the Bible for moral inspiration, dominated public education. Now it has been largely eliminated because of reactions to the Supreme Court's decisions. The second and third concepts, which relegate theism to private schools and humanism to public schools, are unconstitutional. Public schools cannot legally teach humanism and demand theists to sent their children to private schools. Though the Supreme Court specifically stated that "government may not establish a 'religion of secularism,' "[28] its effect of outlawing theism has established the religion of humanism in violation of the very Constitution it aimed to uphold. Dr. Bernard Iddings Bell said in *Crisis in Education* that American education is now more and more conducted so "there is no such thing as religious liberty in American education. There is liberty only to be unreligious."[29]

How did the Supreme Court fall into this trap? Because it is impossible to be morally neutral. The United States was not founded upon moral neutrality; to insist on neutrality leads to contradictory results. If there is any neutrality, it is accommodation-neutrality, which favors religious exercises that do not establish a particular church or sect.

Contradictory Court Decisions

The difficulty with the Supreme Court is that its rulings have been contradictory. In 1947 Justice Black stated in *Everson v. Board of Education*, "The First Amendment has erected a wall between church and state. That wall must be kept high and impregnable. We could not approve the slightest breach."[30] Then in 1976 Justice Blackmun said in *Roemer v. Maryland Public Works Bd.*, "A system of government that makes itself felt as pervasively as ours could hardly be expected never to cross paths with the church. In fact, our State and Federal Governments impose certain burdens upon, and impart certain benefits to, virtually all our activities, and religious activity is not an exception."[31]

Which shall it be? From Supreme Court decisions one could defend either support or a total divorcement between God and government. But when one studies the American heritage, one can *only* support a union between God and government. The Supreme Court justices, instead of adhering to the Constitution as a historical document, have interpreted it according to their own philosophical beliefs. The Court is supposed to hear only those cases concerned with constitutional issues; unfortunately, it has usurped roles never intended by the Constitution.

Supreme Court's Activism

Constitutional lawyer John Whitehead, author of *The Separation Illusion* and *The Second American Revolution*, told me in an interview that judges "take evolution as a doctrine, and if you take evolution as your philosophical base, then all the Constitution is, is what they call a living document. And that's a dangerous statement, because what they are saying is that it is evolving and they don't have to look to history." Whitehead also pointed out, "If history is not any good, then where do we anchor our ship? The Constitution is a contract, and like any contract you have to go back and interpret the intentions of the people who made the contract."

Senator Jesse Helms, speaking before the Senate, proposed a method to stem Supreme Court activism:

Fortunately, the Constitution provides this alternative under the system of checks and balances. In anticipation of judicial usurpations of power, the framers of our Constitution wisely gave Congress the authority, by a simple majority of both Houses, to check the Supreme Court through regulation of its appellate jurisdiction. Section 2 of article III states in clear and unequivocal language that the appellate jurisdiction of the Court is subject to "such exceptions, and under such regulations, as the Congress shall make."

Permit me to point out, Mr. President, that Congress has never doubted its authority to exercise this power. Since the earliest days of the Republic, Members of Congress have proposed and enacted legislation to regulate the appellate jurisdiction of the Supreme Court. . . .

In my view, Mr. President, these arguments against the right of this Congress to regulate the jurisdiction of the Courts of the United States amount to little more than an assertion of judicial supremacy. They are based on the assumption—and it is a false as well as a dangerous one—that once the Supreme Court has taken jurisdiction over a class of cases, that we are thereafter helpless to do anything about it except by constitutional amendment. Such an assumption flies in the face of the theory and language of our fundamental law and totally disregards the democratic character of our system. . . .

For these reasons, I am introducing today a bill which would limit the appellate jurisdiction of the Supreme Court, and the original jurisdiction of Federal district courts, in actions relating to the recitation of prayers in public schools. This bill states simply that the Federal courts shall not have jurisdiction to enter any judgment, decree, or order, denying or restricting as unconstitutional, voluntary prayer in any public school. Implicit in the bill is the understanding that the American citizen will have recourse to a judicial settlement of his rights, but this settlement will be made in the State courts of this Nation, and not in the Federal courts. This is where our religious freedoms have always been safeguarded, until they were nationalized by the Supreme Court just a few years ago. From 1789 until 1962, a period of 173 years, the whole matter of what constitutes a religious establishment in the separate States was determined by our State courts, and if I am not mistaken Americans enjoyed their religious freedom throughout this long period of time. In this sense, then, my bill simply restores to the American people and to their respective States those rights which they possessed until the Supreme Court decided a few years ago, without benefit of statute, that the Justices themselves must take jurisdiction.[32]

Harvard law professor Raoul Berger, in his book *Government by Judiciary*, concurs with Jesse Helms on judicial supremacy: "A democratic system requires adherence to constitutional limits, by courts no less than presidents. Respect for the limits on power is the essence of a democratic society."[33]

We the American people must decide whether we want to return to our historical Constitution. The proposal of Senator Jesse Helms to remove all federal court jurisdiction over voluntary prayers is a step toward restoring what was originally provided in our Constitution. Since schools cannot be morally neutral and the Supreme Court has suppressed the national theistic moral system, many educators choose a secularistic moral philosophy that has eliminated theism in favor of atheistic humanism—a complete reversal from our historical value system.

Reverse Discrimination

Since many children are now forcibly trained in the religion of humanism, the arguments used to defeat prayer and Bible reading can be applied to children of oppressed theists: Children are compelled to accept a religion contrary to their beliefs, students are trained in an environment that is hostile toward theistic religion and prayer, the rights and liberties of the majority who believe in God are violated since they are forced to sustain a religion in which they do not believe in a tax-supported school, and schools are financing and establishing a religion in violation of the First Amendment.

As a result of the Court's action, children who believe in God are now taught in an environment that discriminates against them. If such children ask permission to be excused, they will incur social stigma for refusing to be trained in the religious beliefs of humanism. A strange turn of events! Atheists used the argument of discrimination to support eliminating prayer and Bible reading; now children believing in God have become the victims of discrimination. By ruling in favor of a few offended atheists, the Supreme Court has rejected the majority's constitutional right freely to exercise their faith. The tyranny of the minority!

Not satisfied with having eliminated prayer and Bible reading, humanists also want to eradicate every vestige of our theistic heritage: remove the singing of "America" and "The Star-Spangled Banner" since in these patriotic songs God is honored; remove "In God We Trust" from our currency; eliminate "under God" from our Pledge of Allegiance; throw out prayer at presidential inaugurals; and eliminate any celebration of Christmas and Easter from our public institutions.

Though state-mandated Bible reading for moral instruction was outlawed, Justice Clark stated, in *Abington School District v. Schempp*: . . .It might well be said that one's education is not complete without a study of comparative religion or the history of religion and its relationship to the advancement of civilization. It certainly may be said that the Bible is worthy of study for its literary and historic qualities. Nothing we have said here indicates that such study of the Bible or of religion, when presented objectively as part of a secular program of education, may not be effected consistent with the First Amendment.[34]

Certainly! And teachers ought to take full advantage of this right. However, many individuals have mistakenly rejoiced because schools are now permitted to teach religion. One of my sons took such a course in high school: "The Bible as Literature." The teacher taught religion from an antibiblical point of view. The course destroyed faith in God and promoted the concept of the Bible's being just one book of many myths—take your pick.

In many classrooms today teachers require children to read books that freely blaspheme God's name, yet they forbid books that honor God's name. While substituting in my school for an absent English teacher, I was irritated that students were required to read blasphemous words in J. D. Salinger's *The Catcher in the Rye*. Repeatedly the book used: *crap, ass, sonuvabitch, bastards, Chrissake* and *goddam*; in one seven-page chapter, *goddam* was used 27 times![35]

In one school kindergarten children recited this prayer:

> Thank You for the World so Sweet,
> Thank You for the Food We Eat,
> Thank You for the Birds that Sing—
> Thank You, God, for Everything.

The principal ordered teachers to stop using the prayer. Since the Supreme Court had ruled against state-mandated prayers, the parents went to court on the grounds that this prayer was student-initiated. They lost in the United States Court of Appeals.[36]

Two years later, kindergarten children recited another version:

> We thank you for the flowers so sweet,
> We thank you for the food we eat,
> We thank you for the birds that sing,
> We thank you for everything.

In this prayer God was not even mentioned, but opponents of the prayer brought a case to court stating it violated the Constitution. The lower courts rules this rhyme an establishment of a religion.[37] The Supreme Court refused to hear the case on appeal, creating the impression that it concurs in the decision. Result: Teachers can freely choose books cursing and blaspheming God—but woe to any teacher who in the slightest way prayerfully reveres God's name.

Chapter 17

Schools and the Future of America

"You are a member of the school board of a medium-sized Western city. It is September and the high school must immediately replace a very fine history teacher who died quite suddenly, since high school starts next week. You must make a choice from among four applicants—Don, Jim, Bill and Harry." This problem was presented on a spirit-duplicated sheet to my son's high school speech class. Students were to choose from these four candidates:

1. "Don had an exceptional academic record in teachers college. He is bright and hard-working, well liked and well mannered. However, he is a very stubborn young man—also a confirmed atheist—and does not hide his lack of religious belief. When asked if he intended to teach atheism to his pupils, he replied that he would teach waht [sic] he believed, and no one had the right to ask him not to."

2. "Harry had an average academic record at a small church scool [sic]. His recommendations are just adequate, with the clear indication that some question of competence remains in the minds of his teachers. When the principal asked how well his practice teaching has gone, Harry replied that he did not get through all the material he was supposed to cover."

3. "Jim had an exceptional academic record at a large, well-respected, private university. His recommendations were excellent as far as academic training was concerned. Although well-liked and well-mannered, Jim is very uncomfortable around women and definitely seems to prefer the company of men. Jim admitted that this was true and replied that he was a homosexual but had the situation in full control. Jim said that he would not teach any of his homosexual views but if asked would admit that he preferred the company of men to that of women." Jim contends that "he has his own circle of friends in a town fifty miles away and has never been in trouble with the police, nor was he in any trouble during four years of undergraduate work."

4. "Bill had a sporadic record from a large public university. The principal reports that he is neat, clean and well dressed. He was a campus radical and took part in several protests, on one occasion spending eighteen days in jail because of his activities. His record

also shows that Bill has strong political leanings toward Communism. Upon Questioning [sic], Bill admitted his association with violent factions but assured the principal that he was now ready to settle down and that he would like to teach. Bill said that he would not teach Communist doctrines but would not lie to the students if asked about his beliefs."

On the bottom of the sheet students were asked, "Which candidate should the board select to fill the teaching position in the high school history department?"

Notice the two applicants favoring humanistic life-styles, the atheist and the homosexual, have "exceptional academic" records and are "well-liked and well-mannered"; the communist radical is "neat, clean and well dressed"; and the Christian is of average ability with clear evidence of being incompetent. This is a subtle undermining of our moral heritage. These humanistic attacks are repeated in countless ways in classrooms across America.

Internal Disintegration

America has faced many crises and survived. Today's crisis, however, is unique—it is an internal disintegration. The humanistic attack is demolishing our nation's moral strength, and it is being promoted by government and schools in the name of constitutional liberty. America is vibrant and strong, but no nation is immune from destruction. Unless nations transmit to future generations discipline and moral strength, they will join the graveyard of nations. Though many Americans object to humanistic standards, they are nevertheless forced upon their children. The difficulty in combating humanism is that it comes disguised as love, compassion, freedom, self-determination, and respect for individuality. These concepts have an aesthetic appeal that tends to pacify parents' fear of a dehumanizing and valueless education. It is therefore necessary to look behind the deceptive mask of semantics and examine the true meaning of these humanistic terms.

Although humanism places man on a pinnacle, in the end it debases him into an animal. Since God is dead, man is God; man is the sole determiner of his own values. As with the pragmatic approach of John Dewey, truth is "what works"; therefore, all values are relative. According to humanists, neither God, Freud, nor Marx makes individuals; man makes himself. But since God is dead and there are no moral absolutes, humanism destroys man's dignity. Humanists often cry the loudest for a world of tolerance, compassion and humaneness, but they are often the ones who reveal their "noble" behavior—they advocate abortion, suicide, and euthanasia.

Despite high goals of personal freedom and social responsibility, children reared in humanistic fashion have claimed their inherent right to freedom. Yet in the process they have abrogated social responsibility. Selfishness is characteristic of humanism; one can detect a horrible apathy and callousness in youth trained in permissive schools. Why does humanism breed inhumanity? It fails to produce humans with true compassion because, when self-satisfaction is the goal of living, anything that destroys this feeling of satisfaction becomes evil. "No!" cries humanism; our goal is self-satisfaction plus social responsibility. The dilemma occurs when individuals who express social responsibility must often sacrifice self-pleasure. Since humanism debases man into an animal, the moral imperative is lacking. Therefore, social responsibility is rejected for self-indulgence. Humanism repudiates theism, but it is faith in God that provides meaning for life, dignity to man, and love for neighbor. Since man is not an animal but a created being, man has a future, social responsibility is practiced, and morality has meaning.

Take, for example, theistic and humanistic treatment of criminals. The historical creed of man's fall permitted an insight into both man's potential goodness and his cruelty. Humanism believes man is born only with the capability of doing good; it therefore excuses man's cruelty and blames society or environment or both. Consequently, humanism perverts justice because it acquits the perpetrators of crime, and these criminals in turn prey upon the innocent. Theism blames man's cruelty on his fall but instead of leaving man there it offers him power through faith in God to alter his fallen nature and also offers forgiveness.

Our founding fathers in uniting God and state recognized that, since help was available for individuals to change their deviant behavior, anyone who refused to change and engaged in criminal misconduct was guilty and deserved punishment. Rather than constantly looking for excuses for criminal behavior, theism punishes criminals and offers programs for reform. Our historical criminal justice system is based on this Judeo-Christian ethic. Departure from these concepts has produced the escalating crime wave. We need a new understanding of man's guilt and the right of society to insist on proper moral behavior.

In a Judeo-Christian culture lawmakers and judges do not just look into their own minds to formulate the laws for a safe and just society; they also look into the Bible to determine principles of justice. In 1963 Supreme Court Justice William Brennan stated, "Nearly every criminal law on the books can be traced to some religious principle or inspiration."[1] Many of the evils in today's society can be traced to a breakdown of law. Increasingly we hear of political leaders who advocate law and order, yet upon being elected effect little change. Why? They are not necessarily using law and order themes as political ploys to get elected. Rather, it is often permissive laws and judges that prevent effective criminal procedures from being implemented. This humanistic trend of excusing the guilty has brought about much of the grave criminal crisis in the schools and nation.

Theism and Human Rights

Along with the equitable punishment of the guilty, the theistic heritage has held proper human rights in highest regard. Although theists have often failed to obey the precepts of their faith, yet the potential was there. Humanism, in contrast, is not a protector of human rights; its libertine concepts protect debauchery, lawlessness, and immorality. Believers in the historic Judeo-Christian ethic support human rights and emancipation for the human spirit within the concepts of decency and justice. These rights give dignity to man, along with liberty and happiness.

Carl F. H. Henry says the United States Declaration of Independence "identifies the divine Creator as the transcendent source and sanction of human rights. To a radically secular society, this may seem to be a bit of quaint poetry. But the fact remains that the insistence of the classic American political documents on a transcendent source and sanction of human rights (whether it was ventured on theistic or deistic principles or both we need not argue here) is of immense importance." The writers of the Declaration of Independence did not hesitate to declare God's transcendent claim upon mankind, Henry notes, and "the fact that we today are less disposed to say so indicates how deeply naturalistic secularism has penetrated our own society."

Henry relates how "at a Bicentennial education conference in Philadelphia last year, a key speaker commended the historic American political documents for their distinctive emphasis on human rights. But when I asked whether the philosophy department of any great public university in America today espouses the supernaturalistic world-and-life view presupposed by the Declaration of Independence when it asserts that there are inalienable rights grounded in divine creation and preservation, the answer was crystal clear. What now dominates the intellectual arena is a naturalistic evolutionary philosophy or a radically secular view of reality and life.

"This antisupernaturalistic, anti-God development ought to chill our souls. Neither a utopian evolutionary philosophy nor a radically secular alternative can persuasively maintain the case for human rights. A merely evolutionary view of human origins and development cannot vindicate either the permanent or the universal dignity of mankind."[2]

Constitutional Democracy

It is important to understand the structure of the United States government so one can intelligently promote the national well-being. America does not have a pure democracy; it has a constitutional democracy. In a pure democracy 51 percent of the people rule; if the majority decided that all blacks should be lynched, this would be law and considered right. Pure democracy can become mob rule. Though Pontius Pilate knew Jesus was falsely accused and was innocent, he employed the principles of democracy to escape the unpopular reactions of the multitude by asking them what he should do—the crowd roared, "Crucify him! Crucify him!"

Effective democracy must have some sort of inner control, for democracy by itself does not contain a moral force. For this reason our national founders did not formulate a simple democracy; instead, they formed a constitutional democracy based on theistic faith, which gave America a strong moral cohesiveness. Thus they established certain laws that no simple majority could change.

From what source do America's concepts of human rights come? Not from democratic concepts, but from the Constitution, which provides all citizens the right of freedom of religion, speech, press, assembly, and petition. Because of the Constitution, individuals can stand against the majority, expose its evils, and succeed, and without this right, minorities would be defenseless. Where did the principles of the Constitution originate? In the consciences of the people, who used the Bible as the framework for their values. They could confidently state in the Declaration of Independence, "We hold these truths to be self-evident, that they are endowed by their Creator with certain unalienable rights." The reason freedom of speech, religion, and press was so liberally provided in the founding of our nation was that moral values were well established. When our forefathers spoke of separation of a national church and federal government, it never entered their minds that prayer to God would one day be declared illegal in a public institution; otherwise they would have rejected Benjamin Franklin's proposal. When freedom of speech and press were established, profanity and pornography would never be included because of the moral standards of that day. They would have been universally considered a perversion of freedom.

Perpetuating America's Heritage

America needs to be awakened to the concepts of our constitutional republic that have so greatly prospered the nation. Moreover, our children need to be educated to understand that form of government. Unfortunately, because of humanistic forces many schools are not perpetuating the American heritage. Unless America regains its spiritual basics, it will be wrecked on the rocks of its own freedom. Freedom without control breeds license, for under the guise of freedom, libertarians pedal their degenerate behavior and concepts. At the same time they suppress religious freedom and speech under the guise of separation of church and state.

The Senate Judiciary Committee had a hearing concerning school prayer. Seventeen-year-old Bonnie Bailey, chosen as the 1982 YMCA Governor of Texas, joined Secretary Terrel Bell and others in stressing that schools should permit voluntary Bible study and prayer before or after school hours, just as they do extracurricular sports, dramatics, and other activities. "We can picket, demonstrate, curse and take God's name in vain, but we can't voluntarily get together and talk about God at school," said Miss Bailey, a high school senior from Lubbock. "I can decide if I want an abortion or use contraceptives, but I can't decide if I want to come to a meeting to talk about religious matters before or after school. To me, that just isn't fair.

Previous to the hearing the ACLU won a court case against the Lubbock school board for permitting high school students to gather during nonclass hours for religious purposes. Terrel Bell asked, "If a public school allows students to meet before or after school to discuss or engage in politics, social activism or athletics, why should the rule change just because the students happen to be religious?"

Other students testified before the committee. William F. Kidd, of Anoka, Minnesota, and 11 other students were told that they may be suspended from school and also have their senior diplomas withheld. Their crime? They distributed a self-published Christian student newspaper in school.

Miss Scanlon told how her Christian club could not meet at school during lunch because of school board orders. Yet her school had a special smoking section. Moreover, when one of her teachers was talking about alternative life-styles, a prostitute was invited to speak to the students.[3]

Professor Norval Morris, dean of the University of Chicago Law School, coauthored a book with Gordon Hawkins, *The Honest Politicians Guide to Crime Control*, which outlines ways to "curb" crime. One is "total abolition" of capital punishment. "Capital punishment is irrelevant to the murder, or attempted, murder rate. . . . If, therefore, we are to be sincere in our efforts to reduce violence, there is one type of violence that we can with complete certainty eliminate. That is the killing of criminals by the state."

All drugs are to be decriminalized, including cocaine and heroin. "Neither the acquisition, purchase, possession, nor the use of any drug will be a criminal offense." Remove police units dealing with organized crime. The authors want "to exorcise the myth of organized crime," and they propose that "all special organized crime units in federal and state justice and police departments shall be disbanded." They want drunkenness to "cease to be a criminal offence" and stipulate the eliminating of disorderly conduct and vagrancy laws, removing all criminal statutes against gambling and prostitution, and ending jail terms for the performance of abortion and statutory rape. The abolition of all criminal penalties for sexual behavior, including "bigamy, incest, sodomy, bestiality, homosexuality, pornography and obscenity," is called for. And it is unjust to put anyone in prison for "failure to support one's family." Amazingly, in 1978 the president of the United States of America wanted Professor Morris to head the federal Law Enforcement Assistance Administration (LEAA), which distributes yearly 647 million dollars to combat crime.[4]

Time reports the unveiling of a new humanistic bill:

> While the Vatican was anchoring age-old religious views on sex, those who make a religion out of non-religion were decreeing the opposite in the name of freedom. In the current *Humanist*, a bi-monthly magazine published for the American Humanist Association and the Ethical Culture movement, 34 sexologists have unveiled their "New Bill of Sexual Rights and Responsibilities."
>
> The humanists celebrate "responsible" freedom after centuries of "bondage to church or state." Marriage "where viable" is "a cherished human relationship," but "other sexual relationships also are significant." The 34 signers predict a growing acceptance of premarital, homosexual and bisexual relations. Though prostitution, sadomasochism and fetishism are gently tut-tutted as "limiting," the humanists state that if they are to be discouraged, it should be through education, not laws.[5]

Jefferson rightly stressed that democracy needs an educated populace, but democracy also needs an inner moral force. Education alone can produce intellectual beasts. It was educated Nazis who massacred six million Jews and atheistic communists who slaughtered untold millions. The majority of Americans want transmitted to their children, not only an education, but also their historical theistic culture, and this culture is in direct opposition to the aims of humanism.

Humanism under the guise of human betterment promotes issues that make schools a primary agent of societal change, rather than a primary agent to develop student's intellectual capabilities. These two views are demonstrated by the following statements. The National Education Association says:

> The most controversial issues of the 21st century will pertain to the ends and means of human behavior and who will determine them. The first educational question will not be "What knowledge is of most worth?" but "What kind of human behavior do we wish to produce?"[6]

In contrast, the Policy Book of the Arizona State Board of Education states,

> The schools have neither the chief responsibility nor the means for dealing with all aspects of personal development. . . . It is not the job of the schools to create a new social order. . . . Students can develop the competency necessary to carry on the jobs of society only through the mastery of the skills, knowledge and thought which embody the major achievements of civilization.[7]

Many educational leaders operate on the basis of the concepts of the National Education Association; they believe they have the *right* to change children's values and behavior for whatever they consider the "better." W. W. Harmon, director of educational research policy at Stanford Research Institute, states, in *The Forward Edge of Education*, "As we enter the third half of the 20th century, it is now feasible not just to predict the future but to *DESIGN* the future . . . we can no longer view education solely as the passing on of the culture to the next generation, it is in addition the PRIMARY TOOL for SHAPING the future."[8] But who provides educators the right to change our children? When parents send their children to schools, they expect the schools to educate their children and educators to uphold the common values of society. Parents do not give the schools the license to remake their children into new humanistic social beings.

Collapse of Civilization

Today, our nation is facing its worst crisis because humanism is destroying not only our children but also America's moral foundation. Furthermore, children trained in today's humanistic educational system will become tomorrow's parents and leaders. In the *New York Times News Service* Edward B. Fiske reports, "A group of 41 governors, corporate leaders and other prominent figures asserted here that the poor quality of U.S. public schools was threatening the military, economic and social well-being of the country."[9]

Concerned leaders, seeing the unparalleled deterioration of moral responsibility, raise the terrifying question: Is Western civilization on the verge of collapse? General Douglas MacArthur said, "History fails to record a single precedent in which nations subject to moral decay have not passed into political and economic decline. There has been either a spiritual awakening to overcome the moral lapse, or a progressive deterioration leading to ultimate national disaster."[10]

Arnold Toynbee, author of the six-volume, *Study of History*, stressed the role of religion in major civilizations. Nations encounter and overcome a physical, moral, or military challenge. From this victory a creative minority emerges that offers moral and spiritual leadership, causing the civilization to prosper. Disintegration occurs when either the creative leadership loses its vision or the people refuse to follow.[11]

Traditional moral standards have been eroding in America for decades, but they suffered a devastating blow when the Warren Court ruled unconstitutional state rights allowing teachers to pray and read the Bible. In addition, the Warren Court removed many state laws protecting society from exploitation of sex for mercenary ends. Encouraged by these permissive decisions of the Supreme Court, newsstands began blatantly to expose their pornomagazines, theaters and TV exploited sexual perversions, and massage parlors and topless bars emerged in many cities.

Dr. James Dobson, in his book *Dare to Discipline*, states:

> Not everyone in our society has allowed passion to overrule judgment. There are those who still believe, as I do, that sexual irresponsibility carries an enormous price tag for the momentary pleasure it promises. Despite the reasuring philosophy of Hugh Heffner and his Playmates, sexual "freedom" is a direct thoroughfare to disillusionment, emptiness, divorce, venereal disease, illegitimacy, and broken lives. Not only do promiscuous individuals suffer adverse consequences; history reveals that entire societies begin to deteriorate when free love reaches a position of social acceptance. This fact was first illuminated by J. D. Unwin, a British social anthropologist who spent seven years studying the births and deaths of eighty civilizations. He reported from his exhaustive research that every known culture in the world's history has followed the same sexual pattern: during its early days of existence, premarital and extramarital sexual relationships were strictly prohibited. Great creative energy was associated with this inhibition of sexual expression, causing the culture to prosper. Much later in the life of the society, its people began to rebel against the strict prohibitions, demanding the freedom to release their internal passions. As

the mores weakened, the social energy abated, eventually
resulting in the decay or destruction of the civilization. Dr.
Unwin stated that the energy which holds a society together is
sexual in nature. When a man is devoted to one woman and
one family, he is motivated to build, save, protect, plan and
prosper on their behalf. However, when his sexual interests are
dispersed and generalized, his effort is invested in the gratification of sensual desires. Dr. Unwin concluded: "Any human
society is free either to display great energy, or to enjoy sexual
freedom; the evidence is that they cannot do both for more than
one generation."[12]

America is being destroyed by the new standards of sexual
license, but we should not be shocked at what is happening to
American youth—schools have trained children in this behavior.
Instead of being a bulwark for morality and faith in God, schools
promote immorality and atheism. E. M. Blaiklock, who held the chair
of classics at the University of Auckland, New Zealand, for 21 years
and taught Latin, Greek, and ancient and biblical history for 42
years, said:

> I am now going to be positive. As a historian, I assure you
> that Toynbee was right in this: all human cultures grow round a
> central core of moral ideas and ideals that command obe-
> dience, respect, and general observance. There is right and
> there is wrong, both unquestioned. This is what is called the
> "ethos" of a people, of a culture.
> Early Rome had something called *pietas*. We have borrowed
> the word twice, as "piety" and "pity," neither of which repre-
> sents the old Roman virtue and mainstay of society: a loyalty to
> family and state, a courageous sense of duty, trustiness. Try the
> truth of this in all societies. Some central core holds all
> together. . . .
> But this anticipates. The "ethos" of Western civilization,
> once called Christendom, is the Christian faith, its central
> beliefs, its ethics. Hence the love of liberty of which we boast,
> the reverence for human life, the old stabilities of marriage,
> honor, care for the weak. They derive from the deep truth that
> Christ died to save lost human beings. This moral core, the
> heart of it all, the strength by which it stands, is embedded in
> the Bible, the book that transformed Britain when it was let
> loose upon the people in the days of the first Elizabeth. All this
> is history. It is thus that Britain, indeed the English-speaking
> peoples, rose to stature, leadership, and strength. It is thus that

nations rise and serve their era, and make their contribution to mankind.

And thus they pass away, for commonly in the story of a nation's rise and fall comes the time when the authority of the ideal is questioned. There comes a moment when, in the phrase of the great and mordant historian, the Roman, Tacitus, a group discovers that "what authority had kept hidden" can be challenged and outfaced. There comes "permissiveness." It is the beginning of the end, unless, intelligent enough, frightened enough, dowed sufficiently with courageous leadership, or swept by a revival of faith, a people rallies and returns to strength.

Unless that happens, "as surely as water will wet us, as surely as fire will burn," that people dies. There is always another race, disciplined, moral, rigid in its attitudes, waiting to apply its strong thrust to the crumbling structure.[13]

While the moral core of our nation falters, America is faced by an organized force whose stated goal is to conquer the world. Nobel Prize-winner Aleksander Solzhenitsyn, the noted former Russian political prisoner and author of *The Gulag Archipelago*, said, "The communist ideology is to destroy your society. This has been their aim for 125 years and has never changed; only the methods have changed."[14]

There are two ways to destroy a society: by overpowering it from without by the use of superior military might, or by overpowering it from within by encouraging such forces as will foster internal moral decay. Communist Lenin realized how to conquer a nation without force when he wrote, "Demoralize the youth and the revolution is won."[15] Today's schools are doing an efficient job of demoralizing youth.

How long can the nation survive when permissive leaders are allowed to destroy students with their humanistic values? Representative democracy is an excellent concept, but it is only as good as its people. When youth become immoral, then democracy will lead to disaster. Look at today's society with its rapid mushrooming of divorce, broken homes, pornography, sexual license, unwed mothers, disrespect for authority, juvenile delinquency and crime. It can only lead to national destruction.

Three Value Systems

When as a parent I objected to a high school sex education program because of its lack of moral direction, I was offered the argument "Whose morals shall we teach?" This is a legitimate question, and one that must be answered.

There are three basic value systems for establishing morality:
1. Humanism—man determines his own value system.
2. Communism—the state determines the value system.
3. Theism—God determines the value system.

Let us examine these value systems in the light of a situation that occurred while I was a substitute teacher in an eighth-grade class in a Lower East Side junior high school in Manhattan. I questioned some boys about their life goals in hopes of stimulating them to strive for a good education. Their immediate reaction was that they aimed at an easy life as criminals and pimps. How would each value system answer these pupils?

1. Humanists could not categorically say that crime was wrong; only if the crime injures another is it wrong. They would discourage crime; however, certain humanists could easily rationalize stealing, in view of unemployment and if only the rich were victimized. Humanists are against sexual exploitation, yet working as a pimp could be considered beneficial: Men are made happy, the pimp is making a living, and prostitutes have an income. Humanists favor decriminalization for such "nonvictimless" crimes as using drugs or engaging in pornography, prostitution, incest, and homosexuality. The fact that such acts may destroy a society is unimportant; human happiness is the criterion for morality.

2. Communists would first evaluate whether the state would benefit from crime or prostitution. If they are in the minority, they favor freedom, like the humanists, knowing it will benefit their cause. However, once communists obtain power, they reject crime and immorality because they recognize that these evils harm society.

3. Theists categorically condemn engagement in criminal behavior or prostitution because of God's commandments against stealing and immorality. A theistic culture passes laws that reflect its beliefs and punishes offenders. America's theistic heritage has provided our nation with such a moral framework, yet humanism has become the dominant educational philosophy and has rejected these absolutes.

In pursuing its goals humanism has deified man by making him free to determine his own values, even to the point of his own ruin. In contrast, communism has deified the state instead of man. Nevertheless, the basic concept of communism is humanistic; it concentrates on man's interests and values in his world. The favorite maxim of Karl Marx was: "I believe nothing human to be alien to me."[16] Though this Marxist concept fits perfectly into the humanistic philosophy that "moral values derive their source from human experience" and "ethics are autonomous and situational," in communism the state supersedes man. Because the state is deified, communism has produced a rigid moral system: whatever does not benefit the state must be suppressed.

How can communists be both humanistic and strict moralists? To overcome a nation, communists are the greatest champions for personal freedom and permissive policies. They know that in this atmosphere they can freely propagate their views to cause internal decay. They realize that a strong and vibrant society does not turn to communism; therefore, a nation must first be disrupted for communism to succeed. But once communists gain power, their schizophrenic nature emerges; they become ultra-authoritative and repressive. In order to promote their humanistic utopias, communists have used police spies to control their people, instituted vicious religious persecution, utilized concentration camps, drugged dissidents in mental institutions, used torture chambers, and murdered millions of innocent victims.

Some will charge communists with being inconsistent and criminal, but to themselves they are not. Morality has to do with what benefits the state, and, all morals being relative, any act benefiting the state is good and therefore moral. Human rights mean nothing when they interfere with communistic designs. Humanism is a perfect tool for communists; we need to be aware that such deceptive forces are active in our society to "destroy the establishment." The former leader of the Black Panther party, Eldridge Cleaver, spent several years abroad to avoid a possible prison term. After visiting many communistic countries he turned against communism and voluntarily returned to the United States, even at the risk of serving time in prison. The communists, he said, have a three-way plan to defeat the United States: (1) Isolate America by alienating the developing nations. (2) Achieve military superiority. (3) Promote subversion from within.[17]

An excellent strategy to destroy America internally would be to weaken the foundation of morality by insisting on separation of church and state until every concept of God is eliminated from our national life as it is in communist Russia. Next, slowly begin to attack every vestige of morality by allowing every divergent culture and lifestyle to exist in the name of freedom. Advocate freedom of the media for violence and pornography. Champion the cause for homosexuals, lesbians, and prostitutes. Break down the moral traditions of virginity, marriage, unity of the family, and authority of parents. Promote easy divorce and excessive children's rights. Insist on extreme criminal rights even at the expense of the innocent. Concentrate on supporting school issues that will have the effect of producing ignorant, degenerate, and undisciplined youth. Then, when the nation has become demoralized and defenseless, attack, either by threat or by force.

Dr. Bob Simonds gives this report in his article on "How Humanism Took Over American Thought-Life":

> To augment the educational take-over of America's mind, the Humanists founded the *American Civil Liberties Union* as the Humanist's legal arm. The ACLU was founded by the Humanist Society, and the Ethical Culture Union by Dr. Harry Ward. Dr. Ward's positions on socialism perfectly paralleled those of the Communist Manifesto. William Z. Foster, former head of the U.S. Communist Party, was the founder of the ACLU, along with John Dewey, Clarence Darrow and Corliss Lamont. The U.S. House of Representatives' Committee, investigating communist activities, wrote: "The American Civil Liberties Union is closely affiliated with the communist movement in the United States, and fully 90% of its efforts are in behalf of communists who have come into conflict with the law."
>
> The Humanist Society and the ACLU, declared the 60's as "The Battle for Racial Rights" (to win the support of the common man); the 70's were "The Battle for Sexual (homosexual) Rights and Freedom"; and the 80's "The Battle Against Religious Rights."
>
> The ACLU has fought vociferously against the use of the Bible or the religious study of our American heritage in the public schools. They have tried to remove prayer from government functions (even congress). They have fought the rights of religious freedom of speech, specially on campus. They have fought for sexual freedoms of homosexuals, deviates and child molesters and against the religious rights of students. They have misinformed school administrators across America on every major Supreme Court decision in favor of religion.
>
> They even sent out "U.S. Guidelines" to all the school administrators over the "prayer ban" case, totally twisting the court's rulings. Even though the ACLU has been sternly corrected by the Congress and the courts, many school administrators still use them as law.[18]

George F. Will, Pulitzer Prize-winning columnist, gave this report on how far the ACLU will go to remove any vestige of faith in God in a public institution:

> The U.S. CONSTITUTION has, according to a New Jersey judge and the American Civil Liberties Union, been ravished. The instrument of this outrage is a New Jersey law which the judge says "is unconstitutional on its face and as applied, in that it violates the First and Fourteenth Amendments . . . and

that immediate and irreparable injury will result to plain-
tiffs. . . ."

Whoa! The law that is pregnant with such awfulness says:
"Principals and teachers in each public elementary and
secondary school . . . shall permit students to observe a one-
minute period of silence to be used solely at the discretion of
the individual student, before the opening exercises of each
school day, for quiet and private contemplation or introspec-
tion."

According to the ACLU, that violates the constitutional
guarantee against "establishment" of religion.

What is the injury—the irreparable injury—that a minute of
silence will cause to anyone? No doubt a few children and
parents will find it offensive that someone may use the minute
for prayer. But since when is it an "injury" to be offended by
what might be going on in someone's head? Such chaos is
what a society comes to when it believes that every grievance
should be expressed as a conflict of individual rights, and that
every conflict should be adjudicated.

The ACLU's bullying litigation is designed not to protect the
plaintiff (a student) but to compel others to behave as the
plaintiff prefers. A lawyer for New Jersey's Legislature argues
that the law is constitutional because it is "neutral with respect
to any religious content." The legislator who sponsored it says:
"All we did was provide the opportunity for contemplation,"
and regarding the possibility that someone might silently pray,
he says: "Who has the right, in this day and age, to determine
that any thoughts someone has could violate the Constitution?"

An ACLU lawyer says New Jersey must "prove that nowhere
among the purposes of the law is the opportunity for prayer."
Opportunity? Perhaps the ACLU will soon say that a state
"establishes" religion unless its schools make contemplation
impossible for even a minute. (Many schools do make it
difficult.) But even today, after some bizarre Supreme Court
rulings, the ACLU lawyer may be correct about what New
Jersey must prove. . . .

The ACLU is a political organization pursuing its agenda
primarily through litigation rather than legislation—often an
authoritarian shortcut around the democratic process.[19]

Rebuilding America

For a strong America, our nation needs to return to its spiritual
heritage. It must be decided whether we will accept the theistic ethic
upon which the founding fathers built the United States or the
religion of humanism. In addition, the courts must reflect our

constitutional heritage as found in the Judeo-Christian ethic or else we are in deep trouble. National survival depends on perpetuating the moral values upon which America was founded. Abraham Lincoln wisely said, "The only assurance of our nation's safety is to lay our foundations in morality and religion."[20]

John Witherspoon, one of the signers of the Declaration of Independence, declared, "He is the best friend to American liberty who is most sincere and active in promoting true and undefiled religion. . . . Whoever is an enemy to God, I scruple not to call him an enemy to his country." He concluded, "God grant that in America, true religion and civil liberty may be inseparable."[21]

George Washington clearly brought out the importance of uniting God and state to produce a national morality:

> Of all the dispositions and habits, which lead to political prosperity, Religion and morality are indispensable supports.— In vain would that man claim the tribute of Patriotism, who should labour to subvert these great Pillars of human happiness, these firmest props of the duties of Men and Citizens.— The mere Politician, equally with the pious man, ought to respect and to cherish them.—A volume could not trace all their connexions with private and public felicity.—Let it simply be asked where is the security for property, for reputation, for life, if the sense of religious obligation desert the oaths, which are the instruments of investigation in Courts of Justice? And let us with caution indulge the supposition, that morality can be maintained without religion.—Whatever may be conceded to the influence of refined education on minds of peculiar structure—reason and experience both forbid us to expect, that national morality can prevail in exclusion of religious principle.[22]

Alexis de Tocqueville was a French statesman and political philosopher, whose studies of American democracy and the French Revolution were two of the most original and perceptive books of the nineteenth century. He came to the United States to investigate the American penal system. However, in the beginning of his visit he intended also to study American democracy. His observations resulted in a report on the American penal system, and then he published his first masterpiece: *De la démocratie en Amérique (Democracy in America)*. The work was an immediate success, winning him a seat in the Académie francaise. In his observation of American democratic institutions Tocqueville said that, unlike despotism, liberty cannot "govern without faith."[23]

The Blackout
Many colonial leaders firmly believed that religious faith was

essential for the proper working of our government. However, many Americans today reject its principles and embrace atheistic humanism as their guiding force. An example of this rejection of our civil faith occurred the night of Wednesday, July 13, 1977, when a bolt of lightning triggered a chain reaction that produced a massive 25-hour blackout for New York City. The power loss also triggered a moral catastrophe. Widespread looting and rioting caused 18,000 merchants to suffer losses costing 310 million dollars; 23,722 fire alarms were sounded, involving 900 fires, in one of which 22 firemen were hurt; 3,776 arrests were made; and 123 policemen were injured.

The *New York Times* commenting on the blackout reports: "Throughout the city, groups of 30 to 40 people, mainly teen-agers, gathered outside the vandalized stores, urging one another: 'Lets do it, let's do it.' After breaking into a store, they fled upon hearing a police siren. But, soon after, if not arrested they would smash another window or pull apart a protective door grating.

"Officer Gary Parlefsky of the 30th Precinct in Harlem said that, while trying to arrest looters, he and other officers came under fire from guns, bottles and rocks.

"'We were scared to death,' said the 30-year old policeman. 'Anyone who says he was not is lying—but worse than that, the blue uniform didn't mean a thing.'

"'They couldn't understand why we were arresting them,' continued Officer Parlefsky. 'They were angry with us. They said: 'I'm on welfare. I'm taking what I need. What are you bothering me for?' "[24]

Some looters felt no guilt. "We're doing right," insisted a teenager. "I got a whole bedroom and living-room set. I got a wardrobe. And what I don't need or what I can't wear, I'll give to people who do need it. There's no real big thing about it." A police lieutenant commented, "I'm not surprised at what happened. Here was an opportunity of something for nothing. There was no concept of a moral issue involved. The spirit was carnival."[25] *Time* notes, "A number of looters were robbed in turn by other thieves, who clawed and wrenched away their booty. When two men in Bushwick wearily set down a heavy box of shoes, a band of youths swooped in like vultures and made off with the prize. A teen-age girl on Manhattan's upper West Side complained to friends that some boys had offered to help carry away clothes and radios, then had stolen them from her. Said she, with the skewed logic of the looters: 'That's just not right. They shouldn't have done that.' "[26]

Some people blame the looting on poverty, but of the 176 individuals indicted for looting, nearly 50 percent had full-time jobs, and less than 10 percent were on welfare. One columnist said, "Nor was this an example of people driven by desperation to reach out for necessities. They took toasters, not bread; liquor, not milk; more sports shirts for the sporty than shoes for the shoeless. One of the participants aptly called the evil carnival atmosphere 'Christmas in July.' "[27]

Not only did the looters steal, but what some could not carry they destroyed. A chandelier was smashed to pieces, couches were slashed with knives, glass-topped tables were smashed, bookcases were pulled over, and stores were set on fire. Emit M. Bernath, a Rumanian who survived the Nazi concentration camps, had a furniture and lumber store in Manhattan. He delighted in helping neighborhood schools by providing lumber for the children. His walls were lined with pictures of first- and second-graders and thank-you notes from recipients of his generosity. On the night of the blackout a mob broke into his store and stole thousands of dollars' worth of bookcases, beds, cabinets, tables, and other furniture, leaving his store in shambles. "For 25 years I've helped all the children—black children, white children, Catholic and not Catholic, colored and not colored and all kinds of children," Bernath said. "I went through Aushwitz and Buchenwald—the only difference is that there they wore boots and here they wore sneakers."[28]

The looting was not racial revenge; many of the victims were themselves minorities. *Time* reports, "Stores owned by blacks and Hispanics suffered the same fate as those operated by whites. In Brooklyn, the Fort Green cooperative supermarket—set up by low-income blacks after the 1968 riots—was stripped bare. The store had no steel window guards because, said Manager Clifford Thomas, 'we thought we were part of the community. We were wrong.' "[29]

Throughout this book it has been stressed that lack of discipline and the humanistic permissive policies were destroying the youth of America. The *New York Times* notes that most looters were teenagers;[30] thus they either were still in school or had recently left. The *New York Times* also reported that "the heaviest hit areas were the primarily black and Hispanic neighborhoods of Harlem and East Harlem, the South Bronx, the Bedford-Stuyvesant, Bushwick and Crown Heights in Brooklyn and Jamaica, Queens."[31] It was quite coincidental that prior to this blackout I was a substitute teacher in each of these neighborhoods except East Harlem and Crown Heights (however, some of the schools were very near these areas), and it was in these same schools that I experienced the shocking undisciplined conditions.

The discipline breakdown in the schools has shown itself in a breakdown of neighborhood discipline. These teenagers put into practice the humanistic concept of situation ethics: There are no moral absolutes—each situation determines whether an act is right or wrong. As William Safire points out, "The looters looted because of the spreading non-ethic that stealing is O.K. if you can get away with it, as you usually can; that only a jerk passes up an opportunity to rip off his neighbor: that society not only owes you a living, but the good life."[32]

What transpired was a moral breakdown. New York City has been a bastion for liberal humanism for decades; the seeds just sprouted and bore fruit. Can America continue to sit back and watch as more and more of its cities and youth are destroyed? Will we wake up and learn and take action?

The Silent Majority

When George Gallup took a survey on the religious faith of Americans, an overwhelming 94 percent of the respondents stated that they believed in God.[33] It is time for this silent majority once and for all unashamedly to declare their faith in God and return America to its foundational strengths. Atheistic humanism has clearly taken over the schools, and the guiding light of our theistic heritage has been snuffed out. A few atheists have destroyed in children's minds the principles that made our nation great. No longer can we rightfully say we are "one nation under God"; rather, we are now "one nation under Man."

We have yet to reap the disastrous effects of this permissive immoral education that has been implanted in the hearts and minds of our youth. New York City's blackout was a mere token of future disasters. Much of the good left in America results from the inertia of our historic faith, but this borrowing from the past cannot continue. There must be a renewal of faith to keep America strong.

Since the overwhelming majority believe in the historical Judeo-Christian ethic, it is imperative that they uphold its standards as a code of conduct and resist the small band of humanist educators who try to make us believe we are supporting church and state. Our earlier constitutional democracy inspired nations to emulate us. In recent years, however, since humanism has become the standard for American morality, many nations reject our form of government. Freedom is cherished worldwide, but our present brand of freedom, which results in broken homes, violence, drugs, crime, juvenile delinquency, and perverted sex, is spurned by world leaders.

If the full implications of humanism were evident to the American people, they would overwhelmingly oppose it and our historical theistic faith would be restored. To counteract atheistic humanism, all Americans who believe in our theistic heritage should boldly proclaim their faith in God to revitalize our spiritual roots. Many have felt ashamed to declare their faith in God in a public institution because they themselves have been the victims of the progressive educational experience in which that faith as the foundation of our government was either repudiated or ignored. Humanism has now been exposed. No longer do Americans need to be ashamed to declare their faith in God publicly.

The philosophy of humanism vs. theism is not only an issue for our schools but the major issue of how our country is governed. The future prosperity of America hinges on which philosophy gains ascendance. It is crucial for the dedicated minority who understand that our national values are based upon a theistic heritage to go forth and stir the American people to action. The substitution of humanism for theism for our guiding light has caused the massive deterioration in schools and society. There needs to be a moral cry from every hamlet, town, and city for the restoration of the historical values as provided by our founding fathers to bring our youth and nation out of moral chaos and disintegration.

Part VI

Conclusion

Chapter 18

Tomorrow's Students: Actions for Success

Across the nation widespread disillusionment is evidenced by protesting parents and taxpayers over reported failures and mushrooming expenditures for education. They want more value from the billions of dollars that will be spent annually on elementary and secondary public school students. The "baby boom" is over, and there is a growing danger of a split between the American public and the school establishment. Their disgust is shown by the increasing votes against the spiraling funding for educational programs. The disgust is not unjustified; many of today's youth problems can be traced to faulty educational training: the massive decline in the basics, the increased juvenile violence and crime, and the rampant adolescent moral deterioration.

There are, however, practical solutions.

Educational Solutions

Eliminate automatic advancement by providing a program of achievement promotion that will guarantee minimum competency for each grade.

Institute educational standards and a system of accountability for students and teachers that will ensure mastery of basics.

Adopt reasonable educational standards for high school graduation.

Use ability grouping for effective teaching.

Develop interesting and practical educational programs that will properly prepare students for their future.

Disciplinal Solutions

Insist on proper student behavior so schools can maintain an effective learning atmosphere.

Utilize preventive teaching techniques to avoid discipline problems.

Give teachers the legal right to act *in loco parentis,* which includes the judicious use of corporal punishment.

Remove the few unruly youth who refuse to submit to proper authority.

Create a fair, firm, and loving atmosphere.

Racial Solutions

Eliminate forced busing, which removes children from neighborhood schools.

Provide immediate remedial work to help students achieve rather than lower educational standards for nonachievers.

Insist on quality education in a disciplined environment.

Provide the proven method of fundamental education that expects all children to learn and is beneficial for all races.

Moral Solutions

Provide states the option to permit teachers to pray and to read the Bible in order to teach children that our national moral values are derived from faith in God.

Eliminate sensitivity training and programs that invade the privacy of children for the purpose of desensitizing them for humanistic resocialization.

Promote America's traditional and legal ethical standards in courses and textbooks instead of the immoral concepts of atheistic humanism.

The implementation of these solutions will revolutionize the educational system and the nation. Success can be achieved. However, the difficulty is that public schools are controlled by an entrenched group of progressive leaders who adhere to atheistic humanism as their educational philosophy. The largest group of signers of the 1973 Humanist Manifesto were university-level American educators who continue to perpetuate the progressive concepts of John Dewey. Many leading universities are dominated by these humanists who train the teachers; the teachers in turn propagate these progressive principles to students; and many students incorporate the principles in their life-styles. Instead of transmitting our historical traditional values, which the majority of Americans adhere to, educators subtly substitute their subversive programs to build a new social order.

Restrictive Regulations

Many principals and teachers could have successful schools and classes, but regulations imposed by governmental and educational leaders forbid them to incorporate successful solutions. Dr. Richard Vetterli, commenting on the negative effects of government intrusion in fundamental schools in Pasadena, says, "Because most federal education programs tend to promote progressive education and at the same time inhibit the freedom of the individual school districts through rules, orders, restrictions and regulations, fundamental educators look upon federal aid as counter-productive. The fundamental schools in the Pasadena Unified District reject federal funds outright."[1]

A 12-member panel of well-known scholars sponsored by an independent research foundation spent a year and a half research-ing American education. The diverse participants issued, "The report of the Task Force on Federal Elementary and Secondary Education Policy." They said:

> Before putting forward our proposals for a new federal policy on elementary and secondary schooling, we think it useful to identify what has gone wrong. Why, despite spending more per student than every other advanced nation, is there a growing gap between the goals and achievements of our schools?. . .
>
> All too often, though, the nature of federal intervention has been counterproductive, entailing heavy costs and undesirable consequences. Direct federal outlays accounted, at their peak, for less than 10 percent of total annual spending on the schools, but by resorting to compulsory regulation and man-dated programs the federal government has swelled school bureaucracies, imposed dubious and expensive procedures, and forced state and local governments to reallocate substan-tial portions of their scarce revenues. What is more, its em-phasis on promoting equality of opportunity in the public schools has meant a slighting of its commitment to educational quality. Thus, the federal government has not only had a pervasive influence on the spending of local school districts but has undoubtedly played a part in many of the other troubles of the schools.[2]

The disaster in many of New York City's schools is caused primarily by board of education rules. Students are automatically promoted without mastering the basics, teachers cannot properly discipline students, guidelines permit vulgar textbooks, and sex educators must be nonjudgmental on sexual vices. It is difficult to imagine leaders tolerating undisciplined atmospheres in their schools, but I have witnessed such schools. It is schools like these that produce masses of illiterate and undisciplined youth. Also, humanistic textbooks and sex education classes have trained multi-tudes of youth to become immoral.

Private Schools

Out of desperation, scores of parents have abandoned public schools. In the last decade public school enrollment fell 11 percent in the West, while private enrollment rose 19 percent; in the South, enrollment declined 6 percent, while private advanced 31 percent.

Now one out of every eight students goes to private school. A top federal official estimates that a new private school opens every seven hours. In New Orleans, Buffalo, Providence, and Boston half of the school-age children have defected to private schools. When parents were asked in a *Newsweek* survey whether they ever considered sending their children to a private school, more than half said they did.[3] Many parents are so dismayed over the crime, drugs, vandalism, nondiscipline, lax academic standards, and immorality that they are willing to forsake free public education for private. One minister pointed out, "Schools have gone from religion-sponsored to non-religious, then to anti-religious."

The private school movement has been charged with racism. Yet black and Hispanic families account for 17 percent of the total Roman Catholic parochial enrollment, 13 percent of Lutheran school enrollment, and 9 percent of old-line independent school enrollment. From 80 to 90 percent of all private schools belong to the Council for American Private Education, which requires all member schools to be racially nondiscriminatory.[4]

Sociologist James S. Coleman created quite a stir in a government-sponsored report. His study of 58,728 sophomores and seniors in 1,016 high schools revealed that private schools do a better job of education than public schools. The results were still the same even when affluent family backgrounds were discounted. The achievements were due to tougher courses, lots of homework, and better discipline. The "greatest difference found in any aspect of school functioning between public and private schools was in the degree of discipline and order in the schools." Even though private schools have a lower percentage of blacks, Coleman maintained that in some respect private schools are less segregated than public ones.[5]

What aroused the ire of public school officials is that Coleman supported tuition tax credits for parents of students in private schools. This arrangement, he claimed, would aid desegregation by allowing minorities to enter private schools. John C. Esty Jr., president of the National Association of Independent Schools, says, "In the past, many of us in private education have not advocated tuition tax credits, but now because more low- and middle-income families are turning to private schools, with resulting strains on family and schools' financial-aid resources, we are increasingly interested in new forms of support to equalize the right of families to choose what they deem the best education for their children." Esty notes that "twenty-seven percent of families with children in private schools have an income under $15,000; the average cost per student per year is $820—less than one-half the public school figure."[6]

Opponents of tax credits such as Albert Shanker, who heads the American Federation of Teachers, have warned that such aid would lead to the ruin of American Public education.[7] When Secretary of Education T. H. Bell was asked whether such aid would be a big blow to public schools, he replied, "I don't think so. I don't believe that the credits will be so massive that they're going to make an enormous difference in the family budget and cause a big exodus from the public schools. To have alternatives and to have some contrast and even friendly competition is a good thing."[8] Columnist James J. Kilpatrick puts the challenge squarely:

> We lose sight of fundamentals. Why are we spending all this money anyhow? Our public purpose is not public education; our public purpose is education, period. The object of these vast expenditures is to raise our children to be responsible, literate, knowledgeable citizens, capable of making their way in an adult world. The mechanism by which this aim is achieved is immaterial.
>
> In a free society, the people ought to have a right to buy any kind of schooling that will meet these goals. If the public schools serve the public purpose, fine. But to paraphrase the Founding Fathers, if the public school system is destructive of these ends, it is the right of the people to abolish the existing system and to institute a new system that seems to them more likely to effect their desires. Diversity is generally to be preferred to regimentation, and voluntarism is superior to compulsion. As long as we impose "compulsory education," wise public policies should encourage a variety of choices.[9]

Opponents of private school education have other methods to close private schools—use legislation to overburden these schools in meeting state requirements for educators and buildings. However, private schools are resisting; they recognize that to license is to control, and control means being dominated by humanistic standards. One could understand these attacks if children were in dangerous buildings and receiving a defective education, but private schools with their "inferior" educational buildings and teachers are doing a better job teaching children than public institutions. Many of these schools are in churches, which cannot meet the enormous expenses that state-supported institutions receive from tax revenues. Furthermore, one wonders why these schools are safe for children on Sunday but unsafe on Monday.

To produce quality education Americans should permit a greater percentage of parents the option to put their children into private schools by providing vouchers or tax credits. At the same time, they should encourage educational leaders to restore our traditional value system for public schools. Our economic system allows

competing forces to stimulate productivity, and the spirit of competition has brought Americans their high standard of living. Encouraging a public and private school system will apply that same
beneficial pressure to stimulate both kinds of schools to be productive. Provided with vouchers or tax credits many poor and middle-
class parents will also have the liberty to choose the schools they
believe are most beneficial for their children. To avoid the un-
warranted attack on separation of church and state, parents, not
schools, should receive the tax credits or vouchers. Just as, during
World War II and the Korean War, GI's were given the option to
attend secular or religious colleges, so should children today receive
the same privilege. This aid did not bring ruin to public education.

It has been claimed that a dual school system will encourage
children to be exploited in inferior private schools because of
ignorant parents. But the fact that a few parents choose unwisely
should be no reason to deny millions of other parents the freedom to
choose their child's school. Besides, how many children are now
being ruined by public schools? In addition, a dual educational
system will provide an incentive for public school leaders to implement necessary changes to provide quality and proper moral education
for all pupils. When these educators begin to see frustrated parents
removing their children to private schools because of inadequate
training, they will be forced to change or see a greater exodus.

A Time for Action
A tempting solution has been proposed: a purely secular school
and a parochial school system—but this is not the answer. Even if
private school enrollment reaches 25 percent of the student population, we cannot allow the remaining 75 percent to be destroyed by
progressive educators. America was founded upon a theistic value
system, not a secular one. Public schools should promote a nonsectarian faith in God while leaving private schools free to teach
sectarian beliefs. To this end there needs to be an infusion of new
leaders to guide the schools properly and install successful programs. To incorporate such changes is extremely difficult; it will not
be accomplished because problems have been exposed and solutions presented. Neither will change occur at the top, where educational leaders are ingrained with progressive concepts. Change
must come from concerned parents, individuals, and organizations
that will apply firm pressure on leaders to change or bring in new
leaders with better programs.

Americans are concerned over the rapid deterioration of our
society; but many are unaware that schools are a major source of
this breakdown of the traditional national values. The shocking
school conditions have been exposed and documented, and explicit

solutions have been offered. The next step is action by concerned individuals. Militants, activists, and persons aiming to destroy our society have spoken. Now it is time for the silent majority to become an active force for those issues that have made our nation great. Looking back just a few years one can observe the deplorable decline of schools and nation, and the roots of havoc are spreading rapidly. We can no longer stand by and permit ourselves to become so weak that we are unable to resist the systematic destruction of the virtues and principles that formed our nation. The ruinous policies of the gargantuan humanistic educational system must be eliminated.

The moral disintegration of public education can be seen from a statement made 45 years ago by Elwood P. Cubberley, cited as the principal historian of American public education: It was the "settled conviction of our American people" that nothing "contributes so much to the moral uplift" and "to a higher civic virtue" as the public school system.[10] Who would dare say that today?

What is now transpiring is a minority of educational leaders are permitted to discriminate against the values of the majority of Americans. Constitutional lawyer William B. Ball, member of the New York, Pennsylvania, and United States Court bars, has appeared in numerous litigations producing landmark educational decisions. He says:

> Look again at *Engel*. The prayer was the merest expression of theistic sentiment, which, even if persisted in, was not going to radically alter any child's life. Yet the twenty-two-word prayer is now unconstitutional. Compare that with such programs as MACOS or HEW's latest job, "The New Model Me." These later programs go to the very vitals of a child's existence, probe into his family relationships, directly attack Christian values pertaining to many areas of morality, and are capable of severely disorienting a child psychologically. These programs have innumerable ramifications respecting a child's own privacy and familial privacy. Can we venture to say that a handful of people who didn't like Bible reading and praying have rights superior to other people who do not want their children's moral structure destroyed?[11]

People who believe in our historical theistic culture must act. But if we are unwilling to fight for the right, we have no right to complain about the wrong; we deserve what we receive. Once ignorance could be blamed, but no longer. Swiss author Henri Frederic Amid said, "Truth is violated by falsehood, but it is outraged by silence." John A. Howard, president of Rockford College, has shown what happens when good men do nothing.

To a very great extent, the degeneration of public standards of conduct and the increasingly corruptive character of literary, artistic and dramatic works are simply the result of what the citizens tolerate without voicing their strong objections.

Like the small child who keeps going a little farther to see how much he can get away with, the pace setters of the news and entertainment industries seem impelled to reach deeper and deeper into the cesspools of sensationalism, animalism and degradation. Their success is only possible because of the tolerance of those who know better.[12]

Parental Rights

Parents need to learn about their rights and then insist upon them to promote educational excellence. In many states parents have the right to visit their child's classrooms any time upon notification to the school office, to have their child excused from studying subjects or reading assigned books on religious, moral, or other reasonable grounds, to speak to local public school board meetings, and to appeal certain local school board decisions to higher state authorities. In all states parents have the right to examine all official school policies and to investigate research programs of the Department of Education and the National Science Foundation.[13]

Senator Orrin Hatch had an amendment (Public Law 95-561, Nov. 1, 1978) added to the Elementary and Secondary Education Act that applies to every public school receiving federal funds—that is, basically all schools: "No student shall be required, as part of any applicable program, to submit to psychiatric examination, testing, or treatment, or psychological examination, testing, or treatment . . . without the prior written consent of the parent." This ban applies to "(1) political affiliations; (2) mental and psychological problems potentially embarrassing to the student or his family; (3) sex behavior and attitudes; (4) illegal, antisocial, self-incriminating and demeaning behavior; (5) critical appraisals of other individuals with whom respondents have close family relationships. . . ."[14] Parents now have the needed material to stop the few humanistic Peeping Toms in their psychodrama, role playing, sensitivity programs, touch therapy, and other psychological games. Schools failing to adhere to these restrictions would lose federal funds.

Persistent Action

Individual parents will find it extremely difficult to change the system. Alone they often laugh at their puny efforts. But as concerned individuals unite, they can once again make America a nation of achievement, discipline, and morality. Disagreement will certainly exist among those favoring a fundamental approach to education. Yet if major concepts are accepted, we can bury our differences and band together to bring back excellence to our schools. It has been wisely said, "In essentials unity, in nonessentials charity." The secret of success is unified parental pressure that demands action. There has been a small measure of success, but it needs to be multiplied in every community. It will take much more than an outcry of displeasure to effect a change; it will take time and sacrifice.

One must guard against permissive leaders who by their soft words and fair speeches claim all is well by seizing upon some molehill of gain and ignoring the mountains of failure. Some improvement is not enough. Our educational system needs a dramatic policy reversal. Many educators today are verbally against the term *permissiveness* because it has unpopular connotations. Nevertheless, their actions betray them; they still embrace permissive policies. Parents must insist on specific actions to alter the current educational deficiencies. Sadly, even if radical change does restructure the educational system, society must still pay for generations the damage done to inadequately trained children.

Though solutions are simple, it is extremely difficult to alter teachers, principals and administrators. Persons who endeavor to change schools must be willing to be called everything from far-right ultraconservatives to ignorant bigots suffering from sexual hangups. Parents should not be surprised when educators charge that their methods will set education back 100 years. Ignore the name-calling and ridicule. Let the shocking statistics tell their own story; facts cannot be refuted. We cannot let them embarrass us to silence.

Magical Secrets for Creating Understanding is a communications guide to show educators how to eliminate parental objections. The book is written in storybook fashion: A wise king and his tutors are having problems because some of the subjects have fallen under a spell. These are objecting parents; to deal with them four basic truths are presented:

  I All persons are basically good and seek to learn and also grow in knowledge.
  II Although persons are basically good, it is true that there are evil forces in the kingdom which influence them. Those forces seek to thwart education and to block communication.
  III If an evil spell has befallen a person, the cardinal rule for breaking that spell is to recognize that the person is separate from the spell. . . .
  IV To combat an evil spell and to allow the good within persons

to emerge, a tutor must understand and exercise the principles of communication outlined in this volume.

The book lists various types of complaining individuals whom educators will encounter, then presents instructions in how to deal with their spell. Following are some excerpts:

"Sheriffs" are "overcome with righteous indignation" and speak with a "very authoritative tone."

Antidote

FOG. Fogging is a skill needed in many antidotes to spells. It is the ability to confuse a person acting antagonistically by refusing to argue a point. It is best done by agreeing either (a) in part; (b) in principle; (c) in predictions to the statements the person makes.

Sheriff: "If things don't improve, this whole school will fall apart!"

Responder: "I know there are things we could improve."

If anger increases or shifts to another area of contention, you can be certain that this is a long-term spell. At this point:

Avoid this person, but make your exit politely OR develop instant telephone trouble. "Hello! Hello! I'm sorry. Can you hear that? Can you hear me! Something must have gone wrong with this line (louder each time). If you can still hear me, please call back in ten minutes."

If anger persists, ask what they intend to accomplish with this visit/call. Then ask them to submit it in writing so that their message will not be misunderstood nor forgotten. This will clarify their thinking.

"Messengers" think "they are blessed with superior knowledge"; they desire to "enlighten tutors."

Antidote

Messengers quickly lose their way in a fog. Use the fogging technique to satisfy and short circuit the spell. If possible, especially if the spell seems to be one of long duration, put this person to work. The inconvenience of time and effort will frequently wipe out this or some variant of the "do-goody" class of spells. One wise tutor kept an on-going *ad hoc* committee just for persons falling under this spell. The committee would meet and try to enlighten one another until the spell faded.

"Dumb Spell Bugs" are confused and anxious individuals.

Antidote

If confusion persists, tell the person that you, too, are sometimes confused on the particular matter. Then, promise to mail
information that will clarify the situation. (This will get them out
of the room or off the phone.)

"Loquacious Lecturers" are "able to pour forth incredible volumes
of words."

Antidote

Put them on hold. When you come back on, shift the conversation by beginning with a statement of your own.
In extreme cases, the only way to stop the flow of words is to
create an instant emergency. "Oh, no!" The lights just went off!
I'll call you back!" Breathlessly take the number quickly and
hang up.[15]

So, my dear parent, you are basically good; unfortunately, you
have fallen under an evil spell because you do not like our sex
education program or our humanistic literature program supporting
violence, racism, lying, profanity, euthanasia, infanticide, pornography, prostitution, and homosexuality. We the educator by the art
of skillful communication will endeavor to help you to separate your
wicked spell from your basic goodness. It is all right for you to
express your emotions—we understand how you feel; however, if
you still persist in demanding a solution, we will have you write
down your problem, get you off the phone by offering to mail
information to clarify the situation, put you on a committee to divert
your excess energy, confuse you by our fogging technique, or
downright lie to get rid of you.

Because of tactics like these there is a danger that concerned
parents will become discouraged and settle into defeatism because
of encountering stubborn resistance; but parents must exert the
same persistence as those forces destroying our schools and nation.
We cannot surrender millions of public school children to atheistic
humanism. We must resist becoming psychologically conditioned to
accept undisciplined and immoral behavior. Schools were once
disciplined and moral; there is no reason they cannot return to this
condition.

The program of quality education is not one of instant success. It
takes time and diligent work to overcome failures of permissive

education and to graduate literate and disciplined youth. First there needs to be a crash program to reform the early grades; here success can be quickly realized. As properly educated children move through the school system, the entire educational system will be transformed if standards are maintained. For children ruined by the permissive training, a disciplined program should be immediately implemented to break the syndrome of failure and to salvage as many as possible. Traditionally, public schools were firmly controlled by parents and local school boards; however, state and federal agencies, courts and professional organizations are increasingly controlling them. Fortunately, there is now a new emphasis on getting power back to local rule. Concerned individuals need to encourage such moves and to insist on quality education.

What action can be taken to restore quality education? As Eric Hoffer has said, "It is easy to be full of rage. It is not so easy to go to work and build something." In carrying your hammer, do not just knock—build. Many practical solutions have been offered; use the documented facts to build programs of success. Do not just be negative—be also positive. In being against permissiveness, progressive schools, rights without responsibility, situational ethics, infanticide, euthanasia, abortion, profane textbooks, immoral sex education, anti-Americanism, and atheistic humanism, be certain to stress the positive virtues of discipline, fundamental schools, human rights, honesty, parental respect, decent textbooks, moral purity, patriotism, and America's traditional theistic heritage.

There are public schools where children are receiving a good education. Support these schools. But be alert that there are individuals who want to bring in policies which destroy educational achievement. To promote quality education, elect officials who support sound policies. Write letters to your city and state leaders and members of Congress about issues detrimental to the well-being of children. Inform the public if your school or district is promoting programs that are alien to proper teaching or are promoting immorality. Send items to the press and concerned parent groups. Become aggressive and vocal about important issues and insist on an open educational atmosphere; educational leaders have built high walls of secrecy making it extremely difficult for concerned individuals to investigate their programs. Examine textbooks and insist that they be open to public review before purchase. Stress the illegality of the religion of humanism and programs that promote views violating state and local laws. Guard against invasion of student privacy, sensitivity training, and programs for resocialization of children. Be involved in parent-teacher organizations and especially try to be elected to one of the 16,000 school boards.

Endeavor to gain positions where you can influence positive actions. Refuse to become a rubber stamp of the humanistic status quo.*

Do not let educators silence you by saying it is too expensive to incorporate these changes. The changes—implementing achievement promotion, ability grouping, interesting and practical educational programs, disciplined learning environment, neighborhood schools, programs that expect all children to learn, textbooks that promote decency and patriotism, and voluntary prayer and Bible reading—are not costly to put in place.

America needs a parental revolution to incorporate these changes. Not a revolution of violence, but a revolution to restore quality education. We need to beware of labeling every humanist a communist, even though humanism is a perfect tool for the destruction of our nation. Many teachers are unaware of the ramifications of their teaching methods; they have been trained in humanistic procedures and they continue to follow what they have been taught. Provide them with books and literature that exposes humanism; some teachers will change after being shown the full implications of their teaching methods.

Action by Educators

There are teachers, principals, and administrators who believe in our theistic heritage and value system and are alarmed at the deterioration of our schools. Individually they often feel helpless to change the entrenched humanistic bureaucracy. Nevertheless, they need to speak out boldly for wholesome education and to oppose in every way possible the influence of humanism.

In a meeting with Christian educators I heard one teacher tell how she and another teacher decided they wanted to pray together before school hours. When they asked the principal's permission, he gave his approval. Then the principal told the two teachers to wait because of the pending Lubbock court case in which the ACLU challenged the right of high school students to organize a voluntary Bible discussion group. The teachers acquiesced and did not meet to pray. Unless Christian educators insist upon their rights to express their faith in God, every vestige of America's moral heritage will be removed from public education.

Many of today's educational problems occur because professors at the university level promote humanism. America needs professors

---

*Those interested in starting a parents' group can contact the organization founded by Mel and Norma Gabler: Educational Research Analysts, P.O. Box 7518, Longview, TX 75602. Though they specialize in reviewing textbooks, they can put you in contact with groups or individuals.

to raise intelligent voices in behalf of the ethical core values that promote national moral soundness. All educators, from elementary to university level, need to organize and become an effective instrument for positive education. United effort can have a powerful impact on the future of our nation; statements made by such educators can have a significant effect in combating the entrenched humanistic programs. Their actions will arouse strong opposition, but educators need to be courageous.

There is a national teacher organization that promotes positive values. Christian Educators Association (CEA), formerly National Educators Fellowship (NEF). This organization has been in existence for 30 years. It has members in each of the 50 states, and in many states local chapters in which educators meet to learn and to inspire others to uphold the moral principles that have shaped our nation. CEA has national and regional conventions, city-wide banquets, and a magazine, *Vision*, which has interesting articles for educators and parents.*

This is CEA's stated philosophy:

It is the philosophy of Christian Educators Association of America that the Judeo-Christian ethic is the foundation and the heritage of our great country. Although we would like to see America turn to God and become a truly Christian nation, we do not advocate that Christianity should become a state religion.

America is a pluralistic society, with tolerance toward all religions and political views. *Tolerance* is the key word, not control. When any religion tries to control the government or schools, it is out of step with the laws and purposes of our country. This is precisely why the atheistic religion of humanism is illegal in our schools and government.

However, on the question of "whose religious moral values do we use to teach morality?", it is our philosophy and the hetitage of our country, that those basic values are to be based upon Judeo-Christian principles. This philosophy says: there is but one God; there is right and wrong; every man is born with certain inalienable rights; children must be nurtured and taught moral truth before they can live a life of responsible actions; human life is sacred; sexual permissiveness is damaging and wrong; honesty is proper in all situations; stealing is always wrong; we must respect and honor God and our fellowman. This is the *Christian* philosophy.

---

*To receive further information, write to Christian Educators Association, 1410 West Colorado Boulevard, Pasadena, CA 91105

The philosophy of *secular humanism*, in direct contrast to Christianity, as written out in *The Humanist Manifesto I and II*, says that there is no God; there is no standard of right and wrong; all is situation ethics; man's rights are as each generation and each person sees them; there are no absolutes, so children do not need moral training, for morality is immoral; human life can be taken by suicide or euthanasia (medical elimination of the old or infirm). Humanism is not in the American tradition. It is a religion, not out of our tradition, held by only a handful and damaging to our children. We thus feel this philosophy must be opposed, and we are dedicated to eliminating its propagation within our public school systems.

Education is the glue that holds a democratic society together. When education is wrongfully used, as in the religion of humanism, it becomes self-destructive. CEA believes that public education is absolutely critical to maintaining America intact. Christian schools and all non-Christian private schools combined comprise only 10% of the student population. The church should not abandon the public schools because of the obvious evils of humanism—the church should join in the battle to change the schools by ridding them of humanism.

Christian teachers and Christian students should remain in the public schools and practice Christ's teaching to be the "salt of the earth" and the "light of the world." Christian parents should accept their personal responsibility to teach their own children the Bible and the Christian faith. The schools should teach our national heritage of Judeo-Christian morality and values. Gallup polls and United Press polls in 1982 claim that 97% of Americans believe in God. That means the humanists cannot claim them! Another Gallup poll in 1980 indicated that 170,000,000 Americans accept the morality of the Bible as man's only standard.

We hold that the beliefs of the vast majority of Americans and the heritage of the founding fathers should dictate the basic moral system of our nation's philosophy. . . .[16]

Though there is at present a discernible disgust with the educational system, this new movement of stressing morality, standards, basics, discipline, and patriotism must be more than a backlash return to the "good old days." A mere nostalgia for the past will fail. Historic reinforcement is good, but there must be also pragmatic programs that project into the future. The unparalleled technological advancements of our modern society demand that education keep pace; programs must be innovative and experimental to prepare students for the future. Unfortunately, most experimental programs have implemented permissive humanistic concepts.

Intelligent Action

Voting a tight pocketbook will not solve the educational crisis; while it proves frustration, education still needs funding to educate children properly. Jamming students into oversized classes hinders effective learning. Certainly, there are ways to save money, but blind budget slashing is not the answer.

One of the fastest ways to destroy educational reform is for furious individuals to make foolish demands. There must be intelligent action to restore proper educational procedures. It must be stressed—*be intelligent* in your demands. The crisis is very real. Be logical and factual; avoid nitpicking over every minor issue, or the entire emphasis on educational reform will be thwarted by causing legitimate complaints to go unheeded. Parents should present a positive image by endeavoring to help students, teachers, and administrators. Also, when educators *are* doing good work, let them know!

Successful Actions

Mel and Norma Gabler, founders of Educational Research Analysts, fought many battles to secure proper textbooks and learned many valuable lessons. Following are excerpts from an article they wrote, "A Parent's Guide to Textbook Review and Reform":

> The secret ingredient: Work. Parents need not be highly qualified, skilled or educated, but do need to know their subject. Closely related to work is persistence.
>
> The essential time to protest objectionable books and to propose positive alternatives is before the texts are adopted and purchased. While books are under consideration for adoption, they should be available for citizen review.
>
> It is at the adoption state that victories for positive education are more likely to be obtained.
>
> Learn the textbook adoption procedures in your state and district. Become familiar with procedures concerning citizen participation.
>
> Your thorough knowledge of the textbook is your best offensive weapon. Do not attempt to stop adoption of any book with which you are not personally familiar. Do not rely on hearsay. Obtain the book for yourself and verify what it contains.
>
> One of the best ways to stay on the offensive when school officials try to place you on the defensive as an "emotionally overwrought" parent, is to ask them if they have read the books

thoroughly and to question them on content. If they have not read the book, or have done so only cursorily, they have clearly placed themselves in the absurd position of defending a text with which they are not personally familiar. The question then becomes obvious, "Is it your position with the school system that obligates you to defend this book rather than its actual merits?"

Never start with the worst of your objections, but save some of the most telling material for your rebuttal; thus your argument will not be anti-climactic.

Do not expect victory overnight. Be prepared to lose some battles. Remember that each time you will learn to be better the next time. Sometimes you make gains you know nothing about. It is evident that where parents have been persistent in exposing questionable content, publishers do not submit their more "mature" versions.

Seek out other concerned persons in your area for help. Numbers are important. Objecting parents are frequently told, "you are the only parent who has objected to this material."

In dealing with school board members in particular, a low-key approach is the most effective. Do not be hasty or rude with a school board member. If possible, have different parents contact each of the board members. Tell them you give them credit for having the interest of the children at heart.

One of the most essential steps toward textbook reform is to gain support from leaders in your community. Take the texts in question to as many community leaders as possible.

One effective means to focus attention is to purchase an ad in the local paper featuring quotes from the books. Also consider going on audience participation programs, news or talk shows on TV or radio. An essential tool for dealing with the media is a press release.

Remember again that thorough knowledge of the text is your best offensive weapon.[17]

Here is how Marcia Sielaff of Peoria, Arizona, became involved in the struggle to change schools. "I discovered that our youngest son was not learning as he should. I knew there was a problem, but I wasn't really sure what it was. I wondered if my situation was unique. I spoke to other parents. I read all the articles on education in the media. I visited public schools; I visited private schools. I was looking for a school that would give our son the kind of education we wanted him to have. But, what kind of education was that? Suddenly, I had more questions than answers.

"At first, all I could figure out was that I was looking for a school that had a good phonic reading program and a classroom atmosphere conducive to learning. I found that the public school educators to whom I spoke couldn't be pinned down to answer specific questions. *Their words seemed to have meanings not in my dictionary. . . .*

"I spent a whole summer reading everything I could get my hands on about education. I made trips to the University. I talked to teachers. I wrote letters to the editor, and I answered letters to the editor. I found people who knew more than I who were willing to help me get information. I even took an in-service training course with the teachers from my district. I figured that if I could understand what teachers were being taught about teaching, I could understand what they were trying to accomplish in the classroom.

"I have a patient and long-suffering husband whose inclination, I'm sure, was to put his hand over my mouth because, wherever we went, in town or out, I would talk to people about their schools." Sielaff was a menace at weddings, social functions, and funerals. Finally, after all her searching she concluded that our educational system has switched tracks.

It was the progressive education movement, Sielaff discovered, that "took control of the Professional Associations and today, virtually runs the education show."[18] She started an organization called LITE (Let's Improve Today's Education) to provide information to parents that was not readily available through official sources. Parents obtained a phonics course of study in Arizona; authored a similar version of the Buckley Privacy Amendment as a part of their Parents' Bill of Rights six months prior to the federal law; and opened the textbook selection process so that now educators must make textbooks available for parental review, have an open hearing, and include parents on textbook committees.

In Carlsbad, California, high school students taught fifth- and sixth-graders sex education under the guidance of a school district nurse. In order to learn about the teaching methods, about 150 parents gathered to watch a student peer teacher demonstration. There was a discussion over values:

"But we're not teaching values," protested a teenager. "Nothing's right and nothing's wrong."

"Don't you realize that that in itself is a value?" asked a parent.

The course never mentioned the words *husband, wife,* or *marriage;* the terms *partner* and *the one you love* were used. Many parents opposed the teaching methodology of this sex education course because 16-year-old boys were teaching mixed classes of fifth- and sixth-grade children the facts about menstruation.

Initially, the peer teaching class was to be a health education class exposing the dangers of VD, but it was expanded. The nurse director was influenced greatly by Dr. Sidney Simon, professor of humanistic education at the University of Massachusetts. Dr. Simon frequently visited the area and actively supervised student peer teachers. In values clarification workshops he taught them that all values were of equal worth.

Christine A. Jones, a minister's wife, decided to find out more about this peer teaching class. She says, "Many of the students claimed to have undergone a personality or character change since joining the class. Observers at their demonstrations described the testimonies of these students as euphoric and religiouslike. Often a demonstration would begin with the district nurse asking one of the peer teachers his name. Then followed the question, 'And how long have you been alive?' The student would reply, 'Two years,' or whatever length of time he had been in the class."

Six couples gathered to form a concerned parents group. They decided to use all legitimate channels in a gracious manner. Four major sex education objections and alternatives were formulated, and the material was presented to the Health and Safety Citizens Committee. They wanted educators to know that, though they had a right to their opinion, they did not have the authority to violate parental rights by undermining the values children were being taught at home. To be well prepared these parents thoroughly researched values education, read hundreds of other articles and books, and contacted other parent groups engaged in fighting humanistic values. It was time-consuming, but in the end they knew their subject. Now when they spoke the opponents would have to respect the fact that they were knowledgeable.

Because of the interest generated, the Health and Safety Citizens Committee was expanded from 15 to 90 members. It included doctors and teachers who refused to acknowledge that abortion, homosexuality, and premarital sex were even undesirable. One mother said, "You have so little faith in the children's ability to make right and good choices!"

"We had to agree," Christine Jones said, "and it soon became evident that this was a basic issue that divided the committee. As Christians believing in man's sinful nature, we felt that children need guidelines. Many who did not profess to be Christians supported us, if only because they felt we had a more realistic viewpoint."

A few weeks later Christine Jones and her husband were called to meet the chairman of the school board, the district superintendent, and the high school principal. They were informed that the school district nurse was being transferred to elementary schools and would no longer supervise the peer teaching class. In addition, the Health and Safety Committee met and rewrote the health curri-

culum. Many conflicts were still unresolved, and on some of the
issues compromises had to be made; nevertheless, a number of
positive results were achieved. Though unsettled issues remain,
parents are watching and teachers are more concerned over parental values. Mrs. Jones says, "The furor has diminished, but we will
not lapse into indifference. Our children are too important for
that."[19]

A Maryland family, aroused over what was transpiring in the
schools, became an effective voice for better education. The father,
Malcolm Lawrence, attended George Washington University and
received his M.A. in government and economic policy; for 20 years
he served as a diplomat for the United States foreign service. At
present, Malcolm Lawrence is deputy special assistant to the secretary of state for narcotics matters and is listed in *Who's Who in
Government.* His wife Jacqueline has spoken throughout the United
States on the needs of education.

As a foreign service family with nine children the Lawrences left
the United States in 1958 for a ten-year duty in Europe. During this
time their children attended schools in England, France, Germany,
and Switzerland. The family retained the lofty principles of what it
was to be an American and remembered the high ideals of American
education. While serving in the United States embassy in London,
Jacqueline often spoke on "Education in America."

In Switzerland, Malcolm was a commercial attaché, and he
served as chairman of the board of the English-Speaking School of
Bern, a school for business and diplomatic families. Both Malcolm
and Jacqueline endeavored to promote the best of British and
American educational systems by carefully selecting teachers and
curriculum. Malcolm says, "The beauty of the school was that it
worked. The children learned to read, write and compute; and
nobody's ethnic, nationalistic or religious toes were stepped on.
Discipline was good, and the parents and students were content.
The school did what it was supposed to do—impart a quality
education, with plenty of homework in the process."

When their term came to an end in 1968, the family returned to
Montgomery County, Maryland, near Washington, D.C., one of the
most affluent areas in the United States. "This was a rude awakening!" Malcolm relates. "The education of a decade earlier no longer
existed. The schools had taken a drastic turn for the worse."
Malcolm reveals what they discovered in a thorough investigation of
the schools:

> We found discipline was ragged—student revolt was be-
> coming a fashionable tool for destroying the schools. The
> school board was catering to weakness and succumbing to

every whim of a permissive superintendent and demanding student body, and drug abuse was rampant in the schools. The curriculum and teaching methods had drastically changed. Unevaluated experimental innovations had begun to permeate the schools, crowding out the basics. To keep students "happy," emphasis was shifting from what a child should know (cognitive) to how a child feels about things (affective). There was a loss of scholarly objectivity and academic freedom. Chronological factual history was being replaced by conceptualized social studies. Achievement scores were on the decline; the system was graduating functional illiterates.

We noted the introduction of open-ended, non-judgmental discussions based not on what was right or wrong, but on how students viewed such concepts as lying, cheating, stealing, and expression of human sexuality. Situation ethics and other tenets of the religion of Secular Humanism were invading the schools, with the children being told to consider all options of moral and ethical issues and "make up their own minds." We felt that community ethics and standards were being eroded and that the schools were actually contributing to the delinquency of minors. State bylaws and county regulations were being violated. The classroom materials invaded the privacy of the student and family. Teachers were rolling over and playing dead to the tunes of the new educationist. They complied with instructions to use such psychotherapeutic techniques as role-playing, psychodrama and socio-drama. Without parental permission, teachers were assuming the role of clinicians and therapists—and our children were the patients.

Finding PTAs ineffectual, the Lawrences located other concerned parents and formed a group called Parents Who Care. They took the school system to court and filed a bill of complaint charging the school system with violating state bylaws and the U.S. Constitution. They called "for the removal of Family Life and Human Development curriculum, sensitivity training, selected humanistic social studies and other specified materials and practices that invade the privacy of the students and the home." The judge decided that they must first appeal to the county and state school system. Finally, more than three years from the beginning of their state board hearings, they were able to present their final arguments.[20]

The Maryland state board of education evaluated the charges and recommendations of Parents Who Care. Malcolm Lawrence reports:

While we did not win all of our points, it is gratifying that the State Board of Education went along for the most part with five of our twelve recommendations. This is a good start toward guiding the education establishment down a more wholesome road.

In addition to the State Board rulings, during our five-year battle, the Montgomery County educators have been quietly withdrawing books, issuing internal instructions to staff and teachers, and rewriting curriculum and teachers' guides to avoid the problem areas raised by PARENTS WHO CARE. At long last the teachers are being made aware of the State and local regulations.[21]

Parents Who Care engaged in a long, difficult battle. Though they won some issues and lost others, what is encouraging is that they determined to keep on pressing their demands. What will happen if communities around the nation follow suit? We will see education start to become what it should be.

While we as parents endeavor to promote positive values, we must train our own children and encourage them to stand for their convictions. Many times we parents do not want to create trouble for fear of the negative consequences our children will encounter. But confrontation of immoral issues is necessary even if it causes disturbances. Although your children may have to suffer for moral rightness, years later they will be proud that they took a stand with their parents for morality.

The silent majority needs a creative minority to stimulate the American people to action. Our nation needs leaders who will publicly declare their faith in God and the moral convictions that such faith produces. We need also a vast educational campaign to instruct Americans about the true nature of our government and its theistic heritage. For too long theists have refrained from expressing their moral convictions in our national life. We must now arise in unison and press for the restoration of the value system proposed by our founding fathers. We cannot surrender our public schools to atheistic humanism.

Bill Freeman attended Southern Methodist University and Columbia University Teachers College, where his many liberal professors caused him to abandon his parents' faith and conservative upbringing. Freeman says, "There I was indoctrinated into the permissive philosophy of education and of life." At college he enjoyed the high grades he received, for teachers graded according to the progressive concept that the group had priority over the individual; the nebulous concepts of "group progress, social interaction and future potentialities" determined his grades.

As a teacher and principal in one of the better school systems in Austin, Texas, Freeman pioneered the way to change the curriculum. "I advocated the 'progressive' idea that writing, reading, and arithmetic should be integrated into the social studies program to let these basic skills more or less 'emerge.'"

He received his doctorate from the University of Texas. Then, while teaching at Austin College he told prospective teachers, "Teaching reading was secondary. Of first importance was the child's social development." Freeman tells how "another 'progressive' theory was that all teaching and learning should be fun, exciting, and made easy. If a lesson or skill was difficult, it should be carefully scrutinized because pupils should not be daunted by hard problems."

However, something happened—his two older children awakened him to the "world of evangelism." He took a sabbatical and did a postdoctoral work at L'Abri in Switzerland. He studied and listened to tapes of Francis Schaeffer on the influence of humanism in our culture. "I could understand the truth of what they proclaimed," notes Freeman, "because I had experienced directly or vicariously everything they said." Freeman says, "At L'Abri I found intellectual reasons for believing in the biblical absolutes I had once been taught but had later taken lightly or dismissed entirely." Freeman came to this conclusion:

> Among all the religious and nonreligious philosophies of the world, none compares with the Christian philosophy centered in the teaching of Christ concerning the worth, potential, and responsibilities of each person. Without such a philosophy, parents, educators, and leaders in society often deteriorate in personhood.
>
> I became specially aware of the results of permissivenes in the public schools. I came to see such problems as grade inflation, promotion for merely social reasons, laxity in discipline, lower academic standards, and general disrespect for people and property as reflections of our culture and its system of education.[22]

Men and Women of Action

Restoring prayer and Bible reading will do much to return our nation to its moral strength, but this is just a part of the solution. America needs a total revitalization of its faith in all its institutions whereby parents, educators, businessmen, lawyers, political leaders, and ministers will translate God's truths into the moral fabric of our schools and nation. As theists we need to fight the logics of futility and take leadership roles in giving moral direction to our nation. When the original 13 states were on the verge of disintegration, Benjamin Franklin called for prayer; as America travels the humanistic road to destruction, let us too call for national prayer to save our schools and nation. Then with prayer and faith in God let each one go forth as if the destiny of America hinged on our action.

America need not join the graveyard of nations after her 200 years. We have not reached the point of no return. But the implications of the future of America with humanism as its ideology is horrendous. Every American ought to feel a moral disgust at this atheistic social engineering attempt to brainwash our children to become adherents to this new religion.

It has been said, "What you put into the school will appear in the life of the people of the next generation." Let us provide our children with an education that is in keeping with the standards that have made our nation prosperous. Concerned Americans must act while they are strong. As we proceed, let us go with love and compassion for the youth of America. We should never forget the future distress these children will encounter because of the destructive effects of their indequate educational and moral learning experience. We need to keep the children on our hearts as we patiently champion the cause for academic excellence, disciplined learning environment, racial progress, and moral wholeness.

Who will arise to call America back to her foundational strengths? The issues are clearly marked; the lines are drawn. Our action or inaction will determine America's future. Let each one take the mantel of responsibility to transform American education into: Schools of Accomplishment: Training for Success.

Notes

Publication data for the book titles cites are given in the Bib-liography.

Chapter 1

The Crisis   3

1. "Down, Down, Down for Pupil's Scores," *U.S. News & World Report*, Oct. 20, 1980, p. 12.
2. "Why Johnny Can't Write—And What's Being Done," *U.S. News & World Report*, Mar. 16, 1981, p. 47.
3. "No Tea Party," *Time*, July 12, 1982, p. 53.
4. "Tomorrow," *U.S. News & World Report*, Oct. 11, 1982, p. 18.
5. Marcia Chambers, "New York City Public Schools Open Today," *New York Times*, Sept. 9, 1979.
6. "Bunk as History," *Newsweek*, Nov. 10, 1975, pp. 85, 86.
7. *Ibid.*, p. 86.
8. "Modern illiteracy," taken from New York Times News Service, *Houston Chronicle*, May 16, 1982.
9. "U.S. Report Fears Most Americans Will Become Scientific Illiterates," *New York Times*, Oct. 23, 1980.
10. "An Open Letter to the American People," *Education Week*, Apr. 27, 1983, p. 12.
  Christopher Connel, "Panel Hits Educational Disarmament in U.S.," *Houston Chronicle*, Apr. 27, 1983.
11. Ann Landers, "Teacher's Lament," *New York Daily News*, Feb. 28, 1977.
12. "Terror in Schools," *U.S. News & World Report*, Jan. 26, 1976, p. 54.
  "The Battered Teacher," *Newsweek*, May 30, 1977, p. 83.
13. "Help! Teacher Can't Teach," *Time*, June 16, 1980, p. 59.
14. "A Bitter New Generation of Jobless Young Blacks," *U.S. News & World Report*, Sept. 27, 1976, p. 81.
15. "And, finally, a success story: How one school changes from snake pit to model," *American School Board Journal*, Jan. 1975, p. 36.
16. "Successful Inner-City Schools Don't Follow Theorists' Models," *Today's Child*, Dec. 1971, p. 4.

Chapter 2

Forward with Basics   11

1. "Why SAT Scores Decline," *Newsweek*, Sept. 5, 1977, p. 82.
   "Why Those Falling Test Scores," *Time*, Sept. 12, 1977, p. 40.
2. James Dobson, *Hide or Seek*, p. 89.
3. Louise Bates Ames, "Retention Grade Can Be a Step Forward," *Education Digest*, Mar. 1981, p. 36.
4. *Ibid.*, p. 37.
5. "They Shall Not Pass," *Time*, Dec. 31, 1973, p. 45.
6. "Standards," *Council for Basic Education Bulletin*, Mar. 1976, p. 4.
7. "High Schools Under Fire," *Time*, Nov. 14, 1977, p. 65.
8. *Ibid.*, p. 67.
9. Murray Schumach, "Queens Principal Who Defied School Board Will Chastise It in His Valedictory," *New York Times*, June 20, 1977.
10. A Graham Down, "Why Basic Education," *Education Digest*, Nov. 1977, p. 2.
11. "Standardized Tests Must Go, Herndon Says," *NEA Reporter*, Feb. 1976.
12. "Good News from Here and There," *Council for Basic Education Bulletin*, Feb. 1977, p. 11.
13. "Why Johnny Can't Write," *Newsweek*, Dec. 8, 1975, p. 61.
14. Max Rafferty, "Dallas Teachers Fail Competency Test," *Human Events*, Jan. 13, 1979.
15. R. R. Allen, "Do You Really Want to Know Why Johnny Can't Write, or Read, or Speak, or Listen?" *Vital Speeches of the Day*, Dec. 15, 1976, pp. 149, 150.
16. "They Shall Not Pass," *Time*, Dec. 31, 1973, p. 45.
17. "An End to Social Promotions," editorial, *New York Times*, Dec. 31, 1979.
18. "The Knowledge Isn't There," *Council for Basic Education Bulletin*, Apr. 1976, p. 15.

Chapter 3

Training for Excellence   25

1. "Why 1.4 Million Americans Can't Read or Write—And the Remedies Proposed," *U.S. News & World Report*, Aug. 19, 1974, p. 37.
   "The Right to Read," *Education Digest*, Nov. 1974, pp. 31-33.
2. "Where Money Fails," *Newsweek*, Mar. 29, 1976, p. 86.

3. "What the Schools Cannot Do," *Time*, Apr. 16, 1973, p. 78.
4. James E. Allen, "We *Can* End Juvenile Illiteracy," *Reader's Digest*, Apr. 1970, p. 158.
5. "Find There's No One Best Way to Teach Reading," *Today's Child*, Apr. 1972, p. 4.
6. Rudolf Flesch, *Why Johnny Can't Read*, pp. 9, 10.
7. Samuel L. Blumenfeld, "Twenty Years After Rudolf Flesch," *Vital Speeches of the Day*, July 15, 1975, p. 597.
8. William D. Boutwell, "The Reading Controversy Still Rages," *PTA Magazine*, Oct. 1968, pp. 4, 5.
9. Samuel L. Blumenfeld, "Why America Has A Reading Problem," *Education Digest*, Oct. 1974, p. 27.
10. Joyce Hood, "Children with Problems—Poor Reader—II," *Today's Education*, Sept.-Oct. 1974, p. 39.
11. Frank W. Freshour, "Dyslexia: A Sure Cure," *Education Digest*, Nov. 1974, p. 34.
12. Samuel L. Blumenfeld, "Why America Has a Reading Problem," *Education Digest*, Oct. 1974, p. 24.
13. Rudolf Flesch, p. 23.
14. "Why 1.4 Million Americans Can't Read or Write—And the Remedies Proposed," p. 38.
15. Ronald Schiller, "Where the 'New Math' Went Wrong," *Reader's Digest*, Sept. 1974, pp. 110, 111.
16. John H. Lawson, "Is the New Math Doing the Job?" *Education Digest*, Dec. 1973, p. 17.
17. "High Cost of Schooling—Is It Worth the Price?" *U.S. News & World Report*, Sept. 3, 1973, p. 28.
18. Ronald Schiller, p. 112.
19. *Ibid.*, p. 112.
20. *Ibid.*, pp. 112, 113.
21. *Ibid.*, p. 113.
22. John H. Lawson, p. 17.
23. "New Math: The Ongoing Debate." *American Teacher,* May 1977.
24. "Nobel Winner Says U.S. Has Slipped in Science Teaching," *Houston Post*, Nov. 17, 1982.
25. Paul DeHart Hurd, "Why Johnny Can't Compute," *Education Week*, Nov. 10, 1982.
26. "Low-Tech Teaching Blues," *Time*, Dec. 27, 1982, p. 67.
27. Roger W. Ming, "Meeting the Needs of the Gifted," *Inside Education*, Oct. 1972, p. 8.
28. Susan B. Thomas, "Neglecting the Gifted Causes Them to Hide Their Talents," *Gifted Child Quarterly*, Autumn 1973, p. 193.
29. Gene I. Maeroff, "A New Day for the Gifted." *New York Times*, Apr. 25, 1976.

30. Hilde Bruch, *Don't Be Afraid of Your Child*, pp. 244, 245.
31. Gene I. Maeroff, "Study of U.S. Decline in Precollege Test Scores Arouses a Dispute," *New York Times*, July 10, 1978.
32. Albert Shanker, "Picture of Our City Schools Is Distorted," *New York Teacher*, June 26, 1977.
33. "Whadjaget?" *Time*, Nov. 27, 1972, p. 49.
34. John Holt, *The Underachieving School*, p. 58.
35. Claire Berman, "The Pressure to Win, the Pain of Losing," *New York Times*, Aug. 8, 1976.
36. Joe David, "Some Reasons Why Johnny Can't Read," *Education University of Wisconsin*, Sept.Oct., 1972, Vol. 93, No. 1, p. 26.
37. Howard L. Hurwitz, "What So Vague About 'Excessive Absence'?" *Ridgewood (N.Y.) Times*, Sept. 15, 1977.
38. "What's Being Done About the Dropouts," *U.S. News & World Report*, June 2, 1980, p. 51.
39. "Skilled Manpower Shortage: A Crisis Facing Defense," *Iron Age*, June 22, 1981, p. 51.
40. "Dropouts and Pushouts. The 2.4 Million Children Who Aren't in School," *U.S. News & World Report*, Mar. 22, 1976, pp. 43, 44.
41. "'Three R's' In Schools Now: Retrenchment, Results, Realism," *U.S. News & World Report*, Sept. 6, 1976, p. 50.
42. James E. Allen, p. 158.
43. Robert E. Grinder, *Adolescence,* p. 473.
44. "The Fall of Billy Don," *Newsweek*, Apr. 19, 1982, p. 86.

Chapter 4

The Educational Maze   43

1. A. S. Neill, *Summerhill: A Radical Approach to Child Rearing*, p. 3.
2. *Ibid.*, pp. 4, 5, 29.
3. Herbert C. Rudman, "A Conversation with A. S. Neill," *Education Digest*, Jan. 1973, p. 21.
4. A. S. Neill, pp. 9, 20, 53, 140, 141, 297, 363.
5. Ethel Mannin, *Common-Sense and the Child*, pp. 61, 62.
6. A. S. Neill, pp. 138, 139.
7. Suzanne S. Fremon, "Why Free Schools Fail," *Parents Magazine*, Sept. 1972, pp. 50, 92, 96.
8. "What the Schools Cannot Do," *Time*, Apr. 16, 1973, pp. 78—85.
9. "The Shadow Schools," *Time*, June 6, 1969, pp. 56, 61.
10. *Ibid.*, p. 61.
11. James D. Koerner, "Changing Education—The Gullibility of

Teachers and Administrators," *Vital Speeches of the Day*, Jan. 1, 1974, p. 179.

12. Leslie B. Hohman, *As the Twig Is Bent*, pp. 70, 76.
13. Hilde Bruch, *Don't Be Afraid of Your Child*, p. 239.
14. Arthur E. Salz, "The Truly Open Classroom," *Education Digest*, May 1974, pp. 10, 11.
15. Beatrice and Ronald Gross, Editors, *Radical School Reform*. The Quotation is from "Visions: The School in Society," by Paul Goodman, p. 100.
16. "Does School + Joy = Learning?" *Newsweek*, May 3, 1971, pp. 60, 68.
17. "Briton Says Neo-Progressive Teaching Methods Lowered Literacy Standards," *Today's Child*, Oct. 1973, p. 2.
18. *Ibid.*
19. John H. Hollifield, "Research Clues," *Today's Education*, Mar.-Apr. 1976, p. 10.
20. Judith Weinraub, "New British Study on Education Says Old Way Is Best Way," *New York Times*, May 8, 1976.
21. "Latest in Schools and Colleges," *U.S. News & World Report*, July 25, 1977, p. 75.
22. Mara Wolynski, "Confessions of a Misspent Youth," *Newsweek*, Aug. 30, 1976, p. 11.

Chapter 5

Discipline Problems: The Root Causes   63

1. Joe David, "Some Reasons Why Johnny Can't Read," *Education, University of Wisconsin*, Vol. 93, No. 1, Sept.-Oct. 1972, pp. 25, 26.
2. Sidney Fields, "Only Human," *New York Daily News*, Dec. 22, 1975.
3. "Violence in the Schools," *NEA Reporter*, Feb. 1976, p. 5.
4. *Ibid.*, p. 5.
5. James Dobson, *Dare to Discipline*, p. 109.
6. William C. Morse, "The Crisis-Intervention Teacher," *Today's Education*, Mar.-Apr. 1975, p. 62.
7. Dr. Howard L. Hurwitz, "City Council Seeks to Save Our Sinking Schools," *Ridgewood (N.Y.) Times*, Apr. 21, 1977.
8. "Erasing the Blackboard Jungle, *New York Daily News*, July 8, 1974.
9. Bylaws of the New York City Board of Education concerning corporal punishment, Sec. 90, Subd. 15.
10. Enid Nemy, "Violence in Schools Now Seen as Norm Across the Nation," *New York Times*, June 16, 1975.

11. *Ibid.*
12. "Violence in the Schools," p. 9.
13. Jeremiah Mckenna, "Crime in the Schools," *New York Teacher* (Magazine Section), Dec. 14, 1975, pp. 19–22. Reprinted from *New York Affairs*, 25 W. 45th Street, New York, NY 10036.
14. "Cost of School Crime Exceeds Half Billion Dollars Each Year," *LEAA Newsletter*, May 1975, p. 26.
15. "Violence in the Schools: Everybody Has Solutions, and on the Next Ten Pages, Everybody Offers Them," *American School Board Journal*, Jan. 1975, p. 27.
16. "Violence in the Schools," *NEA Reporter*, Feb. 1976, p. 4.
17. "Help! Teacher Can't Teach," *Time*, June 16, 1980, p. 59.
18. "Delinquency Linked to Schools," Parent's Rights, Inc., Newsletter, 12571 Northwinds Drive, St. Louis, MO 63141, Summer 1977.
19. "All Kinds of Crime—Growing . . . Growing . . . Growing," *U.S. News & World Report*, Dec. 16, 1974, p. 33.
20. "Children and the Law," *Newsweek*, Sept. 8, 1975, p. 66.

Chapter 6

Love and Discipline   79

1. Smiley Blanton, *Love or Perish*, p. 3.
2. Jean Dunaway, "How to Cut Discipline Problems in Half," *Today's Education*, Sept.–Oct. 1974, pp. 75–77.
3. Various sources were used. The main source was: Nella Broddy, *Anne Sullivan Macy: The Story Behind Helen Keller.*
4. Dorothy W. Baruch, *New Ways in Discipline*, pp. 44, 54.
5. "Youngsters in Study Thrive in Strict Home," *Today's Child*, Summer 1969, p. 1.
6. Judy F. Rosenblith, Wesley Allinsmith, and Joanna P. Williams, *The Causes of Behavior: Readings in Child Development and Educational Psychology*, p. 143.
7. Grace Langdon and Irving W. Stout, *These Well-Adjusted Children*, pp. 33, 46.
8. "Drug Addiction Is Called Major Cause of Crime," *Houston Chronicle*, Feb. 14, 1983.
9. "White Favors Mandatory Jail Term If Drugs Sold at School," *Houston Chronicle*, Feb. 3, 1983.
10. "How to Get Tough," *Newsweek*, July 10, 1978, p. 69.
11. Judy F. Rosenblith, Wesley Allinsmith, and Joanna P. Williams, p. 145.
12. Muriel Schoenbrun Karlin and Regina Berger, *Discipline and the Disruptive Child*, p. 35.

13. James Dobson, *Dare to Discipline*, p. 125.
14. "Skills Testing . . . Crime in Schools . . . Salable Diplomas,"
    U.S. News & World Report, Apr. 3, 1978, p. 83.

Chapter 7

Discipline for Excellence   93

1. Diane Divoky, "Learning-Disability 'Epidemic,' " *New York Times*,
    Jan. 15, 1975.
 2. Charles Mangel, "The Puzzle of Learning Disabilities," *New York
    Times*, Apr. 25, 1976.
 3. Diane Divoky.
 4. Arlene Silberman, "If They Say Your Child Can't Learn, "*Reader's
    Digest*, Jan. 1976, p. 152.
 5. "We've Been Asked About Drugs for 'Unruly' Schoolchildren,"
    U.S. News & World Report, Apr. 5, 1976, p. 68.
 6. Paul Francis, "The Survival of the Special Student," *American
    Teacher*, Jan. 1976, p. 24. A book review of Peter Schrag and
    Diane Divoky, *The Myth of the Hyperactive Child and Other
    Means of Child Control*. New York: Pantheon Books, 1975.
 7. "We've Been Asked About Drugs for 'Unruly' Schoolchildren,"
    p. 68.
 8. Ellen Bowman Welsch, "You May Not Know It, but Your Schools
    Probably Are Deep into the Potentially Dangerous Business of
    Teaching with Drugs," *American School Board Journal*, Feb.
    1974, p. 42.
 9. "We've Been Asked About Drugs for 'Unruly' Schoolchildren,"
    p. 68.
10. Ellen Bowman Welsch, pp. 41, 42.
11. Richard Flaste, "Learning for Lollipops," *New York Times*, Apr.
    25, 1976.
12. Frances Templet, "Why Johnny Can't," *Eternity*, Oct. 1977,
    p. 18.
13. Ellen Bowman Welsch, p. 45.
14. "We've Been Asked About Drugs for 'Unruly' Schoolchildren,"
    p. 68.
15. *A Federal Source Book: Answers to the Most Frequently Asked
    Questions About Drug Abuse*, p. 18.
16. Fizhugh Dodson, *How to Parent*, p. 26.
17. John D. Krumboltz and Helen B. Krumboltz, *Changing Children's
    Behavior*, p. 185.
18. John. E. Valusek, *People Are Not for Hitting,* p. 71.
19. "It's Time to Hang Up the Hickory Stick," *Education Digest*, Jan.
    1973, p. 34.

20. *Report of the Task Force on Corporal Punishment*, p. 15.
21. B. F. Skinner, *Walden Two.* New York: Macmillan, 1948, p. 183. Quoted in *Report of the Task Force on Corporal Punishment*, p. 15.
22. *Report of the Task Force on Corporal Punishment*, p. 8.
23. "Hows, Whys, Wheres of Spanking Subject of Conjecture by Physicians," *Today's Child*, Apr. 1967, p. 5.
24. Richard L. Solomon, "Punishment," *American Psychologist*, Apr. 1964, pp. 248-252.
25. Donna M. Gelfand, Editor, *Social Learning in Childhood*, pp. 223-227.
26. Donald M. Baer, "Let's Take Another Look at Punishment," *Psychology Today*, Oct. 1971, pp. 32-37, 111.
27. *Report of the Task Force on Corporal Punishment*, p. 10. Letter to the President, Los Angeles City Board of Education, from Henry A. Waxman (California legislature), Jan. 25, 1972, p. 1.
28. Donald M. Baer, p. 111.
29. Occasional Spanking Is Held Good Medicine," *Today's Child*, Nov. 1959, p. 1.
30. Marilyn Whiteside, "School Discipline: The Ongoing Crisis," *Education Digest*, Mar. 1976, p. 39.
31. "Pittsburgh's Teachers March for Discipline," *American Teacher*, June 1975.
32. "Suing to Prevent Schoolyard Crime," *Newsweek*, June 2, 1980. "Allowing Spanking in Schools?" *U.S. News & World Report*, June 2, 1980, p. 65.
33. "Ruling on the Rod," *Newsweek*, May 2, 1977, p. 65. "The Court: Don't Spare the Rod," *Time*, May 2, 1977, p. 58.
34. Gene I. Maeroff, "Discipline Seen Aided by Spanking Decision," *New York Times*, Apr. 25, 1977.
35. Lesley Oelsner, "High Court Rules Pupil Spankings Are Permissible," *New York Times*, Oct. 21, 1975.
36. Fritz Redl and William W. Wattenberg, *Mental Hygiene in Teaching.* New York: Harcourt Brace and Co., 1951, p. 309. Cited in *Report of the Task Force on Corporal Punishment*, p. 9.
37. "The Court: Don't Spare the Rod," *Time*, May 2, 1977, p. 58.
38. Ross D. Parke, "The Role of Punishment in the Socialization Process," cited in Ronald A. Hoppe, G. Alexander Milton, and Edward C. Simmel, Editors, *Early Experiences and the Processes of Socilization*, p. 81.
39. *Report of the Task Force on Corporal Punishment*, pp. 27, 28.
40. "David Was an Inner-City Victim," *Today's Education*, Jan.–Feb. 1976, pp. 92, 93.
41. Shirley Boes Neill, "Causes of School Violence and Vandalism," *Education Digest*, Apr. 1976, pp. 8, 9.

Chapter 8

Racial Progress   117

1. "Twenty Years After Brown," *Newsweek*, May 20, 1974, p. 95.
   Vernon E. Jordan, Jr., "Busing—A Creative Partnership," *Vital Speeches of the Day*, May 1, 1972, p. 435.
2. Thomas F. Pettigrew, "On Busing and Race Relations," *Today's Education*, Sept.–Dec. 1973, p. 37.
3. "The Agony of Busing Moves North," *Time*, Nov. 15, 1971, pp. 57, 58.
4. "The Road to Integration," *Newsweek*, Jan. 26, 1976, p. 72.
5. "What the Schools Cannot Do," *Time*, Apr. 16, 1973, p. 78.
6. Iver Peterson, "City U. Plan May Cut Down on Minorities," *New York Times*, Dec. 19, 1975.
7. "The Busing Dilemma," *Time*, Sept. 22, 1975, p. 12.
8. Robert Cassidy, "The Pros and Cons of Busing" *Parents Magazine*, Sept. 1972, p. 89.
9. "The Busing Dilemma," p. 15.
10. *Ibid.*, p. 15.
11. *Ibid.*, pp. 14, 15.
12. "Busing: Why Tide Is Turning," *U.S. News & World Report*, Aug. 11, 1975, pp. 25, 26.
13. "Why So Many Say Busing Is a Failure," *U.S. News & World Report*, Dec. 8, 1980, p. 59.
14. "America's Schools on the Spot," *Newsweek*, Sept. 15, 1975, p. 51.
15. Walter Goodman interviews James S. Coleman, "Integration, Yes; Busing, No," *Education Digest*, Nov. 1975, p. 6.
16. "Busing—A Bad Trip," *Reader's Digest*, Sept. 1975, p. 16.
17. "Shifting into Reverse?" *Houston Chronicle*, Mar. 23, 1981.
18. "The Black Conservative," *Newsweek*, Mar. 9, 1981, pp. 30, 31.
19. "Growing Debate 'Reverse Discrimination' Has It Gone Too Far," *U.S. News & World Report*, Mar. 29, 1976, p. 29.
20. William V. Shannon, "The Boston Affair," *New York Times*, June 24, 1976.
21. "The Furor over Reverse Discrimination," *Newsweek*, Sept. 26, 1977, pp. 52, 53.
    "What's Right for Whites?" *Time*, Oct. 24, 1977, pp. 95, 97.
22. "What Price Quotas?" *New York Teacher* (Magazine Section), Feb. 9, 1975.
23. Letter, "'Reverse Discrimination,'" *Newsweek*, Oct. 10, 1977, p. 10.
24. John Hope Franklin, "Great Expectations," *New York Teacher* (Magazine Section), Dec. 8, 1974.

25. David L. Evans, "Making It, as a Black, at Harvard and Radcliffe," *New York Times*, Nov. 24, 1976.
26. Ralph Kinney Bennett, "Colleges Under the Federal Gun," *Reader's Digest*, May 1976, p. 127.
27. "The Furor over Reverse Discrimination," p. 55.
28. Albert Shanker, "Too Bad Carter Backed Down," *American Teacher*, Nov.–Dec. 1977.
29. "The Busing Dilemma," p. 15.
30. "Is Reverse Discrimination Justified?" *U.S. News & World Report*, Oct. 3, 1977, p. 40.
31. Gene I. Maeroff, "Panel Opposes Testing Students to Gauge Minimum Competency," *New York Times*, Mar. 3, 1978.
32. Walt Haney, "Trouble over Testing," *Education Digest*, Nov. 1980, pp. 2, 6.
33. William Raspberry, "Tackling the Real Problem," *Houston Chronicle*, Feb. 21, 1981.
34. "Minimum Competency and Bias," *Council for Basic Education Bulletin*, Feb. 1979, p. 9.
35. "Of Study on Bilingual Education," *New York Teacher*, May 8, 1977.
36. Frank E. Armbruster, *Our Children's Cripple Future*, pp. 6, 7.
37. "Divisive Languages," editorial, *New York Times*, Oct. 28, 1975.
38. "Let Discipline Fit the Offense, Not the Quota," letter to the editor, *New York Times*, Mar. 16, 1981.
39. "Violence in Schools," *U.S. News & World Report*, Apr. 14, 1975, p. 39.
40. Eugenia Kemble, "the Seeds of School Violence," *American Teacher*, May 1976.
41. "The Busing Dilemma," p. 15.
42. "Violence in Schools," p. 39.
43. "No Accord Is Evident on Young Blacks' Job Problems," *New York Times*, July 12, 1976.
44. "A Bitter New Generation of Jobless Young Blacks," *U.S. News & World Report*, Sept. 27, 1976, p. 61.
45. *Ibid.*, p. 64.
46. *Ibid.*, p. 64.
48. *Ibid.*, pp. 64, 65.
48. "Where Amy Will Be Going to School," *New York Daily News*, Nov. 11, 1976.
49. *Ibid.*, and "Valedictorians, Grades and Test Scores," *Council for Basic Education Bulletin*, Oct. 1976, pp. 9, 10.

Chapter 9

Successful Schools 137

1. Much of the material is from a personal interview with Alice Blair and also from "And, Finally, a Success Story: How One School Changes from Snake Pit to Model, *American School Board Journal*, Jan. 1975, pp. 36, 37.
   "Hope for the Schools," *Newsweek*, May 4, 1981, pp. 67–69.
2. "Tale of Two Schools," editorial, *New York Times*, Apr. 20, 1974.
3. George Weber, *Inner-City Children Can Be Taught to Read: Four Successful Schools*, pp. 26, 30.
4. "Inner City Schools," *Education Digest*, Dec. 1980, p. 67.
   "Hope for the Schools," *Newsweek*, May 4, 1981, p. 66.
5. William Raspberry, "Making the Grade in Baltimore,"*Washington Post*, July 30, 1982.
   William Raspberry, "Combining Toughness, Tenderness," *Houston Chronicle*, Aug. 21, 1982.
6. "High Cost of Schooling—Is It Worth the Price?" *U.S. News & World Report*, Sept. 3, 1973, p. 28.
7. Harold H. Webb, "Compensatory Education? Yes!" *Educational Leadership*, Dec. 1972, p. 209.
8. "Advanced School Goes Back to Traditional Teaching Methods," *Today's Child*, May 1961, p. 7.
9. James K. Wellington, "A Look at the Fundamental School Concept," *Vital Speeches of the Day*, Jan. 15, 1977, pp. 216–218.
10. Material for John Marshall Fundamental School is taken from *Marshall Fundamental School, Pasadena, California* [K-8], from *Marshall Fundamental School, Pasadena, California* [9-12], and from "Special Guidelines for Grades 9-12—The Fundamental School-Senior High Division."
11. Richard Vetterli, *Storming the Citadel: The Fundamental Revolution Against Progressive Education*, pp. 48–58.
12. *"An Open Letter to the American People* A Nation at Risk: The Imperative for Educational Reform," *Education Week*, Apr. 27, 1983.
13. Eileen White, "Bell Comission's 'Excellence' Study Acclaimed," *Education Week*, May 4, 1983.
14. Alex Heard, "Studies Urge Renewal of Public-Education System," *Education Week*, May 11, 1983.

Chapter 10

Textbooks for Wholesome Living   155

1. The major sources for the textbook materials are:
   "A Clash over 'Dirty Books' Is Dividing a School Board, Threatening a Superintendent, and Shattering a Community," *American School Board Journal*, Nov. 1974, p. 31.
   "Schoolbooks that Stirred Up a Storm," *U.S. News & World Report*, Nov. 4, 1974, p. 44.
   "West Virginia Uproar—Contesting the Textbooks," *Christianity Today*, Oct. 11, 1974, p. 44.
   Elmer Fike, *Textbook Controversy in Perspective and Other Related Essays.*
2. "West Virginia Uproar—Contesting the Textbooks," *Christianity Today*, Oct. 11, 1974, p. 45.
   "A Clash over 'Dirty Books' Is Dividing a School Board, Threatening a Superintendent, and Shattering a Community," p. 43.
3. "A Clash Over 'Dirty Books' Is Dividing a School Board, Threatening a Superintendent, and Shattering a Community," p. 32.
4. *Ibid.*, p. 41.
5. *New York Times* editorial is taken from Jenkin Lloyd Jones, "Textbooks Aren't Sacred," *Tulsa Tribune*, Feb. 8, 1975.
6. Elmer Fike, pp. 1, 2.
7. "Parents' Rights," *Christianity Today*, Dec. 6, 1974, p. 28.
8. Mel Gabler, "Miners Show Convictions in Text Protest," *Borger News-Herald*, Dec. 23, 1974.
9. The quotation from the *Wall Street Journal* is taken from Noel F. Busch, "The Furor over School Textbooks," *Reader's Digest*, Jan. 1976, p. 126.
10. Botel, Morton, and Dawkins, *Communicating,* Teacher's Edition, Grade 3, p. 76.
11. *Ibid.*, pp. 142, 143.
12. Botel, Morton, and Dawkins, *Communicating*, Teacher's Edition, Grade 6, p. 1.
13. *Ibid.*, pp. 17, 18.
14. Floren Harper, "Blue Denim," *Scripts 3*, p. 99.
15. *Ibid.*, p. 158.
16. *Ibid.*
17. "GPO Draws the Line on Obscenities," *Human Events*, June 19, 1976.
18. Margaret L. Weeks, "Sharply Divided Court Limits Board's Power to Ban Books," *Education Week*, Aug. 18, 1982.

19. "Parents vs. Educators," *U.S. News & World Report*, Jan. 27, 1975, p. 32.
20. Most of the material about Mel and Norma Gabler is taken from: Jimmy Brown, "The Mel Gablers—Textbook Reviewing Is No Small Readout," *Gladewater (Tex.) Mirror*, July 28, 1974. "Gablers Receive Leadership Award," *Gladewater Mirror,* Feb. 15, 1976.
    The Liner, Exxon Pipeline Company, Mar. 1973.
21. Jimmy Brown.
22. James C. Hefley, *Textbooks on Trial*, p. 178.
23. Jimmy Brown.
24. Frank B. McMahon, Jr., and Sarah B. Resnick, *Behind the Mask: Our Psychological World*. Englewood Cliffs, N.J.: Prentice-Hall, 1973, p. 61.
25. Kathy Allen, "Texas Couple Reveal Findings—Text Books Dominated by Filth," *Manchester* (N.H.) *Union Leader*, July 9, 1973.
    The book about George Washington and Marilyn Monroe is William J. Jacobs, *Search for Freedom: America and Its People.* New York: Macmillan (Benziger), 1973, pp. 384–390.
26. James C. Hefley, p. 183.
27. *Ibid.*, pp. 68, 183.
28. *"Censorship on Rise Again in Schools," U.S. News & World Report*, June 4, 1979, p. 51.
29. James C. Hefley, p. 116.
30. *Ibid.*, p. 97.
31. Steven A. Otfinoski, "No Kidding? Kids' Lib Is Coming?" *Read,* Feb. 28, 1975, pp. 2–5.
32. *Ibid.*, Teacher's Edition, p. 2.
33. "Drive for Rights of Children," *U.S. News & World Report*, Aug. 5, 1974, p. 42.
34. "The Facts About Children's Rights Organization," received from Children's Rights Organization, 17½ 65th Avenue, Playa del Rey, Calif.
35. Ethel Mannin, *Common-Sense and the Child*, p. 59.
36. John Holt, *Escape from Childhood*, pp. 1, 2, 117, 169, 194, and 210.
37. *Congressional Record—House of Representatives*, Apr. 9, 1975, H2585–2596.
    Dorothy Nelkin, "The Science-Textbook Controversies," *Scientific American*, Apr. 1976, Vol 234, No. 4, p. 34.
    Report to the House Committee on Science and Technology by the Comptroller General of the United States, *Administration of the Science Education Project "Man: A Course Of Study" (MACOS) National Science Foundation.*

38. *Congressional Record—House of Representatives*, April 9, 1975, H2585.
39. *Ibid.*
40. *Ibid.*, H2585, 2586. MACOS materials are published by Education Development Center, Cambridge, Mass.
41. *Ibid.*, H2588.
42. *Ibid.*, H2592.
43. *Songs and Stories of the Netsilik Eskimos*, p. 43, 44 (MACOS booklet).
44. *Ibid.*, p. 44.
45. Man: A Course of Study, *The Netsilik Eskimos on the Sea Ice*, p. 21.
46. Man: A Course of Study, *A Journey to the Arctic*, p. 38.
47. *Congressional Record—House of Representatives*, H2593.
48. Lee Dembart, "The Proper Study of Mankind. . .," *New York Times*, Apr. 25, 1976.
49. Noel F. Busch, "The Furor over School Textbooks," *Reader's Digest*, Jan. 1976, pp. 127, 128.
50. James I. Kilpatrick, "MACOS: A Teacher's View," *San Antonio Express*, Apr. 28, 1975.
51. John B. Conlan, "The MACOS Controversy," *Social Education*, Oct. 1975, pp. 390, 391.

Chapter 11

Selection Guidelines or Censorship   175

1. "On School Bill, Book-Banning," *New York Teacher*, Apr. 4, 1976.
2. "L.I. Students File Suit to Overturn School Book Ban," *New York Times*, Jan. 5, 1977.
3. Kurt Vonnegut, Jr., *Slaughterhouse Five*, pp. 155, 205.
4. Eldridge Cleaver, *Soul On Ice*, pp. 157, 158.
5. Jane Yolen, "It's Not All Peter Rabbit," *Writer*, Apr. 1975, p. 12.
6. Anonymous, *Go Ask Alice*, pp. 38, 48, 55, 56, 58, 59, 98, 101, 102.
7. "Parents vs. Educators: Battle Over What's Taught in Schools," *U.S. News & World Report*, July 19, 1976, p. 38.
8. "State Board of Education requires textbooks to show U.S. in good light;" *Houston Chronicle*, Mar. 13, 1983.
9. "How Should We Select School Textbooks?" *Council for Basic Education Bulletin*, Dec. 1975, p. 14.
10. Jeffrey St. John, "School Books: Educational Time Bomb," *Tacoma News Tribune*, Oct. 27, 1974.

11. George H. Gallup, "How the Public Views the Schools," *American Teacher*, Jan. 1976, pp. 7, 8.
12. William Murchison, "Flames over Austin," *Dallas Morning News,* Nov. 18, 1982.
13. Mel Gabler, "Miners Show Convictions in Text Protest," *Borger News-Herald,* Dec. 23, 1974.
14. Henry M. Morris, "Creationism Provides the Answers," *Acts & Facts*, Nov. 1975, Vol. 4, No. 9, p. 3.
15. Dorothy Nelkin, "The Science-Textbook Controversies," *Scientific American*, Apr. 1976, Vol. 234, No. 4, pp. 33, 39.
16. "Resolution for Balanced Presentation of Evolution and Scientific Creationism," *Impact Series*, Institute for Creation Research, 2716 Madison Ave., San Diego, CA 92116, May 1979.
17. Steven Silvers, "ACLU and Creation," *Vision*, June/July, 1982, p. 24.
18. John N. Moore, "I Used to Be Darwin's Disciple," *Christian Reader*, Mar.-Apr. 1976, p. 33.
19. "Teaching of Evolution and Bible View Favored," *New York Times*, Nov. 18, 1981.
    "76% Want Schools to Use Both Evolution Theories," *Houston Chronicle*, Nov. 18, 1981.
20. Gene I. Maeroff, "New York Schools Bar Texts: Fault the Handling of Darwin," *New York Times,* June 24, 1982.

Chapter 12

Education for Sex or Immorality   187

1. Ira L. Reiss, *Premarital Sexual Standards*, p. 2.
2. "Sex and the Single Child," *Newsweek*, June 2, 1969, p. 102.
3. Isadore Rubin, *The Sex Educator and Moral Values*, pp. 9, 10.
4. "Why the Furor over Sex Education?" *U.S. News & World Report*, Aug. 4, 1969, p. 46.
5. Gloria Lentz, *Raping Our Children*, pp. 172, 173.
6. Susan Berryhill, Felicia Guest, and Sheryl Richardson, Editors, *What's Happening*, pp. 4-32.
7. William Block, "For Kids Only," PREP Publication, Trenton, N.J. Material received from the Mel Gablers Educational Research Analysts Newsletter, May 1981.
8. Sex course material was quoted from Melvin Anchell, *Second Look at Sex Education*, p. 18.
9. *Ibid.*, p. 79.
10. "What They Think Now," *Time*, June 3, 1974, p. 46.

11. Mary Susan Miller, "Who's Afraid of Sex Education?" *Education Digest*, Apr. 1976, p. 35.
12. "Colleges: Boys and Girls Together," *Time*, May 30, 1969, p. 44.
13. "Dormmates, Bedmates," *Time*, June 3, 1974, p. 45.
14. George Thorman, "Cohabitation: A Report on the Married-Unmarried Life Style," *Futurist*, Dec. 1973, p. 251.
15. *Ibid.*, p. 253.
16. Ken McKenna, "11 Years Old—and Pregnant," *New York Daily News*, Jan. 13, 1977.
17. Gloria Lentz, p. 211.
18. "Why the Furor over Sex Education?" p. 45.
19. Melvin Anchell, p. 45.
20. Patrick J. Buchanan, "Schweiker Hangs Tough on Sex Ed," *Human Events*, Apr. 4, 1981.
21. "Illicit Sex Education," the Mel Gablers Educational Research Analysts Newsletter, May 1981.
22. "Sex Education and the Schools," *LITE*, May 1979, p. 571. (LITE, 9340 West Peoria Ave., Peoria, AZ 85345.)
23. Sol Gordon, "A Strong Case for Straightforward Sex Education in the Home *and* the School," *American School Board Journal*, Feb. 1975, pp. 39–40.
24. "America's Youth—Angry . . . Bored . . . or Just Confused?" *U.S. News & World Report*, July 18, 1977, p. 19.
25. Sol Gordon, p. 40.
26. Rosalie Cohen and Claire Rudin, "How Schools Can Fight the VD Menace," *Education Digest*, Nov. 1973, p. 28.
27. "Sex and the Single Child," p. 103.
28. Eric W. Johnson, "What Do You Want Your Children to Learn About Sex?" *Parents Magazine*, Apr. 1972, p. 62.
29. "Family Living Including Sex Education," *Public Schools of New York City Staff Bulletin* (Special Supplement) Apr. 7, 1969, p. 2.
30. Harold W. Minor, Joseph B. Muyskens, and Margaret Newell Alexander, *Sex Education—The Schools and the Churches*, p. 75.
31. _____, *Family Living Including Sex Education*, pp. 50, 51.
32. *Ibid.*, p. 4.
33. Donald A. Doyle, "But Are the Schools Really the Best Places for Sex Education?" *American School Board Journal*, Feb. 1975, p. 40.
34. Donn Byrne, "A Pregnant Pause in the Sexual Revolution," *Psychology Today*, July 1977, pp. 67, 68.
35. "Values Education and the Politics of Pedagogy," *LITE*, Sept. 1975, p. 2.
36. "Sex and the Single Child," *Newsweek*, June 2, 1969, p. 102.
37. Rhoda L. Lorand, "The Betrayal of Youth," *Education Update*, The Heritage Foundation, Summer 1979.

38. Educational Research Analysts, P.O. Box 7518, Longview, TX 75607, Article T-536. A letter Dr. Rhoda L. Lorand wrote to *Cause* Rt. #2, Box 270-A, Salem, VA 24153, on Feb. 17, 1979.
39. "The New Scarlet Letter—Herpes, an Incurable Virus, Threatens to Undo the Sexual Revolution," *Time*, Aug. 2, 1982, P. 62.
40. "Chronology of AIDS Epidemic," *Houston Chronicle*, May 22, 1983.
41. Melvin Anchell, p. 16.
42. *Ibid.*, pp. 1, 2.
43. Howard L. Hurwitz, "Should Homosexuals Teach in Our Schools?" *Ridgewood* (N.Y.) *Times*, June 9, 1977.
44. "Gay Power in San Francisco," *Newsweek*, June 6, 1977, p. 25.
45. "Family Living Including Sex Education," *The Public Schools of New York City Staff Bulletin*, Apr. 7, 1969.
46. Howard Hurwitz, "Should Homosexuals Teach in Our Schools?"
47. Howard L. Hurwitz, "Should Gay Teachers Be Fired," *Ridgewood Times*, Mar. 24, 1983.
48. Eugene V. Clark, "A Matter of Personal Morality," letter to the editor, *New York Times*, Nov. 5, 1977.
49. Grace Lichtenstein, "Teachers on Coast and in Jersey Lose Disputes Over Homosexuality," *New York Times*, Oct. 4, 1977.
50. Melvin Anchell, pp. 118, 122.
51. "Miami Vote: Tide Turning Against Homosexuals?" *U.S. News & World Report*, June 20, 1977, p. 46.
52. Eunice Kennedy Shriver, "There *Is* a Moral Dimension," *Reader's Digest*, Nov. 1977, pp. 153, 154.

Chapter 13

Values Clarification   207

1. "Moral Education," *Newsweek*, Mar. 1, 1976, p. 74.
2. Amitai Etzioni, "Do as I Say, Not as I Do," *New York Times Magazine*, Sept. 26, 1976.
3. "Do Moral Values Belong in School?" *Newsweek*, June 2, 1980, p. 58.
4. Cecelia M. Dobrish, "Can Values Really Be Learned at School?" *Parents Magazine*, Sept. 1976.
5. Sidney B. Simon, Leland W. Howe, and Howard Kirschenbaum, *Values Clarification*, pp. 290–292.
6. *Ibid.*, p. 290.
7. "Burning Issue—1976, the Impact of Federal Involvement on Public Education," Maryland Federation of Republican Women Study Guide, p. 7. From Mrs. Jacqueline Lawrence, 3807 Taylor Street, Chevy Chase, MD 20015.

8. Sidney B. Simon, Leland W. Howe, and Howard Kirschenbaum, pp. 281–283.
9. Barbara M. Morris, *Why Are You Losing Your Children?* between pp. 26, 27.
10. Sidney B. Simon, Leland W. Howe, and Howard Kirschenbaum, p. 388.
11. Barbara M. Morris, p. 13.
12. "Prying into Kids' Lives," *Council for Basic Education Bulletin,* Feb. 1976, p. 14.
13. Barbara M. Morris, p. 24.
14. "Federal Funds Fuel Sexual Revolution," *Human Events*, Oct. 10, 1981.
15. Richard A. Bauer, Jr., "Teaching Values in the Schools," *American Education*, Nov. 1982, pp. 11–17.

Chapter 14

Moral Disintegration   215

1. *Engel v. Vitale*, 370 U.S. 421 (1962).
2. *Abington School Distrist v. Schempp*, 374 U.S. 203 (1963).
3. *Humanist Manifestos I and II*, pp. 14–19, 21, 23.
4. Sidney B. Simon, Leland W. Howe, and Howard Kirschenbaum, *Values Clarification*, p. 22.
5. "Creation-Evolution Debate Is Stirring Again," *Eternity*, June 1977, p. 6.
6. "Humanists Attack Creationists," *Acts & Facts*, Mar. 1977, p. 1.

Chapter 15

America's Moral Foundation   223

1. Max Farrand, Editor, *The Records of the Federal Convention of 1787,* Vol. 1, pp. 451, 452.
2. Saul K. Padover, *The Washington Papers*, p. 263.
3. *Ibid.*, pp. 302, 303.
4. *Engel v. Vitale*, 370 U.S. 446 (1962).
5. *Ibid.*, 447.
6. *Ibid.*
7. *Ibid.*
8. *Ibid.*, 427, 428.
9. William Warren Sweet, *The Story of Religion in America*, p. 275.
10. *Church of the Holy Trinity v. United States*, 143 U.S. 470, 471 1892).
11. *Vidal v. Girad's Executors*, 2 How.127 (1844).

12. Raymond J. Celada, *The Supreme Court Opinion in the School Prayer Case (Engel v. Vitale): The Decision, the Reaction, the Pros and Cons*, pp. 26, 27.
13. Clarence H. Benson, An Introduction to Child Study, p. 80.
14. Benjamin Weiss, *God in American History*, p. 163.
15. *Ibid.*, p. 195.
16. J. Robertson McQuilkin, "Public Schools' Equal Time for Evangelicals" *Christianity Today*, Dec. 30, 1977, p. 8.
17. *Zorach v. Clauson*, 343 U.S. 306, 313 (1952).
18. *Engel v. Vitale,* 440, statement found in a footnote in Justice Douglas' concurring opinion.
19. *Abington School District v. Schempp*, 374 U.S. 253 (1963).
20. *Cantwell v. Connecticut*, 310 U.S. 296, 303 (1940).
21. Walter Berns, *The First Amendment and the Future of American Democracy*, p. 56.
22. *Ibid.*, p. 71.
23. *Ibid.*
24. Harold O. J. Brown, *The Reconstruction of the Republic,* p. 19.
25. Albert P. Blaustein, and Gilbert H. Flantz, *Constitutions of the Countries of the World.* The USSR Constitution was adopted by the 7th Extraordinary Session of the Supreme Soviet of the USSR (9th Convocation), October 7, 1977.

Chapter 16

A Moral America   235

1. Peter Berger, "Battered Pillars of the American System," *New York Teacher*, June 27, 1976, pp. 21, 22.
2. *Engel v. Vitale*, 370 U.S. 435 (1962), footnote.
3. *Abington School District v. Schempp*, 374 U.S. 205, 211 (1963).
4. *Engel v. Vitale*, 370 U.S. 422 (1962).
5. *Ibid.*, 435.
6. *De Spain v. De Kalb County Community School District* (Illinois), 384 F.2d (1967).
7. *Stein v. Oshinsky*, 348 F.2d 999 (1965).
8. *Engel v. Vitale*, 370 U.S. 446 (1962).
9. "Why High School Students Can't Discuss the Bible," *Christianity Today*, Feb. 18, 1983, pp. 34, 35.
    "Lubbock Case Fails," *Eternity*, Mar. 1983, p. 17.
10. *Zorach v. Clauson*, 343 U.S. 313 (1952).
11. John Laubach, *School Prayers*, p. 70.
12. "Reagan's Remarks on Permitting School Prayer," *New York Times*, May 7, 1982.
13. John Laubach, p. 81.

14. *Ibid.*
15. *Ibid.*
16. "Church-State Commandments," *Time*, Dec. 1, 1980, p. 74.
17. Jesse Helms, "Public Supports School Prayer," *Human Events*, Sept. 13, 1980.
18. "Son of Atheist Leader Issues Apology," *New York Times*, May 10, 1980.
19. "Southern Baptists Back Constitution Amendment on School Prayers," *New York Times*, June 18, 1982.
20. "Prayer Comeback Bid Hasn't Got a Prayer." *Christianity Today*, May 4, 1979.
21. Paul H. Hirst. "Public and Private Values and Religious Educational Content," taken from Theodore R. Sizer, Editor, *Religion and Public Education*, p. 330.
22. *Congressional Record—House of Representatives*, May 12, 1976, Vol. 122, No. 70.
23. *Humanist Manifestos I and II*, preface.
24. *McCollum v. Board of Education*, 333 U.S. 203 (1948).
25. *Zorach v. Clauson*, 343 U.S. 306, 313 (1952).
26. *Ibid.*
27. *Roemer v. Maryland Public Works Bds.*, 49 L.Ed. 2d 187 (1976).
28. *Abington School District v. Schempp*, 374 U.S. 225 (1963).
29. Virgil C. Blum, "Political Action for Liberty and Justice in Education," *Vital Speeches of the Day*, Dec. 15, 1975, p. 150.
30. *Everson v. Board of Education*, 330 U.S. 18 (1947).
31. *Roemer v. Maryland Public Works Bds.*, 49 L.Ed. 2d 187 (1976).
32. *Congressional Record—Senate*, Feb. 23, 1978, Vol. 124, No. 23, S2163–S2165.
33. Eugene H. Methvin, "Should Prayer Be Restored to Our Public Schools?" *Reader's Digest*, Sept. 1979, p. 91.
34. *Abington School District v. Schempp*, 374 U.S. 225 (1963).
35. J. D. Salinger, *The Catcher in the Rye*, chapter 6.
36. *Stein v. Oshinsky*, 348 F.2d 999 (1965).
37. *De Spain v. De Kalb County Community School District* (Illinois), 384 F.2d 836 (1967).
    John W. Whitehead, *The Separation Illusion*, p. 108.

Chapter 17

Schools and the Future of America   253

1. *Abington School District v. Schempp*, 374 U.S. 303 (1963).
2. Carl H. Henry, "Human Rights and Wrongs," *Christianity Today*, July 8, 1977, p. 25.

3. "Texas Teen Defends School Prayer in Hearing," *Houston Chronicle*, Apr. 29, 1983.
4. "Carter's LEAA Nominee Holds Bizarre Views," *Human Events*, Oct. 7, 1978.
5. "Thou Shalt Not—And Shall," *Time*, Jan. 26, 1976, p. 41.
6. Quoted from *LITE* (Let's Improve Today's Education), Parents' Newsletter, p. 3. LITE, 9340 W. Peoria Ave., Peoria, AZ 85345.) Taken from *NEA Journal*, Feb. 1968.
7. *Ibid*. Taken from Arizona State Board of Education Policy Book. Philosophy and Goals.
8. "An Historical Overview of the Philosophy of Progressive Education," *LITE*, Apr. 1973, p. 2.
9. Edward B. Fiske, "Panel Criticizes Public Education in U.S.," *Houston Chronicle*, May 6, 1982.
10. Tim LaHaye, *The Bible's Influences on American History*, p. 20.
11. "Toynbee: Chronicler of Religion in Society," *Eternity*, Jan. 1976, p. 37.
12. James Dobson, *Dare to Discipline*, pp. 168, 169.
13. E. M. Blaiklock, "The Breath of Hell," *Christianity Today*, May 7, 1976, pp. 13, 14.
14. Aleksander Solzhenitsyn, "Wake Up! Wake Up!" *Reader's Digest*, Dec. 1975, p. 71.
15. S. I. McMillen, "How Are We Imprinting Our Children?" *Christian Life*, Feb. 1966.
16. Luther J. Binkley, *Conflict of Ideals: Changing Values in Western Society*, p. 48.
17. Reed Irvine, "Press Freedom Doesn't Guarantee a Free Society," *Human Events*, Mar. 5, 1977.
18. Bob Simonds, "How Humanism Took Over American Thought-life," *Vision*, Jan. 1982.
19. George F. Will, "ACLU Fanatical When It Finds Silence a Menace," *Houston Chronicle*, Jan. 21, 1983.
20. Peter Berger, "Battered Pillars of the American System," *New York Teacher*, (Magazine Section), June 27, 1976, p. 20.
21. James E. Hamilton, "John Witherspoon: Foundations for a Threatened Tradition," *Christianity Today*, Nov. 5, 1976, p. 13.
22. Saul K. Padover, Editor, *The Washington Papers*, pp. 318, 319.
23. Alexis de Tocqueville, *Democracy in America*, Vol. 1, p. 318.
24. Selwyn Raab, "Ravage Continues Far into Day; Gunfire and Bottles Beset Police," *New York Times*, July 15, 1977.
25. "Heart of Darkness," *Newsweek*, July 15, 1977.
26. "Night of Terror," *Time*, July 25, 1977, p. 17.
27. William Safire, "Christmas in July," *New York Times*, July 18, 1977.

28. Deirdre Carmody, "Ravaged Slums Facing a Future of Un-
    certainty," *New York Times*, July 16, 1977.
29. "Night of Terror," p. 17.
30. Selwyn Raab.
31. *Ibid.*
32. William Safire.
33. "The Revival Spirit," *Time*, Aug. 9, 1976, p. 6.

                        Chapter 18

        Tomorrow's Students: Actions for Success   275

1. Richard Vetterli, *Storming the Citadel*, p. 57.
2. "The Report of the Task Force on Federal Elementary and
   Secondary Education Policy," *Education Week*, May 11, 1983.
3. "The Bright Flight," *Newsweek*, Apr. 20, 1981, pp. 66–73.
        "Are Public Schools About to Flunk?" *U.S. News & World
   Report*, June 8, 1981, pp. 59, 60.
4. John C. Esty, Jr., "Private Schools Tax Credits," *New York
   Times*, Feb. 7, 1981.
5. "Private Schools Win a Public Vote," *Newsweek*, Apr. 13, 1981,
   p. 107.
        "Can Public Learn from Private?" *Time*, Apr. 20, 1981, p. 50.
        "High Marks for Private Schools," *U.S. News & World Report*,
   Apr. 20, 1981, p. 12.
        "Coleman Study Supports Tuition Tax Credits," *Human Events,*
   Apr. 25, 1981.
6. John C. Esty.
7. Dan Morgan, "Reports Stir Emotional Debate over Education,"
   Houston Chronicle, Apr. 5, 1981.
8. "Secretary Bell's View of a Department in Transition," *New York
   Times*, Feb. 3, 1981.
9. James J. Kilpatrick, "Tuition Tax Credits a Sound Idea," *Houston
   Chronicle,* Apr. 20, 1981.
10. Walter Berns, *The First Amendment and the Future of American
    Democracy*, pp. 67, 75.
11. William B. Ball, *Litigation in Education: In Defense of Freedom*,
    p. 15.
12. "Outraged by Silence," *U.S. News & World Report*, July 12,
    1976, p. 76.
13. Parent Right Card, received from the National Committee for
    Citizens in Education, 410 Wilde Lake Village Green, Columbia,
    MD 21044.
14. Orrin Hatch amendment, Public Law 95-561—Nov. 1, 1978,
    95th Congress, 92 Stat. 2143.

15. Wayne McClusky and Rusty Palmer, *Magical Secrets for Creating Understanding,* pp. 6, 12–16.
16. "Christian Educators Association—A Reflection on 30 Years," *Vision,* Jan./Feb. 1983, pp. 5, 29.
17. Norma and Mel Gabler, "A Parent's Guide to Textbook Review and Reform," Special Supplement to *Education Update,* Winter 1978. Additional copies are available from The Heritage Foundation, 513 C Street, N.E., Washington, D.C. 20002.
18. "An Historical Overview of the Philosophy of Progressive Education," *LITE,* Apr. 1973, pp. 1, 2.
19. Christine A. Jones, "Sex Without Values," *Eternity,* Oct. 1977, pp. 21–23.
20. Kris McGough, Editor, "A Parent's Perspective," *Social Education,* Mar. 1977, Vol. 41, No. 3.
21. Malcolm Lawrence, "Executive Reports," *Advertiser,* Jan. 26, 1977.
22. Bill Freeman, "Confessions of a Permissive Teacher," *Christian Reader,* Jan.–Feb. 1982, pp. 106–109.

Bibliography

Anchell, Melvin. *A Second Look at Sex Education.* Santa Monica, Calif.: Educulture, 1972.

Armbruster, Frank E. *Our Children's Crippled Future.* New York: New York Times Book Co., 1977.

Ball, William B. *Litigation in Education: In Defense of Freedom.* Center for Independent Education, P.O. Box 2256, Wichita, KS 67201, 1977.

Baruch, Dorothy W. *New Ways in Discipline.* New York: McGraw-Hill, 1949.

Benson, Clarence H. *An Introduction to Child Study.* Chicago: Moody Press, 1942.

Berns, Walter. *The First Amendment and the Future of American Democracy.* New York: Basic Books, 1976.

Berryhill, Susan, Guest, Felicia, and Richardson, Sheryl, Editors, *What's Happening.* Published by Emory University School of Medicine, Department of Gynecology and Obstetrics, Family Planning Program, 69 Butler Street S.E., Atlanta, GA 30303, N.D.

Binkley, Luther J. *Conflict of Ideals: Changing Values in Western Society.* New York: Van Nostrand Reinhold, 1969.

Blanton, Similey. *Love or Perish.* New York: Simon & Schuster, 1956.

Blaustein, Albert P., and Flanz, Gilbert H. *Constitutions of the Countries of the World.* Dobbs Ferry, N.Y.: Oceana Publications, 1982.

Botel, Morton, and Dawkins. *Communicating.* Teacher's Edition, Grade 3. Lexington, Mass.: Heath, 1973.

Botel, Morton, and Dawkins, *Communicating.* Teacher's Edition, Grade 6. Lexington, Mass.: Heath, 1973.

Broddy, Nella. *Anne Sullivan Macy: The Story Behind Helen Keller.* New York: Doubleday, 1933.

Brown, Harold O. J. *The Reconstruction of the Republic.* New Rochelle, N.Y.: Arlington House, 1977.

Bruch, Hilde. *Don't Be Afraid of Your Child.* New York: Farrar, Straus & Giroux, 1952.

Celada, Raymond J. *The Supreme Court Opinion in the School Prayer Case (Engel v. Vitale): The Decision, the Reaction, the Pros and Cons.* Congressional Research Service, Library of Congress, N.D. (Paper written 1/28/63) LCIII 200/273.

Cleaver, Eldridge. *Soul On Ice.* New York: Dell, 1968.

Dodson, Fitzhugh. *How to Parent.* New York: New American Library, 1970.

323

Dobson, James. *Dare to Discipline*. Wheaton, Ill.: Tyndale House, 1970.

Dobson, James. *Hide or Seek*. Old Tappan, N.J.: Revell, 1974.

Family Living Including Sex Education. Brooklyn, N.Y.: Bureau of Curriculum Development, Board of Education of New York, No. 3, 1969–70 Series.

Farrand, Max, Editor. *The Records of the Federal Convention of 1787*. Revised ed., 4 vols. New Haven, Conn.: Yale University Press, 1937.

A Federal Source Book: Answers to the Most Frequently Asked Questions About Drug Abuse. Washington, D.C.: U.S. Government Printing Office, 1971.

Fike, Elmer. *Textbook Controversy in Perspective and Other Related Essays*. Distributed by Alliance for Better Textbooks, P.O. Box 4371, Charleston, WV 25304.

Flesch, Rudolf. *Why Johnny Can't Read*. New York: Harper & Row, 1955.

Gelfand, Donna M., Editor. *Social Learning in Childhood*. Monterey, Calif.: Brooks/Cole, 1969.

Go Ask Alice. New York: Avon Books, 1971.

Grinder, Robert E. *Adolescence*. New York: Wiley, 1973.

Gorss, Beatrice and Ronald, Editors. *Radical School Reform*. New York: Simon & Schuster, 1969.

Harper, Floren. *Scripts 3.*. Boston: Houghton Mifflin, 1973.

Hefley, James C. *Textbooks on Trial*. Wheaton, Ill.: Victor Books, 1976.

Hohman, Leslie B. *As the Twig Is Bent*. New York: Macmillan, 1939.

Holt, John. *Escape from Childhood*. New York: Ballantine Books, 1974.

Holt, John. *The Underachieving School*. New York: Dell, 1969

Hoppe, Ronald A., Milton, G. Alexander, and Simmel, Edward C., Editors. *Early Experiences and the Processes of Socialization*. New York: Academic, 1970.

Humanist Manifestos I and II. Buffalo, N.Y.: Prometheus Books, 1973.

Karlin, Muriel Schoenbrun, and Berger, Regina. *Discipline and the Disruptive Child*. Englewood Cliffs, N.J.: Parker Publishing Co., 1972.

Krumboltz, John D., and Krumboltz, Helen B. *Changing Children's Behavior*. Englewood Cliffs, N.J.: Prentice-Hall, 1972.

La Haye, Tim. *The Bible's Influence on American History*. San Diego: Master Books, 1976.

Langdon, Grace, and Stout, Irving W. *These Well-Adjusted Children*. New York: John Day, 1951.

Laubach, John Herbert. *School Prayers*. Washington, D.C.: Public Affairs Press, 1969.

Lentz, Gloria. *Raping Our Children*. New Rochelle, N.Y.: Arlington House, 1972.

Man: A Course of Study. *A Journey to the Arctic*. Cambridge, Mass.: Education Development Center, 1969.

Man: A Course of Study. *The Netsilik Eskimos on the Sea Ice*. Cambridge, Mass.: Education Development Center, Inc., 1969.

Mannin, Ethel. *Common-Sense and the Child*. Philadelphia: Lippincott, 1931.

Marshall Fundamental School, Pasadena, California [K–8]. Pasadena Unified School District, 1975–76.

Marshall Fundamental School, Pasadena, California [9-12] Pasadena Unified School District, 1975–76.

McClusky, Wayne, and Palmer, Rusty. *Magical Secrets for Creating Understanding*. Region IV Education Service Center, P.O. Box 863, 7200 West Tidwell Rd., Houston, TX 77001, 1982.

Minor, Harold W., Muyskens, Joseph B., and Alexander, Margaret Newell. *Sex Education—The Schools and the Churches*. Richmond, Virginia: John Knox Press, 1971.

Morris, Barbara M. *Why Are You Losing Your Children?* The Barbara M. Morris Report, P.O. Box 412, Ellicott City, MD 21043. N.D.

Neill, A. S. *Summerhill: A Radical Approach to Child Rearing*. New York: Hart Publishing Co., 1960.

Padover, Saul K., Editor. *The Washington Papers*. New York: Harper & Row, 1955.

Reiss, Ira L. *Premarital Sexual Standards*. New York: Human Sciences Press, 1976. (SIECUS Study Guide No. 5, revised ed.)

Report of the Task Report on Corporal Punishment. Washington, D.C.: National Education Association, 1972.

Report to the House Committee on Science and Technology by the Comptroller General of the United States. *Administration of the Science Education Project "Man: A Course Of Study" (MACOS) National Science Foundation*. Washington, D.C.: U.S. General Accounting Office, Oct. 14, 1975, MWD–76–26.

Rosenblith, Judy F., Allinsmith, Wesley, and Williams, Joanna P. *The Causes of Behavior: Readings in Child Development and Educational Psychology*. Boston: Allyn & Bacon, 1972.

Rubin, Isadore. *The Sex Educator and Moral Values*. (SIECUS Study Guide No. 10.) New York: Behavioral Publications, 1969.

Salinger, J. D. *The Catcher in the Rye*. New York: Bantam Books, 1951.

Simon, Sidney B., Howe, Leland W., and Kirschenbaum, Howard. *Values Clarification*. New York: Hart Publishing Co., 1972.

Sizer, Theodore R., Editor. *Religion and Public Education*. Boston: Houghton Mifflin, 1967.

Sweet, William Warren. *The Story of Religion in America.* New York: Harper & Row, 1930.

Tocqueville, Alexis de. *Democracy in America*. New York: Vintage, 1945.

Valusek, John E. *People Are Not for Hitting*. Wichita, Kansas: John E. Valusek, 3629 Mossman, Wichita KS 1974.

Vetterli, Richard. *Storming the Citadel: The Fundamental Revolution Against Progressive Education.* Costa Mesa, Calif.: Educational Media Press, 1976.

Vonnegut, Kurt, Jr. *Slaughterhouse Five*. New York: Dell, 1969.

Weber, George. *Inner-City Children Can Be Taught to Read: Four Successful Schools.* Washington, D.C.: Council for Basic Education, N.D.

Weiss, Benjamin. *God in American History*. Distributed by National Educators Fellowship, Inc., P.O. Box 243, South Pasadena, CA 91030, 1966.

Whitehead, John W. *The Separation Illusion*. Milford, ME: Mott Media, 1977.

Index

Ability Grouping 36, 149, 150, 175, 287
Ability Promotion see Promotion
Abington School District v. Schempp 216, 217, 231, 237, 241, 242, 245, 250
Abortion see Sex
Abt Associates of Cambridge 56
Accommodation-Neutrality 245-247
Activism, Supreme Court see Supreme Court
Adams, John 227
Administrators (see also Teachers) 59, 70, 71, 113, 277, 282, 295
  Chain of Command 90
Allen, James E. 25, 26, 40
Allen, R.R. 20
America 49, 298
  Collapse of Civilization 260-263
  Disintegration 215, 216, 254-256
  Moral Foundation (see also Morals) 223-234
  Perpetuating America's Heritage 257-260
  Rebuilding America 267, 268
  Revolution 224
American Civil Liberties Union 183, 184, 238, 258, 266, 267, 287
American Federation of Teachers 278, 279
Ames, Louise Bates 14
Amid, Henri Frederic 281
Anchell, Melvin 193, 203-205
Anker, Irving 108
Anson, Albert 155
Aristocracy 35
Armbruster, Frank E. 128
Aronfreed, Justin 101-103
Arts, 18, 49, 50, 57
Atheism see Theism
Atomic Energy Commission 33
Author I
Authoritarian see Discipline
Automatic Promotion see Promotion
Autonomous Children see Values Clarification

Baer, Donald M. 103
Bailey, Bonnie 258
Bakke, Allan 123, 124
Ball, William B. 281
Baruch, Dorothy W. 83-85
Basics 17, 18, 20, 55, 149, 217, 275, 277, 289
  Forward With Basics 11-23
Bateman, Barbara 94
Bauer, Richard A. 212, 213
Baumrind, Diana 85, 89
Beberman, Max 31
Becker Amendment 238, 239
Begle, Edward G. 31
Behavior Modification see Discipline
Bell, Alexander Graham 80
Bell, Bernard Iddings 247
Bell, Derek A. 122
Bell, Terrel H. 4, 146, 258, 279
Bennet, Neville 56
Berger, Peter 235
Berger, Raoul 249
Berger, Regina 89
Bernath, Emil M. 270
Berns, Walter 232
Bible (see also Theism) 216, 217, 223, 229-232, 237-245, 250, 251, 255, 257, 258, 262, 276, 281, 287, 297
  Prayer and Bible Reading Statute (see also Prayer) 238-243
  Voluntary Bible Reading 238, 239, 287
Bilingual Education see Race
Bill of Rights see Constitution; Rights
Billingsley, Andrew 132
Bilingual Education see Race
Birch, Edward L. 95
Bird, Wendell R. 183
Birth Control see Sex
Black, Hugo L. 228, 236, 237, 247
Blackmun, Harry A. 246, 248
Blackout, New York City 268-271
Blaiklock, E.M. 262
Blair, Alice 7, 137-139
Blair, Omar 131

Blanton, Smiley 79
Bloch, Alfred 6
Block, William 191
Blumenfeld, Samuel L. 28, 30, 31
Board of Education Island Trees Union
    Free School District No. 26 v. Pico 160
Bonewits, P.E.I. 160
Boston, Bruce O. 35
Boyson, Rhodes 55
Brennan, William J. 231, 255
Bress, Grace Billings 121
Bronfenbrenner, Urie 65
Brown, Bertram S. 96
Brown, Harold O.J. 233
Brown, Jimmy 161
Brown, Linda 117
Brown, Oliver 117
Bruch, Hilde 35, 52
Bruner, Jerome S. 168
Bryan, William Jennings 183
Buchanan, Patrick J. 134
Burgers, Sheilah Cambell 172
Busing see Race
Byrne, Donn 200

Calderone, Mary Steichen 188
Calloway, Ernest 126
Cambridge Conference 32
Camp, L.T. 142
Canter, Lee 88, 89
Cantwell v. Connecticut 232
Censorship see Textbooks
Chall, Jeanne 29
Chambers, Bette 221
Cheating see Textbooks
Children's Liberation see Rights
Chisholm, Shirley 117
Christian Educators Association 288, 289
Christianity see Theism
Church of the Holy Trinity v. United States
    228
Clark, Tom C. 250
Cleaver, Eldridge 265
Code of Student Rights 110
Cohen, Rosalie 196
Cohn, Murry A. 204
Coleman, James S. 118, 121, 122, 139,
    278
Colleges 17
    Failures 16

Remedial Reading 17
Communism 181, 254, 259, 263-265
Compensatory Programs 141
Competency Tests see Race
Competition 37, 38, 49, 280
Computer Science 149
Conlan, John B. 167, 168, 244, 245
Constitution 160, 179, 223-226, 228,
    229, 233, 235, 236, 240, 248, 257
    Bill of Rights 227-229, 232, 233
    Constitutional Democracy 257
    First Amendment, 228, 232, 233, 235,
        250, 266, 267
    Fourteenth Amendment 231-233, 266,
        267
    Reinterpreting the Constitution 231-
        233
    Russian 234
    State Rights 160, 233, 234
Constitutional Convention 224, 225
Copperman, Paul 147
Corner, Harold 40
Corporal Punishment See Discipline
Corwin, Edward S. 233
Council for Exceptional Children 35
Cowan, Morley 166
Creativity 56, 57
Crew, John L. 140, 141
Crime 41, 134, 255, 264, 269-271, 278,
    285
    Assaults on Teachers 6, 76, 106, 107
    Habitation for Criminals 75-77
Crisis, School 3-10
Cuevas, Rosa 124

Darrow, Clarence 183, 266
David, Joe 63
Declaration of Independence 223, 224,
    256, 268
Democracy 257
De Spain v. De Kalb County Community
    School District 237
Dewey, John 52, 54, 83, 193, 217, 254,
    266, 276
Discipline 47, 50, 58, 129, 137, 139, 140,
    143, 149, 151, 158, 217, 277, 278,
    283, 286, 287, 289, 297
    Ancient Wisdom 111, 112
    Authoritarian 82, 83, 91, 113

Index

Behavior Modification 95-97
Chain of Command 90
Classroom Management 90
Concealing Problems 69-76
Corporal Punishment 67, 77, 80, 81, 98-109, 113, 275
Corporal Punishment Banned 108, 109
Crisis Discipline 5, 6
Defiant Students 65-69, 86, 87, 113, 275
Drugs 93-95 see also Drugs
Effective Punishment 101-104
Fair, Firm and Loving 87-90, 275
Freedom and Discipline 58, 85, 86
Habitation for Criminals 75-77
Excessive Punishment 103, 105, 106
In Loco Parentis 109, 110, 113, 217, 275
Investigating Schools 69-75
Issues Unrelated to School 65, 130, 131
Love and Discipline 79-90, 113
Love and Punishment 104-106
Nature 109
New York City's Standards 66-69
Permissive 83-85, 91, 113, 297
Permissive Solutions 109-111
Powerless Teachers 67-69, 77, 108, 109, 277
Preventive 86, 88
Quota Discipline 130-132
Reform School 86, 87
Rejected 44, 45
Root Causes 63-78
Self 49, 58
Solutions 63-133
   Summary 113, 275
Successful Teachers 87-90
Supreme Court 107, 108
Suspension 67, 109
Total Disciplined Environment 90
Training Centers for Proper Social Behavior 77
Violence 5, 6, 63-65, 67, 69-76
Divoky, Diane 93-95
Dobson, James C. 14, 90, 261
Dodson Fitshugh 99
Donovan, Bernard E. 197
Douglas, William O. 238, 246
Dropouts 4, 17, 39-41

Drugs 130, 133, 134, 177, 179, 185, 210, 215, 271, 278, 295
Amphetamine 94, 97, 98
Chemotherapy 97, 98
Encouraging Drugs 75, 76
Learning and Behavior 93-95
Mandatory Prison 87
Duekmejian, George 107
Dunaway, Jean 79
Dyslexia see Reading

Early Grades 12-15
Edmonds, Ronald 140
Educational Solutions 11-59
   Summary 58, 59, 275
Educational Crisis 3-5
Educational Maze 43-59
Educational Research Analysts 161
Educators see Teachers
Egalitarianism 35, 36, 124, 216
Elitism 35
Elsberg, Ted 130
Engel v. Vitale 216, 217, 227, 228, 229, 237, 281
English 4, 11, 40, 49, 50, 59, 129, 147, 149, 297
   Nonstandard 158
   Success 56, 294
   Teachers 20
Ethics see Morals; Humanism
Etzioni, Amitai 207
Euthanasia see Textbooks
Evans, David L. 110, 124, 125
Everson v. Board of Education 247
Evolution 173
   Creationism Censored 184, 185, 221
   Scientific Creationism v. Evolution 182, 185

Falwell, Jerry 202
Family 215
Farson, Richard 164
Federal Government's Investigation of the Schools 146-150
Feynman, Richard P. 33
Fiedler, Bobbi 107
Fike, Elmer 156
Fiske, Edward B. 260
FitzGerald, Frances 163
Flesch, Rudolf 28, 30, 31

Fondy, Al 106, 107
Foster, William Z. 266
Franklin, Benjamin 257, 297
Franklin, John Hope 124
Freedom 58
Freeman, Bill 296
Free Schools 43-48, 50, 51, 217
Free Universities 46
Fremon, Suzanne S. 46
Freshour, Frank W. 30
Freud, Paul 241
Freud, Sigmund 103, 254
Freudian Psychology 100
Fundamental Schools 43, 49-59, 143-
    146, 276, 282, 286
    Evaluated 55-57
    Progressive v. Fundamental Schools
    112, 113, 144-146

Gabler, Mel and Norma 157, 160-163,
    181, 290, 291
Gallaudet, Thomas H. 27
Gallop Poll 125, 127, 180, 198, 207, 242,
    289
Germany 4
Gifted 34-36, 59, 141, 142
Glancy, Fred F. Jr. 93
Glasser, Ira 175
God see Theism
Goldeke, Thomas 209
Goodman, Paul 54
Gordon, Sol 195, 196
Grades 36-38, 58, 297
Graduation 12-15
    Standards 17, 18
Green, Edith 117
Greitzer, Samuel L. 33
Grinder, Robert E. 40
Guines, James 127

Hardy, John 144
Harmon, W.W. 260
Hatch, Orrin 282
Haubner, William P. 178
Hechinger, Fred 142
Helms, Jesse 243, 248, 249
Henderson, Donald 55
Henry, Carl F.H. 256
Herndon, Terry 18
Heterogeneous Grouping 36, 86

Hirst, Paul 244
History 4, 18, 49, 50, 57, 59, 129, 160-
    163, 171, 179, 181, 220, 236, 297
Hoffer, Eric 286
Hohman, Leslie B. 52
Hollifield, John H. 56
Holloway, Ruth L. 31
Holt, John 37, 166, 167
Homework 11, 37, 38, 49, 148, 150, 151,
    172, 217, 278, 294
Homogeneous Grouping see Ability Group-
    ing
Hood, Joyce 30
Hopkins, Mark 46
Howard, John A. 281
Howe, Leland W. 208, 209, 220
Humanism 211, 217, 220, 221, 244-247,
    250, 254-272, 276, 277, 279, 281,
    282, 287, 289, 295, 297, 298
    Ethics 218
    Humanist Manifesto 217-219, 245,
        276, 289
    Individual 219
    Religion 218, 244, 245
    World Community 219, 220
Humanist Manifesto see Humanism
Hunt, James B. 151
Hurd, Paul DeHart 33
Hurwitz, Howard L. 17, 39, 66, 204
Hyperkinetic 94, 95

Illich, Ivan 43
Illiterates see Reading
Immaturity 50, 51
Infanticide see Textbooks
In Loco Parentis see Discipline
Institute for Creation Research 182

Jackson, Billy Don 41
Janis, Jean 193
Japan 4
Jefferson, Thomas 227, 240, 259
Jencks, Christopher 139
Jensen, Arthur 139
Johnson, Lyndon B. 125
Johnstone, Robert 198
Jones, Christine A. 293
Judeo-Christian Ethics see Morals

Kanawha County, 7, 155-159

Karlin, Muriel S. 89
Kasun, Jacqueline 195
Katz, Joseph 193
Kauper, 241
Keller, Helen 80, 98
Kemble, Eugenia 130
Kennedy, John F. 227
Kennedy, Joseph P. 206
Kenward, John F. 104
Kidd, William F. 258
Kilpatrick, James J. 279
Kirk, Russell 125
Kirschenbaum, Howard 208, 209, 220
Klepak, Daniel 139
Kline, Morris 31
Koerner, James D. 52
Krumboltz, Helen B. 100
Krumboltz, John D. 100

Lamont, Corliss 266
Landers, Ann 5, 164, 165
Langdon, Grace 85
Laubach, John Herbert 241
Lawrence, Malcolm and Jacqueline 294-296
Lawson, John H. 32
Learning-disability 93-95
Lenin, Vladimir, I. 263
Levin, Max 203
Lewis, James 156
Lewis Ralph W. 16
Lewis, Verne 14
Lief, Harold I. 188
Lincoln, Abraham 239, 268
Lorand Rhoda 171, 172, 201, 203
Love
  Love and Punishment 104-106
  Loving Discipline 79-91, 140
  Touching 79, 80
Lubbock School Board v. Lubbock Civil
  Liberties Union 238

MacArthur, Douglas 261
MACOS see Textbooks
Macy, Anne Sullivan 80, 98
Madison, James 227
Mainstreaming 34
Man A Course Of Study see Textbooks:
  MACOS

Mangel, Charles 93
Mann, Dale 25
Mannin Ethel 45, 166
Martin, Bernice 55
Marx, Karl 254, 264
Math 3, 11-13, 18, 23, 33-35, 40, 49, 54,
  59, 129, 144, 147, 149, 294, 297
  Calculus 34
  New 31-33
  Success 56, 145
  Teachers 33
McCauley, Al and Mildred 119
McGraw, Onalee 172
McKenna, Jeremiah 75, 76
McKenna, Ken 194
Meland, Bernard Eugene 231
Merchant, Carl 120
Meritocracy 35, 36
Miller, Mary Susan 193
Monroe, Marilyn 162
Moore, Alice 7, 155, 157
Moore, John N. 184
Morals (see also Sex) 18, 179, 185, 249,
  260, 261, 265, 278, 281, 289
  A Moral America 235-252
  America's Moral Foundation 223-234
  Building a Moral Foundation 243-244
  Crisis 7
  Government's Moral Imput 211-213
  Hedonism 213
  Judeo-Christian Ethic 201, 255, 256,
    268, 288
  Moral Breakdown 268-271
  Moral Relativism 195, 206, 212, 213
  Positive 49, 206, 213, 215, 217, 286
  Promoting America's Moral Heritage
    236
  Situation Ethics 189, 210, 217, 218,
    220, 264, 265, 270, 286, 295
  Solutions 276
  Source of Moral Disintegration 215-
    222
  Three Value Systems 263-267
Morris, Barbara M. 209-211
Morris, Henry M. 182
Morris, Norval 258, 259
Morse, William C. 66
Murchison, William 180
Murphy, Kevin 202
Murray, William J. 242, 243

Nairn, Allan 127
National Association of Secondary School
    Principals 39
National Commission on Excellence in
    Education 4, 5, 33
National Education Association 15, 100,
    103, 110, 112, 180, 187, 260
National Institute of Education 91
National Institute of Mental Health 94
National Tooling and Machining Associa-
    tion 39, 40
Navy 147
Neighborhood Schools see Race
Neill, A.S. 43-46, 85
Nelkin, Dorothy 183
Nelson-Denny Reading Test 21, 22
New Math see Math
Nordwall, Ulf 194
Northcott, Kaye 180

O'Hair, Madalyn Murray 242
Open Classroom 145, 217
Open Schools 43, 47-51
Opportunity Classes 13
Organization of American Historians 4
Otfinoski, Steven A. 164

Parents 51, 78, 161, 164, 165, 175, 185,
    210, 282, 283, 285-287, 289-298
    Disrespect 217, 283-285
    Furious 178, 179
    Intelligent Actions 290, 293, 295
    Respect 217
    Rights 178-180, 282, 292
Parents Who Care 295-296
Parke, Ross D. 109
Parlefsky, Gary 269
Patriotism see Textbooks
Permissiveness (see also Discipline, Pro-
    gressiveness) 50, 52, 83-85, 91, 109-
    112, 121, 134, 138, 140, 151, 217,
    263, 283, 286, 295-297
    Permissive Discipline see Discipline
Pettigrew, Thomas F. 117
Phonics see Reading
Piaget, Jean 13
Pilate, Pontius 257
Powell, Lewis 107
Prayer (see also Theism) 216, 217, 223,
    225, 227-229, 237-245, 249, 251,

258, 266, 267, 276, 281, 287, 297, 298
    Prayer and Bible Reading Statute 238-
        243, 297
    Silent prayer 242, 267
    Voluntary Prayer 234, 238-241, 287
Premarital Intercourse see Sex
Preparation 12, 13
Prinz, Joachim 241
Private Schools 121, 242, 247, 277-280,
    289
    Tuition Tax Credits 278-280
Profanity see Textbooks
Progressiveness (see also Permissive-
    ness) 43, 47-58, 150, 151, 207, 216,
    276, 282, 283, 292
    Evaluated 55-77
    Fundamental vs. Progressive Schools
        112, 113, 144-146
    Goals 166, 167
    Leaders 112
Progressive Education Association 83
Promotion
    Ability 135, 150, 217, 275, 287
    Exams 17, 18
    Retention 13, 14
    Semiannual 13
    Standards 12-15, 19, 21, 33, 34, 59,
        149
Prostitution see Sex
Psychotherapeutic see Values Clarifica-
    tion
Punishment see Discipline

Quotas see Race

Race 4, 285
    Bilingual Education 127-130
    Busing 6, 117-122, 143-146, 276
    Crisis 6
    Destroyed Generation 132-135
    Discipline 6, 130-132
    Neighborhood Schools 118, 287
    Private Schools 278
    Progress 117-136
    Quality Education 135, 136
    Quotas 6, 122-126, 135, 136
    Resegregation 121
    Reverse Discrimination 118
    Solutions 276

Success 7, 137-139, 144, 145
Unemployment 132-134
Voluntary Integration 120, 144, 145
Racism see Textbooks
Raspberry, William 120, 127, 140
Reading 3, 11, 13, 18, 35, 129, 138, 297
  Comprehension 15, 16
  Deficencies 11, 19, 57, 73, 144, 145,
    147, 277
  Dyslexia 30, 31, 95
  Gadgets 26
  Illiterates 25, 26, 28, 35, 41, 53, 54
  Look-say 27-30
  Phonics 27-30, 138, 292
  Remedial 17, 28
  Right to Read 25, 26
  Success 7, 56, 145, 294
  Tests 21, 22
Reagan, Ronald 239, 240, 243
Redl, Fritz 108
Reed, Vincent 135
Reform School see Discipline
Regents of the University of California v.
  Allan Bakke 123
Religious Bias see Textbooks
Remedial Reading see Reading
Remedial Work 13, 15, 17, 28, 276
Richman, Sonya 69
Rights 215
  Bill of Rights 227-229
  Children 113, 163-167
  Code of Student Rights 110
  Human 224, 286
  Parents 178-180, 282, 292
  Sexual 259
  State Rights 160, 233, 234
  Theism and Human Rights 256
Roemer v. Maryland Public Works Bd.
  246, 248
Roosevelt, Theodore 90
Rostow, Eugene V. 126
Rubertone, Vincent 63
Rubin, Isadore 187, 188
Rudin, Claire 196
Run Away Youth 215
Russia 4, 34, 234
Rustin, Bayard 123
Ruth, Joseph 135

Safire, William 270

Salinger, J.D. 251
Salk, Lee 37, 38
Salz, Arthur E. 53
Sartre, Jean Paul 238
Saul of Tarsus 238
Schaeffer, Francis 297
Schiller, Ronald 32, 33
Scholastic Aptitude Tests 3, 12, 36, 135
Schrag, Peter 94, 95
Science 4, 18, 33, 34, 49, 50, 59, 147,
  148
Scientific Creationism see Evolution
Seaborg, Glenn 33
Seidman, Stanley 142
Self-esteem 14, 40, 56, 57
Senilicide see Textbooks
Separation of a National Church and
  Federal Government 223, 233, 234,
  257
Separation of Church and State 223, 228
  Russia 234
Sex (See also Morals)
  Abortion 188, 190, 192, 195, 198, 219,
    220, 244, 286, 288, 293
  Adultery 205, 206, 215, 220
  AIDS 203
  Birth Control 188, 190-192, 194, 196,
    200, 205, 207, 211, 219
  Claims of Sex Educators 195, 196
  Coeducational Living 193, 194
  Denmark 195
  Education 7, 187-206, 220, 263, 264,
    277, 285, 286, 288, 292-294
  Herpes 202, 203
  Homosexuality 162, 188, 192, 198,
    199, 203-207, 211, 213, 220, 253,
    259, 265, 266, 285, 293
  Illigitimate Pregnancies 7, 201, 205,
    215
  Introducing Sex Education 196-198
  Masturbation 188-190
  Molesters 67, 74
  Nonjudgmental Sex Education 192,
    193
  Objectives of Sex Educators 198, 199
  Opponents of Sex Education 201-204
  Petting 188
  Pornography 188, 192, 195, 198, 201,
    205, 206, 215, 244, 259, 285
  Premarital Intercourse 188-194, 198-

203, 205-208, 215, 220, 244, 259, 261, 293
Proper Sex Education 205, 206
Prostitution 192, 198, 199, 205, 215, 220, 244, 258, 259, 264, 265, 285
Rape 194
Results of Sex Education 194, 195
Sexual Abstinence 199, 200, 202, 203, 205, 206, 261, 262
Sexual Rights 259
SIECUS 187-189
Stimulation 193, 194
Sweden 194, 195
Three Basic Value Systems 188, 189
Venereal Disease 7, 190, 191, 195, 196, 198-200, 202, 203, 205, 211, 215
Virginity 191, 201, 215
Sex Education see Sex
Sex Information and Education Council of the U.S. See Sex: SIECUS
Shackelford, James M. 33
Shanker, Albert 278, 279
Shriver, Eunice Kennedy 205, 206
SIECUS see Sex
Sielaff, Marcia 291, 292
Silent Majority 271, 272
Simon, Sidney B. 208, 209, 220, 293
Simonds, Bob 266
Simons, William H. 69
Situation Ethics see Morals
Skinner, B.F. 96, 100, 101, 103, 168
Smith, Robert F. 183
Socarides, Charles W. 196
Social Engineering see Textbooks
Social Promotion see Promotion
Solomon, King 111, 112
Solomon, Richard L. 101
Solutions see Discipline, Educational, Morals, Race
Solzhenitsyn, Aleksander 263
Sowell, Thomas 122
Sputnik 31
St. John, Jeffrey 180
Standards, Minimum 16
Stanley, Charles 243
State Rights see Constitution
Stein v. Oshinsky 237
Stewart, Potter 227
Stout, Irving W. 85

Successful Schools 7, 136-154, 286
Achieving and Nonachieving Schools 139-141
Parental Cooperation 138
Suicide see Textbooks
Summerhill 43-46
Supreme Court (see individual court cases.)
Activism 248, 250
Contradictory Court Decisions 247, 248
Prayer and Bible Reading Decisions 216, 217, 223, 235, 237, 251, 281
Sutherland, Herman R. 23
Survey I, 11

Teachers (see also Administrators) I, 5, 20, 33, 297
Accountability 13, 19, 149, 150, 275
Action by Educators 287-290
Battered Teachers 6, 76, 106, 107
Colleges 20
Devoted 16
Frustrated 11, 63, 64, 66, 74, 75, 88, 89
Incompetent 19, 20, 38, 90, 150
Reactions Towards Corporal Punishment 106-108
Removal 19, 90
Standards 59, 90, 150
Student Failures 15, 16
Superior 19, 87-90
Underpaid 19
Technology 146, 215, 216
Television 65
Templet, Frances 96, 97
Tests 17, 18, 36-38, 58, 145, 217
Achievement Tests 149, 150
Minimum Competency Tests 126, 127
Textbooks 155-186, 217, 221, 277, 286
Adoption Procedures 290-292
Censorship 157, 173, 180-185, 221
Cheating 157, 158, 295
Drugs 177, 179, 185
Euthanasia 210, 217, 244, 285, 286, 289
Free Enterprise 163
Gallup Poll 180
Infanticide 168-171, 285, 286
MACOS 167-173, 220, 281
New England Primer 229

New Standards 176, 177
Patriotism 162, 163, 179, 181, 185, 217, 220, 221, 286, 287, 289
Profanity 159, 177, 178, 185, 220, 221, 251, 285
Promiscuity 156, 160, 162, 168, 171 175-179, 185, 221, 244
Promoting Positive Books 236, 286, 287
Protesters 155-157, 221
Racism 156, 159, 175, 176, 179, 185
Reformers 160-162
Religious Bias 158, 162, 179, 185, 220, 221
Selection Guidelines or Censorship 175-186
Senilicide 169, 171, 172
Social Engineering 167-173
Suicide 170, 171, 210, 217, 289
Supporters 155, 156
Trial Marriages 169
Violence 158, 162, 168, 179
Women 161
Thanksgiving Day 226, 227
Theism (see also Bible, Prayer) 217, 223-234, 244, 246, 247, 249, 250, 254-268, 271, 272, 280, 281, 286, 296, 297
Accomodation-Neutrality 245-247
Atheism 217, 218, 220, 221, 244, 253, 256
Christianity 228, 229, 232, 233, 262
Daily Bible Reading 230
Freedom of Religion 227-229
Reverse Discrimination 250, 251
Ten Commandments 242
Theism and Human Rights 256
Thomas, Clifford 270
Thomas, Susan B. 34
Thomson, Scott D. 130
Thorman, George 194
Tocqueville, Alexis de 240, 268
Torcaso v. Watkins 245
Toynbee, Arnold 261
Training for Excellence 25-41
Truancy 11, 39-41
Turner, Tom 133
Tuttmacher, Alan 196

Underwood, Ken 155
Ungraded Classes 13

United States see America
Unwin, J.D. 261, 262

Values Clarification 207-214, 220, 295
Autonomous Children 210-212, 217, 218, 220
Diaries 209, 210
Psychodrama 211
Psychotherapeutic 173, 211, 295
Role Playing 211
Sex 208
Survival Games 208, 209
Valusek, John E. 100
Venereal Disease see Sex
Vetterli, Richard 144-146, 276, 277
Vidal v. Girad's Executors 229
Violence see Discipline
Voth, Harold M. 211, 212

Walker, Sidney 97
Ward, Harry 266
Washington, George 162, 224, 226, 227, 239, 268
Wattenberg, William W. 108
Waxman, Henry A. 103
Weber, George 139, 140, 179
Weiss, Benjamin 230
Wellington, James K. 142
Will, George F. 266, 267
Wilson, Woodrow 82
Wise, Helen 15
Witherspoon, John 268
Wolynski, Mara 57
Writing see English

Yolen, Jane 176
Young, Biloine Whiting 121

Zorach v. Clauson 238, 246